"This is a book that provides students of public administration with an approach that allows them to escape from the issues of classic bureaucracy yet confront issues of structure, process, and complexity. In addition, it places the reader in a world that is both universal and (as COVID-19 has shown) constantly changing. As such, it prepares students for their venture into the field where they are likely to face incredible conflict and demands. It draws on important academic sources and places them in the classic conflict/collaboration dichotomy."

Beryl A. Radin, *Georgetown University, USA*

"The field of collaborative public management and intergovernmental relations lost a giant when Dr. Bob Agranoff passed away. Fortunately, Agranoff left one last parting gift, helped to completion by his co-author Dr. Aleksey Kolpakov, with *The Politics of Collaborative Public Management*, a must-read for any student of how collaboration is essential to pursue public ends. This book provides a much-needed missing piece to our understanding of collaboration: politics. Drs. Agranoff and Kolpakov artfully incorporate the dynamics of politics into the complicated world of the partnership between public organizations working across sectors and levels."

Trevor Brown, *Dean of John Glenn College of Public Affairs,*
Ohio State University, USA

"In this timely volume, Drs. Agranoff and Kolpakov provide an excellent summary of the growing appreciation of collaboration with democratic and bureaucratic contexts. By illustrating the everyday practices of public administrators, they advance an important proposition: that collaboration is neither a new mode of operation nor something to be drawn on just for special occasions. Collaborative management is ubiquitous—from the coordination needed to build a new road or water system to the negotiations needed to carry out more complex intergovernmental relations to the more recent transitions to remote and hybrid workplaces. This is an essential read for anyone looking to build and maintain collaborative capacities for the common good."

Christopher Koliba, *Edwin O. Stene Distinguished Professor,*
University of Kansas, USA

"*The Politics of Collaborative Management* should be a must-read for every CEO of a non-governmental agency that interfaces with a public bureaucracy—if just in the simple context of being a funding recipient. This is a valuable text for public administration students or other applied fields of study. Drs. Agranoff and Kolpakov do an excellent job of sharing and explaining the evolution of simple bureaucratic functioning to the increasing presence of collaborative management structures and relationships. Likewise, the information shared that portrays the evolution from bureaucracy to collaboration via a combination of traditional and emergent ideas is invaluable."

Art Dykstra, *CEO of the Trinity Services Foundation,*
Human Services organization serving children and adults with intellectual
or developmental disabilities or mental illness in the state of Illinois, USA

The Politics of Collaborative Public Management

Although one often thinks of collaborative management and related group problem-solving as different interests coming together in "peaceful harmony," nothing could be further from reality. Collaboration in real-world action requires steering and negotiation in virtually every situation, with a considerable process that precedes agreement. This progression is, in effect, a "mini" political and managerial process we have come to know as collaborative politics and its management. This volume explores the process and operations of collaboration and collaborative politics, from routine transactions—or "small p" politics—to the significant issue forces, or "big P" politics. Collaboration is defined here as the process of facilitating and operating in multiorganizational arrangements for addressing problems and producing solutions through the contributions of several organizations and individuals. Throughout the book, readers are gradually exposed to analysis of key findings in collaborative politics from the long research tradition in policy and political science.

This book adapts a series of stories to highlight some of the dynamics of collaborative politics from a range of jurisdictions. It further analyzes the efficacy of storytelling as a learning tool and contributor to practice in different contexts. With collaborative politics often associated with negotiations among administrative actors, authors Drs. Robert Agranoff and Aleksey Kolpakov demonstrate how interorganizational/interagency collaboration operates and is managed, as well as how it has been modified or adjusted in its fundamental core concepts of bureaucratic organization and hierarchy. *The Politics of Collaborative Public Management* is designed as a core text for undergraduate and graduate classes on collaborative management and governance.

Dr. Robert Agranoff was Professor Emeritus in the School of Public and Environmental Affairs at Indiana University-Bloomington, USA, and Catedrático, Government and Public Administration Program, Instituto Universitario Ortega y Gasset, Madrid, Spain. At IU, he served as a faculty chair, Ph.D. director, and as Associate Dean for Bloomington. He specialized in public administration, intergovernmental relations (IGR) and management, and public network studies. He published widely on collaborative management and intergovernmental relations, including *Collaborative Public Management* (2003), *Managing Within Networks* (2007), *Collaborating to Manage* (2012), and *Network Theory in the Public Sector* (Routledge, 2014).

Dr. Aleksey Kolpakov is Visiting Assistant Professor in the School of Public Administration at Florida Atlantic University, USA. He is the author of two books and numerous technical and program evaluation reports for federal, state, and international agencies such as the United Nations Development Program, United Nations Population Fund Agency, International City/County Management Association, and the UK Department for International Development. His major areas of research expertise include international nonprofit organizations, networks, and collaboration in the public and nonprofit sectors, managing diversity in the public and nonprofit sectors, leadership in the public and nonprofit sectors, and knowledge management in the public and nonprofit sectors.

Public Administration and Public Policy
A Comprehensive Publication Program
Editor-In-Chief David H. Rosenbloom
Distinguished Professor of Public Administration
American University, Washington, DC

Recently Published Books

Social Equity and LGBTQ Rights
Dismantling Discrimination and Expanding Civil Rights
Lorenda A. Naylor

Handbook of Public Administration
Fourth Edition
W. Bartley Hildreth, Gerald J. Miller and Evert Linquest

The Public Productivity and Performance Handbook, Third Edition
Edited by Marc Holzer and Andrew Ballard

Cost and Optimization in Government, Third Edition
An Introduction to Cost Accounting, Operations Management,
and Quality Control
Aman Khan

Contracting for Services in State and Local Government Agencies, Third Edition
Best Practices for Public Procurement
William Sims Curry

Public Management Reform in the Gulf Cooperation Council and Beyond
Mhamed Biygautane

The Politics of Collaborative Public Management
A Primer
Robert Agranoff and Aleksey Kolpakov

For more information about this series please visit: www.routledge.com/
Public-Administration-and-Public-Policy/book-series/AUEPUBADMPUP

The Politics of Collaborative Public Management
A Primer

Robert Agranoff and Aleksey Kolpakov

NEW YORK AND LONDON

Designed cover image: © Getty Images

First published 2023
by Routledge
605 Third Avenue, New York, NY 10158

and by Routledge
4 Park Square, Milton Park, Abingdon, Oxon, OX14 4RN

Routledge is an imprint of the Taylor & Francis Group, an informa business
© 2023 Taylor & Francis

The right of Robert Agranoff and Aleksey Kolpakov to be identified as
authors of this work has been asserted in accordance with sections 77 and
78 of the Copyright, Designs and Patents Act 1988.

All rights reserved. No part of this book may be reprinted or reproduced
or utilised in any form or by any electronic, mechanical, or other means,
now known or hereafter invented, including photocopying and recording,
or in any information storage or retrieval system, without permission in
writing from the publishers.

Trademark notice: Product or corporate names may be trademarks or
registered trademarks, and are used only for identification and explanation
without intent to infringe.

Library of Congress Cataloging-in-Publication Data
Names: Agranoff, Robert, author. | Kolpakov, Aleksey, author.
Title: The politics of collaborative public management : a primer / Robert
  Agranoff and Aleksey Kolpakov.
Description: New York, NY : Routledge, 2023. | Series: Public administration
  and public policy | Includes bibliographical references and index.
Identifiers: LCCN 2022061761 (print) | LCCN 2022061762 (ebook) |
  ISBN 9781032473628 (hardback) | ISBN 9781003385769 (ebook)
Subjects: LCSH: Public administration—United States. | Intergovernmental
  cooperation—United States. | Public-private sector cooperation—
  United States.
Classification: LCC JK421 .A565 2023 (print) | LCC JK421 (ebook) |
  DDC 351.73—dc23/eng/20230307
LC record available at https://lccn.loc.gov/2022061761
LC ebook record available at https://lccn.loc.gov/2022061762

ISBN: 978-1-032-47362-8 (hbk)
ISBN: 978-1-003-38576-9 (ebk)

DOI: 10.4324/9781003385769

Typeset in Garamond
by Apex CoVantage, LLC

Contents

List of Figures	*ix*
List of Tables	*x*
List of Boxes	*xi*
List of Abbreviations	*xiii*
Author Biographies	*xv*
Foreword	*xvii*
DAVID H. ROSENBLOOM	
Preface	*xix*

1	From Bureaucracy to the Politics and Organization for Collaborative Management	1
2	Development of Collaborative Enterprises	28
3	Organizing Government to Meet Collaboration Challenges	65
4	The Processes of Reaching Agreement	98
5	On Power and Operations in Collaboration	126
6	The Politics of It All	149
7	Academic Studies of Collaborative Politics and Management	167
8	Stories in Collaborative Politics	191
9	The Process Challenges and Struggles of Joint Undertakings	205

viii *Contents*

10 Assessing and Improving Collaborative Performance   223

11 The Future Politics of Public Bureaucracy in a Connected Era   249

12 Conclusion: Administering Collaborative Affairs
in the Digital Era   276

Index   *295*

Figures

1.1	Four Approaches to Intergovernmental Relations	13
2.1	Agency-to-Agency Connections—Acts of Networking: Public-to-Public and NGO–Agency Collaborating Model	33
2.2	New River: Governance in River Management: A Study of Collaboration-Based Work Plans	42
2.3	Fifteen Principles of Collaborative Groups	43
3.1	Hypothetical Collaborative Public Agency	73
3.2	Typical Collaborative State Economic and Community Development Department	75
3.3	U.S. Department of Homeland Security	80
3.4	Maine Department of Health and Human Services	83
3.5	Metro School Network Structure	90
4.1	Ten Propositions in Negotiations: How to Negotiate	100
4.2	Internal Collaborative Skills	101
4.3	Network Collaborative Interactive Outcomes	120

Tables

1.1	From Bureaucracy to the Politics and Organization for Collaborative Management	15
2.1	Hierarchical and Collaborative Processes Compared	29
2.2	Collaborative Tools	37
7.1	Explicit Knowledge Management Activities	177
7.2	Tacit Knowledge Management Activities	178
9.1	Challenges of Collaborative Governance	206
11.1	Features of 1.0 and 2.0 Organizations	251

Boxes

1.1	Political Negotiations in Cincinnati	5
1.2	Rural Development Councils	6
1.3	Reorganization in Indiana Family and Social Services Administration (FSSA) in Indiana	6
1.4	Practice and Law in Collaboration	17
2.1	Radius Indiana	29
2.2	Lake Champlain Basin Program	51
2.3	EcoPeace Middle East	52
2.4	Creative Solution Process	53
2.5	Essential Features of Networks as Organized Forms	57
2.6	Anne-Marie Slaughter's Network Power	58
3.1	Special Collaborative Bodies: Joint Terrorism Task Forces	71
3.2	Coordinated Bodies: The Case of Fusion Centers	76
3.3	A Typology of Public Networks	86
4.1	Steps in Collaboration Assessment Rubric (CoPCAR)	116
4.2	Network Managing Activities	119
5.1	Collaborative Leadership	128
5.2	Governance Networks in Operation	132
5.3	Bevir and Rhodes's Decentered Theory of Governance	134
5.4	Possible Dimensions of the "Power To" (P2): The Enabling Dimensions in Collaborative Settings	139
5.5	Practical Suggestions on Power Sharing	142
5.6	Seven Common Barriers to Collaboration	143
5.7	Ten Tips on Playing the Political Game	145
6.1	Public Managers' Role in Collaborative Inclusion	154
6.2	About "big P" Politics	157
6.3	"Small p" Politics Experiential Tips	159
7.1	From Federalism to Local Problem Resolution	187
8.1	Waiver of the Rules in North Carolina	192
8.2	The Budget: Salem, Indiana, 1998	193
8.3	The "Bat Signal" in River Falls, Wisconsin, Until 1960	195
8.4	Home Rule in Ukraine, 2010	196

xii *Boxes*

10.1	Contract Management Connections in Human Service Do Matter	233
10.2	Building Collaboration Into Performance Management	242
11.1	The Future of Bureaucracy/Transformation	269
12.1	CERN: The Importance of Connection	276
12.2	Case Study: Civic Level Connecting—The Automated City	278

Abbreviations

ADA	Americans with Disabilities Act
AD	Area director
AFRINIC	African Network Information Centre
APA	Administration Procedures Act
ARC	Association for Retarded Citizens
AI	Artificial intelligence
BLM	Bureau of Land Management
CALFED	Collaboration Among State and Federal Agencies to Improve California's Water Supply
CoC	Continuum of care
CIO	Chief information officers
CI	Continuous improvement
CIP	Capital improvement project
CIR	Critical internet resources
CO_2	Carbon dioxide
CoPCAR	Collaboration assessment rubric
CP	Collaborative politics
CT	Cultural theory
DDARS	Developmental disabilities, aging, and rehabilitation services
DFL	Democratic–Farmer–Labor (Party)
DHHS	Department of Health and Human Services
DHR	Department of Human Resources
DNS	Domain name system
DOT	Department of Transportation
EC	Educational Council
FSSA	Family and Social Services Administration
GIS	Geographic information system
HCBS	Home- and community-based services
HEW	Health, Education, and Welfare
HHS	Health and Human Services
HUD	Housing and Urban Development
ICMA	International City Management Association

xiv *Abbreviations*

ICT	Information communication technologies
ID/DD	Intellectual and developmental disabilities
IETF	Internet Engineering Task Force
IESG	Internet Engineering Steering Group
IGM	Intergovernmental management
INARF	Indiana Association of Rehabilitation Facilities
IRS	Internal Revenue Service
IOp	Interoperability
KM	Knowledge management
MLG	Multilevel governance
MPO	Metropolitan Planning Organization
NASA	National Aeronautics and Space Administration
NFC	National Incident Fire Command
NGO	Non-governmental organizations
NOAA	National Oceanic and Atmospheric Administration
NPM	New public management
OASIS	Outcome and assessment information set
OPM	Office of Personnel Management
OSHA	Occupational Safety and Health Administration
OSU	Ohio State University
RDC	Rural Development Council
RIP	Regional internet registration
ROD	Record of decision
SBDC	Small Business Development Center
SES	Senior Executive Service
STEM	Science, technology, engineering, and mathematics
TNA	Tennessee Valley Authority
RGI	Rural Governance Initiative
USAID	U.S. Agency for International Development
USDA	U.S. Department of Agriculture
USDA/RD	U.S. Department of Agriculture/Rural Development

Author Biographies

Robert Agranoff, Ph.D. (University of Pittsburgh 1967) was Professor Emeritus, School of Public and Environmental Affairs, Indiana University-Bloomington, USA and Catedrático, Government and Public Administration Program, Instituto Universitario Ortega y Gasset, Madrid, Spain. He joined IU in 1980 from Northern Illinois University Political Science/Public Affairs (1966–1980) and began at Ortega y Gasset in 1990. At IU, he served as a faculty chair, Ph.D. director, and as Associate Dean for Bloomington. He specialized in public administration, intergovernmental relations (IGR) and management, and public network studies.

His published work includes books, journal articles, book chapters, research reports, encyclopedia articles, and government-sponsored studies. He published several books on collaborative management and intergovernmental relations, including *Collaborative Public Management: New Strategies for Local Governments* (Georgetown University Press, 2003), *Managing Within Networks* (Georgetown University Press, 2007), *Collaborating to Manage: A Primer for the Public Sector* (Georgetown University Press, 2012), *Crossing Boundaries for Intergovernmental Management* (Georgetown University Press, 2017), *and Local Governments in Multilevel Governance* (Lexington Books, 2020). In addition to publishing numerous book chapters and journal articles, Dr. Agranoff was a contributor to *The Encyclopedia of Political Science* (CQ Press, 2011), *Encyclopedia of Public Administration and Public Policy* (Routledge, 2011), *The Oxford Handbook of American Bureaucracy* (Oxford University Press, 2010), and *The Oxford Handbook of State and Local Government* (Oxford University Press, 2014).

Aleksey Kolpakov, Ph.D. (Indiana University, 2012) is a Visiting Assistant Professor at the School of Public Affairs, Florida Atlantic University, who holds a Master of Science degree in organizational and social psychology from the London School of Economics and Political Science and a Ph.D. in public affairs (policy analysis and public management) from Indiana University. His research has been published in academic journals such as *Public Performance & Management Review*, *American Review of Public Administration*, *Public Integrity*, *International Journal of Public Administration*, *Journal of Strategic Contracting and Negotiations*, and *Journal of Health Science*.

He is the author of two books and numerous technical and program evaluation reports for federal, state, and international agencies such as the United Nations xvi *Author Biographies*

Development Program, United Nations Population Fund Agency, International City/County Management Association, Technical Assistance to Countries of Independent States, Organization for Security and Co-operation in Europe, Eurasia Foundation, Conrad Adenaur Foundation and UK Department for International Development. His major areas of research expertise include international nonprofit organizations, networks, and collaboration in the public and nonprofit sectors, managing diversity in the public and nonprofit sectors, leadership in the public and nonprofit sectors, and knowledge management in the public and nonprofit sectors.

Foreword

Classical public administration in the United States reached the pinnacle of its importance in the late 1930s. It left an orthodoxy of principles and structural arrangements that—with significant modification—continue to influence and define public administrative practice today. One of its main tenets was that administrative activity could be coordinated by unity of command or by dominance of idea. Collaborative governance fits the latter category. It requires public managers to coordinate focused efforts of two or more entities to promote common purposes in the absence of hierarchical authority. Although government administration remains largely characterized by hierarchical bureaucracies, collaborative arrangements and networks have become increasingly salient to administrative practice. The potential benefits of collaborative governance and the challenges in realizing them are both substantial.

In this book on *Politics of Collaborative Management*, co-authors Dr. Robert Agranoff and Dr. Aleksey Kolpakov masterfully explore and analyze the political dimensions of collaborative governance. They explain that politics "pervades" collaboration (Chapter 6) at micro through macro levels. Determining "who gets what, when, how" (as Harold Lasswell (2018) famously defined "politics") in collaborative relationships involves power relationships; consensus building and maintenance; "collaborarchy"; asymmetrical participants, values, and interests; decentralized decision-making; resource commitments; and distributive, legal, ethical, and moral concerns; as well as positive, negative, and mixed outcomes—and a great deal more. The political complexity of coordinating collaboration in a network of participants who may be equally or more committed to, or dependent on, other networks in which they participate can be daunting. Including, as the authors do, collaborative governance across federal-, state-, and local-level programs, politics are all but unavoidable.

Among its many virtues, the book is very well written and comprehensive. The authors deftly incorporate and integrate academic literature with important real-world examples. They are balanced in not claiming too much for collaborative governance by noting that it augments rather than replaces government through hierarchical bureaucracies, and that it is hardly a panacea for making the public sector work better and committing it to continuous improvement.

xviii *Foreword*

The book was completed through difficult circumstances. Co-author Dr. Robert ("Bob") Agranoff, a professor at Indiana University-Bloomington (IUB) and top leader in the public administration fields of federalism, intergovernmental relations, and collaborative governance, died in November 2019. He left behind a 200-page manuscript under contract with Routledge. In fall 2020, while the pandemic was taking a heavy toll, his wife, Susan Klein, and Bob's friend and colleague, Art Dykstra, thought the manuscript needed additional work and polishing before publication. Susan asked co-author Dr. Aleksey Kolpakov, a highly accomplished scholar in his own right and one of Bob's former doctoral students and co-authors, if he would consider completing the manuscript as co-author. Though ready to take on the project, he initially demurred on being co-author. At Susan's insistence, however, he eventually agreed. His excellent revision and completion of the manuscript was aided by Catherine Overbey, Bob's research assistant at IU, who found the most recent version of the manuscript and "deciphered" (as Susan put it) Bob's handwritten marginal notes. The Routledge Series on Public Administration and Public Policy is very grateful to the commitment of Susan, Aleksey, and Catherine to the book's publication. It is a major contribution to knowledge about collaborative management. I hope readers will find it as valuable as I do.

David H. Rosenbloom
Series Editor
Washington, DC

Reference

Lasswell, H. D. (2018). *Politics: Who gets what, when, how.* Pickle Partners Publishing.

Preface

This work is designed to be a text or professional reading material for many undergraduate/graduate classes that involve collaborative processing/networking among representatives of different organizations. Collaboration is defined here as the process of facilitating and operating in multiorganizational arrangements for addressing problems and producing solutions through the contributions of several organizations.

Although one often thinks of collaborative management and related group problem-solving as different interests coming together in "peaceful harmony," nothing could be further from reality. Collaborative management has "equal potential" for conflict or at least "interest differentials," leading to inaction and/or conflict-laden modified action. In other words, collaborative management is not always the "smooth" agreement, reaching a compromise, that some solutions/agreements are assumed to be when "outcomes" or solutions are announced. In short, collaboration in real-world action requires steering and agreement-reaching in virtually every situation, with a considerable process that precedes collaborative agreement, regardless of a successful outcome or one more negative in nature. This process is, in effect, a "mini" political and managerial process, which is this volume's aim. We call this collaborative politics (CP) and its management.

The book has been written as a text for undergraduate or graduate courses where it can be used as a required or recommended textbook. Its applications are well suited in several fields/courses when multi-interest collaborative management is part of the curricula: public administration, urban studies, development administration, human services, vocational rehabilitation, social work, allied health, special education, criminal justice, and many other applied fields of study. Although the careers of Drs. Agranoff and Kolpakov were formally lodged in the field of public affairs, their work over the years in organized politics, farm associations, human services, international development, and civic activity, among others, has brought exposure to many different fields of applied problem resolution.

This volume begins with a definitional overview of the process and operations of collaboration and collaborative politics, from routine transactions, or "small p" politics, and the significant issue forces or "big P" politics. One or both are likely to be at work xx *Preface*

in CP and collaborative management. The analysis hinges on the critical ingredient in CP: power, the ability to forge action, and its uses in collaboration. Politics in its basic forms in collaboration are then understood from "small p" and "big P" perspectives.

Throughout this volume, readers are gradually exposed to elaborated and extended analysis of key related findings in CP from the long research tradition in policy and political science. A series of stories have been adapted that highlight some dynamics of CP from a range of various types of jurisdictions. The efficacy of storytelling as a learning tool and contributor to practice is also revealed for analyzing CP in different contexts. Since CP is essentially associated with negotiations and adjustments among administrative actors, we look at how interorganizational/interagency collaboration operates and is managed, as well as how it has been modified or adjusted in its fundamental core concepts of bureaucratic organization and hierarchy.

We would like to thank many people who helped us to complete this project. First of all, we would like to thank a number of individuals at the School of Public and Environmental Affairs at Indiana University who have supported the intellectual curiosity of Dr. Robert Agranoff and Dr. Aleksey Kolpakov (while he was a Ph.D. student there) for a long time. Emeriti faculty from Indiana University, Professor Charles Wise, Professor Lois Wise, Professor Edwardo Rhodes, current Professor Claudia Avellaneda, and his Master student Valerie Rinkle have always supported the various research projects of Dr. Agranoff. We need to acknowledge the encouragement of our long-time research partner, Dr. Michael McGuire, a former Professor at Indiana University who wrote several publications with Dr. Agranoff and Dr. Kolpakov which became the foundation for this volume. We also would like to thank Professor Beryl Radin, Georgetown University, retired, who has influenced the work of Dr. Agranoff in the area of integration of human services and federalism. None of the previous works of Dr. Agranoff would be possible without the support of his wonderful wife, Susan Klein, Professor Emerita, Indiana University. Thanks to her support and dedication, this project was brought to fruition after Dr. Agranoff died in 2019.

This particular book project would not be possible without the contribution of Art Dykstra, a colleague of Dr. Agranoff who reviewed the draft of the manuscript and provided valuable comments to make it more practitioner-oriented. We also appreciate the work of Charlene Lynn Abbott and Catherine T. Overbey, who assisted us in preparing the manuscript from day one. The book would not see the light of day without the editorial work of Christopher Marchand, a former doctoral student of Dr. Aleksey Kolpakov at the University of Nevada, Reno. His comments and revisions made the text more practitioner-friendly while maintaining high standards of academic research. Finally, we would like to thank Cynthia Mahigian-Moorhead for assisting us with the book cover.

We would like to dedicate this book to our loved ones: Dr. Agranoff to his loving wife, Susan Klein, Professor Emerita of Special Education Indiana University-Bloomington, and his granddaughters, Zada and Lily Grimley; and Dr. Kolpakov to his grandmother Zoya and his mother Irina, who supported his love for research since he was a child.

1 From Bureaucracy to the Politics and Organization for Collaborative Management

Everywhere we see bureaucracies representing government, but they are no longer the rigid hierarchies and rule-bound structures as they were once portrayed. Today, we also see strategic alliances, partnerships, coalitions, joint ventures, contracts, franchises, networks, and more (Ring & Van de Ven, 1994). There is even a revised bureaucratic response to environmental issues on the Antarctic continent. Backed by numerous governments, the Antarctic and Southern Ocean Coalition bring together more than 30 non-governmental organizations (NGOs) focused on preserving the continent. The most important accomplishment includes a network of large marine protected areas for the Ross Sea and negotiating a legally binding Polar Code that covers all vessels operating in the Southern Ocean (www.seagov.org). The challenge to agency hierarchies involves the flow of information aided by the personal computer, e-mail, and the internet, which have all "allowed ordinary citizens to organize themselves into much larger and dispersed networks than has ever been possible before," observes Niall Ferguson (Ferguson, 2014). Today, there are interagency task forces, interdepartmental task forces, intergovernmental bodies, contractor–contractee connections, multiple agency task forces, interorganizational contracts, leases, services delivery and sponsoring agencies, public–private alliances, and networks of public and private agencies/organizations of all types that interact with every level of local to national bureaucracies.

In the 20th century, bureaucracy was the core organizational concept shaping public organization. Following the influence of Max Weber, Berman (1987) identifies four major features of bureaucracy: (1) hierarchy; (2) continuity with rule-governed procedures; (3) operating with impersonality so that work is interactive without arbitrariness or favoritism by following established rules; and (4) expertise and competency-based neutrality by merit- selected/trained officials. Such strict rule-bound behavior results in considerable inflexibility and hierarchy, which in turn may discourage individual effort and promote overly protective organizational behavior, and limited actions beyond the mandate bureaucracies nevertheless prevailed in their intraorganizational niches to reach their internal and external clients for decades.

Collaboration within and between bureaucracies is everywhere these days. For example, the Indiana Innovation Institute recently formed a consortium called

DOI: 10.4324/9781003385769-1

2 *From Bureaucracy to Politics and Organization*

Radius to promote advanced technology around the Crane U.S. Naval Surface Warfare Center for the meeting of research universities, military and industrial leaders to collaborate on projects that directly connect with the U.S. Department of Defense/Crane. Its space will house more than 40 tenants to solve technical problems in microelectronics, hypersonics, electronic warfare, and other advanced technologies (Bloomington Herald-Times, 2018). Similarly, the Indiana Innovation Institute recently opened a "new collaborative space" in the Crane Technology Park to facilitate universities, military, and industrial leaders to collaborate on projects aimed at the U.S. Department of Defense. It is part of a space that involves 40 other tenants, including Purdue and Indiana universities (Indiana Innovation Institute, 2018). In Philadelphia, neighbors develop green space into gardens (even in alleyways), cleaning up shared space, planting flowers, vegetables, and herbs, making their own compost, and sharing vegetable harvests. This type of collaboration to "green" urban spaces is just one of the thousands of urban collaborative garden efforts (Editorial Board, 2018).

There are also numerous mandatory collaborations, such as those among emergency management agencies at the local level. For example, the U.S. Department of Housing and Urban Development requires local agencies serving the homeless to collaborate on obtaining funding. Identified as a "continuum of care" (CoC), the approach requires four McKinney Act components needed of service: (1) prevention by community outreach and assessment; (2) emergency shelter as a street alternative; (3) short-term transitional housing and supportive services (e.g., employment); and (4) long-term permanent housing (Hafer, 2018). Literally hundreds of such mandated collaborative undertakings flow in the United States from the McKinney Act. They are all part of this volume's focus, that of collaborative politics (referred to as CP).

The contemporary challenge to bureaucratic organization is different, as Watson, Deeming, and Treffny (2009) observe it in relation to contemporary environmental development:

> While government bureaucracies were designed for the disturbed-reactive environment of the last century, they lack the sorts of response capabilities and qualities that organizations need to cope with the turbulent conditions that now exist. Bureaucracy was designed for functional specialization, whereas many present-day societal problems are framed in ways that transcend the conventional categories of economy, society, and environment. The concept of sustainable development is particularly important in this regard. While many governments have adopted sustainability as a fundamental development principle and goal, they continue to rely on bureaucratic structures and processes for policy delivery. Additional concerns about the capacity of bureaucratic systems to cope with emerging conditions revolve around their dependency on professional expertise and objective evidence. Many of the major societal problems that attract public attention, including climate change, are characterized by uncertainty, contested

knowledge, and intense debate. In these sorts of situations, the limitations of expert knowledge are quickly exposed, and therefore "professional expertise" itself does not carry the same sort of authority and legitimacy as it might have carried in the past. Overall what this implies is that bureaucratic arrangements no longer match the prevailing operating environment of public policy. As a result, governments and their bureaucratic organizations have come under increasing pressure to adapt to the new environmental conditions, integrate new holistic framings of societal problems, and respond to the loss of public confidence in government and professional expertise.

(p. 450)

As a result of these conditions, bureaucracy now is considerably less executive-centered in practice and theory (Rosenbloom, 2010) and focuses its work on public problems with a host of connected public agencies and NGOs to meet its challenges (Powell, 1990; Ring & Van de Ven, 1994). Bureaucracies do indeed exist—but in a series of multiagency arenas to meet the challenges of vested interest, uncertainty, contested knowledge, and continuing debate, all leading to new interactive conditions for bureaucracy in the collaborative era.

Collaboration in public management involves the joint efforts of different government and nonorganizational representatives trying to solve problems by joint facilitation and operation in multiorganizational arrangements in their political and managerial arenas. It involves the "ultimate" in crossing organizational boundaries. The aim is to solve problems that cannot be solved or resolved easily by a single organization (Agranoff & McGuire, 2003; McGuire, Agranoff, & Silvia, 2011). While largely engaged by administrators, outside organization agency executives, and officer volunteers, collaboration involves emergent managerial processes.

Collaboration is also political in nature, a less visible but real-world interactive function. Indeed, its development in the United States parallels the American "stable state" development that took shape over time and matured (Stillman, 1998). Simply, where there are governments, there are politics, "the deliberation, commitment, or contestation (s) that are related to governing" (Palonen, 2011, p. 1300). Virtually every organization that collaborates brings its internal and external "political baggage" with it. Politics are ever-present but less visible in practice, less formally taught in workshops and classes, and less publicly obvious in collaborative process instruction or related forums. Politics are not only ever-present in collaboration, as they also promote public value, while administrative process analysis is normally more devoid of overt politics. However, there is considerable empirical evidence that political actors and influences weigh considerably on collaborative engagement (e.g., Margerum, 2011; Lejano & Ingram, 2009). In regard to politics, Machiavelli states in the preface to *The Prince*, "I have not found among my belongings anything that I hold more dear or valuable than my knowledge of the conduct of great men, learned through long experience of modern affairs and continual study of ancient history" (Machiavelli, 1995, p. 3).

4 *From Bureaucracy to Politics and Organization*

Although the traditional view of management is grounded in hierarchical, vertically aligned organizational structures, the chief historical concerns arising have been focused on the limits of rationality and ethical neutrality, and the potentially dehumanizing effects that public bureaucracies once brought to both the people who work in them and those whom they are supposed to serve. The managerial key players in governments are positioned at the top of the public bureaucracy, "to whom" accounts need to be made (Koliba, Meek & Zia, 2019). The role of politics in the administration of public bureaucracies has been a prominent topic in the public administration field, ranging from Woodrow Wilson (1887) and Frank Goodnow's (1900) early calls for the separation of politics and administration to Paul Appleby's recognition that politics plays a big role in the day-to-day practices of most public bureaucracies (Appleby, 1965), to Phillip Selznick's discussion of the role of politics and citizen participation as a form of cooptation (2011). Across these threads of discussion has been the assumption first captured by Karl Mannheim that "bureaucracy turns all political issues into matters of administration" (Mannheim, 1936, p. 118). Echoing this observation, a general consensus has emerged that public administrators are political actors—and, more specifically, policy-makers—when interpreting and enforcing rules and regulations outlined in laws and statutes. Frederick Mosher (1982) discussed the role of politics in the life of public administrators:

> Public administrators are heavily engaged in policy and politics a good share of their time. Still, much of this activity is of a different order of politics from that represented by political parties, elections, and votes in Congress. It is controversy, competition, and negotiation among different factions within the bureaucracy itself. It consists in dealing with, responding to, or resisting clienteles and other interest groups outside the bureaucracy, and dealing with Congressional groups and other individual congressmen.
>
> (p. 95)

James March and Johan Olsen (1996, p. 950) define politics as "aggregating individual preferences into collective actions by some procedures of rational bargaining, negotiation, coalition formation, and exchange." Essentially, "politics both results from and contributes to negotiation and bargaining processes" (Koliba, Meek, & Zia, 2019, p. 314). "Smaller scope politics unfolds as the result of more routine negotiated meaning, positioning, and other "games" (Rhodes, 1997, p. 126) through the phenomena of everyday actors and resource exchanges. Broader politics can be found in the big power plays, electoral processes, the role and influence of political parties, formal lobbying, and the creation of interest group coalitions, in this case, designed to impact the decisions and actions of sovereign governments.

Two brief scenarios involving collaborative management politics illustrate how politics pervades process. First, in Box 1.1, local economic development with heavy intergovernmental overtones tells a lot about the politics of collaborative management.

From Bureaucracy to Politics and Organization 5

Box 1.1 Political Negotiations in Cincinnati

Cincinnati became heavily involved in both political and administrative bargaining and negotiation with state government while under pressure in the mid-1990s by both its major professional sport franchises (the baseball Reds and football Bengals) to build new playing facilities to improve financial arrangements with the city. The city government, including the city manager, was under heavy fire to broker a deal that would keep both franchises in town. Cincinnati saw the opportunity to negotiate with the State of Ohio regarding its Capital Improvement Project (CIP) funds. The CIP program is primarily designed to help communities revitalize their physical infrastructures, particularly either those of general public use or those that connect with state projects through the Ohio Division of Natural Resources, the Ohio Building Authority, the Board of Regents (university), or agencies in the governor's administrative cabinet. Although the CIP is not explicitly designed for retaining sports franchises, city staff initially generated additional local funding criteria to state criteria and then sought local public input on projects. Though the original public hearing list of nine priorities included an aquarium, a park, and conservatory improvements, the city in the end was able to place heavy emphasis on the projects designed to help retain the sports franchises, particularly riverfront improvements near the proposed stadia and for nearby downtown recreation and entertainment. The next stage involved extended back-and-forth negotiations with state officials, who were not initially receptive. After a great deal of give and take, a total of $13.9 million in CIP money was approved, the largest award in the city's history. The city was able to direct a substantial proportion of this state program, primarily intended for other purposes, toward its most pressing priorities at the riverfront site. It would not have happened without mobilization of local support, sublimation of other priorities, and—most importantly—the confidence in formulating proposals and experience-based ability to engage in protracted bargaining with the state government.

Source: Agranoff and McGuire (2004, pp. 504–505)

Cincinnati was able to respond to challenges for change through its political will and ability to play the ultimate political games along with collaboration management. If one does not see politics behind these moves, it would appear that understanding politics may not be their game. It depicts the outcomes of what we would identify as heavy or "big P" collaborative management and politics, played with high stakes.

This second scenario in Box 1.2 also demonstrates that political power is not always distributed equally among collaborative management players. This scenario, from a comparative study of state rural development councils, makes clear that some political interests and their agendas are more prominent than others:

6 *From Bureaucracy to Politics and Organization*

Box 1.2 Rural Development Councils

Lurking behind the overt pretenses of network power sharing was the contesting and sometimes contention or compliance enforcing of the most powerful stakeholders. In virtually every rural council state, the interest or noninterest of the governor's office proved to be a key force in determining the issues that the councils addressed. In one or two states, councils' agendas proved to be their governor's agenda. In other states, the work of councils could come to a halt if their governors were uninterested or unwilling to support it. Under very limited circumstances could most councils thread on the turf of an administration's rural agenda, if one existed. Rural policy agendas belonged to the governor, so councils were relegated to marginal cross-jurisdiction discussions, issue papers, and demonstrations. At a network operating level, most councils also have to defer to the power of their two most important stakeholders, the state departments of economic development (agencies also very close to their governors) and the U.S. Department of Agriculture's rural development unit, housed in each state and headed by a presidential appointee. These two agencies constitute the sources of discretionary funding for rural development projects. In one state, the power conflict within the council between these two major stakeholders was so intense that the rest of the council tried to "mute" it by precluding either party from membership on its steering committee—but this was not a deterrent for either one, because they wielded their operational levers behind the scenes. Most importantly, in this state, the powerful stakeholders limited the council's agenda to issues that did not interfere with their interests.

Source: Agranoff and McGuire (2000, pp. 385–421)

Other cases involve "big P" organization politics. For example, Box 1.3 is a personal story demonstrating the existence of broader or heavy political overtones to collaborative efforts at administrative reorganization to enhance collaboration in human services.

Box 1.3 Reorganization in Indiana Family and Social Services Administration (FSSA) in Indiana

In the early 1990s, newly elected Indiana Gov. Evan Bayh's chief of staff asked one author of this book, Dr. Agranoff, to chair and steer a task force of state cabinet-level human service agency program heads, peak lobby

---

association executive directors/lobbyists, academics, and civic association leaders to integrate the various state government health and human services agencies into a "comprehensive department" of health and human services. This new structure would enable the program-to-program crosswalks to meet complex client needs. Dr. Agranoff was told that he was chosen because of his prior academic work on a leading comprehensive DHHS compendium on the subject (Agranoff & Pattakos, 1979) and his pre-academic political experience as a full-time state political party legislative affairs director in Minnesota. The Bayh task force was a very amicable group of professionals representing administration of in-home support, social welfare, public health, vocational rehabilitation, mental health, developmental, physical disabilities, and others. In the beginning, time was spent on core approaches and working principles, designing how the various "pillars" would remain in basic service departments yet be able to reach across prior separate department boundaries.

As the group was about to "go public" with a working plan before it went to the legislature, a "political bomb" of sorts was dropped. One morning, the chief of staff called (political messages of this type remained by phone) and relayed that the task force had to take the Public Health Department out of the new agency. Why? Because the Indiana State Medical Association (ISMA) objected to its inclusion in the new "umbrella" department, referring to some sort of secondary status. Dr. Agranoff replied that they have virtually no involvement in public health and, under many circumstances, cross-programming is essential. Examples of Medicaid, aging, and disabilities were raised. It would "cut off" the huge state Medicaid program (in the new department) as well as immunizations (which would remain in Public Health), along with a series of small programs that would stay in a freestanding public health department. Moreover, virtually every state that made similar reorganization moves always included its public health system. The reply was simple. The ISMA would lobby against the entire proposal if we retain Public Health.

Source: Robert Agranoff

There was no choice in the face of politics of the powerful medical interest group. The Public Health Department (without Medicaid) was dropped from the bill, and over a quarter-century later, it remains independent. At the same time, the combined department continues with the other programs, including Medicaid. The ISMA's move in 1991 clearly represents what one can call the "big boys" of politics or "big P" politics. At the time, the inclusion of public health obviously would have risked a fatal blow to the entire reorganization bill.

8 *From Bureaucracy to Politics and Organization*

Whatever collaborative results may emanate, the process—state rural development councils—is designed to: (1) deal with the politics; and (2) reach some sort of state-based rural strategy involving collaborative management.

These three incidents underscore the pervasiveness of collaborative politics (CP) in management, whether internal or external to a program. It is possible that supranational, national, subnational, and local politics are also somehow in program mixes. Many issues and concerns are thrown into administrative, ideological and advocacy groups, party, and power of office fights as the politics of these issues "bubble down" to local/program level concerns due to the interconnections among these politics (Agranoff, 2018). Indeed, behind the façade of government, politics are likely to be almost everywhere and not often obvious or in the visible picture.

A contemporary example relating to disabilities programs illustrates the more "hidden hand" of politics. Governments in many countries are now encouraged to adhere to international standards for the disabled living in their communities; for example, the intellectual/developmentally disabled, physically disabled, the impaired elderly, and persons with mental illness. The United Nations Convention on the Rights of Persons with Disabilities includes these standards in the codified form (United Nations, 2006). This convention is supported by the International Council on Disabilities and endorsed by numerous countries' disability and veterans organizations (Agranoff, 2018). The council uses local government advocates to promote accessibility, independent and community living, employment and education opportunities, and healthcare (Brown, 2015).

The Americans with Disabilities Act (ADA) of 1990 has incorporated these international standards and includes many anti-discrimination provisions which are now interlaced into federal rules and standards of funding and providing financial grants to the states (Agranoff, 2013). ADA is not presumed to be a "who can oppose it?" law. Local officials and experts interpret and wrestle with the federal government over measures that are not necessarily technically legal but have political elements, pressures, and discretion-seeking activities, resulting in ADA politics. The political factors are then compounded at the local government and NGO levels, where networks and those who wish to make anti-discrimination easier are constantly at work. Because the ADA (and state-level anti-discrimination issues) are interwoven with program/funding issues, disability groups and agencies at the local level are administratively and politically involved in the push and pull of the ADA (and state-level anti-discrimination issues). Some of these worries may be dialed down along the way, especially if local activists disagree with the state and/or federal government policies and concerns in other ways. As a result, anti-discrimination concerns must be viewed from political and administrative perspectives.

From a government perspective, "hidden" politics often deeply involves policy/program concerns as collaboration/deliberation in multilevel governance (MLG) unfolds. Similar to the disability rights issue, the political dimension could also be identified in environmental, economic development, K–12 education, workforce development, infrastructure building, and many other policy contexts (Agranoff,

2018). Like the example mentioned previously of programming for people with disabilities, none of these policies are purely apolitical in nature. The issue is that legal clauses, negotiations, and program standards are visible to everyone. They are usually written as laws, regulations, financing rules, program standards, written expectations, and evaluation criteria. Thus, while not often the foci of collaborative studies, politics are present there but less detectable and considered, and therefore need to be examined to understand the larger collaborative management picture (Gazley, 2010).

The politics of collaborative management is much more than these "big-picture" issues. In the "small p" category are also the stresses, strains, pressures issues, and issue avoidance of organizational-agency delegates and representatives who struggle to work across agency lines in ways without the assistance of rigid hierarchy, mission certainty, and deliberative goals familiar to organizations. Indeed, in addition to the normal agency politics, CP encompasses these issues across organizational lines. Often mission compatibility is at stake. Scarce in-house resources are expected to be shared across organizations. Internal processes become external. New ways of public engagement are deliberated and engaged. Increasingly, power of decision is across or between and continuing internal power configurations. This is also a growing phenomenon in Western Europe (Wollmann, 2012). As will be demonstrated, all of this reflects *dispersed power* out of bureaucracies and its manifestations—changing boundaries—that pervade the collaborative venture. Many of these issues are "within" the interactions of the deliberative processes of collaboration but rarely in the most visible form. Presently, they are the essential aspects of the changing state or what is termed *governance* (Rhodes, 1997, 2014).

In many ways, these political considerations are not obvious but are nevertheless present and relevant. In the same way that most of the details of Shakespeare's life must be teased out by reading his plays, one needs to find the basics of politics in collaborative management-related reports and agreements. For example, in 1606, it was *King Lear*, along with the influences of Plutarch's *Life of Anthony*, that offers a glimpse of court politics via Shakespeare's role as Groom of the Chamber, which offered him a view of the court. According to James Shapiro (2015), a look at his works in 1606 allows us to see *Shakespeare* traveling back in time to tease out his politics, as he illuminates in his *The Year of Lear: Shakespeare in 1606*. Indeed, in this work, Shapiro takes a closer look at the political forces that contributed to his plays, as they were ever-present in Lear and Anthony. In many ways, it represents an exercise in governmentality or the reflections on how best to govern through facilitated and structured freedom of persons, groups, and organizations (Foucault, 2001).

Politics as a Positive and Negative Force

It is not unusual for persons involved in CP to see politics as an ever-present and negative force. Questions are raised such as: what led to the breakdown of the process, and why are unsuccessful outcomes easily written off as "political" in

10 *From Bureaucracy to Politics and Organization*

resonance? In the earlier identified case of the Family and Social Services Administration (FSSA) in Indiana, the resistance of the ISMA was really overshadowed by many other cooperating elements and departments, e.g., Mental Health and Developmental Disabilities, Income Support, Rehabilitation, Children's Services, and others that were constructively in support of making some form of combined structure work. Moreover, many leading state interest groups were in full support. They represented essential core political support factors. Indeed, the result was the same program outcome: collaboration patterns as in other states engaged in program organization realignment and waivers. It would never have happened without general support. Sometimes, people tend to forget the political positives.

It is also important to note that some CP actors consistently avoid necessary politics. For example, the experience of one author of this book who facilitated the work of various collaboratives in Nevada and Ohio (Dr. Aleksey Kolpakov) and the study of 14 networks by the other author of this primer (Agranoff, 2007a) suggests that some collaboration networks virtually avoid overt politics by coming together to exchange information about mutual interests but always sweep aside both positive and negative politics by convening to simply report on what the disparate parties are doing of "joint interest" areas, taking absolutely no real actions as a network. One such network involves the Darby Partnership in western Ohio. It meets quarterly and issues a newsletter regarding watershed conservation management practices but takes no action as a group; for example, on any regulated planning and zoning of problems, presumably to avoid legal and political objections, among other features, to its agency-established missions and operations (Agranoff, 2007a; Koontz, 2004).

Politics can be real and a pervasive force in collaboration. Collaboration Among State and Federal Agencies to Improve California's Water Supply (CALFED) is a California-based water quality network operated through formal and informal operations of many different organizations (Innes, Connick, & Booher, 2007). In contrast to Darby, its development shows that this water quality network hit many political obstacles. Michael Hanemann and Calvin Dyckman (2009) conclude that it is nearly impossible for CALFED to reach its potential as a water resource management network due to the presence of the strong political opposition of core involved interests, major water users such as water supply firms and agricultural organizations. Constant political pressure by these various interests led to thwarted water-conservation efforts. It was a clear inhibiting factor. The network designers thus came to a calculated decision leading to voluntary solution frameworks as the designed best chance of success. Its fundamentally fallacious reliance on these voluntary agreements to reconcile deep differences proved to be the "Achilles' heel" of the collaboration. The overarching limiting factors were political decision-makers' loss of interest, refusal to engage with the agency, and jurisdictional fragmentation. For example, state legislative unwillingness to get too deep in the process and exercise leadership, along with the basic passivity of the State Water Resources Control Board, to take on the water control risks as an administrative agency. The study

From Bureaucracy to Politics and Organization   11

authors conclude that the politics of the matter is compounded by property rights disagreements and the perception by many parties that to "engage in this process [is] to place them in zero-sum games where the risk of negative outcomes proved not worth playing" (Hanemann & Dyckman, 2009, p. 712). To environmental policy observers, collaboration in such networks must depend on political networking that is not necessarily tied to political/elected office or administration. "A political network needs the agency to coordinate activities and allow the resources as well as provide network support functions" and also to follow with implementing activities (Margerum, 2011, pp. 299–300). Success is often problematic without the complex political manifestations worked out, as was in CALFED.

Collective Action

Collaborative management involves what Elinor Ostrom—the late colleague of one author and former professor of the other author, the only female Nobel Prize winner in economics and Professor in the School of Environmental and Public Affairs at Indiana University who founded the Workshop in Political Theory and Policy Analysis—called collective action (Ostrom, 1990). In self-governing, common-pool resource appropriations and shared norms such as trust are key. They have the effect of decreasing the costs associated with monitoring, building commitment, and rule creation that oversee the collective effort. Additional supportive forces—such as repetitive face-to-face communication, symmetry in individual assets and successes, longer time horizons, involvement in rule-setting, graduated transactions, and learning from the process—may also enhance collective action. In general, collective action problems facing NGO and government partners in CP is a very important arena of study (Bielefeld, Perry, & Thomson, 2010), as bureaucracy is "part of a repertoire of overlapping, supplementary, and competing forms of coexisting in contemporary democracies, and so are market organization and network organization" (Olsen, 2006, p. 18).

Government Into Governance

The collaborative organizational metamorphosis, for example, into CP, now involves governance systems as more and more actors enter the public stage to carry out government functions and programs (Torfing, 2014). What is less understood is the continuing "central" or core working role that government plays. It remains a viable and authoritative entity as it interacts with other governments and non-governmental actors in emergent governance systems in many respects through collaboration (Offe, 2009). Literally thousands of governments and NGOs exist in the United States, making policies and seeing that such policies are transformed into public programs at the delivery level. Governance largely comes in with the latter functions, "a mix of all kinds of governing efforts by all manner of sociopolitical actors, public as well as private; occurring between them at different levels, in different governance

12 *From Bureaucracy to Politics and Organization*

modes and orders" (Kooiman, 2003, p. 3). Moreover, governance has expanded the traditional bureaucracy concept (Piattoni, 2009). As this volume documents, contemporary collaborative management involves real-world human interaction management. Currently, "it entails more than officials representing governments; it includes NGOs and other groups that interact with governments as advocates or in contractual, legal, collaborative and working partner connections" (Agranoff, 2017, p. 3). These forces constitute the heart of collaborative management.

Collaboration theory and practice need to consider government policy and administration's evolving and ever-changing development while maintaining established government institutional processes (Agranoff, 2017). This enterprise "journeys through evolving relationships that include law and state-building, working interdependencies among governments, partnerships with NGOs, and complex multisector networks, as certain verities of political science remain as part of the story—in particular, how government institutions and later NGOs interact to shape politics" (p. 3), government externalization, and transactional management across sectors: devolution, coordination, and distribution of power (Piattoni, 2009). It shows the ongoing interplay between change, like the variety of stakeholders influencing the organization, administration, and evaluation of programs, and permanent conditions. Specifically, in his four volumes of administrative history (1948, 1951, 1954, 1958), Leonard White examined the activities of actors involved in the government processes, which subsequently led to the art of administration. These research studies examined "service delivery under intergovernmental programs within the basic parameters regarding the type of services to be financed, to whom they may be delivered, and with whom programs are fixed in law and regulations" (Agranoff, 2017, p. 3). Those parameters are seldom modified. However, as practice of collaboration expands administratively, it becomes evident that the old is very rarely and completely replaced by the new (Bovaird, 2005). In reality, the new is built on the foundation of the old. Thus, any theory of CP follows suit.

Four Phases of the New Governing

As government has moved into governing, with its multiple actors dealing with programs that cross boundaries, new actors in CP are exercising coordination and control in collaboration. As a result, agencies engage in emergent forms of managing, culminating in linkages across governments at different levels and with NGOs. Rhodes (1996, p. 195) concludes that "government is searching for a new operating code as a result of these forces." These changes involve government and its interlocutors in what are now regarded as governance systems.

Governance implies many working actions and transactions across governments and participants outside government. This situation has existed for some time, but as the multiplicity of participants and acts have become increasingly mutually contingent, these actions have become denser and more intense (Agranoff, 2017). From an operational standpoint, the four approaches to collaborative governing are summarized and analyzed in Figure 1.1 as intergovernmental relations approaches.

From Bureaucracy to Politics and Organization   13

> 1. Interdependence between organizations. Governance is broader than government, including non-state actors. Changing the state's boundaries means the boundaries between public, private and voluntary sectors become shifting and opaque.
> 2. Continuing interactions between participants, caused by the need to exchange resources and negotiate shared purposes.
> 3. Game-like interactions rooted in trust and regulated by rules of the game negotiated and agreed upon by network participants.
> 4. A significant degree of autonomy from the state. Networks are not accountable to the state; they are self-organising. Although the state does not occupy a privileged, sovereign position. it can indirectly and imperfectly steer networks.

Figure 1.1 Four Approaches to Intergovernmental Relations
Source: Rhodes (1996, p. 660)

The dominant paradigm has included but moved from building integral states or separate subnational jurisdictions that are minimally related to one another and eventually included not only divided but mixed jurisdictional NGO competencies. The more involved NGOs are partnering with governments in operations that function in many ways like public service markets. The resulting complexity has led to more intensive collaborative activities, a sort of metagovernance that occurs both inside and outside the boundaries of governments and NGOs.

To the degree that there was traditional management, the earliest intergovernmental directions were predominantly top-down, from central bureaucracy to local level. When this activity initially accelerated, new actors—for example, governments promoting procurement from suppliers and contractors—became the first non-governmental agents for those governments as principals. As this activity grew, new tools—contracts, loans, vouchers—entered what later became known as part of governance. In turn, this led to both top-down and bottom-up collaborative activity that ultimately generated horizontal systems of different programs.

As maintained, CP has always been interwoven with politics but it becomes more convoluted with more players. It moved later to administration, in a phase that blended in political interjurisdictional concerns and extended to focus more on citizen involvement through grassroots politics, from partisan and electoral concerns to protect and promote growing aid programs and government association lobbying at the policy enactment stage (Agranoff, 2018). Many public administration researchers and practitioners are aware that CP encompasses the big picture and political shifts at the transaction level, such as over grant and contract negotiations and rules, standards, and interaction practices. Meanwhile, CP lobbying has gradually become a political process.

CP's actions have always been rooted in legal enactment. Responsibility was assigned at the earliest stages to deal with program growth and cases of program overlapping. As time went by, NGOs became more and more responsible for the

14 *From Bureaucracy to Politics and Organization*

larger part of operational programming and became heavily involved in service delivery. As a result, government agencies and NGOs gradually realized the importance of working together, which subsequently gave birth to collaborative management (Agranoff, 2018).

Meanwhile, judicial involvement in CP expanded from performing the original constitutional role of each level, especially in federal programs, to enriched multilevel involvement by considering the operational concerns of subnational governments. Then, it covered the needs of NGOs to separate public responsibilities from non-public responsibilities without clearly specifying the roles and rights of citizens and clients. In short, one can observe the expansion of CP beyond traditional actors in IGR to NGOs that can deliver services to their clients. Consequently, "the concern went beyond the intergovernmental actions of governments to those of NGO delivery agencies and their clients" (Agranoff, 2017, p. 229).

If one now looks down the column in Table 1.1 labeled "Continuing Roles" of government agencies, one sees that public agencies retain important powers— outsourcing and networking notwithstanding. These responsibilities include, but are not limited to, ultimate legal authority, financial dominance, and key supervision, funding, compliance, and enforcement responsibilities (McGuire & Agranoff, 2010). As such, the "partners" of public agencies in effect work for and with them when engaging public agencies, not the reverse. The explanation is quite simple. Collaboratives and networks do not possess formal authority to exercise the state's sovereign authority. The essential elements of government work that have been contracted out as alternative service delivery networks as grantee, recipient, and delivery are associated with subnational governments and nonprofit and for-profit agencies. Thus, the transactional core of network/collaborative operations—including funding, standards writing, and auditing—largely lies outside most collaboratives' normal deliberations. Even in the most well-defined network of public/non-governmental organization connections, government agencies are not replaced but redirected. Under these circumstances, it is impossible to embrace the principle that networks and organized non-governmental actors replace government agencies or "hollowing out" as the key governance agents. They are not.

While governments once had near-exclusive authority for operating programs, their operational control is shared and/or decreasing. "Ultimate legal authority with regard to regulations and standards, along with court guidance, remains" (McGuire & Agranoff, 2010, p. 379). The majority of funding is still public, but it is increasingly flowing downward through governments and outward to for-profits and nonprofits. Despite this, public finance continues to dominate due to the greater scope and capability of public revenue. Although the agency's budgetary mechanism is still the usual legislative appropriation procedure, contractors outside of government are now at the end of the money transmission belt as well—with government agencies serving as contract principals in many cases (McGuire & Agranoff, 2010). Thus, the public role remains substantial.

From Bureaucracy to Politics and Organization 15

Table 1.1 From Bureaucracy to the Politics and Organization for Collaborative Management

Element	Traditional Roles	Emergent Roles	Continuing Roles
Powers	The hierarchical, mostly legal authority for government-operated public programming	Legal authority remains; less directed control over public program operations	Delegation of administrative powers and some programs, not an ultimate legal authority with agencies, their regulations, and standards-court guidance
Financing	Tax-based near-exclusive financing of public programs	Money flows through the operating set of public and NGOs, subnational governments	Finance domination of the public sector-broad scope of revenue capacity
Service Operations	Delivery through public service agencies in government departments	Outsourcing to an increasing number of NGOs and subnational governments that are in day-to-day operational control	Substantial oversight of implementation services delivery
Oversight	The flow of service and fiscal outputs up the line to separate in-house reporting and auditing functions	Basically unchanged except for self-reports and minimal external program evaluations, and public–NGO auditing	Fiscal and program audits for governmental NGOs
Transaction of Legitimization	Agency legislative program enablement/ appropriations	Implementation organizations public–NGO-designated recipients	Bureaucratic donor to non-bureaucratic outsources
Fiscal Mechanism	Agency appropriations	Contracted agents outside of the government	Government agencies arc contract principals
Organization	Hierarchy of line and staff units appointed administrative program heads	Non-bureaucratic actors are participants, advocates, shared administration, plus many delivery agents	Government officials participate with NGO actors, enforce programs

Source: Robert Agranoff

Notes: As indicated in the table, service operations have changed from hierarchical or divisionalized government departments directly delivering services or products to imposed outsourcing to subnational governments and NGOs with operational control. However, government is still largely responsible for oversight (or review) of contracted services or products (McGuire & Agranoff, 2010). Even though the fiscal and program reporting and auditing requirements have been delegated to subnational governments, private and nonprofit organizations for self-originated reporting, and for-profits, the government still bears a large responsibility for auditing. During this process, "agency organizing involves more than line and staff units within an organization; it includes non-agency, participant actors who are engaged in service delivery, as well as advocates for programs, working together with government officials to enforce the rules and make programs" (p. 379). The table captures these changes.

16 *From Bureaucracy to Politics and Organization*

Government bureaucracy slowly became more "external" in focus under a CP transformation. As Agranoff (2017, p. 229) notes:

> Hierarchical and administrative roles changed as transactional interactions across governments and agencies increased and NGO executants were recognized as both agents and stewards of public programs that worked conductively or interactively between government and NGOs. Administrative tasks cumulatively evolved as well, moving from less formal oversight review and fiscal post audits to more standardized grant reporting and auditing, and to government–NGO contract management. Ultimately interactive organizations began working horizontally and vertically in joint learning and problem-solving activities. In sum, more regular and more relational interactive processes emerged and became standardized parts of administrative behavior.

Consequently, the most notable transactions moved from older program reports to newer complex and involved agreements and electronic services exchanges (Agranoff, 2017). They "were followed by even more detailed contract-related and results-oriented concerns" (p. 229). Business approaches, e.g., leases and contracts, were imprinted on the public sector to some degree as newer public management approaches. This led to CP's multiple participants undertaking network-based knowledge management and other multiorganization designs and operations. Finally, CP style further evolved into continuing operating partnerships. These arrangements will become clear as the text moves through CP in action.

Collaboration and Law

The framework of public law related to collaborative management is an often-overlooked dimension in action. It has become particularly relevant as an increasing number of public programs are externalized yet legally enabled. For example, David Rosenbloom (2018) has observed that the federal courts have interpreted the U.S. Constitution to affect contractor (i.e., NGOs) relationships in three ways: (1) racial and ethnic classifications in contracting are subject to strict scrutiny (*Adarand Constructors vs. Pena*, 1995); (2) contractors and those engaged in transactional relationships with governments retain their First Amendment rights; and (3) except for the Thirteenth Amendment, the Constitution does not govern relationships among purely private parties—however, under certain circumstances, contractors can become "state actors" when engaging in, public functions or otherwise exercising public purposes (*Brentwood Academy vs. Tennessee Secondary School Athletic Association*, 2001). Thus, the law brings NGO actors into public regulation.

In a comprehensive overview of the role of law in collaborative governance, Lisa Blomgren Amsler (2016) provides a core of the legal frameworks for collaborative governance. She notes that scholarship generally does not explicitly look at the public law framework shown in Box 1.4, which summarizes the practical conclusions from Amsler's introduction to law and CP. Amsler concludes that the practice of the law related to collaboration must be considered to be a key public value.

From Bureaucracy to Politics and Organization   17

Box 1.4   Practice and Law in Collaboration

Practitioner Points

- In designing public engagement and collaborative processes, public managers must consider the legal framework that governs their actions.
- Relevant law varies across the federal, state, and local arenas and shapes design choices.
- Collaboration itself is an important value to the public and stakeholders.
- Public managers must acquire an understanding of basic constitutional and administrative law to plan effective public engagement and collaborative governance.
- In seeking to innovate, public managers should consider what the relevant legal framework is and consult with legal counsel. However, they should also consider the likelihood that in-house counsel may be risk-averse.
- When innovation presents a case of first impression, one for which there is not case law, managers should ask not whether they can innovate by using participatory and collaborative processes but how to do it consistent with their legal authority.

Source: Amsler (2016, p. 700)

Advancing Networks as Core Collaborative Solutions

The emergent phenomenon of governance now means dealing with collaborative management as a consciousness of networking and networks that are permanent or semi-permanent structures of interdependence representing the efforts of persons from multiple organizations working to solve particular problems. In business, networks represent some midway point between open markets and hierarchies, whereby relationships are established and maintained over time. Walter Powell (1990) famously labeled these approaches to be neither those of markets nor hierarchies:

> In network modes of resource allocation, transactions occur neither through discrete exchanges nor by administrative fiat but through networks of individuals engaged in reciprocal, preferential, mutually supportive actions. Networks can be complex: they involve neither the explicit criteria of the market nor the familiar paternalism of the hierarchy. A basic assumption of network relationships is that one party is dependent on resources controlled by another and that there are gains to be had by the pooling of resources.
>
> (p. 270)

To analysts like Powell, network participants ideally put aside the right to pursue their own interests for the benefit of the whole. To others, networks present another vehicle to pursue one's interest while working with others, and the possibility that

18 *From Bureaucracy to Politics and Organization*

other interests may be derived from the network process. In short, networks are an important means of collaboration but are not as inherently politically neutral as sometimes assumed.

As important as they are to solving complex interunit problems, through the potential linkages of networks of different types, most remain as "voluntary" structures. Importantly, it has been maintained that they are not replacing governments but working with them. For example, in a recent volume on necessary connections in the digital world, Anne-Marie Slaughter, in *The Chessboard and the Web* (2017), concludes that while we must accept the ubiquity and power of networks and internalize their opportunities and threats, governments are also at work. Networks are thus not replacing governments, and neither is their dominant influence. Indeed, networks often arise out of government needs and challenges. Contemporary governments (chess boards) operate, exert power, and interact both traditionally and in a networked fashion (web). Governmentality theory helps to explain how state power persists everywhere—governing is increasingly devolved, and allows for activists to shape new spaces in a classic essay on institutional relations (Taylor, 2007). Moreover, DiMaggio and Powell (1983) conclude that increased organized isomorphism means that networks who are likely to discover new forms of intersectional coordination together when governments work through and with other non-key government organizations. Indeed, working together network behavior has become among the emergent organized mechanisms.

This coexistence of networks and collaborative bodies working with governmental hierarchies is a fundamentally important consideration as the politics and management of collaboration are analyzed (Sørenson & Torfing, 2005). Some analysts observe, even fear, that collaboration like government contracting of service delivery outside of government and the existence and operation of networks have "hollowed out" public agencies in the same fashion as that of many corporations (Milward, Provan, & Else, 1993). Others do not go that far but fear that extensive "externalization" has led to a loss of accountability, a condition that is linked to government agencies no longer being the central steering actors in policy processes (Klijn, 1997) as networks replace hierarchies (Beierle & Konisky, 2001; Papadopoulos, 2010; Castells, 1996; Klijn & Koppenjan, 1997).

In the *Oxford Handbook of American Bureaucracy* (Durant, 2012), one of the authors of this volume and Michael McGuire point to a very different way of thinking (McGuire & Agranoff, 2010). Networks have *not* eclipsed or displaced the power or centrality of government agencies, at least in the United States. The empirical evidence from prior research on U.S. bureaucracy in general, and networks in particular, is too mixed to support such a contention. In reality, neither networks (or the for-profit organizations and nonprofit agencies within them) nor government agencies prevail in these partnerships (McGuire, 2011).

> Despite the very broad range of network activity in the United States, the ability [of non-governmental actors] to influence the public agency domain is real but

From Bureaucracy to Politics and Organization 19

quite limited in scope . . . accommodations are made, decisions are influenced, strategies are altered, resources are directed, intensive groups, exert undue influence, and public responsibility is indirectly shared.

(p. 439)

Derived from prior research on networks, this argument's logic is straightforward. First, while networks and the other types of non-governmental organizations that work with public agencies influence policy and have a role in management, those organizations and agencies that comprise these "networks" work with governments as the latter continue to maintain some important abilities that guide public action. Second, while an interactive interdependency has emerged within networks crossing many boundaries, public agency–NGO connections seem to overlay the hierarchy—often known as collaborative governance regimes—rather than act as replacements for government action (Agranoff, 2007b; Agranoff & McGuire, 2003; McGuire, 2002; Salamon, 1995; Scott & Thomas, 2017). Third, a recent review of various federal and state statutes indicates that none were drafted to "authorize agencies to collaborate in networks with others" (Bingham, 2008, p. 258). As a result, the agencies retain their authority under the law. Fourth, networks are not considered the only form of collaborative government or non-governmental relations. Lester Salamon (2002) lists several standard tools of government, such as cooperative agreements, loans, grants, and insurance guarantees, which bring public, private, and nonprofit agencies together to form networks (Agranoff, 2012; McGuire & Agranoff, 2010) without the employment of networks. Finally, not all public sector managers tend to use networks in government operations. Except for traditional "boundary spanners," who are constantly engaged in the cross-boundary work on a day-to-day basis, many public administrators spend as little as 15%–20% of their total work time in collaborative activity (Agranoff & McGuire, 2003). Clearly, the limits on some networks identified here, like Darby or the struggles among interests of CALFED as a collaborative, suggest that while increasingly present, notable networks are not at all replacing hierarchies, particularly in relation to government agencies.

In his update of the early ground-breaking article (O'Toole, 1997) defining networks, Laurence O'Toole (2010) insists that networks have attracted the attention of both scholars and practitioners of public administration while cautioning public managers to be wary of the general application of networks in practice and be aware that networks can produce both positive and negative—or even disastrous—outcomes. Networking often results in different levels of commitment and conflict of organizational cultures (Agranoff, 2016). Generally, public management includes tasks, skills, and behaviors to interact both within and outside the organizational boundaries. Government agencies frequently have the "final word," as in the case of CALFED, the environmental network. Finally, some networks are built for "dark motives," such as excluding some interests to protect agency monopolies or limit activity scope. Given this dual nature of networks, "we need to know much

20   *From Bureaucracy to Politics and Organization*

more about how networks and networking behavior can shape performance and affect the most salient values in our governance systems" (O'Toole, 2015, p. 368). These include political, as well as administrative, values. It includes power politics aside from any dark sides; thus, a serious assessment of networks' "other side" is clearly in order—and will be for some time to come.

Although many regard politics as something "shady," sinister, or even illegal, they are not necessarily so. As maintained, politics can be supportive or unsupportive to a cause. Politics are inherently neutral, and to many experienced in collaborative politics, they are employed as means to facilitate agreement. "It's all politics" is often a means of writing off any resistance, nonagreement, or various forms of conflict. On the other hand, we tend to think less of politically based decisions—for example, compromises—which are sometimes "tainted" with sinister motives. Actually, politics can be laced with very benign and constructive motives. Politics then needs to be regarded as operationally neutral and with considerable collaborative potential. To be the bearer or facilitator of the collaborative agreement, employing political strategies is inherently neutral, potentially constructive, and potentially essential to collaborative processing.

Power in Politics

Politics are based on the exercise or non-exercise of power, which involves achieving values in collaboration with and in opposition to opposing others. In collaboration, power can be an end in itself, but it is primarily instrumental in accomplishing other objectives (Lentner, 2011). Case analyses and incidents like "The 'Big Boys' of Politics" (Chapter 8) or "Political Negotiations in Cincinnati" (Box 1.1) highlight power's potential and actual exertion. There are many phases and aspects of power. In this volume on CP, we necessarily emphasize the importance of the "power to" along with the "power over"—both are instrumental in understanding collaborative management. Indeed, power is an inherently neutral concept, facilitating the ability or inability to achieve results across agency/organizational lines (Saz-Carranza & Ospina, 2011).

The positive aspects of power emanate from the original community power studies investigating how the "power to" overcomes challenges in urban communities (e.g., Stone, 1989, 2015). This concept has been further refined by Ann-Marie Slaughter (2017), who distinguishes between hard and soft power, with the latter being that of more informal influences advanced by actors, who do not directly get involved in conflicts but whose presence influences outcomes. For example, both are normally at work in U.S. foreign policy. In addition, Slaughter introduces power brought on by engagement or connection, a new aspect of power that operates differently, like electrical currents, made by many, more open, participating, and peer-driven. Indeed, CP has underscored emergent dimensions of power that have joined the scene of power over and power to accomplish joint tasks.

One face of power emphasized in this volume is the emergence of "deliberative power," the notion that working together on a multiagency solution can support and enhance problem-solving and value creation. Yet, despite the resistance of the ISMA in the previous FSSA story, the process results, in general, cannot be overlooked. Both soft and hard power were at work here. The level of agreement—rarely unanimous—was remarkable given the disparate human services public agencies and interest groups involved. For example, Medicaid, a purchase of service model that remained in the new structure, opened up access to various services not previously or easily available to clients and their families. In addition, the new department facilitated the 1915c Medicaid Waiver program, further analyzed in Chapter 4. In short, one can never completely cast out the influence of deliberation or the "power to."

That is also true in CP concerning agency power. In collaboration, each participating agency has its mission, goals, resources, and programs that it wishes to advance and protect to some degree. We will see this when "mission incompatibility" in collaboration is discussed. Daniel Carpenter's (2001) work on bureaucratic autonomy concludes that "Bureaucrats take actions consistent with their own wishes, actions, to which politicizing and organized interests defer even though they would prefer that other actions (or no action at all) be taken" (p. 4). Short of bureaucrats' wishes, "their actions can constitute leverage, based on their reputation for expertise, efficiency, or moral protection and uniquely diverse complex of ties to organized groups, the media, and with political actors" (p. 4). In this sense, ongoing agency power is rooted in officials' and representatives' multiplicity of ties to political organizations (Carpenter, 2001).

Another dimension of power that is very real and operative is legal power. In CP, one must also consider the impact of legal powers. Most programs at stake in CP are based on law or are legislatively delegated, administered by agencies, and later audited, both their program and fiscal aspects. In most cases, what is at stake is the power of law and regulations that can further or inhibit collaboration. For example, the Medicaid Waiver statute is generally open to public agency purchasing services approaches. Since its inception in the 1960s, state agencies have externally purchased medical, dental, speech, hearing, disability, support equipment, and many allied services, such as respite care. The requirements, however, once pre-empted respite care in clients' homes or care of any kind by family members. Until 2011, regulation could not change it, thus exerting power over the ability to facilitate one of the most central aspects of habilitation. The fear by Congress and the federal bureaucracy was that home/family-provided care of habilitation would invite too much fraudulent behavior. With "tight guidelines," home care is now allowable under certain limited circumstances. This type of legal power can be both facilitating and inhibiting, and its use in innovation is an important dimension of CP.

Finally, there is the power of knowledge in collaborative processing. One of the core functions of collaborative bodies is to learn more about the dimensions of the various problems faced and how to deal with and investigate potential solutions. For example, many land management programs (e.g., trusts, forest alliances, state and federal agencies) are often faced with the processing of timber cutting

22 *From Bureaucracy to Politics and Organization*

on public land and land held in trust. The ability to make rational and scientific decisions about stands of growth versus cutting, clear-cutting in particular, is often based on scientific growth management data, particularly when comparing "sustained growth" versus "clear-cutting." Scientific data can assist collaborating partners in making decision. No doubt, however, there can be conflicts between the timber industry and conservationists. They cannot be avoided as both sides exert their power. A solution could well be reached based on sustained yield forestry data studies that allow for some cutting, short of clear-cutting. "Knowledge power" is often in the mix in many deliberative processes.

Subsequent analysis of power will then incorporate deliberative, agency, legal, and knowledge power, along with the simple power over and power to. In different ways, they are core aspects of most collaborative processes. As will be demonstrated, collaboration and power go hand in hand. Acting together with others through debate and deliberation to agree on common arrangements and objectives proved as the base dynamic for accumulating power (Lentner, 2011).

Plan of the Book

Subsequent chapters will elaborate on the various types of power and politics and their impact on management, particularly "small p" and "big P" politics in collaboration, along with the multiple dimensions of multistakeholder power. The aim of this volume is straightforward. In order to cope with and deal with collaboration and its management, certain issues must be underscored and confronted since they unfold as real-world phenomena. The game is complex because of the multiple interests and organizations involved. As much as power politics may be or might be psychologically avoided, politics *will* always impact one or another. Moreover, while real and ever-present and difficult to battle, it is always better to understand politics than avoid them when collaborating. After all, it is maintained here that understanding and playing political games are part of the "winning" strategy.

Chapter 2 further introduces the politics of collaborative processes by looking at various collaborative enterprises. As such, it anchors practice in legal, program, and agency mission politics, bringing out the "primacy of collaboration" as a political and a managerial process. Chapter 3 explores various forms of organizational means of collaborative management, including interagency and cross-organizational taskforces and special units that bring agencies together, and newly erected comprehensive government departments like the U.S. Department of Homeland Security. Chapter 4 follows how these emergent structures work together to reach an agreement through means that rarely involve raw majority voting but involve many different means encompassing deliberation and creative resolution/nonresolution. It covers both organized and informal transactions. Chapter 5 then looks at the various forms of power by examining how the operations in collaborative bodies unfold and how "small p" and "big P" considerations and transactions play out. It demonstrates how important forces like agency and knowledge-based power, for example, weigh heavily in decisions/agreements.

From Bureaucracy to Politics and Organization 23

Political experiences from the field are then identified in Chapter 6. The "Politics of It All" further demonstrates the inherent-political nature of most collaborative agreements. A number of related political situations are revealed. Whereas these political situations are not particularly partisan, they provide valuable learning opportunities. Then the examination of CP shifts to learning enhanced by academic studies in Chapter 7, which is what we know about governing transactions from research in the field. The primary academic bases are public administration and public policy. Chapter 8 follows with adapted stories and narratives from the field. While they focus on collaboration, they look at situations working across agencies and governments. They reflect how collaboration became a core function of contemporary administration, both minor and major interorganizational moves/incidents. Chapter 9 then looks at CP's political and managerial opportunities and barriers, ranging from mission sensibility and process fatigue issues to outright political/organizational disagreements. Also, it will be demonstrated how "operational localism" or implementing jurisdictions handles programs, putting their own locally based shape interpretations on programs.

Chapter 10 focuses on understanding and improving collaborative performance management. This chapter thoroughly examines managerial roles and actions related to understanding and improving collaborative performance. Chapter 11 then looks at how CP in governance has changed classical bureaucracy into more conductive or externally interactive bodies. It also proposes a set of new connective operating demands and expectations for the "new bureaucrat" in CP. Finally, the concluding Chapter 12 provides experiential guidance on organizing and being a better operative in CP, particularly with innovation supports like artificial intelligence (AI). It includes a "top ten" of operating links on how one might play the CP game based on interpersonal and electronic reports by administrators; the aim is to use the knowledge and future technology captured in this volume to work and play at current collaborative politics and management.

References

Agranoff, R. (2007a). *Managing within networks: Adding value to public organizations.* Georgetown University Press.

Agranoff, R. (2007b). Intergovernmental policy management. In M. Pagano & R. Leonetti (Eds.), *Dynamics of federalism.* Palgrave.

Agranoff, R. (2012). *Collaborating to manage: A primer for the public sector.* Georgetown University Press.

Agranoff, R. (2013). The transformation of public sector intellectual/developmental disabilities programming. *Public Administration Review, 73*(s1), 127–138. https://doi.org/10.1111/puar.12101

Agranoff, R. (2016). The other side of managing in networks. In R. D Margerum & C. J. Robinson (Eds.), *The challenges of collaboration in environmental governance: Barriers and responses* (pp. 81–107). Edward Elgar Publishing.

Agranoff, R. (2017). *Crossing boundaries for intergovernmental management.* Georgetown University Press.

24   *From Bureaucracy to Politics and Organization*

Agranoff, R. (2018). *Local governments in multilevel governance: The administrative Dimension.* Lexington Books.

Agranoff, R., & McGuire, M. (2000). Administration of state government rural development policy. In J. J. Gargan (Eds.), *Handbook of state government administration.* Marcel Dekker.

Agranoff, R., & McGuire, M. (2003). *Collaborative public management: New strategies for public management: New strategies for local governments.* Georgetown University Press.

Agranoff, R., & McGuire, M. (2004). Another look at bargaining and negotiating in intergovernmental management. *Journal of Public Administration Research and Theory, 14*(4), 495–512. https://doi.org/10.1093/jopart/muh033

Agranoff, R., & Pattakos, A. (1979). *Dimensions of services integration: Service delivery, program linkages, policy management, organizational structure, human service monograph series 13, project share.* US Government Printing Office.

Amsler, L. B. (2016). Collaborative governance: Integrating management, politics, and law. *Public Administration Review, 76*(5), 700–711. https://doi.org/10.1111/puar.12605

Appleby, P. H. (1956). *Big democracy.* AA Knopf.

Beierle, T. C., & Konisky, D. M. (2001). What are we gaining from stakeholder involvement? Observations from environmental planning in the great lakes. *Environment and Planning C: Government and Policy, 19*(4), 515–527. https://doi.org/10.1068/c5s

Berman, H. J. (1987). Some false premises of Max Weber's sociology of law. *Washington University Law Quarterly, 65,* 758.

Bielefeld, W., Perry, J. L., & Thomson, A. M. (2010). Reluctant partners? Nonprofit collaboration, social entrepreneurship, and leverage volunteerism. In R. F. Durant (Ed.), *Handbook of American bureaucracy* (pp. 421–446). Oxford University Press.

Bingham, L. B. (Ed.). (2008). *Big ideas in collaborative public management.* ME Sharpe.

Bovaird, T. (2005). Public governance: Balancing stakeholder power in a network society. *International Review of Administrative Sciences, 71*(2), 217–228. https://doi.org/10.1177/0020852305053881

Brown, A. (2018, October 2). Research institute launches collaborative space, consortium. *Bloomington Herald Times.*

Brown, S. W. (2015). International agenda and disabilities and human rights. In J. A. Racino (Ed.) (2014), *Public administration and disability: Community services administration in the US.* CRC Press.

Carpenter, D. (2001). *The forging of bureaucratic autonomy: Reputations, networks, and policy innovation in executive agencies, 1862–1928* (Vol. 173). Princeton University Press.

Castells, M. (1996). *The information age* (Vol. 98). Blackwell Publishers.

DiMaggio, P. J., & Powell, W. W. (1983). The iron cage revisited: Institutional isomorphism and collective rationality in organizational fields. *American Sociological Review,* 147–160.

Durant, R. F. (Ed.). (2012). *The Oxford handbook of American bureaucracy.* Oxford University Press.

Editorial Board. (2018, July 25). Will Philly's new Rail Park help create a neighborhood for all? *Philadelphia Inquirer.*

Ferguson, N. (2014, June 9). Networks and hierarchies. *The American Interest.*

Foucault, M. (2001). *The order of things: An archeology of the human sciences* (2nd ed.). Routledge.

Gazley, B. (2010). Improving collaboration research by emphasizing the role of the public manager. In R. O'Leary, D. M. Van Slyke, & S. Kim (Eds.) (2011), *The future of public administration around the world: The Minnowbrook perspective.* Georgetown University Press.

Goodnow, F. J. (1900). *Politics and administration: A study in government.* Macmillan.

Hafer, J. A. (2018). Understanding the emergence and persistence of mandated collaboration: A policy feedback perspective of the United States' model to address homelessness. *The American Review of Public Administration, 48*(7), 777–788. https://doi.org/10.1177/0275074017729877

Hanemann, M., & Dyckman, C. (2009). The San Francisco bay-delta: A failure of decision-making capacity. *Environmental Science & Policy, 12*(6), 710–725. https://doi.org/10.1016/j.envsci.2009.07.004

Indiana Innovation Institute. (2018, October 2). *Indiana Innovation Institute (IN3) opens collaboration space, launches new consortium*. https://in3indiana.com. https://in3indiana.com/indiana-innovation-institute-in3-opens-collaboration-space-launches-new-consortium/

Innes, J. E., Connick, S., & Booher, D. (2007). Informality as a planning strategy: Collaborative water management in the CALFED Bay-Delta Program. *Journal of the American Planning Association, 73*(2), 195–210. https://doi.org/10.1080/0194436070897615

Klijn, E. H. (1997). Policy networks: An overview. In W. J. Kickert, E. H. Klijn, & J. F. Koppenjan (Eds.), *Managing complex networks: Strategies for the public sector* (pp. 14–32). Sage.

Klijn, E. H., & Koppenjan, J. F. (1997). Public management and network management. In W. J. Kickert, E. H. Klijn, & J. F. Koppenjan (Eds.), *Managing complex networks: Strategies for the public sector* (pp. 35–61). Sage.

Koliba, C., Meek, J. W., & Zia, A. (2019). *Governance networks in public administration and public policy*. Routledge.

Kooiman, J. (2003). *Governing as governance*. London: SAGE.

Koontz, T. M. (2004). Nonprofit facilitation: The Darby partnership. In T. T. Koontz, J. A. Steelman, Carmin, K. S. Korfmacher, C. Moseley, & C. W. Thomas (Eds.), *Collaborative environmental management: What roles for government* (pp. 49–64). Resources for Future.

Lejano, R. P., & Ingram, H. (2009). Collaborative networks and new ways of knowing. *Environmental Science & Policy, 12*(6), 653–662. https://doi.org/10.1016/j.envsci.2008.09.005

Lentner, H. H. (2011). A realist's view of ethics. *American Foreign Policy Interests, 33*(4), 153–157. https://doi.org/10.1080/10803920.2011.605716

Machiavelli, N. (1995). *The prince and others: Political writings*, edited by S. Milner. Everyman.

Mannheim, K. (1936). *Ideology and Utopia*, translated by Louis Wirth and Edward Shils. New York: Harvest.

March, J. G., & Olsen, J. P. (1996). Institutional perspectives on political institutions. *Governance, 9*(3), 247–264.

Margerum, R. D. (2011). *Beyond consensus: Improving collaborative planning and management*. MIT Press.

McGuire, M. (2002). Managing networks: Propositions on what managers do and why they do it. *Public Administration Review, 62*(5), 599–609.

McGuire, M. (2011). Network managemeny. In M. Bevir (Ed.), *The Sage handbook of goverance* (pp. 272–295). Sage.

McGuire, M., & Agranoff, R. (2010). Networking in the shadow of bureaucracy. In R. F. Durant (Ed.), *The Oxford handbook of American bureaucracy* (pp. 272–295). Oxford University Press.

McGuire, M., Agranoff, R., & Silvia, C. (2011). *Putting the "public" back into collaborative public management*. Public Management Research Conference, Syracuse, NY.

Milward, H. B., Provan, K. G., & Else, B. A. (1993). What does the hollow state look like? In B. Bozeman (Eds.), *Public management: The state of the art* (pp. 309–322). Jossey-Bass.

Mosher, F. C. (1982). *Democracy and the public service*. Oxford University Press.

26 *From Bureaucracy to Politics and Organization*

Offe, C. (2009). Governance: An "empty signifier"? *Constellations, 16*(4), 550.

Olsen, J. P. (2006). Maybe it is time to rediscover bureaucracy. *Journal of Public Administration Research and Theory, 16*(1), 1–24. https://doi.org/10.1111/j.1467-8675.2009.00570.x

Ostrom, E. (1990). *Governing the commons: The evolution of institutions for collective action.* Cambridge University Press.

O'Toole, Jr., L. J. (1997). Treating networks seriously: Practical and research-based agendas in public administration. *Public Administration Review, 57*(1), 45–52.

O'Toole, L. J. (2010). The ties that bind? Networks, public administration, and political science. *Political Science and Politics, 43*(1), 7–14.

O'Toole, Jr., L. J. (2015). Networks and networking: The public administrative agendas. *Public Administration Review, 75*(3), 361–371. https://doi.org/10.1111/puar.12281

Palonen, K. (2011). Politics. In G. T. Kurian (Eds.), *The encyclopedia of political science* (Vol 4, pp. 1299–1301). CQ Press.

Papadopoulos, Y. (2010). Accountability and multi-level governance: More accountability, less democracy? *West European Politics, 33*(5), 1030–1049. https://doi.org/10.1080/0140 2382.2010.486126.

Piattoni, S. (2009). Multi-level governance: A historical and conceptual analysis. *European Integration, 31*(2), 163–180. https://doi.org/10.1080/07036330802642755

Powell, W. W. (1990). Neither market nor hierarchy: Network forms of organization. *Research in Organizational Behavior, 12*(1), 295–336.

Rhodes, R. A. W. (1996). The new governance: Governing without government. *Political Studies, 44*(4), 652–667.

Rhodes, R. A. W. (1997). *Understanding governance: Policy networks, governance, reflexivity, and accountability.* Open University.

Rhodes, R. A. W. (2014). Waves of governance. In D. Levi-Faur (Eds.), *The Oxford handbook of governance* (pp. 294–308). Oxford University Press.

Ring, P. S., & Van de Ven, A. H. (1994). Developmental processes of cooperative interorganizational relationships. *Academy of Management Review, 19*(1), 90–118.

Rosenbloom, D. H. (2010). Reevaluating executive-centered public administrative theory. In R. F. Durant (Eds.), *The Oxford handbook of American bureaucracy* (pp. 101–127). Oxford University Press.

Rosenbloom, D. H. (2018). *Administrative law for public managers.* Routledge.

Salamon, L. M. (1995). *Partners in public service: Government-nonprofit relations in the modern welfare state.* John Hopkins University Press.

Salamon, L. M. (2002). The new governance and the tools of public action. In L. M. Salamon (Eds.), *The tools of government* (pp. 1–42). Oxford University Press.

Saz-Carranza, A., & Ospina, S. M. (2011). The behavioral dimension of governing interorganizational goal-directed networks: Managing the unity-diversity tension. *Journal of Public Administration Research and Theory, 21*(2), 327–365. https://doi.org/10.1093/jopart/muq050

Scott, T. A., & Thomas, C. W. (2017). Unpacking the collaborative toolbox: Why and when do public managers choose collaborative governance strategies? *Policy Studies Journal, 45*(1), 191–214. https://doi.org/10.1111/psj.12162

Selznick, P. (2011). *Leadership in administration: A sociological interpretation.* Quid Pro Books.

Shapiro, J. (2015). *1606: William Shakespeare and the year of lear.* Faber & Faber.

Slaughter, A. M. (2017). *The chessboard and the web: Strategies of connection in a networked world.* Yale University Press.

Sørenson, E., & Torfing, J. (2005). The democratic anchorage of network governance. *Scandinavian Political Studies, 28*(3), 195–218. https://doi.org/10.1111/j.1467-9477.2005.00129.x

Stillman, R. J. (1998). *Creating the American state: The moral reformers and the modern administrative world they made*. University of Alabama Press.

Stone, C. N. (1989). *Regime Politics*. University Press of Kansas.

Stone, C. N. (2015). Reflections on regime politics: From governing coalition to urban political order. *Urban Affairs Review, 51*(1), 101–137. https://doi.org/10.1177/1078087414558948

Taylor, M. (2007). Community participation in the real world: Opportunities and pitfalls in new governance spaces. *Urban Studies, 44*(2), 297–317. https://doi.org/10.1080/00420980601074987

Torfing, J. (2014). Governance networks. In D. Levi-Faur (Ed.), *The Oxford handbook of governance* (pp. 294–308). Oxford University Press.

United Nations. (2006). *Convention on the rights of persons with disabilities*. A/RES/61/10.

Watson, N., Deeming, H., & Treffny, R. (2009). Beyond bureaucracy? Assessing institutional change in the governance of water in England. *Water Alternatives, 2*(3), 448–460.

White, L. (1948). *The Federalists: A study in administrative history*. Macmillan.

White, L. (1951). *The Jeffersonians: A study in administrative history, 1801–1829*. Macmillan.

White, L. (1954). *The Jacksonians: A study in administrative history, 1829–1861*. Macmillan.

White, L. (1958). *The Republican era, 1869–1901: A study in administrative history*. Macmillan.

Wilson, W. (1887). The study of administration. *Political Science Quarterly, 2*(2), 197–222.

Wollmann, H. (2012). Local government reforms in (seven) European countries: Between convergent and divergent, conflicting and complementary developments. *Local Government Studies, 38*(1), 41–70. https://doi.org/10.1080/03003930.2011.638710

2 Development of Collaborative Enterprises

This extended chapter focuses on some of the sociopolitical and legal-governmental processes that form the context of CP. They often comprise a basic part of the organized understanding and thus contextualize reaching collaborative agreements. While not totally political and governmental, the politics and management of agreement formation clearly present a substantial part of the CP picture—a core aim of this volume. For example, one group of scholars who study rural community development astutely observed that cross-sector collaboration occurs on social frontiers, spaces where diversely positioned people work together toward collective ends, often marked by law, conflict, negotiation, and resource constraints. One way to characterize it as community leaders holding regular meetings, identifying areas of mutual benefit, and drawing from organizational assets. Miller, Scanlan, and Phillippo (2017) also point to involved/related political processes. While their study identified some rural/urban development differences, the organizing experiences demonstrated the important need to contemplate and work through the deeper political and social aspects of organizing collaborative efforts.

Collaborative undertakings involve different norms and practices from traditional hierarchy to hierarchical collaborative problem resolution processes. It will become clear that leadership in collaborative efforts involves: "broad community participation, public enterprises, and NGOs; strategies are undertaken that are not at all clear at the outset; and subject and content expertise is also based on tactical or positional approaches" (Chrislip & Larson, 1994, pp. 129–130). A clear first principle of CP is that authoritative-based resolutions are not usually a clear part of the solution equation in the absence of hierarchy. This leads to many of the differences pointed out in Table 2.1 between typical hierarchical and collaborative processes. It is not presented as an exhaustive list, but the table calls attention to many key differences from hierarchy in the collaborative process. It demonstrates that real differences emerge without the ability to make program decisions within an organizational structure that hierarchy affords. Table 2.1 indicates that collaborative processes are more open to interaction, mutual understanding, and participatory decisions/agreements. In general, collaborative process is more interactive, relational, and less authoritative. Contrary to some beliefs of collaboration as mutual

DOI: 10.4324/9781003385769-2

Development of Collaborative Enterprises 29

Table 2.1 Hierarchical and Collaborative Processes Compared

Features	Hierarchical Processes	Collaborative Processes
Auspices	Government entity, relatively closed and identifiable boundaries	Conductive entity, open and flexible boundaries
Boundary-spanning activity and resources	Supportive effort	Core effort
Oversight monitoring	After-the-fact auditing, periodic oversight	Continuous feedback
Principal-agent contact	Periodic review	Constant interaction
Procedural adaptation	Principally by managers	By all administrative, operating, and support personnel
Decision participants and style	Managers and administrators, at points in time	By all operatives when issues emerge
Resource acquisition	Legislative authorized budget, agency delivery of agents	Multiple sources, wherever they can be accessed
Organizational structure	Hierarchical, based on authority	Adaptive, based on connective need

Source: Agranoff, R. (2012). Collaborating to manage: A primer for the public sector. Georgetown University Press. p. 188. Copyright 2012 by Georgetown University Press. www.press.georgetown.edu. Reprinted with permission.

and automatic agreement, the politics in CP shifts among and between sets of independent or semi-independent parties.

One loose collaborative illustration of an active economic and regional development partnership is Radius Indiana, a regional development partnership centered in and around the Crane U.S. Naval Support Activity in southwest Indiana. It promotes regional growth, education, and development with multiple working partners (Box 2.1). It was originally supported by a $42 million Lilly Endowment grant to support Radius's Region Opportunities Initiatives, launch a strategic planning process, and prepare for the next wave of AI development to help what it sees as leading in the era of the "Internet of Things," whereby electronics, software, sensors, actuators, and connectivity will allow for new products to connect, interact, and exchange. One way demonstrates the political nature of Radius; during the formation, it has been led by Becky Skillman, former two-term lieutenant governor of Indiana.

Box 2.1   Radius Indiana

Radius Indiana (www.radiusindiana.com) is a regional economic development partnership representing eight counties in southern Indiana. Formed in 2009, Radius Indiana also serves as a point of contact in Indiana for Naval Support Activity Crane and leads regional collaboration by leveraging the diverse assets of southwest central Indiana to drive attraction, retention, and expansion of business, thereby increasing employment and investment opportunities and quality of life within the region.

Throughout the year, the Radius Indiana team hosts, visits, and responds to site selection advisers and corporate decision-makers throughout the United States. Radius Indiana provides a central location for site selection needs. It offers custom searches and site tours; comprehensive up-to-minute data; contacts to local, regional, and state organizations; and access to gap and intellectual property (IP) funding for regionally beneficial programs.

Additionally, Radius Indiana works to grow the U.S. defense and national security industry by serving as the lead economic development entity outside the gates at Naval Support Activity Crane, the world's third largest naval installation. Radius also works to grow advocacy, connect the community, and coordinate defense resources for Crane within our region.

Radius Indiana serves as a regional catalyst for government, business and academic collaboration to market and promote the area as a highly competitive, vibrant region with an increasingly attractive quality of life.

Community and business leaders have worked collaboratively with the Radius region to establish an economic development partnership at work for the region to ignite prosperity in the heart of southern Indiana.

Radius does the following.

- Enhances awareness of the region's assets.
- Positions the region competitively for the retention, expansion, and attraction of jobs and investment.
- Assists companies from outside the region to find the best location in the Radius region for their needs.
- Supports local communities through development programs to help entrepreneurs, start-ups, and existing businesses succeed and grow in the region.
- Serves as the lead information broker, providing the most accurate and up-to-date data on the region.
- Works with regional communities to support local initiatives that improve and maintain quality of place.

Radius projects have included the following.

- Purdue@WestGate. The opening of the WestGate Academy, growth at WestGate@Crane Tech Park, and the news that Purdue University would be joining forces for the Purdue@WestGate initiative as significant educational opportunities surrounding NSCW-Crane.

- The creation of the Battery Innovation Center (and Bright-Volt) and East Gate Business and Technology Center supported technological advances, as well as Department of Defense contracts.
- The Vincennes University Center of Technology, Innovation and Manufacturing, as well as the creation of Regional Impact Fund, to grow economic development efforts in the area.
- Growth and expansion of the nearby French Lick Resort made it the largest private convention center in the state.
- The state of Indiana named both Bedford and Huntingburg as recipients of its Stellar Communities grant program. In addition, the cities of Bedford and Jasper were both named Communities of the Year.
- The opening of Interstate 69 from Evansville to Bloomington helped logistics and transportation, spurring development in Washington, Indiana, which capitalized on the fact that I-69 would run right through it. Washington, too, was considered a success story because of how it prepared from the development, capturing several new industries.
- Business growth throughout the region including investments at General Motors, Kimball Corp., Farbest Foods, and a $600 million new manufacturing facility for Lehigh Cement Co.

Sources: https://radiusindiana.com/about/; https://radiusindiana.com/author/amanda/

It will become clear that collaborative structures like Radius Indiana—within organizations and between them—are increasingly involved in the interconnective activity. As far back as the late 1960s, Karl Weick offered in *The Social Psychology of Organizing* (1969) that smaller loosely coupled organizations, brought together by smaller participatory elements, could be disconnected and reformed in response to contemporary challenges and can be more innovative. Later observers also called for smaller teams that were more flexible and innovative than rigid bureaucratic structures. That led to the thinking like, "Creativity requires that we encounter and internalize previous sparks of insight, and it requires elaboration time for groups of agencies to unfold," suggests Keith Sawyer (200, p. 167). The key is to create the right balance of planning and innovation.

Types and Aims of Collaborative Agreements

The literature increasingly identifies "networks" as a collaborative universal, a panacea, or a catch-all. Figure 2.1 clarifies that they are not the only collaborative game in town. In reality, networks of different types represent just one broad category of agency-to-agency connections. Truly, various collaborative linkages have been developed because of the need for interdependency linkages (Agranoff, 2012). Three

32 *Development of Collaborative Enterprises*

categories of collaborative linkages are presented in Figure 2.1, ranging from the more informal to formalized or official connections, depending on the normal degree of engagement, minimum or maximum, and the frequency of interaction, intermittent or regular. One of the authors, Robert Agranoff (2012) developed this classification. Even though some experiential linkages may seem to fit into several categories, they are situated in the most suitable category for demonstration purposes. Most importantly, this classification demonstrates that not all collaborations are alike or can be overly broad from the heavily overused labeling of "networks": "Some are not involved and are infrequent, some are not involved but are frequent, others are less involved but require more contact, and still others require high levels of interorganizational commitment on a regular basis" (p. 13), e.g., like some networks.

Because these are examples, the entire Figure 2.1 does not require a complete explanation. To highlight the first category, informal and minimal engagement—normally with intermittent interaction—would include the numerous information and interpretation contacts that administrators make across organizations, sectors, and contacts for grants of various types that tend to be "front-loaded," with far less contact over the life of the grant (Agranoff, 2012). The second category, collaborative tools, "normally with regular interaction, includes all types of vehicles for information exchanges, even networks, and councils that frequently meet among themselves but rarely, if ever, have the authority to make any kind of decisions" (p. 13). The third category, formal interaction, normally with maximum engagement, "includes collaborative devices with less interaction time (e.g., periodic meetings or occasional transactions), but the partners are normally limited to regular types of interactions" (p. 13). A public–private development partnership, for example, may organize meetings regularly, but its main purpose is to report what the staff has been up to or to sanction the parties' occasional transactions like contracts, payments, and audits (Agranoff, 2012). Also included in this category of maximum engagement with regular interaction is a slew of collaborative tools in which one party's work—"even if it's only exchanging program or policy information" (p. 13)—is regularly influenced by the activity of others. This category includes program or policy councils and interoperative networks of multiple agencies engaged in joint programming.

Figure 2.1 illustrates the many different ways that managers can utilize "synergy as a logic to network or otherwise collaborate in collaborative connections, alliances, partnerships, or other sorts of exchange relationships" (Agranoff, 2012, p. 15). The usage of the term "network" in this volume mirrors the widely accepted definition in the public management and administration literature. Agranoff (2007, 2012), O'Toole (1997, 2015), and Koliba, Meek, and Zia (2010) define the action of "*to network*" as engaging in a variety of goal-directed collaborative activities that are not limited to the distinctly organized chartered and non-chartered networks that are also goal-directed (Agranoff, 2012). As a result, network activities include a wide range of regular and purposeful interorganizational contacts and spontaneous interactions (Agranoff, 2012). Formal network activity of different stripes is thus one version of collaboration, commonly used to describe some form of interaction between agencies and other types of organizations (Kilduff & Tsai, 2003).

Development of Collaborative Enterprises 33

I. Informal practice linkages

A. Informal discussions and sharing of information—nonbinding exchanges by personnel of two or more agencies* focused on some program purpose.
B. Informal cooperation—a nonbinding connection (required by law, contract, written exchange) between two agencies to improve programming services.
C. Parallel action—an agreement, usually formally adopted, between two or more agencies or operations to pursue a common course of action. The decisions are agreed on jointly, but their implementation requires individual action by the agencies or organizations involved.
D. Continuous, public, open-source facility use—one organization makes sustained noncontractual use of another public facility, such as public schools, libraries, and museums; small city governments and county planning agencies; community organizations and public buildings; small town leaders; agricultural extension services; chambers of commerce; and small business development centers in colleges.
E. Conference approach—a bringing together, at regular intervals, of representatives of given agencies or organizations within an area to discuss common problems, exchange information, and develop agreements on issues of mutual interest.
F. Shared staff—specialists and professionals on loan from another agency perform certain tasks or services for a cooperating agency while remaining on the payroll of the sending agency.
G. Outreach and liaison staff—employees of one organization assigned work primarily or exclusively with another agency: police in schools, social workers in mental health centers, occupational health and safety specialists in shipyards, ambulance crews in fire stations, and so on.

II. Collaborative tools of government

A. Dedicated task forces—multisector, ad hoc bodies charged to examine, study, and research a particular problem and to propose tentative solutions that cut across multiple populations, jurisdictions, communities, and so forth.
B. Interagency agreements—written collaboration support between two or more code departments or agencies within the same government: social services and parks and recreation departments, economic development and tourism, and the like.
C. Joint venture—two or more agencies seek to invest in and launch an auxiliary operation (for example, a business or spin-off café or service station) based on shared risk capital and with shared liability as part of their respective programs while maintaining the rest of their operations on an independent basis.

Figure 2.1 Agency-to-Agency Connections—Acts of Networking: Public-to-Public and NGO–Agency Collaborating Model

Source: Agranoff (2012, pp 38–39); reprinted with permission

Note: The term "agencies" in this figure refers to both NGO organizations and government agencies.

34 *Development of Collaborative Enterprises*

D. Joint-stock venture—similar to a joint venture but the participating agencies raise capital by selling stock in the operation, and their liability is limited to the joint venture.

E. Joint commissions—private multi-organization bodies that evaluate standards of operation, entry and exit to a field, and sometimes outcomes that are licensed or "franchised" under public auspices, such as the accreditation of hospitals, rehabilitation facilities, geographic information systems specialists, and social workers.

F. Limited powers and intergovernmental public-private organizations—area-based multi-government or super municipal or county representative bodies that have limited or no formal powers over aspects of planning or programming. Examples are transportation metropolitan planning organizations, Area Agencies on Aging, workforce development boards, regional planning boards, rural development councils, and museum or zoo authorities.

III. Formal public and NGO arrangements

A. Advisory boards—citizens, community leaders, service clients, students, and parents representing different organized and non-organized interests meet with public officials, provide advice, respond to proposals, and actively participate in plans and proposals.

B. Councils or federations of agencies—information sharing, information creation, and sometimes pooled fund-raising, with no or few decisional controls over an agency's operations.

C. Compact—two or more agencies or organizations undertake mutual obligations, such as serving clients from neighboring communities where no services are organized.

D. Transfer of functions—shifting an agency's particular services, such as nursing, intake, or case management, to another agency with more adequate knowledge, experience, and resources.

E. Limited partnership—two or more agencies or organizations formally agree to work together and integrate certain functions, such as fund-raising, public relations, financial management, or supportive health services, while remaining separate in their core operations.

F. Formal agreements with a philanthropic body—written compact to work with a philanthropic entity for research, funding, and public relations purposes.

G. Integrated services and partnerships—two or more agencies or organizations contractually, or legally, agree to unify one or more of their services into one operation while operating separately on the other functions. Normally it involves intake and assessment, case management, evaluation and assessment, support, or management services.

Figure 2.1 (Continued)

Development of Collaborative Enterprises 35

In this world of "increased multiprogram pressure to innovate through interorganizational cooperation" (Borins, 2012, p. 176), there are thus many various types of "collaborative activities for which the definitional boundaries are sometimes difficult to determine" and include more than networks (Agranoff, 2012, p. 13). The range, as Mandell (2000) suggests, is from "loose linkages and coalitions to more lasting structural arrangements" (p. 130). As Agranoff (2012) gives an example of such collaborative activity:

> Take, for example, a public agency such as a state government department of tourism or a city department of economic development. Both will have legal or statutory connected relations and nonlegal collaborative connections. Legal collaboration could be by grant arrangement; contract for service; procurement contract; formal interagency agreement with another (state) department or adjacent (city) jurisdiction; and direct agreements or contracts with NGOs, along with the participation of informal networks. Indeed, today many public agency collaborative contacts are between departments within the same government or between one level of government (e.g., the U.S. federal government) and other levels, including state and/or local governments. These are called intergovernmental contacts, and they include collaborative contacts between governments and NGOs (Agranoff, 2008). They range in formality from informal contacts for information and minor adjustments on program management matters to such formalized structures as working partnerships and joint services networks (Agranoff & McGuire, 2003; Agranoff, 2007) (p. 13).

To address these problems, government agencies are transitioning into more conductive organizations or organizations that organize themselves to match internal challenges with exterior expectations and opportunities, particularly those involving collaborative relationships. These operations are "added on" to the public agency's otherwise internal job. As a result, government agencies, like other modern organizations, have had to adapt their structures. As a result, they have flattened or become less centralized as they have become more "de-differentiated" (Clegg, 1990). As a result, organizations take on new forms by combining knowledge and people into frameworks that prioritize human capital. For example, a more boundaryless or centerless organization is flatter, with a network of interdependent or policy information, and is frequently and greatly affected by the activity of others, rather than rigid hierarchies with all the departmental, line staff, headquarters, and superstructure trappings (Agranoff, 2012).

The Tools or Instruments of Collaboration

Only a handful of government agencies—such as state taxation departments, public pensions, the U.S. Social Security Administration, and state weights and measures departments—are public programs that primarily involve a single unit of government that only deliver a program or programs by themselves (Agranoff, 2012).

36 *Development of Collaborative Enterprises*

Governments at the various levels are more complex, and nearly always network with other organizations—public and private—to reach their goals in carrying out programs. For example, more than 70% of U.S. federal government dollars are spent by agents other than that at the federal level (Agranoff, 2012). The government today mostly functions through grants, contracts, loans, and other means of externalized services. These tools have been named by Lester Salamon (2002, p. 9, emphasis in original) as the "*tools* or *instruments* through which public purposes are pursued." The most venerable tool of collaboration is the contract for goods and services, some of which have become complicated and interactive within and between contractors, subcontractors, and government (Brown, Potoski, & Van Slyke, 2013; Girth & Lopez, 2019). In the United States, contracts have expanded in number and scale since the 1960s. Most importantly, public, private, and non-profit organizations started developing contacts with each other, which resulted in plethora of operational arrangements across organizational and sectoral boundaries (Salamon, 2002). That is the nature of the current government administration.

Eleven tools or instruments are briefly described in Table 2.2, highlighting the various exchanges that are the product of implementation by each tool or instrument (Agranoff, 2012). These tools have been hypothesized from real-life programs, and the dynamic, collaborative exchanges typically reflect the potential consequences of using a particular tool or instrument. Agranoff (2012) provides such an example:

> [C]ities are eligible for loans to upgrade and place into compliance their water systems under the U.S. Clean Drinking Water Act. Federal loans—for example, the State of Nebraska's water loan programs—normally require a supplemental or matching loan from a local bank or other lending institution. Normally, these projects are paid back with a combination of higher water fees and special local tax assessments, which results in multiple involvement from citizens, businesses, local lending institutions, local government (or a quasi-government water authority), and state and federal governments.
>
> (p. 30)

Similarly, each of the other ten tools or instruments described in Table 2.2 generates an array, or networks, of possible external organizations engaged in program operations.

With contemporary overlapping and shared authority, plus implementation by many different actors, these tools are "legally based and can and often are intergovernmentally interactive in a rather complicated and overlapping fashion" (Agranoff, 2012, p. 32). To demonstrate how the legal base can shape a collaborative endeavor, the updated framework for the Lower Platte River Corridor Alliance watershed regulatory study shows the importance of the legal framework as a starting point (Agranoff, 2012). In this circumstance, it acted as a guide for any mitigation effort on the Lower Platte River. Four federal arenas, nine separate state regulatory arenas, and several land-use, planning, zoning, and preservation concerns at the local level make up the regulatory framework. The document's contents prompted federal, state, and natural resource districts and county and city officials to propose various

Table 2.2 Collaborative Tools

Collaborative Tool	Description	Hypothetical Example	Core/Sponsor Jurisdiction	Major Partners	Other Involved Organizations
Direct Government Services	Good or service by public agency	Jefferson County Public Health Department operates an inoculation program	County government	F/S/L	Schools, home nurses' associations, and other voluntary organizations
Regulations	Standards-setting, prohibitions	Municipal clean drinking water standards	Federal government	F/S/L/NP/FP	Homeowners, contractors, school districts, counties, and other voluntary organizations
Grants	Awards, cash payments	Temporary Assistance for Needy Families	Federal government block grants to states	F/S/L (in some states)	Education and training organizations, child care, food stamps, Medicaid, and NGO voluntary associations
Contracting	Payment for goods or direct service delivered	Columbus refuse collection and recycling pickup and disposal	Municipal government	S/L/FP/county waste district programs	Citizens, neighborhood organizations, businesses, institutional clients
Direct Loans	Cash for a project, normally at lower than market rates	Fillmore City, Nebraska, borrows $950,000 to upgrade its water system	Federal–state government	F/S/L/private lending institution	Business and homeowners through special assessments
Loan Guarantees	Interest buy-downs and backups of private loans	Oskaloosa town builds a new community center	State government/ private lending institution	S/L/private lending institution	Community organizations, chamber of commerce, local economic development corporation
Insurance	Protection against unusual risks/costs	Federal–state unemployment insurance in Wisconsin	Federal–state government	F/S/employers	State chambers of commerce, statewide business associations, local offices of state employment service

(Continued)

Table 2.2 (Continued)

Collaborative Tool	Description	Hypothetical Example	Core/Sponsor Jurisdiction	Major Partners	Other Involved Organizations
Tax Expenditures	Cash incentives to encourage a project or program outside of government	Chico, California, provides 15% of the cost of a new office complex in the core of the city	City/county government, private developers	L/private sector	Contractors, building materials companies, labor unions, Downtown Chico, Inc.
Fees, Charges	Payments by users of services, full or partial	Medicare Part B payments, client copayments	Federal government	F/medical and hospital industry/ pharmaceutical industry	Other FP and NP health and allied health organizations
Vouchers	Authorization for access to government goods or services	Food stamps	Federal–state–local governments (in some states)	FM/food vendors	Local social welfare organizations, local case managers
Government Corporations	Special government entities, normally for one purpose, quasi-public agency	Des Moines Transit Authority	A special unit of local government under state government authority	F/S/L	Paratransit contractors, area planning agency, county governments, 13 municipal governments

Source: Agranoff (2012, p. 31). Copyright 2012 by Georgetown University Press. Reprinted with permission.

Notes: F = federal government; S = state government; L = local government; NP = nonprofit; FP = for-profit; NGO = non-governmental organization

Development of Collaborative Enterprises 39

coordinated initiatives. It served as a crucial regulatory first step in their "public policy research," allowing them to move on to mitigation measures and land-use and zoning changes aimed at preserving the river. They show different levels of regulatory engagement in the search for collaborative management.

Tools like these are not always the exclusive domain of the sponsoring level of government or the collaborative body. Many levels of government provide some direct services or interests, with local governments sponsoring most services (Agranoff, 2012).

> All levels regulate and award contracts. Most offer grants and become engaged in loans, offer tax expenditures, charge fees, and establish government corporations. Some are included with insurance and vouchers. But that is not the point here, simply to demonstrate the multiple partnerships for sponsorship and the greater number of organizations involved in most programs. As we begin to look at the ins and outs of collaborative management, the implications will become clear. Salamon (2002, p. 13) observes that many of diverse organizations have little experience in working with each other when the tools are initially enabled. Each organization has its own interests and frame of reference. They are interdependent, but in an asymmetrical, or independent way, and their relationships face constant change.
>
> (p. 32)

To manage within the current interprogram system is "thus to engage both *vertically* and *horizontally* through networks and grants, contracts, and other tools in a highly interdependent and overlapping political system that remains based on law and jurisdiction" (Agranoff, 2012, p. 30, emphasis added). Most recent public collaborative endeavors are, to some degree, shaped by the intergovernmental developments highlighted here in this section.

The Politics of Technological Changes

The past decades have brought on many technological changes that have impacted collaborative possibilities as the cost of collecting and processing information has markedly diminished. This makes it easier for interactive contacts, personal and organizational. For example, while labor union membership may have been declining in the United States, it is increasing among large, particularly tech, industries where union activists apply new ways of electronically contacting and organizing workers.

The use of social media is taking the place of faced-based meetings through "connective action." Platforms like Facebook, Twitter, Reddit, and WhatsApp, along with support tools like Hustle (a texting service), allow union groups to collect information, coordinate workers, and promote externally oriented campaigns. Despite working independently, workers like Uber drivers are now active in chat groups and other online forums. This ride-calling firm often tests new features on

40   Development of Collaborative Enterprises

a small group of drivers, even without informing them they are part of an experiment. Online communications are partly to overcome Uber drivers' inherent disadvantage in communication and part of an initial move to organize. Coordination, in essence, is the initial step in any form of collaborative activity, using global crowdsourcing platforms by such means to talk about career development, how to avoid scams, and comparing prices. Again, this is a prelude to further organizing. For example, one study by Oxford University reported that 58% of independent-based workers were in digital contact with other workers at least once a week (Economist, Nov 17, 2018, p. 14).

In regard to coordination, a basic building block for collaboration, employees, e.g., teachers, have set up Facebook groups among colleagues. For example, nearly 70% of the U.S. state of West Virginia's 35,000 teachers joined in. It became the core of discussions on what to demand and how to organize protests. Again, this group then became the potential collaborative building blocks of any union/worker and management of joint undertakings. Broadening the word among unionists/potential unionists then was accomplished in West Virginia by a Facebook group, as it transformed into a production site for hashtags and "memes"—memorable images or video clips—that spread online. It has been particularly useful in the teachers' situation and other larger organizations where employees have been eager to change worker rules and restrictions that cut deep into worker interests.

The next challenge involves specialty digital applications (apps) designed for labor groups. Since 2013, Coworker.org "helps workers condense their demands in a petition and spread them on social media" (Economist, Nov 17, 2018, p. 26). Other platforms are used to recruit labor organization members, present worker issues, promote crowdfunding for financing organizations, facilitate job-finding activities, explain employee rights sites, link with old and established unions, compare work conditions on different crowdsourcing platforms (Fair Crowd Work), set up innovation units for experimentation and engage workers with dependents, e.g., childcare workers (Fair Care Jobs).

The potential for electronic collaboration in unions among geographically dispersed workers has great potential. The next steps are systems that can mine data that can retrieve information about its union members and from the sources that will allow them to press for employer payment increases, use of algorithms as to when to ask for pay raises, the anticipation of layoffs, information about new executives and union reactions, and how to work with management in a collaborative activity. Newer apps are also coming, such as Mystro, an app for ride-hailing services like Lyft and Uber. It allows users to switch easily between services, evaluate trip requests and reject unprofitable ones, and otherwise enable drivers to make better decisions (Economist, Nov 17, 2018, pp. 24–26). As these tools expand, so too will trade unions similarly be strengthened. Technological change in these venues will undoubtedly bring certain unions to the collaborative management discussion table and enable other employees of large organizations—private and nonprofit—to participate in work discussions among governments, NGOs, and even

Development of Collaborative Enterprises 41

associations of independent workers. In this sense, technology will become very important for supporting collaboration and its impact on CP in the very beginning.

Governance at the Core

Whereas many social, economic, and cultural forces pervade any collaboration program or policy, it is clear that decisions made and executed are at the core. That is the essence of governance. One analysis by the Rural Governance Initiative (RGI) points to four aspects of governance nature: (1) pressures on small governments and their leaders; (2) flaws (openers) in the current governing system, e.g., through globalization and industrial restructuring; (3) opportunities through independent silos, non-comprehensive/isolated governance innovations; and (4) acknowledgment that governance issues and relationships are tremendously complex that is making collaboration happen as protracted processes (Stark, 2017). At any rate, "RGI must use emergent governance to overcome traditional ways of doing things" (p. 6).

In this process, RGI identifies the following eight core principles of rural governance that include aspects of collaboration, citizen engagement, leveraging resources, and strengthening the abilities of local officials.

1. Crossing sectors (public, private, and nonprofit).
2. Crossing political boundaries and recognizing regions.
3. Welcoming new voices (especially underrepresented individuals and youth).
4. Visioning a different future (bottom-up process).
5. Analyzing a region's competitive advantages (focus on strengths and identify clusters).
6. Strengthening competencies of local elected officials.
7. Engaging key intermediaries.
8. Investing in local capital.

Importantly, governance emphasizes the value of collaboration, as in "New River: Governance in River Management: A Study of Collaboration-Based Work Plans" in Figure 2.2.

This mini-study underscores the core underlying value of *connection* in dealing with the forces of politically mobilizing those forces that need to and are willing to collaborate. Complex relationships are increasingly based on broad, interactive connections in this age. We must develop, as Anne-Marie Slaughter (2017, p. 13) maintains, "new 'playbooks' for which the old power games of competing organizations must give way to building deep links."

To Warren Bennis and Patricia Ward Biederman (1997), this is done by people who are working in "great groups" that are much more than a collection of great minds who jointly engage in "creative collaboration" (p. 197). They identify some 15 principles of such groups, summarized in Figure 2.3.

42 *Development of Collaborative Enterprises*

In 1997, New River community leaders in the mountains of North Carolina, Virginia, and West Virginia came together to identify critical issues and develop a shared vision of working together for the future of the river. This unprecedented regional effort was sparked by the Clinton Administration's American Heritage Rivers Initiative. The Initiative was designed to help Americans protect their waterways and revitalize their communities through natural resource protection, cultural resource preservation, and economic revitalization. The New had a history of river enthusiasts, but this was the first time that citizens joined together, across a broad region, to work for something positive.

Leaders set out to build support for nominating the New as an American Heritage River. The "heritage" part was easy—the New is thought to be the oldest river in North American and second oldest in the world, predating the formation of the Appalachian Mountains and the Atlantic Ocean. But the organizing work was tough. Over late night suppers, early morning breakfasts, and kitchen table talks throughout the region, local leaders met, "broke bread," told stories, "swapped lies," and planned for the future of the river they love. Residents from all walks of life came together: economic developers, conservationists, farmers, tourism leaders, artists, elders, and young people.

The New River nomination competed with 125 other rivers across the country. Elected officials from both parties endorsed the designation. Dozens of letters of support from citizens were submitted, along with hundreds of signatures on petitions that had been circulated at regional community festivals. Creative writing students wrote stories, poems, and essays that painted a literary picture of life along the New River. New River leaders were relentless in their pursuit. In the end, the New was one of 14 Heritage designated rivers.

Since 1998, more than 2,000 citizens and numerous elected officials from 21 counties in three states have worked to develop and implement the New River work plan. More than $20 million in public and private funds have been secured to support sustainable agriculture projects, purchase conservation easements, plant buffers along the river and streams, clean up and restore degraded mines, develop riverfront parks and visitor centers, promote downtown revitalization and heritage tourism development, collect oral histories, and develop youth corps programs

Figure 2.2 New River: Governance in River Management: A Study of Collaboration-Based Work Plans

Source: Stark (2017, p. 12)

Development of Collaborative Enterprises   43

1. Recruiting the most talented people, have original minds, are problem solvers, are willing to engage in new relationships and new and better ways of doing things.
2. Most nonterritorial problems require collective solutions. Great groups need leaders who invent a leadership style that suits them, but it is almost always in command and control. Leaders have to act decisively but never arbitrarily.
3. Every great group has a strong leader. Whereas, great groups are made up of people with rare gifts working together as equals, yet in virtually every one, there is one person who acts as a maestro, organizing the genius of the others, yet has to have the respect of the people, some of whom may have greater genius than them.
4. Great groups are headed by people confident enough to recruit people better than themselves. They revel in the talent of others. The talented smell out places full of promise and energy, the areas where the future is being made.
5. Great groups are full of talented people who can work together on tasks that can only be performed collaboratively. It is madness to recruit people, however gifted, who are incapable of working side by side toward a common goal. Such groups are more tolerant of personal idiosyncrasies than are ordinary groups. Moreover, people engaged in groundbreaking collaborations have high regard for people who challenge and test ideas.
6. Great groups always believe they are doing something vital. They are filled with believers. The psychology of these high-minded missions is clear. They know going in, they will expect to make sacrifices, but they know they are working on something monumental, worthy of nothing other than their best selves.
7. Great groups become their own world, physically removed and isolated from the world they are trying to change, free from its distractions but still able to tap into its resources. They can create their own culture, with distinctive customs, jokes, dress, even a private language.
8. Great groups see themselves as winning underdogs who will snatch the prize from competitors.
9. Great groups always have "an enemy" or a competitor. They do not lose hope in the face of complexity. Indeed, the difficulty of the task adds to their joy.
10. People in great groups have blinders on. They are not distracted by peripheral concerns. Instead, they are people with a vision, struggling to turn a vision into a tangible outcome.
11. Great groups are optimistic, not realistic. They believe they can do things others cannot. Indeed, the "can do" people are those who combine reasonable talent with the ability to keep going in the face of defeat.
12. The right person for the right job; people with unique talents—gifted people— can not be forced into roles they are not suited for. The person and the task need to be properly matched.

Figure 2.3 Fifteen Principles of Collaborative Groups

Source: Adapted from Bennis and Biederman (1997, pp. 196–218)

Development of Collaborative Enterprises

> 13. People working in great groups want a worthy challenge, which allows them to explore the whole continent of their talent. Talented people need to transcend trivial duties and expectations—where anything is filed in triplicate—nor are they necessarily in fancy facilities.
> 14. Successful collaborating involves dreams with deadlines. They are places of action, not think tanks or retreat centers devoted solely to generating ideas. Moreover, great groups continue to struggle until the project is brought to a successful conclusion.
> 15. Great work is its own reward. The reward is the creative process itself. Problem-solving douses the human brain with chemicals that make it feel good. Since intellectual explorers do a creative collaboration, most great groups are temporary. Also, members of creative groups can be convened to develop moral or unworthy tasks. You can't think so hard in a great group that you forget to think.

Figure 2.3 (Continued)

Engaging in Collaborative Governance

How do people engage in collaborative governing in the real world? Allison Gash (2022, p. 497) concludes, "Despite a widespread belief in the power of collaboration to solve society's ills, however, we know little about what collaborative governance is, how it works, and whether it lives up to its promise." Just as policy problems involve widespread problems and interests, solutions are proposed and implemented by disparate sets of actors. Such vexing policy dilemmas will require multiple modes of attachment, not by a meeting but by melding the minds of representatives of many fields to accomplish real solutions.

Allison Gash (2022) reminds us that CP must begin by narrowing the space of what is at hand to create a "network of partners" that represent diverse interests: institutional, geographic, cultural, and political.

1. The collaborative as a unit must have the authority and autonomy to govern (ability that varies in practice).
2. A problem-driven approach is needed to identify and address (program) policy shortfalls. Entities must integrate and prioritize flexibility and innovation into any decision-making structures they develop to identify, diagnose, and manage unanticipated obstacles.
3. Mutual understanding and consensus should be promoted. This creates a process whereby learning and evaluation are at a premium, as stakeholders work together on all aspects of policy/program development and management—from problem definition and planning to implementation and assessment.

The context for collaborative governance, suggests Gash (2022), is heavily based on the quality and strength of the relationship between stakeholders. Their

Development of Collaborative Enterprises 45

communicative activity relies on information exchange and *joint learning and discovery*, surrounded by an atmosphere of mutual respect and interdependence. The following conditions may be present for success.

1. Time needs to be spent on developing mutual trust.
2. Existing institutional focus, e.g., government, must be understood and respected. Collaborative governance compliments do not supplant existing structures.
3. "From the initial agenda-setting and problem definition to program design and implementation, each element of a collaborative work plan must be addressed through shared learning and exploration" (p. 501).
4. "Shared learning, however, cannot be achieved without a concomitant focus on developing tools and opportunities that foster interdependence" (p. 502).
5. "Collaborative entities must develop the capacity to foster deliberation and debate, and in so doing, promote credibility and legitimacy among their participants" (p. 502). Partners need to remain invested, even to the degree when personal (and organizational) goals are sacrificed.
6. Strong leadership is essential but not the typical kind of hierarchy. Facilitative leadership concentrates on building and maintaining relationships: recreating the need of actors, massaging tensions among participants, promoting an effective dialogue among participants, safeguarding the regulation of the collaboration among participants and supporters. In addition to managing the collaborative, it helps partners build support among home agencies. "Early and exacting leadership selection, then, helps steer the collaborative in ways that will preserve its horizontal governing structure while encouraging horizontal governing also while encouraging constant relationship-building and idea generation" (p. 502).

Given the connective, non-hierarchical, non-market forms of operatives engaging in collaboration, it entails several challenges. For example, Gash (2022, p. 503) reminds us that "[w]hen you supplement the complicated policy environment that often invites collaborative governance with the tentative administrative structure used to secure relationships and promote credibility, the obstacles multiply" and lists the following challenges to collaboration:

1. Although partner organization mission and personal diversity clearly inspire solutions, tension and dissatisfaction can follow aspects of the process. For example, joint processing coupled with issue complexity can lead to disagreements far exceeding siloed approaches within partner organizations.
2. The double goals of flexibility and inclusion may also cause conflict. Indeed, collaborative governance can create obstacles to participation in those communities or interests with no connections to organized stakeholders.
3. Since collaborative governance is normally (except for legal mandates) voluntary in participation, intention includes: (1) porous entry and exit policies; (2) leaders and partners are attuned to stakeholder dissatisfaction; and (3) at the-ready recruitment strategies to counteract the effects of the revolving door.

46 *Development of Collaborative Enterprises*

4. Collaborative governance may fail under the weight of high or differing participants and expectations, particularly when participants enter with overblown hopes of what collaborative governance can achieve or specifications about the dynamics of collaboration.

Collaborative management, concludes Gash (2022, pp. 504–505), presents the following managerial complications.

1. "The elements of collaborative governance must be tailored to suit the specific needs and conditions of the policy environment" (p. 504). Normally "the 'how-to' component of collaborative governance rests on the unique attitudes of the stakeholders and the political, social, and fiscal environment" (p. 504).
2. To meet diversity and consensus goals, different forms of knowledge are needed, some of which are alternatives to the standard forms that participants possess. Some will be needed to overcome information exchange.
3. The collaborative will almost always face obstacles regarding person-based and technology-based inputs that will be part of the process. Foremost are those inherent in law and government. The problem is that although the collaborative cannot be a puppet of the state, it cannot ignore the state.
4. "[T]he fluid procedural landscape for collaborative management makes it difficult to enge in meaningful evaluation and assessment" (p. 505). It has become difficult to agree on the elementary assessment or its value. While there is some description/narrative on process agreement on performance-related results, they have yet to be agreed upon.
5. "[C]ollaborative governance may be uniquely vulnerable to programmatic changes and shifts that stem from any policy environment" (p. 505). The perceived value of the effort is based on complex forces like the policy environment, the vulnerability of funding shortages, process change risks, and participant agency challenges. In collaboration, these forces compound problems that relate to any individual agency that leads to "combined risk."

These forces, conclude Gash, make collaborative efforts high-risk, high-reward endeavors. They involve lots of groundwork to launch and manage these endeavors, and "if *implemented well*, it can produce significant substantive and participatory rewards. However, in the absence of established characteristics, goals, markers or standards, collaborative governance practitioners risk flying blindly, undercutting the promise of collaboration in the process" (Gash, 2022, pp. 508, emphasis in original).

Spotlight in the Real World: Interlocal Agreements in Nebraska

Many U.S. state governments authorize and encourage their constituent governments, particularly county governments, to engage in various forms of collaborative engagement by legally authorizing and promoting interlocal agreements. Counties

Development of Collaborative Enterprises 47

and cities use interlocal agreements to mutually engage services in law enforcement, rural community extension services, road maintenance, mowing and snow removal, and ambulance and related health services. School districts use interlocal agreements for distance learning cooperatives, personnel sharing, employee insurance, alternative education, shared facility use, distance transportation, utility agreements, equipment/supplies procurement, and fund management (Shank, 2014). In addition, states promote this type of collaboration through startup grants and loans for shared capital projects and various taxation and bond authority incentives advantages.

Nebraska is a model for interlocal agreements; its Interlocal Cooperation Act of 1963 (13 Nebraska Revised Statute §§801–827[10,63]) allows public entities and NGOs to enter into agreements to provide services and share in facilities for mutual benefit. It is a method of operation under state-imposed tax restrictions, among other incentives. Quite importantly, Park, Maher, and Ebdon (2018) have studied the impact of interlocal collaboration on local fiscal outcomes at the state government-wide level, particularly the sections that promote greater state incentives and for local cost-saving purposes.

Nebraska counties that provide the Park, Maher, and Ebdon (2018) unit of analysis were selected because of their motivation for interlocal collaboration due to existing revenue constraints and available state fiscal incentives. Specifically, in 1999, state lawmakers adopted a property tax rate limit of 0.45%, and limited annual revenue growth to 2.5% (Blair & Janousek, 2013). Along with the adoption of these limits, the state provides fiscal incentives for interlocal collaboration. The state incentive program, enacted in the 1999 Nebraska Joint Public Agency Act, has two different layers. First, expenditures for interlocal collaboration are exempted from the revenue limit. Second, counties that have interlocal agreements may levy an additional property tax levy of $0.05. Given that fiscal constraints have generated within-state variation in Nebraska county fiscal burdens (Park, Maher, & Ebdon, 2018), demand for state fiscal incentives may also vary depending on each county's experience with the budgetary limits (p. 21).

Their study revealed three important conclusions. First, state-legislated incentives do matter. After the establishment of a special property tax in 1999, participation had grown from 61 to 87 counties. The average spending on interlocal activities increased from 2.5% to 5.83% of total expenditures. Second, the program does lead to revenue savings. For every percentage of expenditure on interlocal activities, spending on other services decreased by 1.6%. Indeed, some counties spent up to 8% of their budgets on interlocal activity, suggesting collaboration may encourage more efficient services. Third, collaboration has a differential effect: interlocal activities have little impact on spending for those counties close to the state maximum property tax rate. Interlocal actions lead to lower overall county spending for those below the maximum rate. The latter suggests that collaboration can lead to more efficient service delivery. The three authors conclude that despite any limitations on their research, a look at interlocal collaboration has "great potential to look at means of local efficiency" (Park, Maher & Ebdon, 2018, p. 21). Current state incentive structures focus on action-based objectives, which need to be elaborated in more detail in other contexts.

48 *Development of Collaborative Enterprises*

Reaching Small, Interacting Group Agreements

Years of small group decisions or agreement-reaching like those in Nebraska have indicated that several process analyses lead to a rather straightforward, step-by-step process. This type of problem-solving has been called a plan to be shared with group decision-makers. The following collaborative "agenda" has been followed with adaptations for a particular problem, environment, or group.

1. Define the problem that outlines the exact nature of the issues, with a focus on delineation of the major concerns and culminating in a problem statement.
2. Limit the problem, making initial decisions related to the most critical aspects of the problem to be considered.
3. Analyze the problem, a core agreement-related problem, avoiding rapid jumps to any potential conclusions but collecting evidence to help describe and clarify the scope and dimensions of the problem.
4. Problem formula figure/reformulation, setting specific objectives or criteria that may be derived from the problem analysis, deciding the most important and most relevant.
5. Suggest possible solutions, moving toward the most relevant or specific criteria, e.g., using brainstorming, modifying any partial solutions, or piggybacking on partial solutions suggested by others.
6. Check solutions against the previously established criteria. Focus on ideas rather than a personality. Evaluate the most favorable proposals.
7. Implement the solution, which appears as one of the most important but often overlooked processes. If a solution is not to be implemented, the problem has not been solved.
8. Evaluate the implementation of the agreement/solution, including looking for potential modifications.

(Barker et al., 2000, pp. 109–115)

Sources of group information include relying on participants' personal experience, recorded decisions, surveys, personal interviews, printed materials/journals, newspapers, project reports, reference materials, and electronic media (e.g., online sources or film, radio, or television documentaries, etc.).

Mandatory Collaboration: Government to Government

A collaboration share can often involve mandatory joining up. Unlike the Nebraska voluntary situation, or what (could) be called required collaboration, it is also part of the CP landscape, particularly between separate public agencies. Working across agency government legal boundaries is sometimes required, particularly among government officials. Explicit mandates in legislation, policy, or leadership directives require connections and other officials in government and NGOs. In many situations, they can relate to implicit value-based mandates: some agency

Development of Collaborative Enterprises 49

cultures value a collaborative approach (O'Leary & Gerard, 2012). For example, a study of 304 federal executives by O'Leary and Gerard (2012) found that reasons for mandates to collaborate included: expectations of higher-level administrators, agency-based directives, legislative mandates, the influence of organizational culture, one's personal values as an implicit force, and simply persons reporting it was the "right thing to do." One example described by O'Leary and Gerard (2012) involved the payment of economic stimulus benefits to qualified retirees and unemployed railroad workers between the Social Security Administration and the Department of Veterans Affairs, including coordinated tracking, notification, payment, data, and procedural systems. Another situation involved the Producer Price Index program with another program that produced a different price index. After several months of collaboration, the dual agency task force identified projects, wrote charters, recruited team members, and engaged in a series of systems development efforts. Also, the Office of Personnel Management (OPM) worked to reform federal hiring practices by bringing OPM together with the Department of Defense, the Nuclear National Regulatory Commission, and the Department of Homeland Security.

To many federal administrators, "to collaborate" was a natural or implicit element of their job. As O'Leary and Gerard (2012) clarify:

> For many federal executives, collaboration has become a natural way of carrying out the business of government. Our survey respondents say that "collaboration is a normal part of what we do," "part of our everyday function," and "how we do business." Some implicitly mandated collaborations are driven by the need to overcome scarce resources; others indicate an awareness of interdependency that makes working together a given. One federal executive comments,
>
>> Nearly everything I did in the Environmental Protection Agency required collaboration, such as Hurricane Katrina, American Samoa tsunami response ... and the Deepwater Horizon oil spill. An effective federal response to nearly any incident requires more than one agency to respond, hence collaboration becomes critical to mission success.
>>
>> (2012, p. 13)

Citizen-driven collaboration proved to be another driver. An agency executive explains that multiple agencies in his work serve citizens.

> Therefore, citizens are disadvantaged if agencies do *not* work together. For the past four years, his organization has engaged in redesigning all the key systems in its hospitals through collaborative groups, including representatives from the Department of Veteran[s] Affairs, to better meet the needs of wounded warriors.
>
> (O'Leary & Gerard, 2012, p. 13)

50 *Development of Collaborative Enterprises*

In a related sphere of activity, a project involving the U.S. Internal Revenue Service (IRS), the U.S. Environmental Protection Agency (EPA), the Department of Agriculture, the Occupational Safety and Health Administration (OSHA), the Department of Defense, a U.S. senator's office, and the Small Business Administration (SBA) has the common goal of providing better information and services to small businesses. "Citizen focus is behind another example involving the National Oceanic and Atmospheric Administration, the IRS, and state-level authorities who aim to understand the impact of a recent oil spill on the fishing industry" (O'Leary & Gerard, 2012, p. 13).

O'Leary and Gerard (2012) also identify cross-agency and intergovernmental connections among agencies:

> Some Senior Executive Service (SES) federal executives describe a new way of doing government-wide business through ongoing councils of agency administrators who identify issues related to performance and to catalyze collaborative efforts. One specific result of council work is a major effort to identify information technology systems that might be shared across federal agencies. Other executives see their agencies as embracing collaboration as the "right thing to do." The National Aeronautics and Space Administration (NASA) is engaged with the Baltimore City Public Schools, a research university, and a teaching university to improve science and technology education. What began as a modest effort with the city has expanded to include multiple actors and may provide NASA with future talent. Similarly, a Health and Human Services (HHS) agency collaboration, the Health and Human Services Coordinating Committee on Women's Health, expanded its work to a larger collaborative of over 100 organizations including academic groups, nonprofits, advocacy groups, private-sector professionals, governments, and faith organizations to develop a new agenda for women's health in the 21st century.
>
> (p. 13)

Finally, O'Leary and Gerard (2012) found that federal managers used collaborative management "to establish shared processes and procedures to promote greater efficiency" (p. 4). They cite the efforts to create interoperability standards for a geoscience data project among federal and state agencies, industries, and universities.

Voluntary Collaborative Projects

The three voluntary collaborative bodies illustrated in Box 2.1, Box 2.2, and Box 2.3 are representatives of today's non-mandated interorganizational collaborative undertakings. First, none of the three collaboratives are completely outside government, but governments are core and active partners and co–decision-makers. The Lake Champlain group (Box 2.2) is notable in this regard. Second, none of the three are either markets or hierarchies but represent the coming together collaboratively of many public/NGO agencies, such as Radius in Box 2.1, to serve a common purpose. Third, their work is project work, as in EcoPeace (Box 2.3), serving commonly agreed-upon needs. Fourth, these bodies do not merely meet and decide, but rather

Development of Collaborative Enterprises 51

use knowledge and solution exploration to reach accommodation and consensus. This is clearly the case with regard to all three projects. Strictly voting in some "raw" sense is rarely a typical agreement or decision mode, as with the case of Radius. Fifth, their work tends to be project-oriented, such as those of EcoPeace.

Box 2.2   Lake Champlain Basin Program

The Lake Champlain Basin Program (LCBP) works in partnership with government agencies from New York, Vermont, and Québec, private organizations, local communities, and individuals to coordinate and fund efforts that benefit the Lake Champlain Basin's water quality, fisheries, wetlands, wildlife, recreation, and cultural resources.

These efforts are guided by the plan Opportunities For Action (OFA). The LCBP works with its program partners, advisory committees, and local communities to implement this plan through a variety of federal, provincial, and local/municipal funds. Core funding for the LCBP is through the U.S. Environmental Protection Agency.

The LCBP is administered jointly by several agencies: the EPA (New England and Region 2), New York State Department of Environmental Conservation, and the Vermont agency of the New England Interstate Water Pollution Control Commission. The roles of partner agencies and the process for coordination of the Lake Champlain Steering Committee are governed by the following memoranda of agreement.

- Memorandum of Understanding on Environmental Cooperation on the Management of Lake Champlain Among the Gouvernement du Québec, the State of New York, and the State of Vermont.
- Memorandum of Understanding between the Federal Partners for Cooperation and Coordination to Implement Opportunities for Action (1996 version).

Opportunities for Action (OFA) is a plan for managing the Lake Champlain watershed. It is a strategic planning tool used to coordinate the efforts of a diverse group of stakeholders as represented on the Lake Champlain Steering Committee. The Steering committee develops the LCBP's annual budget and guides its work to improve and restore water quality and ecosystem integrity.

The 2017 version of OFA is its fourth iteration. Conditions and issues have continued to change since the plan was first endorsed by the governors of New York and Vermont and the regional administrators of the EPA in 1996. Progress has been made in many areas, and priorities for action have evolved to reflect the dynamic nature of human interactions in a complex ecosystem. Like previous updates in 2003 and 2010, the 2017 version addresses the latest challenges and opportunities related to nutrient loading, aquatic invasive species,

52   *Development of Collaborative Enterprises*

habitat conservation, cultural heritage preservation, and other issues. As with past versions, the 2017 plan also includes a letter of support from Québec demonstrating Québec's commitment to Lake Champlain management efforts. Opportunities For Action 2017 lays out objectives and strategies to address four goals that are the core of the LCBP's work: clean water, healthy ecosystems, thriving communities, and an informed and involved public. It also includes task areas for each goal that represent priorities for action going forward. Specific tasks are identified and supported through the LCBP's annual budget process.

Source: www.lcbp.org/

Box 2.3   EcoPeace Middle East

EcoPeace Middle East is an organization that brings together Jordanian, Palestinian, and Israeli environmentalists. The primary objective is the promotion of cooperative efforts to protect a shared environmental heritage. In so doing, it seeks to advance both sustainable regional development and the creation of necessary conditions for lasting peace in the region. EcoPeace has offices in Amman, Ramallah, and Tel-Aviv.

The people and wildlife of the region are dependent on many of the same natural resources. Shared surface and sub-surface freshwater basins, shared seas, common flora and fauna species and a shared air-shed are some of the characteristics that necessitate regional cooperation. The Jordan River Basin (a major source of freshwater in a water-scarce region), the Gulf of Aqaba (a highly sensitive ecosystem giving life to arguably the world's most beautiful coral reef), and the Dead Sea (the lowest point on earth and the world's saltiest non-shallow body of water) are all examples of unique shared ecosystems in the region which necessitate regional cooperation if they are to be preserved.

EcoPeace is a project-oriented NGO, using both a "bottom-up" (grass roots/community) approach coupled with a "top-down" (advocacy) strategy that has proven to be a very effective work model.

In addition, we approach cross-border environment and peacebuilding issues by first developing a regional strategy. We hire local researchers—Palestinian, Jordanian, and Israeli—to gain a regional understanding as to the root cause of the problem and then develop a common vision as to how we might be able to influence decision-makers, the media, and the general public. A key to success has been that once the common vision has been developed, staff from the respective offices take the same vision and present it to their respective audiences: Palestinian to Palestinian, Jordanian to Jordanian, and Israeli to Israeli.

Our projects can be categorized according to the following themes.

Geographical context—the Dead Sea Rift Valley runs from the Gulf of Aqaba/Eilat, in the south, along the Arava Valley, through the Dead Sea, up

Development of Collaborative Enterprises 53

the Jordan River into the Sea of Galilee and beyond, connecting the peoples of the Eastern Mediterranean. Many of our projects are located along this shared, complex ecosystem.

Socioeconomic-based projects focus on issues such as sustainable water use, water privatization, trade, sustainable development, water as a human security issue, developing renewable energy, and healthy food practices.

Climate change stands on its own as one of the greatest environmental, social, and economic threats facing the planet today, especially to our scarce water resources.

EcoPeace employs 60 paid staff and involves hundreds of volunteers through its "Good Water Neighbors" community program. Projects are carried out by staff in our three regional offices, led by a director in each office, office staff, and more than two dozen field staff.

Through our projects we cooperate and coordinate with a wide range of official and civil society groups whose work has an impact on environmental protection and peacebuilding.

Source: www.ecopeaceme.org

Box 2.4   Creative Solution Process

Most of the emphasis on creative thinking and the brainstorming in the collaboration process has been derived from Alex Osborn's text *Applied Imagination* (1962). Osborn and his colleagues conducted considerable research using brainstorming techniques that, in most situations, were found to be up to 44% more effective than traditional problem-solving methods. The major premise behind the brainstorming method is that everyone should experience total freedom to express ideas without fear of personal embarrassment or criticism from others. Osborn suggests the following rules for engaging in the brainstorming process.

1. Defer judgments on all ideas presented until everyone has had a chance to contribute.
2. Seek to obtain the greatest possible quantity of ideas.
3. Use the "chain reaction" technique associated with "freewheeling" (i.e., let your mind flow freely without pre-censoring ideas).
4. Try to combine and improve on the ideas of others.

In general, groups employing the brainstorming process will want to set a specific time limit for this phase of the solution-generating (or criteria-generating) process. Generally, a brainstorming session should last for no longer

54 *Development of Collaborative Enterprises*

> than 5–7 minutes. During this intensive ideation period, one or two persons may be asked to serve as recorders of ideas. If two people are recording ideas, they can take turns recording in order to more efficiently commit to paper the suggestions that have been made
>
> *Source:* Barker et al. (2000, p. 119), based on Osborn (1962)

Remember that the brainstorming session suggested in Box 2.4 is a true verbal free-for-all. Criticism—at least initially—is ruled out, and all ideas are permitted without condemnation or ridicule. Instead, the group should go through the process of trial and error to accept new ideas without criticizing them first (Kokemuller & Media, 2015). If possible, groups should pick topics with simple solutions to practice in preparation for engaging in brainstorming concerning more complex problems. Finally, decision-making modes described in the following list are generally part of group decision-making or agreement (Barker et al., 2000, p. 182).

1. The five decision-making strategies are: force, majority vote, compromise, arbitration, and consensus.
2. Force, generally, is an ineffective decision-making strategy because group members often do not support decisions that they do not make.
3. The majority of votes can save time when a quick decision is necessary, but the strategy can be destructive when group members take losses as personal defeats.
4. With compromise solutions, no one completely wins and no one completely loses. If group members feel as though they gave more than they gained and/or that the problem is not completely solved, motivation to implement the decision may be low for both sides of the controversy.
5. During arbitration, the group brings in a disinterested third party to make the decision. Sometimes arbitration has the same effects as compromise in that no one completely wins and no one completely loses.
6. Consensus initially centers on goals rather than alternatives, and the group attempts to formulate a new solution that will meet the goals of both sides of the controversy.

Within these processes, power in CP is nuanced. For example, the power of new ideas, new technology, or presentation of new formulaic approaches presents great opportunities to act collaboratively. Thus, the power dimension needs to be expanded to include the power dynamics inside the collaborative undertaking itself, a principle that is not well recognized nor understood.

To summarize, collaborative activity involves at least the following four nuanced power dimensions that tend to appear in various combinations.

(1) the familiar power, including pre-established solutions, that the partner brings to the agency, (2) the internal operational power that results from

Development of Collaborative Enterprises   55

agency inputs and interactive processes within the collaborative process related to its maintenance and operations, along with, (3) knowledge-based power pursued by each cross-organization participants operating as a technical core, (e.g., how they process information), and (4) the deliberative power of generating new agreement possibilities generated by the search for technical solutions and outcomes that address multiorganization and interagency problems.

(Agranoff, 2012, p. 166)

Indeed, it is a dynamic and complex process. As a result, power can be a considerably difficult and protracted undertaking. Because all of these CP power dimensions are likely to be present in various forms analytically, they can and have served as positive forces to facilitate overcoming those negative synergies of doses of agency power used in resisting joint agreement or action. These processes can be understood as possible to "jump-start" and maintain "agreement power" needs in collaborative processes. In the absence of hierarchical authority and/or legal power, more of these interactive forces "substitute" or work in place of hierarchy. Nevertheless, they are important distinctions in collaborative management.

Conflict is inevitable in reaching collaborative agreement. It becomes part of the interorganizational process. Clearly, participants need to sit down and talk. Moreover, conflicts cannot be managed unless the key communication channels are open. Avoiding differences or abruptly ending the process will not solve anything. Perhaps participants could eliminate an issue or at least take it off the agenda, but that move may have its costs. Communication is almost always the key. As a result, it is always important to have each party identify their problems and issues, lay out individual issues and preferred preferences, be tactful in expressing disagreement, listen actively, persuade others of the value of a constructive conflict, and work at developing intragroup trust, avoiding taking disputes personally, and demonstrating cooperativeness, even in the case of your idea being rejected (Barker et al., 2000, p. 185). Moreover, understanding how to operate in a connected world will require a "seventh sense" for operating within and between networks (Ramo, 2016, p. 28).

At the community development level, we are talking about what Cornelia and Jan Flora (2003, p. 217) refer to as "*bridging capital*": the vital connections among diverse groups, including those not part of the community. To them, an effective process also needs "*bonding capital*" (among similar persons) plus bridging capital. Intermediaries are among the different jurisdictions and organizations outside the community that provides key bridging capital. These key intermediaries include government and NGOs, civic organizations, foundations, or other funders, along with issue-based organizations and locally based community and technical colleges. These connections are part of the contemporary give and take that can bring together and hold organizations to work on problems and issues together.

56 *Development of Collaborative Enterprises*

Hierarchy and Networks

In a thick and insightful history of hierarchies and networks in a "figurative" sense of networked connections in the global sphere, Niall Ferguson (2014) identifies the following several insights of network theory that have profound collaborative implications in general.

1. No person is isolated. Individuals need to be understood in terms of their relationships to other nodes—the task edges connect them.
2. Birds of a feather flock together. Because of homophily, social networks can be understood partly in terms of "like attracting like."
3. Weak ties are strong. It also matters how dense a network is and how connected it is to other clusters, even if it only through a few weak links—but can it be considered as a part of larger network?
4. Structure determines virality. Some ideas are viral because of the structural features of the network through which they spread, which are less likely to spread in hierarchical and/or top-down structures.
5. Networks never sleep. They are not static but dynamic and evolve into complex adaptive systems, such that adding just a few changes can radically alter the network's behavior.
6. Networks network. When networks interact, the result can be innovation and intervention. "When a network disrupts an ossified hierarchy, it can overthrow it with breathtaking speed" (Morrisey, 2018, p. 1). But when a hierarchy attacks a fragile network, the result can be the collapse of networks.
7. The rich get richer. Because of preferential attachment, most social networks are profoundly inegalitarian.

These core insights of network science are being dynamically multiplied and made increasingly familiar. Ferguson (2014, p. 48) maintains that a present era is one when "superannuated hierarchical institutions have been challenged by novel networks, their impact magnified by the new technology." The future holds far more network-related and/or collaborative disruption of hierarchies. Chapter 7 will address how such collaboratives, including network-based management, have changed with electronic contact and how administrators and staff cope with multiple network challenges.

The Basics of Networks in Operation

A first principle of networks is differentiated in both purpose and range of public action. In practice, they range from non-decision networks that exchange information and ideas like many environmental networks to those that make legally based authoritative decisions, as in federally chartered transportation metropolitan policy organizations (MPO).

A summary of fundamental issues of network operation is provided in Box 2.5. It overviews five essential features of networks as organized forms (Agranoff, 2012). First,

Development of Collaborative Enterprises 57

different networks serve distinct tasks, and some serve many. Second, networks necessitate distributed leadership, which entails many people in many roles. Third, in these information-society arrangements, the discovery of beneficial knowledge is a driving factor. Fourth, networks act in tandem with existing organizations, facilitating concerns that these organizations bring to them. Finally, networks can be essential contributors to public endeavors in various ways other than only public problem-solving (Börzel & Heard-Lauréote, 2009; Rhodes, 1996; Torfing, 2005; Klijn, 2008).

Box 2.5   Essential Features of Networks as Organized Forms

1. Not all networks are alike. Some exchange information, some build partner capacity, some "blueprint" strategies and process interorganizational programming, and some make policy and/or program adjustments. Some do more than one of these things.
2. Networks are non-hierarchical but are organized into "collaborarchies" that blend today's conductive bureaucracies with voluntary, organization-like structures. The key is not the official leaders but their champions, vision keepers, technical cores, and staff members. They are mainly organized around work and working groups as communities of practice.
3. The most important function of these communities is to discover, organize, and engage in knowledge management. The knowledge management process binds the network as it approaches problems of a multiorganization, multijurisdictional orientation.
4. Networks are overlays on the hierarchies of participating organizations. They influence—but do not control—home agency decisions. The core work of the public agency goes on, but in an increasingly conductive manner.
5. Networks do add public value. To varying degrees, they help multiple organizations engage in problem identification and information exchange, identification of extant knowledge, adaptation to emergent technologies, engagement in knowledge management, building of capacity, developing joint strategies and programs, and adjusting policies and programs.

Source: Agranoff (2012 p. 135). Reprinted with permission.

According to several scholars, network management is viewed "as consisting of exercises in managing a set of interorganizational games" (Agranoff, 2018, p. 141). Klijn and Koppenjan (1997, p. 47) write that

network management, conceived as the steering of interaction processes, may involve activating networks to tackle particular problems or issues (network activation), establishing ad hoc organizational arrangements to support interaction (arranging), bringing together solutions, problems, and parties (brokerage),

58 *Development of Collaborative Enterprises*

promoting favorable conditions for joint action (facilitation) and conflict management (mediation and arbitration).

Mandell (2008, p. 71) similarly denotes the purpose of network management as

a process that includes relative equality and power among stakeholders, who share an overriding mission, work toward a broad perspective or "view of the whole," establish common values, develop new relationships built on trust, and work toward systems changes.

Koppenjan, Koppenjan, and Klijn (2004, p. 10) explain further that the nature of these processes

searches wherein public and private parties from different organizations, [levels of] government, and networks jointly learn about the nature of a problem, look at the possibility of doing something about it, and identify the characteristics of the strategic and institutional context within which the problem solving develops.

Agger, Sørensen, and Torfing (2008) added other processes to the list of network management including facilitation of coordination among relevant players, identification of stakeholders' needs, wants and demands, and conflict mitigation based on mutual learning by all interested parties.

Anne-Marie Slaughter compares the contrasting bases of network and hierarchical power in Box 2.6. Importantly, she emphasizes the importance of non-hierarchical connections and open limits beyond rigid organizational structures. Also, she emphasizes the centrality of exercising the "power to" in networked connections. Slaughter is a former director of policy planning in the U.S. State Department and former dean of Princeton's Woodrow Wilson School of Public Affairs.

Box 2.6 Anne-Marie Slaughter's Network Power

1. Networks allow for non-hierarchical information flow that is efficient and reliable, supplementing forms/chains of command of organizations.
2. Networks are highly adaptable; they build relationships rather than routines. They are typified reciprocal patterns of exchange, incorporating elements of hierarchy and centralization.
3. Networks are scalable, the ability to grow rapidly at relatively low cost. They feature loose agendas with wide appeal, and possess a powerful narrative.
4. Power in networks flows from connectedness: the number, type, and location of connections. Power in hierarchies, by contrast, flows from the ability to command or manipulate others, which requires a position at the top. In networks, the most control nodes have the most connections and have the highest likelihood of gaining more.

Development of Collaborative Enterprises 59

5. Brokering power also means bargaining power. Those who operate in and at the connections; e.g., betweenness centrality provides greater opportunity for brokering/bargaining.
6. The power of exit. Non-bargaining or brokering to participants most often exhibits fewer embedded nodes in the network.
7. Networks often exercise the "power with" rather than the "power over." Power over is power of many to do together what no one can do alone. It is not a liability but an emergent property; it can really be exercised in connection with others. Power with can only be practiced, like a discipline.

Source: Adapted from Slaughter (2017, pp. 168–174)

Although participants operate nonhierarchically in networks and related collaborative activities, politics and the exercise of power are usually real. Focused research indicates that there usually proves to be a non-hierarchical power structure. In collaboration, power is more distributed and usually includes differentiated management core. "This means that the exercise of power by stakeholder interests and agencies is plural and uneven in operation" (Agranoff, 2018, p. 143). For example, Barbara Gray (1989, p. 113) warns us that "although it is essentially an exercise in sharing power over defining a problem and solving it, various interests can exert unequal influence and introduce their own decisions at the access (to political decision-makers), agenda-setting, and agreement stages." During the process of collaboration, even when participants bring power potential that turn out to be unequal,

the power dynamics associated with collaboration generally involves a shift from the kind of elitist decision making to more participative, equally shared access to the decision-making arena. It is important to remember that collaboration always opens up control over access and agendas to wider participation.

(p. 20)

The pioneering studies of Provan and Milward (1991, 1995) linking the structure of mental health networks and performance emphasize the connections between lead agencies working together to achieve common objectives. Provan and Kenis (2008) classify three forms of network governance: participants' governance, lead organization governance, and network administrative organization governance. Recent research on control in networks (Agranoff, 2018) discovers a number of substitutes to network governance:

the interacting viability of small groups of managers, bureaucratic rules, and regulations; networks that hold participants accountable to achieve successful outputs; cultural controls of cooperation norms and values; and the desire of participating organizations to achieve control by enhancing their reputation.

(p. 144)

60 *Development of Collaborative Enterprises*

One or more of these forces have been identified as critical features of managerial practice (Kenis & Provan, 2006). McGuire (2009) also emphasizes the significance of professionalized emergency management agencies in participating in collaborative management, an area where "control" is as difficult as working in networks. He argues that "A command-and-control model of management . . . is not associated with collaborations" (p. 91).

Agency or organizational power is real in networks despite any aura of equality of influence as partners. As will be subsequently developed, political reality must be faced as the analysis of internal management proceeds. As one reads about the implications of power being wielded in the context of rural development networks, it is clear that power is a force that either prevents or facilitates action. Network collaboration can include restructuring power inequity or leveling off the symmetries of resources used to maintain power in networks (Gray, 1989). Schapp and van Twist (1997, p. 66) describe it as individual veto power used in networks since "actors in the network are able to cut themselves off from the steering interventions of other actors." This type of veto power can be employed in networks in several ways to exclude or marginalize certain actors' interests, in effect to exclude serious consideration of certain outlooks or frames of reference, to withhold important information and or services, or to push certain actors out of the network action (Schapp & van Twist, 1997). In short, network participants have hardly proved to be collections of apolitical actors in the public sphere.

Conclusion

The many books and manuals about community development point to networking/collaboration and networks as actively being operationalized to solve problems that cut across many entities (Agranoff & McGuire, 2003; Crosby & Bryson, 2005; Cigler, 2001; Koliba, Meek, & Zia, 2010; McGuire & Agranoff, 2012; O'Toole, 1997; Rhodes, 1996; Senge, 1990; Wenger, 2000). In the following, we provide a summary by identifying Beverly Cigler's (2001, pp. 78–81) findings from multiple collaboration case studies.

1. A problem or crisis triggers thinking about resource dependence.
2. Capacity building is important: state or federal government, foundations, and professional associations.
3. The presence of collaborative skills-building leadership internally in the community was also an important precondition—particularly the various voluntary organization board members or local government committee members who possess skills in such areas as planning and finance, but also participation in government visioning and strategic planning exercises.
4. Collaboration is also coordinated by the presence of a policy entrepreneur or teams of entrepreneurs, which are similar to network champions. Combining their energies, talents, and knowledge of local problems and context sparks

Development of Collaborative Enterprises 61

up the collaboration process (Agranoff, 2012). In addition to knowledge, they should mobilize the necessary internal and external support by combining political, analytical, and people skills.

5. Build a political constituency for cooperation. Politics does really matter in the various types of policies and issues. Therefore, gaining political support is a must. Such broad-based political constituencies are uncommon or non-existent. They must be nurtured—or, as Agranoff and McGuire (2001) argue, "they require activation skills in order to tap knowledge and resources in order to gain the money, information, and experience needed to manage across agencies and organizations" (Agranoff, 2012, p. 163).

6. Early and continued support by elected local officials additionally facilitates collaboration. Local officials do not only serve as experts; they can be brokers for needed politics. Most collaborative solutions require the approval of some authority—a nonprofit board, a city or county council, a state legislature, or the like—before they can take action, and failing to involve one or more key officials in collaborative processes on a proactive basis can result in a lack of support later on.

7. Legitimacy-raising and related preconditions facilitate cooperation. One precondition promoting cooperation is a demonstration of the benefits of collective action by collaborative leaders to the general public and community, which moves the potential networks to join the collaborative effort as a result of a "better future vision." The other precondition requires focusing on visible, effective strategies early in the process, which, in turn, "helped build interested and supportive constituencies." (Cigler 2001, p. 81)

Cigler concludes that although future collaborative ventures will rely on inter-organizational actors that will be expected to chart their own courses, it does not necessarily mean that they do not need external help or that the existence of a catalyst is only enough. Importantly, she reminds us that "politics, public support, and process experience can be as important as technical expertise" (2001, p. 83). As Chapter 6 will elaborate, no matter how technically elegant a collaborative undertaking might be, a designed solution has to garner the agreement of more than a small core of agreeing technical experts. It must also please those political and governmental decision-makers that normally make and implement the ultimate agreements/decisions. Political opportunity, capability, and process development are also essential preconditions; without settling these concerns, they can lead to failure to launch many collaborative efforts. That is part of what makes the process highly political.

Chapter 3 looks deeper into the dynamics of how collaborative management in governments is organized, and Chapter 4 looks deeper into how collaboration is approached and internally managed and assisted, from both internal and external control standpoints. Finally, it seems that collaborative decision and operational mechanisms help collaborating participants find out how to approach and operate problem solutions and, of course, their politics.

62 *Development of Collaborative Enterprises*

Finally, this chapter offers a beginning—not an end—to understanding surface collaborative government–NGO processes as it analyzes the hidden and overt forms of CP. To work together, people from different entities are working out programs and services that cross lines and deal with the politics of the complexities of multiagency multiprogram involvement. Rarely on the surface but nonetheless real, a useful summary of the top ten tips for operating politically within collaboration across agencies and programs was introduced earlier in this chapter. Authoritative decision structure and process without hierarchy must find working substitutes, identified in this volume as collaborarchy with alternative bases of power—agency, operational, knowledge, and deliberation—that can potentially be positive or negative forces. Subsequent analyses in this book deal with specific CP situations from the field, stories of politics, barriers to solutions, and key political experiments and experiences. Together, these foci will hopefully extend the political power bases identified in this chapter. As Professor Norton Long concluded long ago, "Attempts to solve administrative problems in isolation from the structure of power and purpose in the polity are bound to prove illusory" (1949, p. 264).

References

Agger, A., Sørensen, E., & Torfing, J. (2008). It takes two to tango. *Civic Engagement in a Network Society, 15.*

Agranoff, R. (2007). *Managing within networks: Adding value to public organizations.* Georgetown University Press.

Agranoff, R. (2008). Collaborating for knowledge: Learning from public management networks In L. B. Bingham (Eds.), *Big ideas in collaborative public management.* ME Sharpe.

Agranoff, R. (2012). *Collaborating to manage: A primer for the public sector.* Georgetown University Press.

Agranoff, R. (2018). *Local governments in multilevel governance: The administrative dimension.* Lexington Books.

Agranoff, R., & McGuire, M. (2001). Big questions in public network management research. *Journal of Public Administration Research and Theory, 11*(3), 295–326.

Agranoff, R., & McGuire, M. (2003). Inside the matrix: Integrating the paradigms of intergovernmental and network management. *International Journal of Public Administration, 26*(12), 1401–1422. https://doi.org/10.1081/PAD-120024403Barker, L. L., Wahlers, K. J., Watson, K., & Kibler, R. (2000). *Groups in the process: An introduction to small group communication.* Prentice-Hall.

Bennis, W., & Biederman, P. W. (1997). *Organizing genius: The secrets of successful collaboration.* Nicholas Brealey.

Blair, R., & Janousek, C. L. (2013). Collaborative mechanisms in interlocal cooperation: A longitudinal examination. *State and Local Government Review, 45*(4), 268–282. https://doi.org/10.1177/0160323X13511647

Borins, S. F. (2012). Making narrative count: A narratological approach to public management innovation. *Journal of Public Administration Research and Theory, 22*(1), 165–189. https://doi.org/10.1093/jopart/muq088

Börzel, T. A., & Heard-Lauréote, K. (2009). Networks in EU multi-level governance: Concepts and contributions. *Journal of Public Policy, 29*(2), 135–151.

Development of Collaborative Enterprises   63

Brown, T. L., Potoski, M., & Van Slyke, D. M. (2013). *Complex contracting*. Cambridge University Press.

Chrislip, D. D., & Larson, C. E. (1994). *Collaborative leadership: How citizens and civic leaders can make a difference* (Vol. 24). Jossey-Bass.

Cigler, B. (2001). Multiorganizational, multisector, and multicommunity organizations: Setting the research agenda. In M. Mandell (Ed.), *Getting results through collaboration: Networks and network structures for public policy and management* (pp. 71–85). Quorum Books.

Clegg, S. (1990). *Modern organizations: Organization studies in the postmodern world*. Sage.

Crosby, B. C., & Bryson, J. M. (2005). *Leadership for the common good: Tackling public problems in a shared-power world*. John Wiley & Sons.

Economist. (2018, November 17). Workers of the world, log on! *Economist, 429*, 24–26.

Ferguson, N. (2014, June 9). *Networks and hierarchies*. The American Interest.

Flora, C. B., & Flora, J. L. (2003). Social capital. In D. L. Brown & L. E. Swanson (Eds.), *Challenges for rural 30 America in the twenty-first century*. The Pennsylvania State University Press.

Gash, A. (2022). Collaborative governance. In C. Ansell & J. Torfing (Eds.), *Handbook on theories of governance* (pp. 497–509). Edward Elgar Publishing.

Girth, A. M., & Lopez, L. E. (2019). Contract design, complexity, and incentives: Evidence from US federal agencies. *The American Review of Public Administration, 49*(3), 325–337.

Gray, B. (1989). *Collaborating: Finding common ground for multiparty problems*. Jossey Bass.

Kenis, P., & Provan, K. G. (2006). The control of public networks. *International Public Management Journal, 9*(3), 227–247.

Kilduff, M., & Tsai, W. (2003). *Social networks and organizations*. Sage.

Klijn, E. H. (2008). Governance and governance networks in Europe: An assessment of ten years of research on the theme. *Public Management Review, 10*(4), 505–525. https://doi.org/10.1080/14719030802263954

Klijn, E. H., & Koppenjan, J. F. (1997). Public management and network management. In W. J. Kickert, E. H. Klijn, & J. F. Koppenjan (Eds.), *Managing complex networks: Strategies for the public sector* (pp. 35–61). Sage.

Kokemuller, N., & Media. (2015). Importance of mission and vision in organizational strategy. *Small business*. http://chron.com/missionstatement/

Koliba, C. J., Meek, J. W., & Zia, A. (2010). *Governance networks in public administration and public policy*. CRC Press.

Koppenjan, J. F. M., Koppenjan, J., & Klijn, E. H. (2004). *Managing uncertainties in networks: A network approach to problem solving and decision making*. Psychology Press.

Long, N. E. (1949). Power and administration. *Public Administration Review, 9*(4), 257–264.

Mandell, M. P. (2000). A revised look at management in network structures. *International Journal of Organization Theory & Behavior, 3*(1/2), 185–209. https://doi.org/10.1108/IJOTB-03-01-02-2000-B006

Mandell, M. P. (2008). New ways of working: Civic engagement through networks. In E. Bergrud & K. Yang (Eds.), *Civic engagement in a network society* (pp. 65–84). InfoAgePub.

McGuire, M. (2009). The New professionalism and collaborative activity in local emergency management. In R. O'Leary & L. B. Bingham (Eds.), *The collaborative public manager: New ideas for the twenty-first century*. Georgetown University Press.

McGuire, M., & Agranoff, R. (2012). Networking in the shadow of bureaucracy. In R. F. Durant (Eds.), *The Oxford handbook of American bureaucracy* (pp. 372–395). Oxford University Press.

Miller, P. M., Scanlan, M. K., & Phillippo, K. (2017). Rural cross-sector collaboration: A social frontier analysis. *American Educational Research Journal, 54*(1_suppl), 193S–215S. https://doi.org/10.3102/0002831216665188

64 Development of Collaborative Enterprises

Morrisey, D. (2018, March 23). Thomas Friedman's world may be flat, but no one else's is. *Law & Liberty*. https://lawliberty.org/thomas-friedmans-world-may-be-flat-but-no-one-elses-is/

Nebraska Revised Statute §§801–827(10,63) Interlocal Cooperation Act of 1963.

O'Leary, R., & Gerard, C. (2012). *Collaboration across boundaries: Insights and tips from Federal Senior Executives*. IBM Centre for the Business of Government.

Osborn, A. (1962). *Applied imagination*. Scribner.

O'Toole, Jr., L. J. (1997). Treating networks seriously: Practical and research-based agendas in public administration. *Public Administration Review, 57*(1), 45–52.

O'Toole, Jr., L. J. (2015). Networks and networking: The public administrative agendas. *Public Administration Review, 75*(3), 361–371. https://doi.org/10.1111/puar.12281

Park, S., Maher, C. S., & Ebdon, C. (2018). Local property tax limits in Nebraska. *Public Administration Quarterly, 42*(3), 328–371. www.jstor.org/stable/26892943

Provan, K., & Kenis, P. (2008). Modes of network governance: Structure, management, and effectiveness. *Journal of Public Administration Research and Theory, 18*(2), 229–252. https://doi.org/10.1093/jopart/mum015

Provan, K., & Milward, H. B. (1991). Institutional-level norms and organizational involvement in a service-implementation network. *Journal of Public Administration Research and Theory, 1*(4), 391–418. www.jstor.org/stable/1181744?seq=1#metadata_info_tab_contents

Provan, K., & Milward, H. B. (1995). A preliminary theory of interorganizational network effectiveness: A comparative study of four community mental health systems. *Administrative Science Quarterly, 40*(1), 1–33.

Ramo, J. C. (2016). *The seventh sense: Power, fortune, and survival in the age of networks*. Little, Brown.

Rhodes, R. A. W. (1996). The new governance: Governing without government. *Political Studies, 44*(4), 652–667.

Salamon, L. M. (2002). The new governance and the tools of public action. In L. M. Salamon (Eds.), *The tools of government* (pp. 1–42). Oxford University Press.

Sawyer, K. (2008). *The future of learning in the age of innovation*. Beyond Current Horizons.

Schapp, L., & van Twist, M. J. W. (1997). The dynamics of closedness in networks. In W. J. Kickert, E. H. Klijn, & J. F. Koppenjan (Eds.), *Managing complex networks: Strategies for the public sector* (pp. 62–78). Sage.

Senge, P. M. (1990). *The fifth discipline: The art and practice of the learning organization*. Doubleday.

Shank, N. (2014). *Inter-local agreements: A tool for expanded learning opportunities?* Issue Brief 2014-01. University of Nebraska Public Policy Center, Lincoln, NE.

Slaughter, A. M. (2017). *The chessboard and the web: Strategies of connection in a networked world*. Yale University Press.

Stark, N. (2017). *Effective rural governance: What is it? Does it matter?* Rural Governance Initiative.

Torfing, J. (2005). Governance network theory: Towards a second generation. *European Political Science, 4*(3), 305–315.

Weick, K. E. (1969). *The social psychology of organizing*. Topics in Social Psychology. Reading, Mass, 22.

Wenger, E. (2000). Communities of practice: The key to knowledge strategy. In E. Lesser, M. Fontaine, & J. Slusher (Eds.), *Knowledge and communities* (pp. 3–21). Routledge.

3 Organizing Government to Meet Collaboration Challenges

As a partner in collaborative management, government involves more than the usual multiparty collaboration meetings. Today's joint connections are regular, organized, and focused on bringing together public agencies and their external partners to examine and develop solutions that respect and involve multiple needs, potential actions, and problem roots. To Donald Chisholm, in a situation wherein the components of organizations are fundamentally interdependent, the resulting uncertainty creates pressures for coordination (Chisholm, 1992). Everywhere we see hybrid organizations that involve collaboration, from local neighborhood watches to joint efforts like Oceana, a conservation alliance that, among others, involves Google, a division of Alphabet; Sky Truth, a charity that uses remote sensing; plus the U.S. government's National Oceanic and Atmospheric Administration (NOAA), and the European Union function that involves radar data. Together, they form Global Fishing Watch, a vessel-based data action system that provides information on illegal fishing (Ryder, 2018). Governments now regularly combine with NGOs in this way. Many organizations have to position themselves now internally to work externally. This chapter looks at this "organizing" issue from a public agency-external standpoint, responding to complexity, operating in a world of interaction with other organizations' information systems, and altering standard legal and related hierarchical structures to do collaborative work (Bevir, 2004; Börzel, 2010; Stone, 2010; O'Leary et al., 2015).

Administrative Rules Impacting Collaboration

Part of the role that governments play in collaborative management involves the rule of law that impacts the actions of administrators as they interact with NGOs. Most control is based on the core that has evolved as a result of the U.S. Administration Procedures Act (APA) 1946 as amended over the years that created the fundamentals that, as Rosenbloom (2015, p. 185) concludes, have endured:

> Congress's key point in enacting it was that public administration should incorporate the democratic-constitutional values of representation, participation, transparency, fairness, accountability, and limited government intrusion

DOI: 10.4324/9781003385769-3

on private activity. Major subsequent administrative law initiatives—including negotiated rulemaking, freedom of information, alternative dispute resolution, paperwork reduction, and legislative review—have been intended to advance these values. If folding them into administrative law and practice is sometimes bumpy, it is not because they run counter to the APA's initial purposes—in fact, national security policy aside, it is difficult to think of a single post-1946 administrative law statute that undercuts the APA's intent.

Within the APA framework, public managers can "reasonably expect stability in the larger purposes of administrative law" (p. 185); however, changes in particular laws may occur regularly.

Most relevant for CP would be various types of rulemaking. Generally, there are three types of rules: (1) legislative rules like statutes, which have the force of law; (2) procedural rules, which govern an agency's internal operations and organization; and (3) interpretation rules, which are essentially policy statements and guidelines establishing agencies' understanding of their statutory mandates. Examples of legislative rules are those related to workplace hazards and substances by OSHA and motor vehicle safety rules under the National Highway Traffic Safety Administration. For example, procedural rules relate to employee challenges and equal employment opportunity complaints. Interpretive rules explain the operational meaning of established procedures under the 1964 Civil Rights Act; e.g., rules eliminating hiring and promotional exams. There are many more examples of federal rules, as David Rosenbloom's (2015) comprehensive text outlines. Federal government rulemaking is inventorial through the Unified Agenda of Federal Regulatory and Deregulatory Actions. It provides uniform reporting of regulatory rulemaking related to federal government actions, as rules are numerous—in the thousands. States also have their own rules, sometimes parallel and sometimes differing from federal practices, leading to a seemingly infinite number of variations from the 50 individual states. Most relevant are the Model State Administrative Procedures Acts of 1961, 1981, and 2010 wherein procedural guidelines are established for "public" nongovernmental involvement in rulemaking, plus guidelines in 2010 for negotiated rulemaking (Amsler, 2016).

Law and Collaboration

The role of public law in the process is often overlooked in the core role of government in collaborative management. Public agencies are involved in interactive, interagency transactional processes through enabling statutes and executive orders leading to rules and regulations that manage programs and projects (Rosenbloom, 2015; Amsler, 2016; McGuire, 2006). These regulatory powers allow for adopting rules and regulations that will enable involvement in programs and thus affect the legal rights of active litigants and the public and program stakeholders. In this regard, David Rosenbloom (1983) provides

Organizing Government to Meet Collaboration Challenges   67

a broad, general view of public administration theory and public management, introducing the three lenses of executive, legislative, and judicial functions of government: (1) management, focusing on effectiveness and efficiency; (2) politics, which focuses on legislative representativeness, responsiveness, and how interest groups shape policy and its implementation; and (3) law, which focuses on "accountability procedural integrity, individual constitutional rights, and judicial review" (as cited in Amsler, 2016, p. 1). Regarding the latter, the law's values incorporated constitutional integrity, various components of rights, and procedural due process (Rosenbloom & Gong, 2013; Rosenbloom, 2015).

The role of law in CP is an often-overlooked facet of analysis and action. In a seminal article in *Public Administration Review*, Lisa Blomgren Amsler (2016, p. 702) captures the essence of law in collaboration:

> Collaboration, like participation, is indeed a process, and it has instrumental value as a means to an end. However, it also has intrinsic value as an end in itself, unlike conflict or adversarial governance. As an end, collaboration represents broader acceptance of a policy or decision. Omitting collaboration from public values is significant because collaboration is both explicit and implicit in constitutional and administrative law. It is inherent as an end in the constitutional structure for separation of powers, which prevents meaningful action absent collaboration within and across the branches of U.S. government. The *Federalist Papers* illustrate that the founders anticipated and designed for collaboration in government's work (Bingham & O'Leary, 2011). In sum, the ongoing dialogue on management, politics, and law has not sufficiently addressed rules as independent variables or collaboration as a public value in collaborative governance.

Concerning CP, law differs from hierarchical "command and control arrangements in its use of negotiation, dialogue, deliberation, and consensus" (Amsler, 2016, p. 702) and public and stakeholder voices influencing decisions across the policy continuum.

Lisa Amsler's comprehensive overview identifies the Administrative Procedures Act and related rulemaking and adjudication procedures, transparency standards and regulations, federal advisory committees, negotiated rulemaking and dispute resolution, the Paperwork Reduction Act, E-government, and E-rulemaking and public participation in administrative hearings. Plus, overviewing state regulatory schemes needs to be factored in (See also Amsler & Nabatchi, 2016). Amsler (2016) concludes that

> collaboration is embedded in the law as an independent public value, an end in itself and not simply a process. The law shapes what public agencies do and how public managers manage; it reflects the process of representative politics . . . it is time to build that back into our research designs in public administration.

(p. 709)

68 *Organizing Government to Meet Collaboration Challenges*

Forms of Collaborative Organizing

There's much more to organizing for CP than just following the regulations. Beyond the silos of bureaucratic organizations, several formal organizational methods now exist to enhance program/agency coordination. Priority about these adaptation concerns in the United States began in the 1960s when metropolitan problems became a national concern. At the time, state administrations were seen as insensitive to center city decline, fast suburbanization, and difficulties and concerns that cut across multiple jurisdictions (Agranoff, 2012). Metropolitan problems, according to Roscoe Martin (1963), were essential concerns for the entire country because they were national in scope, required federal government responses, established a floor on program quality, and upgraded management in urban governments that could achieve specified national goals and resulted in a significant increase in the practice of cooperative management. Due to this difficulty, Martin (1963) and others (Advisory Commission on Intergovernmental Relations, 1962) began to investigate existing forms of collaboration in urban regions in the form procedural and structural mechanisms for addressing the issues caused by governmental fragmentation in urban areas.

It is no surprise, but many changes have occurred in the metropolitan system since the mid-1960s. Governments and special government units, as well as NGO involvement, have all accelerated. As states get more involved in government matters, they become more involved in federal programs that flow from the federal government to state governments and communities (Agranoff, 2016). As a result, multiple means of organizing, informal and formal, involve a range of actions "to organize," as this chapter will feature. It begins with looking at forms of collaborative organizing, including an update of the Roscoe Martin inventory, then some basics of departmental connections and how government agencies are now organized for collaboration, followed by a look at unique organized intergovernmental structures, then how agencies are consolidated for collaboration. The latter includes a look at a combined department of health and human services and then the introduction of public–private alliances. Next, consolidated public bodies' main activities and accomplishments are introduced, plus coverage of special task forces. Finally, the chapter looks at non-structural connective actions in Ohio's Office of Health Transformation, a varietal means of structuring.

Many informal collaborative organizing mechanisms exist, but the dedicated organizing structures identified in this chapter result from the inability of informal joint structures to work well without further organizing. Charging agencies to work together to solve multiprogram challenges does not mean they will. For example, the Department of Defense, NASA, and NOAA were charged with managing polar satellites used for various data and research purposes during the administration of former U.S. President Bill Clinton. In a short period, concludes Michael Lewis in the best-selling book, *The Fifth Risk*

Organizing Government to Meet Collaboration Challenges   69

(2018), it was caught up in a lack of leadership. He relates that one NOAA official concluded that:

> Three agencies is hard. Because when you are busy or something annoys you, you can't just assume or pretend that someone else will handle it. It's also hard because nobody wants to be responsible when things go badly. It's hard to control headlines and explain complicated things. Congress sends agencies very mixed signals, changes budgets, moves on to new things, speaks with many voices . . . . Everybody blames someone else, and whoever is better at the blame game usually comes out on top.
>
> (quoted in Lewis, 2018, pp. 192–193)

During the administration of former U.S. President Barack Obama, the arrangement was broken up. The three-agency arrangement—the entire project—was handed to NOAA, as the collaborative undertaking did not go well. One indicator is that by charging two or more agencies to be given responsibility does not necessarily ensure coordinated action.

There are also numerous organized "partnerships" or other formal connections around the United States that bring together jurisdictions and/or government bodies for various purposes. One such partnership is Radius Indiana (www. radiusindiana.com), a regional economic development partnership involving eight southern Indiana counties. Operating since 2009, Radius Indiana has focused on recent strategic planning that includes leadership development, tourism promotion, educational courses, focus on defense industry growth strategies (a large U.S. Navy support facility is nearby in Indiana), veterans recruitment, promoting regional job opportunities, hosting "pitch" competitions for aspiring entrepreneurs, and facilitating site selection trips to promote the area. The current Radius CEO is former Indiana Lt. Gov. Becky Skillman, who works with a board comprised of various finance, business, industry, and local government officials.

As indicated in Chapter 2, Medicaid-financed services are implemented through state-initiated partnerships with private and nonprofit organizations on a contractual basis: hospitals, physicians, nursing homes, managed care companies, community health organizations, home health agencies, and community health centers (Agranoff, 2017). In some states, private organizations are even responsible for managing overall care cases based on public–private partnerships (PPPs). Having once served in the capacity of just issuing checks to those providers, states are currently responsible for conducting negotiations and monitoring these contracts (Agranoff, 2017). As Frank Thompson (2012, p. 17) observes. "state bureaucracies that receive grants from the federal government to operate Medicaid face formidable implementation issues." The implementation of such grants is based on connective or partnership forms in many U.S. states.

As was discussed in Chapter 2, there are many and varied forms of collaborative organizing. Even though they represent undoubtedly an incomplete model

70 *Organizing Government to Meet Collaboration Challenges*

of the universe, one can easily understand why using such terms as "network" or "networking" can be confusing and deceptive. You have probably noticed that there are a variety of ways to connect public and private entities to form a formal network, including the more well-known contracting, service exchanges, interagency agreements, shared staff, federated councils, and service partnerships, as well as less well-known parallel actions such as the use of open sources, joint ventures, integrated services partnerships, and "limited powers" intergovernmental public–private organizations (Agranoff, 2012). Thus, the more accurate meaning of the phrases "the network" or "to network" denotes various forms of action linking public, private, and nonprofit organizations together (see also Mandell, 1999).

Why have so many means of collaboration involving public and public-serving organizations arisen? The earlier discussion can provide a clear answer to that question. Governance consists of expanding government at all levels—more governments, more laws and regulations, more NGO government agents or partners, more programs, and more managerial concerns. For example, the United States is in an era during which the law and jurisdictional boundaries are maintained. Yet, the welfare state broadly understood reaches deeper into the world between governments, where government works with non-government partners, and the quest to connect and "network" in different forms is necessary. The variety of organized vehicles discussed in Chapter 2 (see Figure 2.1) has emerged to meet such challenges.

Combining Departments: The Umbrella Organization

There is a venerable tradition of organizing in anticipation of future necessary collaborative results. This approach places considerable emphasis on the assumptions to manage, placing similar units together hierarchically or those whose missions necessarily have to interact quite frequently under the same organization's roof. These "combined departments" put together similar agencies or those frequently interacting under/or proximate to the same hierarchical leadership. For example, it promotes what is called in public administration "umbrella" departments. The movement began particularly with health and human services (Agranoff & Pattakos, 1979) but has moved to other areas: internal security, natural resources/ conservation, economic development, urban development, rural development, transportation, and others.

Collaborative management in practice involves many more actions than creating new departments. Indeed, many engaged in these reorganizations experience that reorganization is often the first step toward many more connective activities. In other words, collaborative management entails many subsequent acts of linkages creating new forms of organizing including combined departments and coordinated structures discussed in the next section. An example of a combined department is shown in Box 3.1.

Box 3.1 Special Collaborative Bodies: Joint Terrorism Task Forces

The U.S. Federal Bureau of Investigation (FBI)'s Joint Terrorism Task Forces, or JTTFs, are our nation's front line in the fight against terrorism: small cells of highly trained, locally based, passionately committed investigators, analysts, linguists, SWAT (special weapons and tactics) experts, and other specialists from dozens of U.S. law enforcement and intelligence agencies.

When it comes to investigating terrorism, they do it all: chase down leads, gather evidence, make arrests, provide security for special events, conduct training, collect and share intelligence, and respond to threats and incidents at a moment's notice.

The task forces are based in 104 cities nationwide, including at least one in each of the FBI's 56 field offices. A total of 71 of these JTTFs have been created since 9/11; the first was established in New York City in 1980.

Today, the JTTFs include approximately 4,000 members nationwide—more than four times the pre-9/11 total—hailing from over 500 state and local agencies and 55 federal agencies (the Department of Homeland Security, the U.S. military, Immigration and Customs Enforcement [ICE], and the Transportation Security Administration [TSA], to name a few).

The JTTFs provide one-stop shopping for information regarding terrorist activities. They enable a shared intelligence base across many agencies. They create familiarity among investigators and managers before a crisis. And perhaps most importantly, they pool talents, skills, and knowledge from across the law enforcement and intelligence communities into a single team that responds together.

Their contributions are more than could possibly be captured here, but JTTFs have been instrumental in breaking up cells like the "Portland Seven," the Lackawanna Six," and the Northern Virginia jihad. They have foiled attacks on the Fort Dix Army base in New Jersey, on the JFK International Airport in New York, and on various military and civilian targets in Los Angeles. They have traced sources of terrorist funding, responded to anthrax threats, halted the use of fake identification documents (IDs), and quickly arrested suspicious characters with all kinds of deadly weapons and explosives. Chances are, if you hear about a counterterrorism investigation, JTTFs are playing an active and often decisive role.

The task forces coordinate their efforts largely through the interagency National Joint Terrorism Task Force, working out of FBI Headquarters in Washington, DC, which makes sure that information and intelligence flows freely among the local JTTFs and beyond.

Source: Adopted from www.fbi.gov/investigate/terrorism/joint-terrorism-task-forces

72 *Organizing Government to Meet Collaboration Challenges*

Coordinated Structures

In coordinated structures, departments remain primarily intact but are "housed" together, at least informally, to encourage collaboration. For example, the Boise, Idaho-based National Interagency Fire Center's Wildland Fire Management Strategy coordinates five federal agencies, multiple state governments, state-based NGOs, and sizable private forest holdings to combat large-scale fires. Along with the U.S. Government Accountability Office (GAO), the Fire Center sees the challenges as identifying and defining problems; establishing coordinated goals and standards that respect the state, regional, and local differences and needs; and determining the roles of various entities at the federal, state, and local government levels.

The Fire Center's coordinated policy involves ten broad overlapping goals: bringing together disparate resources and agencies; documenting agency and organization sequences and procedures; developing a problem or incident command-and-control structure; establishing an agreed-on management strategy; finding a resource redeployment sequence; setting an agency "donated" staffing sequence; agreeing on and setting common standards, policies, and procedures, including equipment deployment; settling incident response policies and procedures; forming and operating a council, or "networked" organized structure; and negotiating and setting interorganizational policies and procedures (U.S. Department of Homeland Security, 2005) (Agranoff, 2017, p. 144).

Using the perspective of the U.S. Department of Homeland Security, William Jenkins (2006) uncovers the challenges of collaboration for separate organizations. Additionally, he recommends clear problem identification, setting collaborative goals, and describing respective responsibilities in structures and procedures that provide incentives and rewards for collaboration, consultation, and support for executing critical goals.

Basics of Departmental Connections

Many possibilities exist in the broad context of how most public agencies work collaboratively with other entities. For example, Figure 3.1 is a graphic representation of a more or less standard or an imagined public agency (Agranoff, 2012). Such agencies can be found at any federal, state, or local government level. This figure sheds light on the internal and external interactions of the agency. It also shows the variety of organizational forms based on collaboration. Legal authority and hierarchical operations, POSDCORB (planning, organizing, staffing, directing, coordinating, reporting, and budgeting) or standard operations, mission-pursuit operations, and resource inputs/outputs are all part of the agency's hierarchical or core operations. Both legally and statutorily related contacts and nonlegal collaborative relations, such as signed interagency agreements, are tied to its working core. "Grants, procurements, contracts, loans, and other legal ties to other governments and NGOs; formal interagency agreements with lateral agencies; direct agreement and contacts

Organizing Government to Meet Collaboration Challenges   73

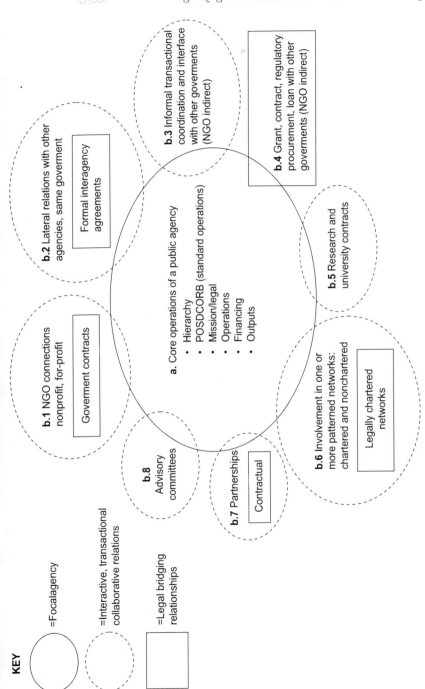

Figure 3.1 Hypothetical Collaborative Public Agency

Source: Agranoff (2012, p. 57). Copyright 2012 by Georgetown University Press. Reprinted with permission.

74 *Organizing Government to Meet Collaboration Challenges*

with NGOs; legally chartered networks; formal partnerships; university contracts; and advisory bodies" (Agranoff, 2012, p. 58) are among the former, which are represented by solid squares or rectangles in Figure 3.1. The dotted circles that overlap the core agencies represent less formal but real collaborative activity, such as lateral relationships with other agencies at the same level of government, connections with NGOs, informal transactional coordination efforts with other governments, and participation in one or more chartered (some of which have legal standing) or non-chartered networks. Clearly, this hypothetical agency's non-core operations make it highly conductive.

In Figure 3.1, part "a" depicts the core functions of imagined agency using a standard form of bureaucracy, whereas parts "b.1"–"b.8" show the more extensive terrain of various collaborative linkages and mixes them with the traditional core functions of the agency (Agranoff, 2012). In actuality, these collaborative linkages cut through the heart of the agency's activities, resulting in hybrid portions "ab" or "ba" rather than "a" or "b." However, it is vital to recognize that the majority of normal or hypothetical government activities can be classified as "a"—"only because, except entirely externalized agencies, conductive relations supplement but seldom replace sections of the government organization's basic activity" (p. 58). In theory, all these linkages are conveniently called "network connections." In practice, network relationships (b.6)

> represent just one of several bureaucratic connections, the others being direct NGO connections (b.1), lateral contacts with other agencies of the same department (b.2), informal transactional coordination with other governments (b.3), grant/regulatory/procurement/loan connections with other governments (b.4), research and university connections (b.5), partnerships with other governments and NGOs (b.7), and partnerships with various advisory committees (b.8).

Therefore, a great variety of forms of interorganizational collaboration exists, reaching the established notions of formal networks and informal networks

What does a real collaborative public agency look like? Figure 3.2 looks at a typical state Community Economic Development (CED) program. It does not include the employment and training and/or unemployment functions that are sometimes included in these departments. The core agency is small, with as few as 30 professional staff members administering a restricted number of state development programs: loans, grants, leadership development, information, planning, and promotion, depending on the size and scope of its purpose (Agranoff, 2012). Going clockwise, one can see first interactions of other state agencies, especially with transportation and the environment. There are numerous connections with federal government agencies, including USDA/RD (U.S. Department of Agriculture/Rural Development), the Department of Commerce (Small Business Administration, Economic Development Administration), Housing and Urban Development (HUD), and state-run Small Cities Community Development Block Grants,

Organizing Government to Meet Collaboration Challenges 75

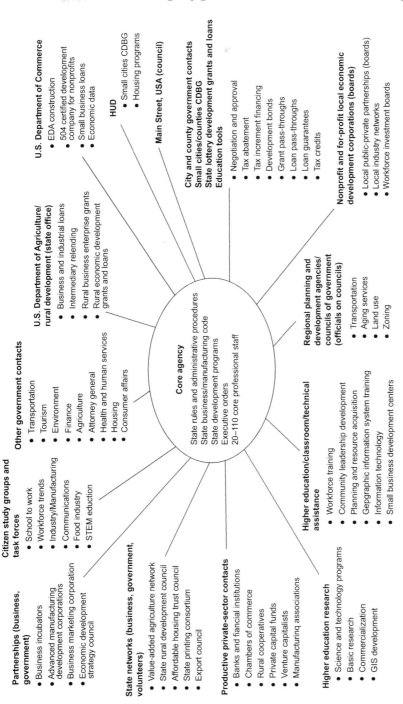

Figure 3.2 Typical Collaborative State Economic and Community Development Department

Source: Agranoff (2012, p. 62). Copyright 2012 by Georgetown University Press. Reprinted with permission.

76 *Organizing Government to Meet Collaboration Challenges*

housing, and special programs like Main Street. Then one can observe the CED connections with city and county governments "over state and federal pass-through programs, and interactively over various economic development tools, for example, tax credits or loans" (Agranoff, 2012, p. 61). Contacts with local economic development organizations would be formed in the same way. On issues such as planning and program development, aging, transportation, land use, and zoning for small communities, other interactions are made with substate planning and development agencies and/or government councils.

Because economic development also involves leadership and skilled workforces, higher education interaction is constant regarding leadership training and curricular issues. Some departments are also in contact with higher education for basic research; for example, projects that might be commercialized and/or with some technology applications. The next key contacts are with representatives of the state's productive sector: banking and financial institutions, chambers of commerce, rural cooperatives, venture capitalists, and manufacturing associations.

Most state agencies also have some involvement in a series of networks/committees in various areas, ranging from an export council to affordable housing. Along with networks are a series of partnerships, typically formal agreements for business promotion and industrial development. Finally, many departments have citizen boards or study groups that examine intractable policy problems, such as school-to-work and/or science, technology, engineering, and mathematics (STEM) education, and most recently, AI applications. These boards make recommendations through the agency/department.

Box 3.2   Coordinated Bodies: The Case of Fusion Centers

Fusion centers operate as state and major urban area focal points for the receipt, analysis, gathering, and sharing of threat-related information between federal, state, local, tribal, territorial (SLTT), and private sector partners. The National Network of Fusion Centers (National Network) brings critical context and value to homeland security and law enforcement that no other federal or local organization can replicate. Fusion centers accomplish this through: (1) their information sharing hubs that provide comprehensive and appropriate access, analysis, and dissemination that no other single partner can offer; (2) independence from federal partners which allows fusion centers to provide partners with a unique perspective on threats to their state or locality, contributing to the national threat picture; and (3) status as the primary conduit between frontline personnel, state and local leadership, and the rest of the homeland security enterprise, filling a significant security gap identified by the 9/11 Commission.

Because state and major urban area fusion centers are locally owned and operated, the relationship between the National Network and the U.S. Department of Homeland Security (DHS)—as well as other homeland security partners—is a coordinated partnership. DHS is committed to maturing its relationship with fusion centers and enhancing information sharing across the homeland security enterprise. As part of this commitment, DHS manages the Fusion Center Performance Program (FCPP) which is designed to evaluate the capability and performance of the National Network. The FCPP also helps DHS and other federal agency partners to improve the quality and effectiveness of federal government support to fusion centers. Beyond the FCPP, DHS, along with other federal partners, also provides significant resources to fusion centers through training, technical assistance, information systems access, guidance, and other support.

Moreover, the DHS Office of Intelligence and Analysis (I&A) deploys field personnel—to include intelligence officers (IOs), reports officers (ROs), and regional directors (RDs)—nationwide in support of state, local, tribal, territorial, and private-sector SLTT partners. I&A field personnel support these partners by facilitating the intelligence cycle at the local level and fostering information sharing between all homeland security stakeholders. Field personnel provide intelligence collection and reporting, integrated intelligence analysis, threat sharing and reporting, and overall engagement with their SLTT and fusion center partners. The I&A office has also deployed the Homeland Secure Data Network (HSDN) to over 70 fusion centers. HSDN enhances the ability of SLTT partners to receive federally generated classified threat information. Fusion centers can also leverage DHS—vis-à-vis their mission advocates or I&A's deployed field personnel—to obtain access and use of the Homeland Security Information Network (HSIN) for specific mission needs. Finally, in coordination with the Department of Justice (DOJ), DHS has conducted hundreds of training and technical assistance workshops and exchanges on topics including risk analysis, security, privacy, civil rights, and civil liberties since 2007 (DHS: 9/31/18).

Source: Adapted from U.S Government Accountability Office; U.S. Department of Homeland Security, www.dhs.gov/fusion-centers

As described in Box 3.2, fusion centers represent coordinated bodies directly motivated by federal action. Following the 2004 publication of the 9/11 Commission's report, DHS encouraged fusion centers to coordinate data sharing among public and nonprofit organizations by providing access to local and national intelligence. In return, the DHS assisted fusion centers by providing technical assistance and training, supporting activities, and providing security clearance access to federal

78 *Organizing Government to Meet Collaboration Challenges*

systems, information technology, and grants (Agranoff, 2017). Some fusion centers were sponsored by the DHS and were developed from existing law enforcement groups, such as the FBI's JTTF and state and municipal anti-drug trafficking programs. The GAO estimates that states' fusion centers used $426 million in DHS grant monies between 2004 and 2009. The fusion center receives about 60% of its funding from federal grants, 30% from state monies, and 10% from local sources (U.S. Government Accountability Office, 2010).

Another typical coordinated body like the fusion centers is in the environmental area. The Lower Platte River Corridor Alliance (LPRCA) represents a consortium of three natural resource districts and seven state organizations in the state of Nebraska. The U.S. Army Corps of Engineers and the U.S. Geological Survey (USGS) joined efforts to promote natural resource management locally in the geographic area of LPRCA. The LPRCA was formed in 1996 after an interlocal agreement was passed (Agranoff, 2017). Members contribute to an administrative budget, which would initially total $65,000 per year, to support the Alliance's coordinator, and they pledge to give technical and other help through the coordinator within their authority. Quarterly meetings are held to share status reports on all of the participants' programs and projects.

The LPRCA aids counties and local communities along the Lower Platte River to become fully informed about the impact of their decisions on natural resources and promote conservation in the river corridor area. The Alliance provides a discussion platform for concerned, interested citizens and local elected public officials to exchange their different perspectives on managing local natural resources and find joint solutions (Agranoff, 2017). The Alliance's goals are to promote a better understanding of the Lower Platte River's resources, support local efforts to achieve comprehensive and coordinated land-use planning, protect the river's long-term vitality, and foster cooperation among federal, state, and local—both private and public—organizations to meet the needs of the river corridor's many and varied interests.

The LPRCA provides easy and reliable access to relevant information on important issues and proposed projects, opportunities for dialogue and discussion for individuals wishing to influence the decision-making process, and a forum for consensus. Community involvement is part and parcel of this collaboration process. River tours, the Water Quality Open golf tournament, stakeholder summit meetings, and regional planning workshops and charrettes are some ways the general public can become involved (intensive planning sessions). The outcomes of this collaboration demonstrate the importance of information technology in promoting communication between governmental, corporate, and nonprofit players. The LPRCA has produced numerous data sheets and guides, public policy evaluations, web-based GIS presentations, water and wastewater studies, and conservation and mitigation suggestions over the course of its nearly two decades (Agranoff, 2017). The network recently worked with the USGS to offer real-time water quality data and produced a comprehensive recreation strategy with the Nebraska Game and

Organizing Government to Meet Collaboration Challenges 79

Parks Commission. Other initiatives include collaborating on an environmental appropriateness assessment, building a water quality monitoring network, designing a watershed management plan, supporting a sandbar monitoring study (in collaboration with the USGS), and completing a cumulative impact study. The partnership also collaborates on coordinated land-use planning with cities and counties.

Connections between persons and organizations in collaborative bodies/organizations have been expedited by the rapidly increasing use of contemporary information and communications technology (ICT) (Castells, 1996). The previously mentioned fusion centers and the LPRCA represent excellent examples of using ICT to facilitate intergovernmental operations based on collaboration (Raab & Kenis, 2009). For more than 60 years, local governments, business associations, and economic development agents have been connected by tight and sparse collaboration linkages, extending their connections to upper-level governments to develop and maintain local economies (Agranoff, 2017; Agranoff & McGuire, 2003; Rhodes, 1997). Nowadays, people can do more for less in the internet-based social networks connecting millions of personal users. In sum, these collaborative interacting bodies operate for different aims, such as manufacturing and commerce, by bringing together affiliated sides in many ways. Similarly, public and nonprofit agencies collaboratively interact for four general purposes: (1) exchanging information; (2) enhancing one another's capabilities; (3) smoothing interactions of services; and (4) promoting program policy solving and problems (Agranoff, 2007).

Consolidated Bodies

Many state and federal agencies attempt to improve collaborative action by consolidating existing departments/organizations into more unified structures while retaining existing organizational/program authority, even reducing specific measures of departmental autonomy. Such consolidation is a move that has been in existence since at least the 1970s.

A consolidated agency allows separate program units to keep a significant portion of their administrative and program responsibility (e.g., hierarchy) while creating an agency or function to coordinate activities and programs, at least, at the "top." It is organized along traditional program lines with top agency management and an administrative unit that assists the agency head/staff in establishing policy, goals, budgeting, and planning, and encouraging program coordination. The agency head has little direct authority over agency operations. An organizational chart depicting this type of organization is illustrated in Figure 3.3. The U.S. Department of Homeland Security (DHS) agency was created by transferring all or most administrative and program authority of previously autonomous programs to a new agency. It is designed along "traditional program lines with agency management and administrative units, which usually perform several agency-wide functions; the agency head has statutory authority over program direction, budgeting, coordinated planning, and evaluation, and generally over appointment and removal of program directors"

80 *Organizing Government to Meet Collaboration Challenges*

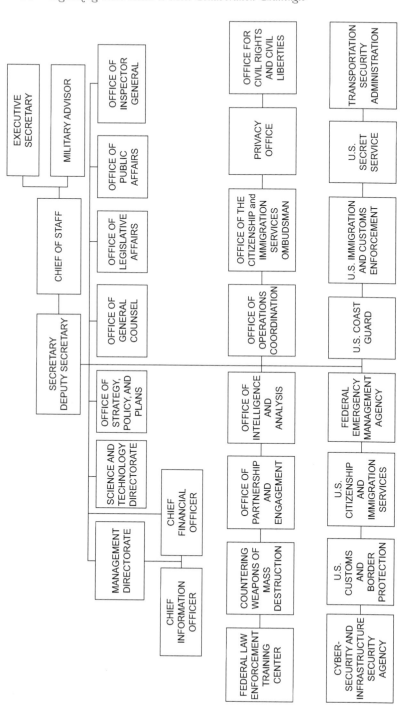

Figure 3.3 U.S. Department of Homeland Security
Source: DHS (2018)

Agranoff & Pattakos, 1979, p. 121). The organizational chart of DHS depicts a consolidated agency.

> From a prescriptive point of view, our conclusions are sobering. Our analysis shows how the merger adversely affected even those legal mandates plainly relevant to homeland security. More generally, we explain how decisions about whether to create a new security agency, what scope and size to give it, and how to organize congressional jurisdiction over it are unlikely to have been driven primarily by meaningful prescriptive concerns. Yet, such decisions are also unlikely to be merely *symbolic*. They can powerfully (and covertly) reshape how laws are implemented while making it more difficult for government to achieve broadly shared prescriptive goals. Marginal improvements depend on solving problems of legislative oversight and on whether competent bureaucrats will succeed in forging autonomy and capacity in a world unlikely to support it. While these scenarios remain elusive, our analysis does not yield a blanket condemnation of bureaucracies created through high-profile reorganizations. Bureaucracies forged in crisis may not be inexorably doomed to fail in carrying out their legal responsibilities, and there may yet be reasons to defer to their legal interpretations. Instead, we highlight the difficulties in averting such failure.
>
> (p. 679)

The authors of this extensive study do not maintain that DHS failed in operating, for example, during Hurricane Katrina. Still, its creation entailed "transition costs of uncertain duration and extent" or that DHS creation led to difficulties faced by the U.S. Transportation Security Administration (TSA) and FEMA (p. 679). Indeed, the authors conclude that political questions were clearly at the heart of the problems, particularly its multiple Congressional support constituencies and matters of presidential control incurred. They conclude that observers must resist the temptation to promote publicly appealing but conceptually unsound statutory fixes (p. 755). Without post-consolidation action, these bureaucratic practices have usually been doomed to a fate that such combined at the top organizations succumb to outcomes that prove short of reorganization goals.

A contemporary example of a state-consolidated department is that of the Maine Department of Health and Human Services (DHHS). It claims to serve one-third of the people of the state, including healthcare and social services support for children, families, the elderly, the disabled, people with mental illness or substance abuse issues, and low-income persons. DHHS also operates two state mental health hospitals, provides public health information, guidance, and management of the Maine Center for Disease Control and Prevention, and provides oversight regulation of hospitals, nursing homes, and other healthcare facilities through its licensing and regulatory services. The Department has more than 3,400 employees and is headed by a commissioner who also provides direct oversight of public welfare programs, including "Temporary Assistance for Needy Families (TANF),

82 *Organizing Government to Meet Collaboration Challenges*

Medicaid eligibility, the Supplemental Nutrition Assistance Program (SNAP), Disability Determination Services, and Child Support Enforcement" (Maine Department of Health and Human Services, 2018). Figure 3.4 provides an organizational chart of the Maine consolidation. The Maine DHHS is one of the many states that have combined their health and human services programs; e.g., North Carolina, Indiana, Louisiana, and Michigan.

A more profound concern in the movement of consolidating agencies and programs in seemingly related areas is evident that consolidating is merely the first step in a series of potential "intradepartmental" or cross-agency moves that follow such consolidations. In the 1970s, the Departments of Human Resources (DHR) were studied by many researchers to understand the integration of human services. Agranoff and Pattakos (1979) provide a comprehensive analysis of the then Departments of Health, Education, and Welfare (HEW). Many involved in the founding consolidations believed that creating the DHRs would automatically equal some idealized state of human services integration. When it always did not, somehow, the studies became the objects of severe criticism. These contentions were true to an extent; all DHRs are different, and some integrate services more than others. What distinguishes each, and each is really unique, is how a government's traditions, political forces, and primary aims in reorganization have combined to create a particular departmental configuration of linking structures, both informal and formal. One essential difference is that the programs within each new structure have entirely different political constituencies, not to speak of varying constituency/interest group support. Some were some what unfairly misaligned since the reorganizations they described were rapidly changing and challenging to understand.

Moreover, the study was conducted to synthesize knowledge on the present state of affairs in the area of state human services agencies in the 1970s. Despite the criticisms, it is fair to say the Council of State Governments' study (1974) created a classificatory lexicon about DHR which makes it difficult for interested observers, including critics (and one of the authors of this book), to avoid using this three-part (coordinated, consolidated, integrated) analysis; e.g., in this chapter. Moreover, despite the criticisms and disillusionment in some quarters with the creation of organizational structures as a vehicle toward services integration, the movement—for example, the creation of the internal security of the DHS—continues.

This line of earlier research of human services consolidation means that these numerous departments were accomplished while under "umbrellas," as is the case of the Maine Dept of Health and Human Services or USDHS.

1. Joint planning: two or more component units formulate plans for shared policies.
2. Joint evaluation: cross-program; e.g., interdivisional assessments that cut across division lines.
3. Advisory councils: focus on jurisdiction-wide issues and problems under the department's jurisdiction.

Organizing Government to Meet Collaboration Challenges 83

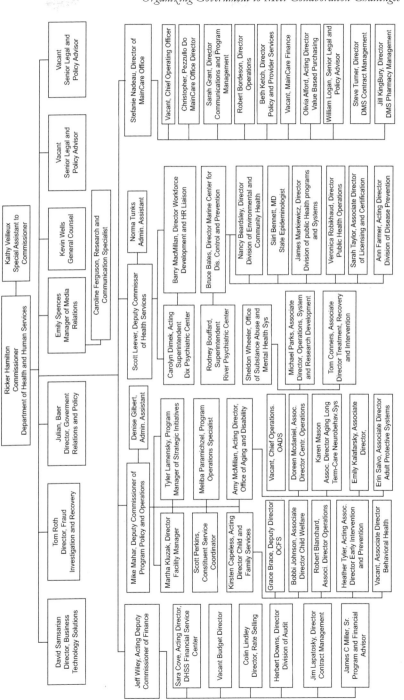

Figure 3.4 Maine Department of Health and Human Services

Source: Maine Department of Health and Human Services (2018)

84 *Organizing Government to Meet Collaboration Challenges*

4. Work toward a unified departmental policy that addresses complex problems that cut across programs and jurisdictions.
5. Intra-agency coordination: developing ways for programs to interact and hopefully become interoperating to solve problems and organize services that require linkages as they cut across programs.
6. Development of centralized or department-wide administrative services, e.g., centralized budgeting, unified support services (e.g., audit, date, personnel, accounting, grants management, purchasing, general services, training of information technology [IT], etc.).
7. Joint client information services include accommodating different client requirements, confidentiality requirements, records/information standards, incompatible electronic records, and program personnel assistance.
8. Purchase services/vouchers; e.g., across different programs that follow this model, such as Medicaid, Medicare, Vocational Rehabilitation, and other coordinated arrangements.
9. Joint training: particularly of new department practices, emergent outlooks of new management support, related programs, and other intradepartmental exchanges.
10. District (substate) administration: decentralized units that, when combined, represent respective state programs.
11. Joint programming: particularly to help solve nettlesome cross-service problems whereby one program impacts another, particularly related to family problems, mental health, substance abuse, etc.
12. Joint funding: funding "contributions" or other fiscal agreements from contributing organizations that are implemented by a single agency.
13. Coordinated/joint/linked services: e.g., by colocation, central intake, unified case management, unified client tracking, support services (daycare, transportation, training).
14. Policy and program management: a look at the programming of departmental procedures and their operations, particularly those that cut across functions of the broader agency.
15. Creation of linkages between programs that are operationally related to one another in service delivery.
16. Services delivery consolidation: a rarely undertaken function, but consolidated departments have undertaken those functions in some cases.

(Agranoff & Pattakos, 1979, pp. 132–152)

The new consolidated organizations must begin by repeating a theme that has permeated this chapter in action. *Integration by organizing must be evaluated in terms of degree rather than absolutes.* Consolidations like Maine DHS are integrative structures designed to facilitate most of the 16 actions described here. They also have another function: other forces being equal, program aims can achieve economies and efficiencies in administering a host of agency programs.

Organizing Government to Meet Collaboration Challenges 85

According to Agranoff and Pattakos (1979), consolidated agencies should be better understood through the analysis of their positive and negative sides:

> They are large in size and highly visible agencies. It is not unusual for such agencies at the state level to consume one-half of a jurisdictions' total budget and over one-third of its employees. It is the focal point for dozens of interest groups ranging from business vendors to high-income and powerful health and social services providers. They require continuing political support. Their large operations are highly visible to legislative bodies who often place more emphasis on saving money, improved accountability, or more and better specific services than on the direct aims of services integration. The chief executive (Governor, mayor, manager, or executive) also has to present an agenda for the agency. The focal point of all the internal and external activity is the head of the agency, who must somehow combine expertise in management, disparate programs, and heavy-duty politics. Moreover, the agency head's actions in achieving goals are constrained by federal and other rules such as compliance requirements, categorical eligibility and service restrictions, organizational and structural requirements, funding guidelines, etc., not to speak of any funding constraints.
>
> (p. 153)

The previously mentioned factors are accompanied by the notion that "each jurisdiction's consolidated organization was created by and operated within its history and traditions, regulations, legal and constitutional framework, and dominant political forces" (Agranoff & Pattakos, 1979, p. 153). There is an enormous variance of organizational design among consolidated organizations depending on "changes in authority patterns, communication, incentives, or decision flow" (Agranoff, 1977, p. 80). Special attention is paid to "various dimensions of integration, management efficiency, the services included in the umbrella, as well as the seriousness with which the new departments like Maine or USDHHS pursue their stated aims are very different" (Agranoff & Pattakos, 1979, p. 153). To put it another way, each form of consolidation encompasses a variety of complex organizational configurations.

In the 1970s, a team of seasoned human resource management professionals found out that the most modest aim is improved operation of the existing system as the most generally successful consolidation outcome with the 16 moves (see above). Smoothing out the rough edges of the various programs, making them work a little better together, was generally agreed to be an essential and solid accomplishment. They identified other achievements of consolidated organizational forms that were contingent on the goals and activities of the human service agencies, with the most important being as follows.

1. Increased ability to understand and use resources: reorganization had enhanced ability to put resources—in both availability and distribution—into a more coherent perspective.

86 *Organizing Government to Meet Collaboration Challenges*

2. More efficient—but not necessarily economical—management, including both policy management and administrative services. The question of saving money was often unanswerable.
3. Flexibility in access, both to group development of broad goals and to services. Groups focused on problem-wide—rather than broad—service concerns, and the client's ability to get a wider range of services increased.
4. More ease in focusing on complex problems and including programs.

(Agranoff & Pattakos, 1979, pp. 153–154)

Networks Are Not All Alike: A Typology

Not all networks are alike, as other researchers have also discovered (Alter & Hage, 1993). One typology of public networks developed by one of the authors of this book is summarized in Box 3.3.

Box 3.3   A Typology of Public Networks

1. *Informational networks*: partners come together exclusively to exchange agency policies and programs, technologies, and potential solutions. Any actions that might be taken are entirely up to the agencies on a voluntary basis.
2. *Developmental networks*: partner information and technical exchange are combined with education and member service that increases member capacity to implement solutions within home agencies or organizations.
3. *Outreach networks*: partners come together to exchange information and technologies, sequence programming, exchange resource opportunities, pool client contacts, and enhance access opportunities that lead to new programming avenues. Implementation of designed programs is within an array of public and private agencies themselves.
4. *Action networks*: partners come together to make interagency adjustments, formally adopt collaborative courses of action, and/or deliver services, along with exchanges of information and technologies.

Source: Agranoff (2007, pp. 45–46). Reprinted with permission.

Regarding the networks examined for their various actions in one multinetwork study: some limit their interorganizational activities to the exchange of information. The previously mentioned Lower Platte River Corridor Alliance is one prime example. Many environmental or natural resource networks (e.g., Lower Platte) and the Indiana Economic Development Council (IEDC) are included in this category.

These informational networks are made up of a huge number of stakeholders—many of whom hold diametrically opposed viewpoints—who get together to exchange information, study the depths of a problem, and consider specific actions that stakeholders might take (Agranoff, 2003). These actions are never mandated and are always optional. As a result, these networks are more often than not wide convening groups or "listening boards," rather than decision-making entities. With one exception, they are similar to state and local level councils (a state or municipal health and welfare council, for example). Informational networks, unlike these councils, do not make decisions.

In stark contrast, other networks represent a more enhanced form of collaboration usually used in partnerships and joint ventures. The Des Moines Metropolitan Planning Organization (DMMPO) has created interactive working methods to adopt regional programs jointly and implement them through component entities. DMMPO is an example of an action network. According to Agranoff (2003), action networks are heavily engaged in information sharing, capacity development, and uncovering new programming opportunities, but they are differentiated by their ability to participate in decisive collective action. On the one hand, an element of decision-making makes action networks more distinguishable from other types of networks. On the other hand, these networks encounter problems in achieving collaboration goals since the governmental, private, and nonprofit organizations are engaged in playing "zero-sum" games in the decision-making process while implementing their programs on a shared basis with these organizations.

The other two types of networks are positioned right between information and action networks: development and outreach (Agranoff, 2003). Development networks engage partner organizations in information exchange and capacity building. The Iowa Geographic Information Council is an excellent example of a developmental network wherein partner organizations are responsible for implementing information exchange strategies and enhancing organizational capacities within the boundaries of the network. In other words, this type of network goes beyond merely exchanging information. Outreach networks are involved in more than just capacity building. They also carve out programming strategies for clients (for example, finance packages with usable technologies) that the partner usually carries out. An example of an outreach network is the Ohio Small Communities Environmental Infrastructure Group (SCEIG). This network unites federal, state, and local government organizations with local nonprofit organizations and service providers to satisfy the water and water infrastructure needs of small communities in Ohio (Agranoff, 2007). In another way, these networks develop potential actions without formally adopting them, like in the case of DMMPO. The actions developed by the outreach network merely have a suggestive nature. Managerially, both of these types of networks—developmental and outreach—are like consortia or confederations whereby information and potential action is collectively determined. Both types of networks experience most of the managerial challenges of all types of networks, except that they stop short of those binding decisions that involve joint action of any kind.

Network is characterized as "displaying a higher willingness to work with other organizations, a higher willingness to engage these entities, and a greater focus on increasing the longevity of those relations" (Gulati, 2007, p. 257). All types of networks involve many different parties with different interests. Working together, they become mutually dependent. Most of them reach agreements or make decisions more participative than in the hierarchical/organizational settings. This is based on two critical network features (De Bruijn & Ten Heuvelhof, 2018, p. 13):

- Content unpredictability: a problem's content and solution shift continuously, and in addition, solutions can determine the problem's definition rather than the other way around. New problems and solutions can be brought in during decision-making, and existing problems and solutions can be eliminated.
- Process unpredictability: the decision-making has no clear starting and finishing points and proceeds in rounds, which follow each other irregularly. The process has no distinct phases, as suggested in many consultancy-type and project-based models. There is also no logical sequence of problem signaling via analyses and decision-making regarding a solution to be implemented. In models, the decision-making progresses linearly; in practice, decision-making is a meandering process.

Networks are most often broken down by their parts or "nodes." In this sense, they are considered by their parts and the sums of their parts. According to Koliba, Meek, and Zia (2019, p. 51):

As we consider the relationship between the parts of a governance network and the governance network as a whole, we will need to view a governance network as being more than the sum of its parts. The extent to which the characteristics and actions of individual nodes (e.g., the network's parts) help to shape the actions of the network as a whole is an extremely important, albeit complicated, consideration. Networks need to be treated of their volition. The joint, coordinated actions that occur between nodes of networks need to eventually be understood in terms of acts of the network as a whole. The matter gets complicated by the challenges posed by differences in scale that can occur between nodes in social network.

Thus, Koliba, Meek, and Zia (2019) describe governance networks in terms of their organizational nodes and the set of relationships between nodes.

Introducing Networks in Action

The key to better understanding networks in action is to look at one that functions by linking network structure and activity (Meier & O'Toole, 2003; Provan & Milward, 1995). Here we look deeper at a complex organized network and how it operates. Metro School in Columbus, Ohio, is a unique STEM network organization that brings together various public and nonprofit organizations (Kolpakov, Agranoff, & McGuire, 2016). This school operates on the principle of the accelerated mastery of subjects required for graduation by the State of Ohio. The major participating organizations include the Educational Council representing 16 Franklin County school districts (public sector); The Ohio State University (OSU); another public organization, KnowledgeWorks (national and state Coalitions for Essential Schools); and Battelle Corporation (a nonprofit research organization). Metro School's governing and management structure constantly evolves, combining network policy and management, instructional programming, and operational processes. As Figure 3.5 indicates, the Metro School operation has much more complexity, including important learning sites that provide opportunities for internships, projects, field placements, and regular classes. The PAST Foundation plays a pivotal role as the knowledge management center in the operations of Metro School by managing research and field learning of students and disseminating advances in STEM learning to the 16 Franklin County school districts. OSU provides student counseling, educational resources, and OSU Library services for Metro School students as the main library. The complex network of learning partners of Metro School is supported by different community levels, including the industry/educator curricula taskforces, teachers, parents, and students.

The governance of the Metro School is carried out by the Educational Council (EC) with the special recommendations of the Metropolitan Partnership Group (MPG), a network governance entity managed by the Metro School administration and Educational Council staff members (Kolpakov, Agranoff, & McGuire, 2016). Approximately 100 students are admitted to each class based on an interview and an admissions-related lottery distributed across the 16 districts based on the school population.

The Metro School is an exemplary case of public management networks since it perfectly blends formal and informal linkages for providing public goods and services. From the administrative point of view, Metro has a formal organizational structure to achieve well-defined goals and objectives by following clear procedures jointly formulated by participating organizations. At the same time, Metro comprises many informal or social relationships among individuals that go beyond the established boundaries of organizations and sectors. Metro was designed to bring together a significant number of network actors by multiple linkages to engage them in the processes of negotiation and coordination (Kolpakov, Agranoff, & McGuire, 2016). Metro network is operated based on the principle of "soft guidance" when the decisions are made and implemented by the multiple focal nodes (Windhoff-Héntier, 1992). This kind of guidance resembles direct supervision in hierarchical organizations. Even though the most prominent and important participants, the Metro School principal and the CEO of the Educational Council, are located in the heart of information exchange and planning in Metro, they do not reach joint decisions.

90 *Organizing Government to Meet Collaboration Challenges*

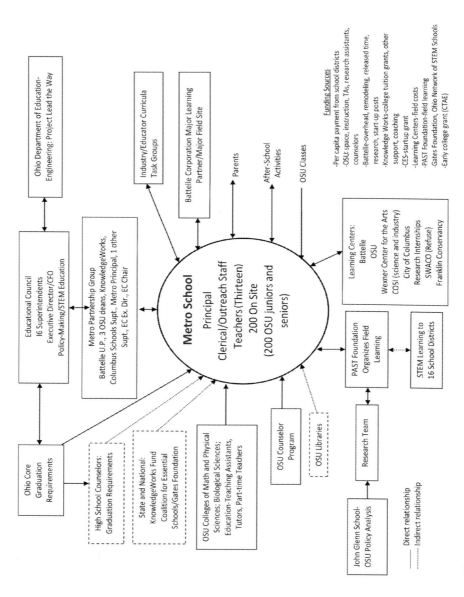

Figure 3.5 Metro School Network Structure

Source: Agranoff (2012, p. 189). Copyright 2012 by Georgetown University Press. Reprinted with permission.

Organizing Government to Meet Collaboration Challenges 91

Operating in a network generally involves many more managerial actions across boundaries than the mere designing of organizations (Agranoff & Pattakos, 1979). Also, working with multiple organizational structures in separate (analytical or real-time) networks/networking as distinct entities is clearly in order (Agranoff, 2007).

As such, it is important to identify their decision-making, structural, and information components. For example, concerning the Incident Command System (ICS) fire control system, the following four key functions are core and go beyond that of "command" and promotes interactive decision-making.

1. Operations to manage all tactical activities.
2. Planning, gathering, and evaluating current and forecasting information.
3. Logistics to provide ongoing support for network participants.
4. Financing administration to track money and time on handling situations.
   (Howitt, Leonard, & Giles, 2009)

These functions are differentiated in large, complex systems and single-agency/hierarchical commands. In networks like Metro School, they are usually highly diffused among network actors in transaction processing. Typically, such systems are distinguished by

> a set of processes and procedures through which information about the system is assembled and analyzed, predictions are made about how things will evolve, options are developed and decided on, and plans are formulated. Regular briefings and planning cycles are the hallmark of a network in action.
> (Howitt, Leonard, & Giles, 2009, p. 135)

Furthermore, the majority of studies on emergency management networks downplay the importance of utilizing mechanisms that foster trust, assembling and developing timely information and communications technology, and working toward mutual goal adjustment among interorganizational actors with divergent goals (Kolpakov, Agranoff, & McGuire, 2016).

Further network operational research in interoperability (IOp) is clearly needed to understand this phenomenon. Public networks involve organizational representatives operating across domains, using the principle of "soft guidance" to move toward mutual reciprocation—as core or as specialized, exchanged organization-based information—is transcended across the boundaries (Kolpakov, Agranoff, &McGuire, 2016). They involve processes that involve knowledge seeking and implementation that precedes joint action. As operational interactions emerged in the Metro research, line contact operations slipped out of the IOp network, while a planning network subgroup was clearly differentiated from a core leadership group. The example of Metro suggests that network learning is transformed across various organizational borders. What has emerged from the Metro experience is the transformation of network *learning* across different organizational domains. This

92 *Organizing Government to Meet Collaboration Challenges*

is confirmed by Bruns's (2013) empirical study on scientific research coordination, whereby she finds that type of network coordination takes place as the result of combining and arranging three types of coordination practices: (1) expert practice, yielding special contributions; (2) coordination practice, arranging cross-boundary contribution; and (3) collaborative practice, modifying expert practices. As a result, separate scientific contributions become more compatible and interoperable (Agranoff, 2018; Kolpakov, Agranoff, & McGuire, 2016). Networks in action will considerably broaden working knowledge about organizing collaborative activities in the future (see, e.g., Koliba, 2014; Koliba & Gajda, 2009).

An Alternative to Combined Agencies and Networks: Ohio's Health Transformation Office

Former Ohio Gov. John Kasich created an alternative to consolidating agencies by creating an Office of Health Transformation (OHT) upon his inauguration in 2001. The OHT (htts://www.healthtransforation.Ohio.gov) effort keeps departments in place. Still, they have established a new unit to operate as a force to bring the various healthcare-serving departments and offices together to work on reforms and long-term health improvements. Among the primary agencies are Health, Mental Health and Addictions, Jobs and Family Services, Veterans Affairs, Administrative Services, and representatives of the private insurance market. In addition, the OHT was charged with developing reforms and bringing long-term health improvements by getting departmental executives to sift through the complex day-to-day operational problems and create interprogram reforms that cut across many programs and sectors in healthcare.

The cornerstone of the effort was facilitated by Kasich's efforts to expand Medicaid under the Affordable Care Act of 2010, allowing states to expand coverage to include people up to 138% of the federal poverty line, as 33 states have, which substantially decreased the number uninsured in Ohio by an estimated 650,000 people (Disability Rights Ohio, 2013). First, the office developed an integrated referral and eligibility system linking Medicaid clients with food assistance, childcare, child welfare, and cash assistance. Most importantly, OHT expanded behavioral health options and community mental health services, ensuring that the state's neediest recipients received care that served them well. That also included raising rates for providers' services to discourage mental health providers from excluding clients.

The real muscle of OHT is its convening power. Problem-oriented teams of leaders from around the state were convened to deal with crosscutting problems, e.g., expanding community-based care for people with long-term health problems. Teams were formed to take an intense look at issues, e.g., dealing with new background check standards or more efficient reimbursement measures. Again, OHT convened multiple stakeholders to agree on the most urgent population health goals. These were settled on: mental health, addictions, chronic diseases, and maternal and infant health. Providers now receive bonuses for meeting employee-based

Organizing Government to Meet Collaboration Challenges 93

goals in those areas and "enhanced payments" in certain administrative changes that help keep people well, e.g., same-day appointments, providing 24/7 (24 hours a day, seven days a week) care, and priority appointments based on risks.

OHT's current priorities include to: (1) modernize Medicaid to improve care coordination, prioritize home and community-based services (HCBS), rebuild community health system capacity, enhance community intellectually/developmentally disabled (I/DD) services; (2) streamline governance, and simplify and integrate eligibility determination; and (3) engage partners to align payment innovation, implement episode-based payments, provide access to primary care, coordinate health information technology infrastructure, and support regional payment reform initiatives.

The overall goal of OHT work includes reducing the number of uninsured citizens, connecting people "with better healthcare, and shifting from a payment model based on the number of services provided to one based on the value and quality of care" (Quinn, 2018). The Ohio model is an alternative to combining or coordinating existing agencies and creating networks.

Conclusion

As the examples in this chapter have presented, this primer clarifies that reorganizing is important but only a first step. The Ohio OHT example illustrates where the agency sits on an organization hierarchy is much less important than *what it does* to engage and interact with collaboration. As Rachel Fleishman concludes, the importance of "political interest is and should be positively and consistently correlated with participation" (2009, p 47). Chapter 11 will demonstrate how the new bureaucracy, existing or dramatically reorganized, must become increasingly interactive/connective—or what here is called conductive externally—by opening its boundaries to needed connections and determined needs.

The largest part of the activities of contemporary bureaucrats working in public agencies is associated with program implementation. In this view, bureaucrats are responsible in their job both to the law they are enforcing and to the hierarchical supervision of politically selected superiors and those in line order of supervision (also defined by law) (Agranoff, 2017). According to John Kingdon (1995), bureaucrats rely on three important political resources that can be tapped within the hierarchy of public agencies. First, the longevity of bureaucrats in an agency allows them to influence political appointees and their superiors, chief executives of public agencies. Second is that their expertise, which is based on professional training and experience in administering programs, including their experience in dealing with the various political stakeholders such as interest groups and legislative representatives. Third are the working sets of relationships that bureaucrats maintain with persons who can influence program implementation, including legislative bodies, interest groups, and other governments. Increasingly, this work involves contact and collaborative operational roles with administrators. This list of

94 *Organizing Government to Meet Collaboration Challenges*

stakeholders also includes the representatives of nonprofit, quasi-government, and private organizations. Although these stakeholders have moved administrative and professional staff into the plane of collaborative programming, they still maintain existing roles and functions.

The new type of public organization with open boundaries can promote collaboration by becoming conductive, as the Ohio OHT operates. A conductive organization is a type of organization that "organizes itself to work 'outside' the agency as well as inside it" (Agranoff, 2012, p. 17). Saint-Onge and Armstrong (2004, p. 213) define this type of organization as "that continuously generates and renews the capabilities to achieve breakthrough performance by enhancing the quality and flow of knowledge and by calibrating its strategy, culture, structure, and systems to the needs of the customers and the marketplace." Even though the concept was initially coined for private-sector organizations, it can be equally applied to public organizations (Agranoff, 2011). As they are for private-sector organizations, creating partnerships, building alliances and coalitions, forming and restructuring cross-functional and cross-organizational teams, and actively managing interdependences are important collaborative activities for contemporary public agencies and organizations. These connective forms will be thoroughly examined with regard to bureaucracy in Chapter 11. Organized collaborative activities are important nowadays because added value is created every time an organization's employees interact with the outside world, and collaboration can serve as a platform for human capital to increase the value created for employees from other organizations and service clients (Agranoff, 2012). In addition, Metro School and Ohio OHT are prime examples of conductive organizations. Management today involves connection, i.e., a more "integrated" approach, so to speak. A vital connection step is by organizing for conductivity.

References

Advisory Commission on Intergovernmental Relations. (1962). *Factors affecting voter reaction to governmental reorganization in metropolitan areas; an information report.* Advisory Commission on Intergovernmental Relations.

Agranoff, R. (1977). *Coping with the demands for change within human services administration.* American Society for Public Administration.

Agranoff, R. (2003, March). *Leveraging networks: A guide for public managers working across organizations: Collaboration: Using networks and partnerships.* The IBM Endowment for Business of Government.

Agranoff, R. (2007). *Managing within networks: Adding value to public organizations.* Georgetown University Press.

Agranoff, R. (2011). Collaborative public agencies in the network era. In D. Menzel & H. White (Eds.), *The state of public administration: Issues, challenges, and opportunities* (pp. 272–294). M.E. Sharpe.

Agranoff, R. (2012). *Collaborating to manage: A primer for the public sector.* Georgetown University Press.

Agranoff, R. (2016). The other side of managing in networks. In *The challenges of collaboration in environmental governance* (pp. 81–107). Edward Elgar Publishing.

Agranoff, R. (2017). *Crossing boundaries for intergovernmental management.* Georgetown University Press.

Agranoff, R. (2018). *Local governments in multilevel governance: The administrative dimension.* Lexington Books.

Agranoff, R., & McGuire, M. (2003). *Collaborative public management: New strategies for public management: New strategies for local governments.* Georgetown University Press.

Agranoff, R., & Pattakos, A. (1979). *Dimensions of services integration: Service delivery, program linkages, policy management, organizational structure, Human Service Monograph Series 13, Project Share.* U.S. Government Printing Office.

Alter, C., & Hage, J. (1993). *Organizations working together* (Vol. 191). SAGE Publications, Incorporated.

Amsler, L. B. (2016). Collaborative governance: Integrating management, politics, and law. *Public Administration Review, 76*(5), 700–711.

Amsler, L. B., & Nabatchi, T. (2016). Public engagement and decision-making: Moving Minnesota forward to dialogue and deliberation. *Mitchell Hamline Law Review, 42*, 1629.

Bevir, M. (2004). Governance and interpretation: What are the implications of postfoundationalism? *Public Administration, 82*(3), 605–625.

Bingham, L. B., & O'Leary, R. (2011). Federalist no. 51: Is the past relevant to today's collaborative public management? *Public Administration Review, 71*, s78–s82.

Börzel, T. (2010). European governance: Negotiation and competition in the shadow of hierarchy. *JCMS: Journal of Common Market Studies, 48*(2), 191–219.

Bruns, H. C. (2013). Working alone together: Coordination in collaboration across domains of expertise. *Academy of Management Journal, 56*(1), 62–83.

Castells, M. (1996). *The information age* (Vol. 98). Blackwell Publishers.

Chisholm, D. (1992). *Coordination without hierarchy: Informal structures in multiorganizational systems.* University of California Press.

Cohen, D. K., Cuéllar, M. F., & Weingast, B. R. (2006). Crisis bureaucracy: Homeland security and the political design of legal mandates. *Stanford Law Review, 59*(3).

Council of State Governments. (1974). *Human services integration: State functions in implementation.*

De Bruijn, H., & Ten Heuvelhof, E. (2018). *Management in networks.* Routledge.

Disability Rights Ohio. (2013). *Disability Rights Ohio applauds Governor Kasich's budget plan to expand medicaid and simplify the eligibility process.* https://www.disabilityrightsohio.org/news/disability-rights-ohio-applauds-governor-kasichs-budget-plan-to-expand

Fleishman, R. (2009). To participate or not to participate? Incentives and obstacles for collaboration. In R. O'Leary & L. B. Bingham (Eds.), *The collaborative public manager: New ideas for the twenty-first century* (pp. 31–52). Georgetown University Press.

Gulati, R. (2007). *Managing network resources: Alliances, affiliations, and other relational assets.* Oxford University Press on Demand.

Howitt, A. M., Leonard, H. B., & Giles, D. (Eds.). (2009). *Managing crises.* Sage.

Jenkins, W. O. (2006). Collaboration over adaptation: The case for interoperable communications in homeland security. *Public Administration Review, 66*(3), 319–321.

Kettl, D. F. (2004). *The department of homeland security's first year: A report card.* Century Foundation.

Kingdon, J. W. (1995). *Agendas, alternatives and public policies* (2nd ed.). Harper Collins.

Koliba, C. (2014). Governance network performance. In R. Keast, M. P., Mandell, & R. Agranoff (Eds.), *Network theory in the public sector: Building new theoretical frameworks.* Routledge.

Koliba, C., & Gajda, R. (2009). Communities of practice as an analytical construct: Implications for theory and practice. *International Journal of Public Administration, 32*(2), 97–135.

Koliba, C., Meek, J. W., & Zia, A. (2019). *Governance networks in public administration and public policy.* Routledge.

Kolpakov, A., Agranoff, R., & McGuire, M. (2016). Understanding interoperability in collaborative network management: The case of Metro High School. *Journal of Health Science, 4*(10), 318–332.

Lewis, M. (2018). *The fifth risk: Undoing democracy.* Penguin U.K.

Maine Department of Health and Human Services. (2018). Retrieved July 20, 2021, from www.maine.gov/dhhs/images/aboutus.shtml

Mandell, M. P. (1999). Community collaborations: Working through network structures. *Review of Policy Research, 16*(1), 42–64.

Martin, R. C. (1963). *Metropolis in transition: Local government adaptation to changing urban needs.* Housing and Home Finance Agency.

McGuire, M. (2006). Collaborative public management: Assessing what we know and how we know it. *Public Administration Review, 66*, 33–43.

Meier, K. J., & O'Toole, Jr., L. J. (2003). Public management and educational performance: The impact of managerial networking. *Public Administration Review, 63*(6), 689–699.

O'Leary, R., Gerard, K., Keast, K., Mandell, M. P., & Voets, J. (2015). Collaboration and performance: Introduction to symposium on collaboration. *Public Performance Management Review, 38*(4), 573–577.

Provan, K., & Milward, H. B. (1995). A preliminary theory of interorganizational network effectiveness: A comparative study of four community mental health systems. *Administrative Science Quarterly, 40*(1), 1–33.

Quinn, M. (2018, October 16). How a tiny office in Ohio is transforming health care. *Governing.* www.governing.com/archive/gov-ohio-medicaid-kasich-health.html

Raab, J., & Kenis, P. (2009). Heading toward a society of networks: Empirical developments and theoretical challenges. *Journal of Management Inquiry, 18*(3), 198–210.

Rhodes, R. A. (1997). *Understanding governance: Policy networks, governance, reflexivity and accountability.* Open University.

Rosenbloom, D. H. (1983). Public administrative theory and the separation of powers. *Public Administration Review,* 219–227.

Rosenbloom, D. H. (2015). Congress and the judiciary's twentieth-century progress. *Public Administration and Law, 60*(1), 48.

Rosenbloom, D. H., & Gong, T. (2013). Coproducing "clean" collaborative governance: Examples from the United States and China. *Public Performance & Management Review, 36*(4), 544–561.

Ryder, B. (2018, September 6). The fight against illicit fishing of the oceans is moving into space. *Economist.* www.economist.com/science-and-technology/2018/09/06/the-fight-against-illicit-fishing-of-the-oceans-is-moving-into-space

Saint-Onge, H., & Armstrong, C. (2004). *The conductive organization.* Elsevier.

Stone, C. N. (2010). *Critical urban studies: New directions.* SUNY Press.

Thompson, F. J. (2012). *Medicaid politics: Federalism, policy durability, and health reform.* Georgetown University Press.

U.S. Department of Homeland Security. (2005). *A comprehensive and sustained approach needed to achieve management integration.* U.S. Government Printing Office. GAO-05-139.

U.S. Department of Homeland Security. (2018). *Organizational structure of homeland security.* https://www.dhs.gov/sites/default/files/2023-02/23_0221_dhs_public-organization-chart.pdf

US Government Accountability Office. (2010). *Opportunities to reduce potential duplication of government programs.* GAO.

Windhoff-Héntier, A. (1992). *The internationalization of domestic policy: A motor of decentralization.* European Consortium for Political Research Joint Sessions, Limerick, Ireland.

4 The Processes of Reaching Agreement

This chapter looks at several alternatives to the majority rule in collaborative management. First, most of us who grew up in the United States and other democratic countries are familiar with and have experienced reaching an agreement by majority rule–based voting. For example, a majority vote selected elementary school room officers. The winner became class president, and the loser(s) remained among the crowd, so to speak. In ways, this mini-democracy majority process made many other class (group) decisions. The simple, ingrained process of majority rule in the U.S. government became how everyone kept and maintained a demeanor for the majority order, from homeroom elections to U.S. offices. It is natural for us to follow this order–except for U.S. president, as we learned in 2016, when a candidate with a minority of popular votes but an Electoral College majority was elected. However, most of the time, we follow the majority rule, which is ingrained in our "procedural psyche." It represents good old social-level democracy.

In CP, however, the majority rule in practice is rarely adequate or realistic to cooperate for several real-world reasons. First, when people represent different agencies, organizations, and interests, they have come together to "represent" what they have to contribute—resources or knowledge—to participate, contribute, discuss, and settle, but not necessarily to be voted down or be on the "losing" side. A model of democratic decision-making discourages workable courses of action. In contrast, collaborative decision-making involves first discovering workable actions by reaching the accommodations needed to have ideas and practices that often interoperate or "work together." Second, in collaboration, people represent their programs with their home agency–based missions, rules, standards, controls, and legal and/or statutory guidelines in the public sector. Third, rules and regulations and related priorities and standards are part of CP considerations; many are thought of as "hard and fast" and in some way must be recognized, considered, and somehow incorporated. They cannot always be merely voted down in process deliberations for collaboration to work. Third, there are professional practices in most programs that in some way need to be built into joint efforts. For example, building construction programs usually require or expect a civil engineer's report on the proposed site. It must not be voted out of the procedure if a group chooses to skip a step, ignore standards and safety practices, and save money. Fourth, a joint effort usually

DOI: 10.4324/9781003385769-4

requires allocating some resources, e.g., broader services for clients or money. These are not easily transferred or politically may not be easy to blend or even transfer to another unit. In reaching a collaborative agreement, raw majority voting has many additional associated drawbacks, particularly in selecting joint processes with complicated steps (Stone, 2005; Voets, Van Dooren, & De Rynck, 2008).

As a result, alternate processes of decisions are necessary to facilitate group movement, which is the operational focus of this chapter. One must remember that collaboration is a "purposive" relationship designed to solve some problem or set of related issues by creating or discovering a solution within a given set of constraints, e.g., knowledge, time, money, regulations, competition, and connections (Agranoff & McGuire, 2003, p. 4). In the collaborative decision, a number of these forces are at work. As a result, CP collaboration participants must be aware of the decision-related "forces" at work.

This chapter will attempt to demonstrate several examples of the collaborative decision/agreement process. First, the essence of negotiations in an increasing complexity flow is revealed through Michael Watkin's (1994) experiential "ten principles of negotiations" amid complexity. Second, one of the authors' experiences demonstrates how a common intake/assessment process was developed and proposed as a companion to merging nine separate departments into a single "umbrella" comprehensive agency in Indiana. As in the case of the other examples, they are models of reaching consensus that, in turn, lead to collaborative operation, as in the ten propositions in negotiation in Figure 4.1. Third, examining the extreme consensus-based and largely "rule-absent" process of name/buyers code formulation for the consensus process based on the model at Laura DeNardis's *The Global War for Internet Governance* (DeNardis, 2014). Fourth, the homeland security SAFECOM and fire security continuum of agreed-upon approaches based on integrated operations (U.S. Government Accountability Office, 2004) are examined. Fifth, the process examination looks to citizen engagement-based decisions by focusing on an intergovernmental management (IGM) report on citizen-initiated decision-making. Sixth, the interactive process within which complex product-based processes are reached in the U.S. Coast Guard (USCG) as it moves forward on integration procurement for their ships and air vehicles. As introduced in Chapter 3, it is not some voting procedure but based on a set of knowledge-based integrations, C4ISR. Seventh, we demonstrate a more focused look at a series of complex agreements based in communities of practice as small self-learning communities (Lubell, 2013). In particular, we look at "stewardship contracting" in forest management and other creative contract-based efforts. Then rural development councils, sponsored by the USDA, demonstrate how disparate intergovernmental state-led bodies can examine rural approaches. Then the processes of communities of practice in school improvement at the local level are detailed as a decision/agreement process, followed by managing in networks as agreements are displayed. The primary methodological focus here is that of the community of practice (CoP), whose group of participants share concerns related to a set of problems or a passion about "a topic, and who deepen their knowledge and expanse in this area by interacting on an ongoing basis" (Wenger, 2000, p. 4). The purpose of displaying

100   *The Processes of Reaching Agreement*

these seven alternate models is not for process replication but for activists to be aware of some variety of the potential forces in collaborative decisions to simple majority rule. Finally, process elements of managing within networks are discussed.

The Watkins principles/experiences in Figure 4.1 are process-oriented. They exhibit the importance of process of value creation, exploring the unknown,

---

The following propositions lay out the key dimensions of complexity in negotiations and put forward some observations about what it takes to be effective in negotiation in a complex world. These propositions are as follows:

I. Negotiations rarely have to be win-lose, but neither are they likely to be win-win. Skilled negotiations tailor their tactics to the type of negotiation, seeking both to create value and to claim value by crafting creative deals that bridge differences.

II. Uncertainty and ambiguity are facts of life in negotiation. Skilled negotiators seek to learn and to shape perceptions through orchestrated actions taken at and away from the negotiating table.

III. Most negotiations involve existing or potential sources of conflict that could poison efforts to reach mutually beneficial agreements. Skilled negotiators often are called upon to mediate even as they negotiate, and intervention by outside parties is commonplace.

IV. Interactions among negotiators are fundamentally chaotic, but there is order in the chaos. Skilled negotiators find opportunity in the fog of negotiation.

V. While negotiations occurring in diverse contexts may appear to be very different, they often have similar underlying structures. Structure shapes strategy, but skilled negotiators work to shape the structure.

VI. Most negotiations are linked to other negotiations, past, present, and future. Skilled negotiators advance their interests by forging and neutralizing linkages.

VII. Negotiations are fragmented in time, and movement occurs in surges. Skilled negotiators channel the flow of the process and work to build momentum in promising directions.

VIII. Most important negotiations take place between representatives of groups. Just as leaders often are called upon to negotiate, so too are negotiators called upon to lead.

IX. Organizations often are represented by many negotiators, each of whom conduct many negotiations over time. Success in setting up organizational learning processes contributes to increased effectiveness, both individual and collective.

X. Negotiation skills can be learned and they can be taught. Expert negotiators possess skills in pattern recognition, mental simulation, process management and reflection-in-action, and these skills can be developed through carefully structured experience.

Figure 4.1 Ten Propositions in Negotiations: How to Negotiate

Source: Watkins (1999, p. 248)

The Processes of Reaching Agreement 101

- Management for accountability, management for legitimacy, management of conflict, management of design, and management of commitment.
- Establishment collaboration as a legitimate organizational form to listen to the voices of participants.
- Determine which structural governance forms would be most appropriate for success.
- Skill sets and personal attributes include: group process skills strategic leadership skills.
- Personal attributes include interpersonal skills, group process skills, strategic leadership skills, and substantive/technical expertise.
- Attitudes: Open-minded, patient, charge-oriented, flexible/unselfish, persistent, diplomatic, honest, trustworthy, respectful, empathetic, goal-oriented, decisive, friendly, and having a good sense of humor.
- Interpersonal skills: good communication, listening, and ability to work with people.
- Group process skills: facilitation; interest-based negotiation; collaborative problem solving; skillful understanding, group dynamics, culture, and personalities; compromise, conflict resolution, and mediation.

Figure 4.2 Internal Collaborative Skills

Source: Adapted from Amsler and O'Leary (2017, pp. 626–639)

mediation, order-seeking, leadership orientation, and more. Importantly, they are oriented around organizational learning, particularly group or collective learning. Finally, Watkins underscores the process elements of pattern recognition and management of the entire process. These are handy principles to bring into many collaborative negation agreement processes.

What interpersonal and/or managerial attributes and skills are needed to manage within the collaboration? In addition to the four roles of champions, leaders, activists, and participants, a number of these skills and attributes are listed in Figure 4.2. Amsler and O'Leary (2017) believe that they are focused "on the human element and interpersonal skills" (p. 632), with more emphasis on people skills (less emphasis on task skills) (McGuire & Silvia, 2009). It is clear that collaboration is dependent on participants—public officials, public managers, and technical specialists—most have some mix of interpersonal/managerial skills, specialized knowledge, and integrating knowledge and expertise with the interactive dynamics required in successful collaboration.

Common Intake/Assessment in Human Services

A Steering Committee on Indiana Human Services integrated this interactive decision process, comprised of heads (lobbyists) of state associations and state department heads/chief operating officers (COOs) of major state departments/divisions. The initially represented departments were: Mental Health and Developmental Disabilities, Public Health, Welfare, Child and Family Services, Title XX Social Services,

102   *The Processes of Reaching Agreement*

Physical Disabilities Services, Services for the Blind, and the "treatment" aspect of rehabilitation or portions of special education. Some 35 people were part of the "decision force." While the association heads brought their staff in, most department heads at the table had the authority to articulate and negotiate the specifics related to their services area. The process proceeded as the following summary indicates.

Month 1

Convene public sector program executives and include primarily advocacy groups. Each representative was invited to present their basic intake/assessment (I/A) process(es). They were also asked to designate the relevant staff who would be part of a working group called a CoP. It was comprised of staff and lobbyists. One author was a resource person and convener/presiding partner for the entire reorganization process.

Months 2–3

Formation of workgroups into several CoPs—at least one representative from each department, chiefs of services, common criteria: administration; mandated (legislative) information, presenting problems, treatment problems, etc. Submit existing product forms.

Month 3

Articulation meeting: presentation and exchange of ideas, federal and state mandates—listing fixed and flexible intake/assessment ideas. Outcome areas of flexibility (to a common process form and areas of inflexibility). Services *group* status reports.

Months 4–5

CoP articulation conferences: (1) reports from workgroups; (2) search for similar practices in other state combined departments: Wisconsin, Georgia, Louisiana, Florida, Delaware, Oregon; (3) presentations; and (4) CoP ground rules in broken down processes with *discussion and initial purposes.*

Months 6–7

Consultation with departments. Public Health backed out of the process (later, they reentered after major accommodations).
Departmental proposals are based on a sense of related department articulation conferences. Sifted ideas and made final recommendations by the combined committee.

Month 8

Articulation conference—based on proposals—outcome: rough draft—outcome template for actual changes. Presentation and questions answered from State of Georgia, which was most representative, by teleconference.

Month 9

Draft report to a group of waiting program administrators. A two-day meeting to make final adjustments to the draft, then a 24-hour turnaround review by principals from each department. After review, final proposals are prepared to be included in the final combined department bill.

It took around nine months for this "community of practice" to reach the necessary agreements and make the required adjustments to make it all work. Committee chairs and program heads reported that *almost no votes were taken* during the process. Instead, processes were worked out interactively, or portions of processes were "detailed" with no real combination of existing processes. Some practices did not work when combined and were left with free standings. Thus, the other departments joined the proceedings except for Public Health, which ultimately partially exited. Moreover, most disparate functions or representatives were all to come together. For example, the common intake/assessment process demonstrates that simple working and voting by majority rule could not work in the real world. Rarely, if ever, does it work, and that collaborative agreement can be a protracted process like this one, in which decision is considerably a "more deliberative" than by simple majorities or related voting (Agranoff & Pattakos, 1979).

Consensus: The Internet Domain Name System

Internet governance—not government—is distributed and multistakeholders-oriented, involving traditional public authorities and international agreements, new institutions, and information governance functions enacted via private ordering and arrangements of technical architecture (DeNardis, 2014, p. 23). Typically, standards organizations focus on technical goals over social or policy aims or consequences. Nevertheless, persons working on standards like the Indiana common intake approach have been concerned with such public values as openness, accessibility, anonymity, and robustness. There have been policy concerns that such issues have been raised after standards are raised and agreed upon. Morris (2011, p. 8) has suggested that more direct public policy concerns should be injected into the policy process that caution to avoid the unconsidered private and commercial agendas being impacted into the standards process: "Effective public advocacy within the technical standards bodies requires the right mix of technical knowledge (or ability

104   *The Processes of Reaching Agreement*

to learn) with public policy experience, which sometimes limits the pool of possible advocates" (DeNardis, 2011, p. 9).

Nevertheless, most internet governance functions have not been the domain of governments. Still, they have been exerted via private ordering, technical design, and new institutional forms enacted in historically specific technical/social contexts. For example, it is distributed and multistakeholder-oriented. Furthermore, the unique alphanumeric codes with internet domain names make websites easily locatable and facilitate routing or navigation.

Part of the odyssey involves how domain names are decided in the province of the IETF (Internet Engineering Task Force).

> The IETF's primary mission is the development of Internet protocol drafts. The organization has no formal membership. Participation is uncompensated activity and open to anyone. Agreement about standards does not involve formal voting but is based on what has long been termed in the ITEF as "rough consensus and working code." Most work is accomplished in working groups organized around key problem areas via electronic mailing lists, although the IETF usually holds three annual plenary meetings. An area director (AD) leads each working group. These A.D.s, along with the chair of the IETF, comprise a governance body called the Internet Engineering Steering Group (IESG), which presents Internet draft standards to the Internet Architecture Board for consultation as formal Internet standards.
>
> (DeNardis, 2014, p. 69)

It is a primary example of how *governance* works without a government body by exercising raw majority voting. The domain name system (DNS) follows a similar pattern.

> Describing how the DNS works is a prelude to explaining what institutions and entities operate the DNS. Examining the technology explains why the administration of the internet's domain name space has always been a critical and central task of Internet governance. The internet would not function without DNS. It is one of the few areas of Internet technical architecture that, as designed, requires consistency, hierarchy, universality, unique name identifiers, and, therefore some degree of centralized coordination.
>
> (DeNardis, 2014, p. 44)

The system allows for participant/user power, which is critical.

> Control over Internet names and numbers is considerable power. CIRs (Critical Internet Resources) are necessary preconditions for being on the internet. Their underlying technical requirements of universality, globally unique identification, and hierarchical structure have necessitated forms of governance that

are paradoxically both globally distributed and centrally coordinated. Unsurprisingly, authority over the administration of the internet's names and numbers has been a contentious area of global Internet governance.

(DeNardis, 2014, p. 46)

The Internet Corporation for Assigned Names and Numbers (ICANN) members are the primary governing body.

ICANN has fundamental governing authority for both internet domain names and addresses. This authority, and its contractual linkage with the U.S. Department of Commerce, has been a contentious and central question of Internet governance. The IANA function under ICANN is still responsible for allocating Internet addresses for regional assignment; overseeing the assignment of domain names, although delegated to other organizations; and administering the root server system and maintaining the root zone file governance.

(DeNardis, 2014, p. 48)

The internet is increasingly privatized:

The RIR (regional internet registration) system is another example of a privatized Internet governance area that is neither market-based nor under government oversight. RIRs are not intergovernmental organizations. Instead, they are primarily private, nonprofit institutions responsible for managing the distribution of number identifiers allocated to them by IANA. Each RIR is driven, financially and procedurally, by its extensive collection of mostly private member organizations. Membership is generally open to anyone but is fee-based and typically composed of private operators and other corporations to which RIPs allocate addresses. As a rough example of the fee structure, AfriNIC charges an annual membership fee of $20,000 for RIRs with a relatively large address allocation. RIR membership directly elects the executive boards of these organizations. For example, RIPE NCC members elect the individuals who comprise the organization's executive committee. These board members guide the RIRs senior management team, which has final procedural and operational decision-making power.

RIRs have a significant public policy function in determining the allocation and pricing of Internet addresses in their respective regions. Sovereign governments in these regions rarely have formal, special influence over these allocations. The stakeholders with the greatest influence over RIRs are the primary corporate entities who make up the RIR membership. So the RIRs have some direct accountability to the networks and customers they serve but do not necessarily have direct accountability to broader publics.

(DeNardis, 2014, pp. 54–55)

106 *The Processes of Reaching Agreement*

Thus, the internet system is a prime example of how decisions under *governance* can work. Decisions/agreements in this context virtually always occur outside of formal government. DeNardis (2014) relates that, as in the case of domain names, the process operates by *rough consensus and broad agreement*. As a result, participants are asked to devise standard-setting processes through a blend of technical expertise, working success-based standards, and "procedures that adhere to democratic principles of openness, accountability, and participation" (p. 84). Finally, the internet system resembles the concept of regulatory regimes, defined as the full set of actors, institutions, norms, and rules that are important for the process and outcomes of public regulation in a given sector (Eberlein & Grande, 2005, p. 91).

Interoperable Coordination Policy for Fires and Emergency Security Among Federal Agencies

The joint efforts of a multidimensional interoperative system of interoperability (IOp) agencies illustrate domestic safety through governance structuring plus the development of standard operating procedures, use of technology, joint training and exercises, and targeted usages within the system. SAFECOM, as it is designated, involves "limited leadership" and a great deal of information sharing. The goal is maximum IOp of systems, equipment, and training-based exercises. Unfortunately, there tends to be almost no voting on the involved parties.

Regarding this issue, the U.S. Government Accountability Office issued a report describing the National Interagency Fire Center (NIFC) wildland fire learning process. Five federal agencies, multiple state governments, and state-based NGOs participate in this learning process. The NFC policy involves ten broad overlapping steps related to interoperability (Agranoff, 2018): (1) bringing together disparate resources and agencies; (2) recording agency/organization rules and procedures; (3) establishing a command-and-control structure; (4) developing a consensus-based management strategy; (5) establishing a resource redeployment sequence; (6) setting an agency "donated" staffing procedure; (7) agreeing and developing general standards, policies, and procedures, including recording equipment utilization; (8) agreeing upon and developing incident response policies and procedures; (9) establishing and operating a "council" or networked-based organizational structure; and (10) negotiating and developing interorganizational operating policies and procedures.

For those who do not participate in this process, it seems that only the tenth NFC step concerning policies and procedures would be resorting to bargaining and negotiations as a quick solution (U.S. Government Accountability Office, 2006). On the surface, it appears to be the essence of IOp, but in reality, it is a more complicated endeavor with many participating sides. From a decision-making perspective, IOp "is a form of an operating community of learning, as people share a common and repeatable linked methodology, focusing on using similar terminology and techniques based on pooled experiences" (Harpst, 2008, p. 187). In reality,

The Processes of Reaching Agreement   107

the steps promote the idea that IOp is a drawn-out, time-consuming, and stressful process (Agranoff, 2018).

Another decision application are Tactical Interoperable Communications Score-cards, which measure interoperability in 75 U.S. metropolitan areas. It looks at how quickly first responder agencies (emergency, medical, fire, and law enforcement) can provide on-scene, incident-based, mission-critical voice communications as required by the incident (Agranoff, 2018). In addition, the U.S. DHS has provided grants to communities to improve these systems. Finally, the process examines how multiagency communications have been managed across different jurisdictions, attempting to localize existing communications strategies (Figure 4.2).

As indicated in Chapter 3, this type of interoperable management can also be distinguished from its close administrative relations: (1) interoperational consulta-tion aims at obtaining information or advice across organizational lines regarding a singular practice" (Agranoff, 2018); or (2) interoperable transactions, such as over a grant or contract of a bi-agency recipient that "regularly shares information or client referrals but does not plan or operate program internally on an interactive basis" (p. 161). In contrast, IOp denotes "regularized programming involving two or more entities for which operating policies and processes have been extensively articulated and are interactively executed by multiple parties (p. 161).

The federal government chief information officers (CIOs) have been struggling with the issues of rendering foundational IOp support. Richard Spires, a former staff member of the Department of Homeland Security (DHS), explains how IT is easily incorporated into IOp systems:

> The typical model for I.T. management in the 1980s and 1990s was first to set up a program in a departmental agency and then develop the I.T. applications for that program. This resulted in stovepiped I.T. systems that largely consisted of duplicated investments for the same capabilities, yet with little interoperability or ability to share data. Moreover, the technology approaches used today allow us to flip that model, especially for foundational commodity I.T. systems (e.g., email systems and common software applications such as Microsoft Office). By doing this, you create a standardized commodity I.T. layer that reaches across the entire enterprise, and all users must migrate to this new platform.
>
> (DHS, 2014, pp. 15–16)

In addition, Spires states that "departmental chief information officers (CIOs) have authority over and 'own' a department's commodity I.T. and related services" (Agranoff, 2018, p. 168). In contrast, joint development of human resources is recommended when linkages are requested with other parameters.

Governance for the IT components includes at least three tiers that support IOp: (1) *strategic*, centered on mission goals and objectives, strategic planning, and documentation across organizational lines; (2) *portfolio*, either by (organizational-, operational-, or mission-related organizational delivery, with internal governance

108 *The Processes of Reaching Agreement*

structures including main stakeholders; and (3) *program*, in this case, specific operations implemented across organizational lines (Agranoff, 2018). These highly interactive processes involve convening, exploring, problem identification, learning, and joint contraction of solutions (Agranoff, 2007)

Public Contracts

Amanda Girth and Lauren Lopez (2019) identify four types of contracting: fixed price, post-reimbursement, time and material, and incentive contracts. They vary in simple and complex situations. Trevor Brown and his associates (2008, 2013, 2016) have written a great deal about the difficulties of complex contracting, whereas purchasing many products—e.g., office supplies—involves simple exchanges. A more relationship-based arrangement is needed to facilitate the complex and involved human interactions in making many contract decisions. In this case, the USCG's building of ships, helicopters, and related transit vehicles is illustrative. Such complex interactive arrangements involve: (1) buyers and sellers do not know the real performance parameters and costs; (2) the exchange involves contractor investments in assets that lose the value of the exchange if it is not executed; and (3) the contract for the exchange is incomplete so that the buyer/seller have room for discretion (and negotiations) (Brown, Potoski, & Slyke, 2016). Dealing with such payoff uncertainty involves more than having the power of the payer nor the testimonial ability of the executant to complete the project. Thus, both parties need some form of interactive adjustment/agreement.

Brown, Potoski, and Slyke (2008) explore these ideas with regard to the USCG's Deepwater Program (ships, vehicles, etc.), which involves multiple mission efforts in designing the service's operations that poses many challenges "in the interaction of the multiple missions of safety (marine, search and rescue, navigation security, drug interdiction, migrant interaction, defense readiness, other law enforcement) and stewardship (marine environment protection, living marine resources)" (Agranoff, 2018, p. 163). In addition, it was organized to acquire a system of systems (SoS), interoperable components whose borderless communication and coordination would have a synergetic effect. A coordinated approach led this interrelated system to government/private-sector programs in a state of command, control, communications, computers and intelligence, surveillance, and reconnaissance system, known as C4ISR.

The program includes "a series of complex products since its design specifications, performance standards, costs, and mission impacts proved to be difficult to pre-establish" (Agranoff, 2018, p. 164). Unfortunately, the USCG could not predetermine cost estimates without the knowledge of all components of systems and specifications of the final products. As a result, it created a challenge in terms of systems design and execution due to the complexity of the government-based product/program.

For the U.S. government, the Deepwater Program became known as "system of systems" contracting, including a lead systems integrator (LSI) in integrating each

The Processes of Reaching Agreement   109

important part (Agranoff, 2018). Each system consists of several discrete systems aimed at the overall goal, whereas components pursue their own goals. Various components such as boats, helicopters, and airplanes can act independently or be part of a larger system. As Brown, Potoski, and Slyke (2008) conclude:

> Concerns about the SoS strategy have less to do with the approach and more to do with who is tasked with designing and producing the macro-system, namely the LSI. On the one hand, LSIs are simply general contractors, linking together systems elements—the boats, airplanes, and helicopters—and ensuring that they are able to coordinate to form the system. In this way, governments buy from LSIs all the time. When the military acquires a fighter jet, for example, it does not typically order wings, landing gear, a cockpit, and other component parts from separate suppliers that arrive in boxes marked "some assembly required." Instead, the military turns to a vendor that delivers a fully functional fighter jet. On the other hand, LSIs may move beyond simply performing product or system integration functions and take on a task and function that is inherently governmental, that is, the function.
>
> (p. 19)

LSI contractors are generally responsible for complex products, including output-based outputs that are challenging to specify in advance (Agranoff, 2018). As a result, integrated project teams of various stakeholders are assembled to work together and share information in order to determine project-related product specifications and requirements during production. These teams analyze, negotiate, and modify specifications and outcomes jointly at various stages of the program.

The massive array of assets for the USCG blends the systems' design and engineering capacities inside and outside of government into one IOp network system. Agranoff (2018, p. 164) argues that the Deepwater Program is designed around "built-in systems that allow for parts of the process to move forward as design changes and prices are agreed upon" (p. 164). This IOp process combines legally based flexibility and utilization of various private-sector contractor management tools by the USCG, including earned value management (EVM), which allows comparing costs with performance.

This case of IOp provides

> a means for the government to be interactive in conducting an extremely complex multistage decision process while maintaining these core concerns of contracting, maintaining public interests and values, respect for and working within institutions, laws, and organizational arrangement, and enjoying the services and their markets that are to activate stakeholder value.
>
> (Kolpakov, Agranoff, & McGuire, 2016, p. 330)

In the USCG's C4ISR system, it is the outcomes of an LSI integrating interactions—mostly by adjustment, rarely by voting. Instead, the key is *exchange* and the

110   *The Processes of Reaching Agreement*

rules and procedures that emanate from their leading to what has become known as *relational* contracting; that is, instead of a more detailed formal contract, the contract is more informal, allowing the buyer and seller to have a more engaged relationship grounded in norms of trust and reciprocity (Brown, Potoski, & Slyke, 2016, p. 303).

The Essence of Stewardship Contracting

The U.S. Bureau of Land Management (BLM) and the U.S. Forest Service (USFS) has a history of using stewardship contracting to implement forest and watershed restoration projects. These contrasts focused on developing federal and state connections with 3,000-plus county-level conservation districts nationwide. Starting from 2010, the USFS moved to "stewardship contract templates that encourage relationships and local participation among" forest and watershed restoration project stakeholders (Agranoff, 2017, p. 163). The collaborative goals are "to identify common ground and barriers and to seek solutions" (Moseley, 2010, p. 11). Instead of using the antiquated system of timber sales, a new system was designed that would enable payment for each additional service activity like restoration and soil conservation by integrating timber harvests and service activities in a single contract (Agranoff, 2017).

Having studied several pilot projects in stewardship contracting, Cassandra Moseley (2010, pp. 30–35) identified four common strategies for building partnerships.

The first strategy is building relationships over time and space. Partners find common ground by talking, meeting conversations, meetings, and going to field tours, establishing more sustainable formal financial relationships over time.

The second strategy is changing the rules to encourage collaborative work. Moseley recommends several tactics: finance the implementation of those agreements that are made through genuine collaboration, provide frontline personnel the autonomy to make fine-tuned decisions and agreements, regularly update all protocols, and remove any obstacles to cooperation.

The third strategy is creating incentives for agency or organization staff to collaborate and punish non-collaborations. The BLM and the USFS specified local circumstances to make collaboration important across the agency. The agencies also developed guidance for frontline staff on building partnerships. The engagement of mid-level and senior staff in collaborative management facilitated the collaboration process. Forming partnerships should be an integral part of decisions regarding performance expectations—in some cases, even establishing goals and objectives for respective units for collaborative contracts.

The fourth strategy is investing in the stewardship capacity building of both governmental and non-governmental actors. In order to support the organizational health of partner organizations, this effort entails developing a cadre of personnel who are prepared to use stewardship tools (such as providing startup funding to fledgling NGOs), training staff and partners in process-specific modules, and continuing to develop peer-to-peer learning processes to facilitate process and information sharing.

The USFS and BLM processes provide important long-term contracting and partnering lessons. Moseley (2010, p. 36) concludes that stewardship requires concerted efforts on behalf of public officials:

> Many of the changes needed to encourage greater use of collaboration came from places in the agency that do not initially appear to have much to do with the collaborative process, such as budget formulation and allocation and performance management, which also need to support frontline collaboration. Moreover, successfully keeping collaboration requires that senior executives themselves engage in collaborative and iterative learning by creating systems to take lessons from the frontline staff and stakeholders and turn them into new guidance, which improves practices and procedures and reflects innovations and changing conditions on the front line.

Having analyzed the stewardship partnership arrangement in the contract work, one can conclude that inward-looking administration models are not well configured to address problems crossing organizational boundaries (Freeman, 1997; Goldsmith & Eggers, 2004; Fernandez, 2009) and require new and different management skills (Agranoff, 2017).

Complex Contracting: How to Execute

One of the most significant contributions to collaborative contract management is those aforementioned involving Trevor Brown, Matthew Potoski, and David Van Slyke on complex contracting (2018, 2016, 2013). They argue that simple contracts— e.g., procuring stationery, office supplies, restroom supplies, finished office machinery, etc.—are different from "complex products" or services that are hard to define in advance and produce according to plan (Brown, Potoski, & Slyke, 2013, p. 29). Examples would be fighter planes, Coast Guard ships, bridges, public buildings, and superhighways. Moreover, complexity is overwhelming in procurement of goods and services that are interrelated and also follow complicated sets of rules and regulations, and when the fine details of a final product/service are unknown in advance.

Complex public contracting puts a high premium on *interactive processes* among cooperating producers and the procuring government. In essence, Brown and his associates describe the process as involving:

> a conceptual managerial framework to guide purchasing the complex products that are often so critical to public organizations' core missions. Drawing on perspectives from across the social sciences, our framework provides guidance for how managers can harness the upsides of complex contracting while avoiding its pitfalls. Our framework helps identify conditions that increase the likelihood of positive

outcomes for the purchasing government and the vendor—the win-win. One set of conditions focuses on rules that allow parties to incentivize cooperative behavior. A second complementary set of conditions focuses on how different relationship dimensions can promote cooperation. Relationships that incorporate repeated play and external reputations increase the likelihood of win-win outcomes. Finally, mutual understanding between the two parties improves the prospects of better outcomes by facilitating more effective contract rules and relationships. Win-win outcomes are more likely when the buyer and the seller understand the contract rules and the relationship in the same way. Along the way, we discuss the planning, coordinating, monitoring, negotiating, and relationship-building investments that can increase contract success. Finally, to illustrate our framework, we offer examples of successful and failed acquisitions for complex products such as transportation projects, social service systems, and information technology systems.

(2018, p. 740)

Brown and associates also propose straightforward steps to manage contracts involving complex products. Job One is to understand the complexity of the end product by discussing with the end-user what the need is and how they will use it. For example, computer products have rather specific needs yet are constantly changing. Some issues in services involving many uses—e.g., subcontractors, clients' delivery organizations, local governments, and so on—make properly functioning services. Another feature is the building of trust "born of goal alignment," born of interactions between the exchanging parties, "If the buyer and seller are in a relationship in which they repeatedly interact over time, each party's behavior can promote future cooperation should they take steps to cooperate at the start" (p. 744). Ways to build such exchanges among the parties include sharing of information to increase transparency, involving a third party to perform independent validation and verification; overseers, e.g., legislative committees auditors, can be helpful networks and promoters of cooperative behavior. In short, contracting for a complex product requires not only entering such connections and relationships by investing in that relationship to learn reciprocal motivations and behaviors.

Brown and associates conclude that process in complex contracting may be as critical as the product.

Win-win outcomes are difficult to achieve in contracting for complex products. The combinations of product uncertainty and specialized investments create the conditions for one party to pursue its own self-interest at the expense of the other party's interests. We have argued that the combination of understanding the product's risks, crafting collaborative contractual rules, building reciprocal relationships, and developing mutual understanding between the exchange partners increase the chances that both sides are made better off throughout the life of the exchange.

(2018, p. 746)

The Processes of Reaching Agreement   113

It is important to understand that complex contracting is not restricted to exotic weapon systems or information technology systems but is also involved in infrastructure for human services systems, participants'/clients' complex data, reporting, recording, and procurement items acquired by government levels.

Rural Development Councils

The near-invisible state-level rural development councils (RDCs) have been in existence since the early 1990s. They do not "decide" on state rural policy but raise issues and explore various courses of action for a state's rural sector. But, again, they exchange rather than "vote," virtually always in a less visible fashion. Most council actions are really not actions or policies or programs. Council delegates are substantial and deliberate leaders in their field of exploring strategies. One of their primary products involves working papers and reports. Councils rarely vote *but interactively* reach sets of joint recommendations to state and local decision-makers.

This sustained rural development initiative appeared in the 1990s from various federal administrations, and they have not disappeared after subsequent federal administrations took over the office (Agranoff, 2017). Based on the interviews with participants who were members of rural councils, the effort was an example "of what can be achieved through a modest investment, coupled with determined action to bring about a new way of conducting the public's business" (Radin et al., 1996, p. 3). The USDA created the project, which supported and seed-funded state-level RDCs to coordinate rural development activities among federal departments and agencies and build partnerships with local, state, and federal governments, as well as with the corporate sector (Agranoff, 2017). The project was based on six components:

> a President's Council on Rural America, a Working Group on Rural Development as a subgroup of the cabinet-level White House Economic Policy Council, a Rural Development Technical Assistance Center and Hotline, a rural development demonstration program, and an effort to target rural development programs on the specific activities.
>
> (p. 204)

The RDCs were then established as pilot programs in eight states: Kansas, Maine, Mississippi, Oregon, South Carolina, South Dakota, Texas, and Washington. By mid-1994, RDCs were functioning in 29 states and were being organized in ten other states. In addition, the National Rural Development Council—a Washington, DC-based interagency entity, was established in 1990 and included representatives from 60 agencies. This movement merged two existing views—the enhancement of rural intergovernmental relations (IGR) and intergovernmental management (IGM), combined with the promotion of more integrated rural development policies (Radin et al., 1996).

114 *The Processes of Reaching Agreement*

Each state's RDC embodies systemic efforts at program-related networks and networking. Specifically, RDCs removed barriers disturbing policy and program implementation within and across public and private organizations, thus creating a venue "for building collaborative strategies and outcomes" (Agranoff, 2017, p. 205). In fact, RDCs were primarily oriented toward collaborative problem-solving. As networks, the RDCs focused on the following activities (Radin et al., 1996, p. 155).

- Changing rural development policy.
- Statutory relief.
- Regulatory relief.
- Management improvement systems.
- Demonstrations and development projects.
- Database development.
- Community information improvements.
- New funding sources.
- Cooperative ventures.
- Outreach activities.
- Leadership development.

RDCs were not established to change basic rural policy or start major new program initiatives. Instead, their main tools included relieving existing programs, enhancing program effectiveness, establishing databases, supplying information, and conducting experiments to support rural development. According to Radin et al. (1996), the RDCs engaged in numerous collaborative activities in the capacity of state-level networks: (1) strategic planning, leadership training and development, and framing and visioning; (2) direct and indirect intergovernmental contacts, including information seeking, guidelines, and interpretations of standards; (3) grant acquisition and administration; (4) regulation processing and management based on results of program evaluation of various efforts of policy and program adjustments; (5) operating through waivers, model program efforts, and related types of special programming; (6) shared or collaborative policy-making, involving joint investigation, and strategy formulation and adoption; and (7) use of network-level or council-level state and efficiency approaches requiring intergovernmental cooperation, such not limited to services consolidation, decentralization of services, cooperation agreements among entities, and governmental consolidations (p. 155).

As formal networks, the RDCs represent both vertical and horizontal intergovernmental entities, including representatives of all levels of government and the business sector. Even though they were responsible for rural development, the real potential was so broad because of their involvement with so many programs (Agranoff, 2017). Their activities were clearly based on intergovernmental programming, allowing the RDCs to remove certain program impediments and solve particular problems on a collaborative basis.

The RDCs' most essential operations entail bringing together the separate rural political and economic actors. At first, the right actors associated with the problem arena were identified to meet together to discuss possible courses of action. Rural development encompasses various stakeholders from "the community or communities impacted, local governments and the private sectors; statewide nonprofits and interest groups; and state and federal governments" (Agranoff, 2017, p. 206). The RDCs provide platforms for bringing all stakeholders together by bringing together federal and state officials, responsible for critical policy and program adjustments, and for teaming up local-level officials and those of private organizations with state and federal officials to address rural development issues. In addition, the RDCs provide an existing template for comprehensive interagency collaborative action within a given arena. Each council delegate represents their department: Agriculture, Economic Development, Highways, Education, University Extension, University Research, and others, depending on the state. Also, each council was assigned an academic investigator as part of a research team whose members primarily studied the process, interacted with council delegates, and provided guidance on intergovernmental processes. In many ways, each council attempted to engage in knowledge management—"objectivist" and practice-based—at all times attempting to share essential explicit and tacit knowledge of the rural sector (Hislop, 2003).

The department representatives mainly related to research team members for review and advice. The ultimate aim was proposals that involved new programs that would bring the various programs together (Radin et al., 1996).

More on Essential Learning by Communities of Practice

Earlier in this chapter, the idea of a community of practice was introduced as the Indiana health and human services advocates came together with state department officials to propose a joint or common intake assessment form to add to pending legislation that was to help coordinate or merge departments. It was facilitated by the various parties collaborating by forming CoPs. Here we extend that elaboration involving collaborative management developed by an extensive use of CoP by Gajda and Koliba (2007). Initially, the authors identify six key aspects of interpersonal collaboration: (1) shared purpose; (2) cycle of inquiry; (3) dialogue; (4) decision-making; (5) action; and (6) evaluation.

Next, the authors developed a CoP collaboration assessment rubric (CoPCAR) that articulates the elements of interpersonal collaboration in a brief and accessible format, which led to theoretical constructs. Each of these elements is explained in the original article.

The CoPCAR displayed here captures the six basic characteristics of intraorganizational interpersonal collaboration: dialogue, decision-making action, and evaluation ranging from loose networks to the creation of a professional learning community. Then clear markers of success, which then guided the program. CoPCAR was developed as follows (Box 4.1). Its lessons are important for those who

116 *The Processes of Reaching Agreement*

need to fathom further that one does not simply meet, vote, and move on. Four CoP steps proved to be useful for collaboration in the different settings. The four steps are shown in Box 4.1.

Box 4.1 Steps in Collaboration Assessment Rubric (CoPCAR)

Step 1: Increase Collaboration Knowledge Among Participants

Evaluators working with organizations that seek to rise to the challenge of creating and sustaining professional learning communities will need to increase collaboration literacy among stakeholders. This can be facilitated through a process whereby the term collaboration is rendered useful, both conceptually and semantically, before engaging in more formal assessment activities. For example, evaluators working in business or non-school settings may reference *The Collaboration Challenge* by James Austin of the Harvard Business School. This book is a compelling and comprehensive read that could generate a common language of collaboration among a range of nonprofit and private organizations. Frey et al.'s (2006) recent article, "Measuring Collaboration Among Grant Partners," is a useful reference point for stakeholders of interagency programs, particularly those supported by time-restricted grant funding.

Step 2: Identity and Inventory CoPs

When an organization's members acquire a degree of conceptual and semantic clarity about the nature and characteristics of collaboration, they inevitably become curious about the dynamics of their own practice. Organizational stakeholders start to ask, "Where and to what extent are we a community of practice? What communities of practice am I in? Are they professional learning communities or just networking opportunities? How will I know?" Evaluators can help to answer these important questions by using a process to identify and inventory intraorganizational CoPs. The goal in this step is for the evaluator(s) to systematically establish who is working with whom, the number and type of existing CoPs, and a concrete picture of the CoP constellation within the stakeholder organization. The identification and inventory process can be used to generate a summary of CoP names, the aggregate number of CoPs, and the nature (purpose) of CoPs and determine the range in CoP membership, the extent of CoP formality, and CoP longevity (Gajda & Koliba, 2007, p. 36).

Step 3: Formatively Assess the Quality and Development of CoPs

Once stakeholders identify their CoPs, it becomes important to gauge their relative quality systematically so that program officials can make informed midcourse corrections and allocate targeted resources for their improvements. In addition, the collection, analysis, and reporting of quantitative and qualitative data regarding the development of intraorganizational collaboration was a primary task for which we were contracted in our school improvement evaluation work.

To examine interpersonal collaboration at work within a school-based setting, we utilized quantitative and qualitative survey techniques across multiple CoPs within a school community. Our methods were threefold. First, we asked individual CoP members of purposefully selected CoPs (identified through the inventory process in Step 2) to rate the quality of their CoP cycle of inquiry using the CoPCAR. All individual members of these CoPs were asked to select the number on a scale of 1 to 6 that most closely characterizes the nature of their CoP's DDAE (Dialogue, Decision making, Action, and Evaluation). Third, scores for individual CoPs were computed by aggregating and then averaging individual member scores. Second, we interviewed purposefully selected CoPs regarding the nature and characteristics of their group DDAE by asking questions that elicited an elaboration of their initial numerical CoPCAR responses. Third, we have used a survey protocol in the formative evaluation of interpersonal collaboration . . . . The focus group questions are intended to solicit perspectives from the members of individual CoPs about the quality of their cycle of inquiry. The resulting findings are intended to be used by program leaders to develop intraorganizational collaboration strategically.

Step 4: Analyze Research Outcomes

Because interpersonal collaboration has been an underoperationalized construct in the fields of evaluation and organization learning, there are relatively few empirical studies that explore the relationship between quality of collaboration and organizational outcomes. In the school improvement literature, student achievement scores, teacher retention, measures of school safety and climate, and other variables related to essential school outcomes have not yet been consistently correlated with collaboration, although in our evaluation context, we have seen some emerging evidence to suggest that such a correlation exists. A school district affiliated with Teaching All Secondary Students that targeted the bulk of its professional development resources on the cultivation of collaboration has experienced significant positive organizational outcomes.

118   *The Processes of Reaching Agreement*

> Student academic performance scores on the New Standards Reference Exam increased each year in nearly all categories following the school's restructuring into professional learning communities, and after four years, the dropout rate decreased 4% to 2.1%, the lowest in the state. However, the correlation between collaboration and organizational outcomes has not yet been empirically studied in this case, and historical, and other intervening variables have not been ruled out. We believe there is great potential for evaluators to make a significant contribution to the field of organizational development by designing utilization-focused studies that examine the correlation between CoP quality and development and the attainment of essential organizational outcomes in educational and other nonprofit and business settings
>
> *Source:* Gajda and Koliba (2007, pp. 34–40). Reprinted with permission.

Gajda and Koliba (2007) thus suggest that the four-step process based on the six fundamental steps (purpose, cycle of inquiry, dialogue, decision-making, action, and evaluation) is one way—however protracted—to advance collaboration. Not only does the Gajda and Koliba approach demonstrate how collaborative decision has become more "horizontal" and less based on rigid hierarchy, but it also emphasizes the move to network-based organizing in order to improve operations in collaborative organizations (see, e.g., Kolpakov, Agranoff, & McGuire, 2016; Agranoff, 2018).

Gajda and Koliba (2007) recommend this four-step process that has proven to be beneficial in the evaluation of initiatives that seek to "do" collaboration and "be" collaborative. Six fundamental characteristics of interpersonal collaboration (purpose, cycle of inquiry, and DDAE) were elucidated and used to frame these steps.

> We suggest that evaluators of collaboration in any organizational context start by facilitating a process whereby collaboration literacy is increased among stakeholders. Evaluators can render the term conceptually accessible and semantically clear by displaying and discussing pictorial representations of CoPs and the cycle of inquiry. This can be done through a combination of direct instruction about terminology and the use of purposefully selected readings that provide the basis for discussion. Second, organizational stakeholders benefit from identifying and inventorying their existing CoPs. Evaluators can help members of the organization see their CoPs, who are working with whom, and for what purpose. In the third step, the quality of CoPs is examined. We have used a survey and interview process in which a scoring rubric (the CoPCAR) and interview protocol are aligned and used to probe the nature of a CoP's DDAE. Last, we recommend that evaluators work collaboratively with program stakeholders to develop research designs in which the relationship between quality of interpersonal collaboration and essential organizational outcomes is empirically determined.

(p. 41)

The Gajda and Koliba mode of using CoPs to reach an agreement has much to offer in advancing collaboration.

Managing in Networks: A First Look

As will be demonstrated throughout the remainder of this volume, an operational and strategic approach to network operations requires a manager's action. For example, McGuire (2002, p. 602) and Agranoff and McGuire (2001, 2003) have identified four goal-directed behaviors/processes: activation, framing, mobilizing, and synthesizing (see Agranoff, 2017, pp. 202–203).

As the Saz-Carranza (2012) immigration study has developed, empirically facilitating is aimed at developing interaction among participants or activating, framing refers to establishing procedures and organized design, and mobilizing and synthesizing involves network agreement and implementation, respectively, as high degrees of interaction takes place (p. 67).

Management-in-networks refers to the outward management dimensions of managers of member organizations. Activities dealing with internal network issues are inward activities. Reaching conceptually out to the network domain is important because the boundaries of a network tend to be fuzzy, since, in real life, it is difficult to tell when an interaction arena starts and finishes. Moreover, given the broad and indivisible problems the networks are dealing with (in this case, immigration), introducing a layer beyond the network itself—the level of the domain.

Saz-Carranza demonstrates the interaction of facilitation by diagramming the four functions of network management—activation, framing, mobilizing, and synthesizing—in dynamic interaction (See Box 4.2). These managerial actions will be revisited in Chapter 9 and Chapter 10 when examining collaborative performance and large projects.

Box 4.2   Network Managing Activities

Framing: network structuring or imprinting formal rules and implicit values for the network's functioning; i.e., creating infrastructures for collaboration rules, values, and perceptions.

Facilitating: organizing interaction among participants and motivating network participants, along with managing the inevitable inequalities among participants.

Activating: embracing supporting actors who might wish to or are needed to further the network's purposes, e.g., knowledge, management procedure, program resources.

Mobilizing: capturing the necessary resources and support for the network to a degree modifying the structure of the network, as relevant actors are sought both internally and externally.

Source: Saz-Carranza (2012, pp. 65–66). Based on Agranoff and McGuire, (2003, Ch. 8).

---

120   *The Processes of Reaching Agreement*

Goal aims are different among networks. Some are created voluntarily, and others are managed by law or hierarchical order. Some are limited to mutual exchange of information (informational), others deal with information exchange, and still others perform these functions and provide member services (developmental); a third type blueprints agreed-upon strategies that are carried out by network organizational (outreach), and finally, there are those that perform the other forms of functions plus make actual program and policy decisions (action) (Agranoff, 2007).

Do collaboratives always reach decisions? The four-part classifications of networks, ranging from those that merely interactively consult and independently implement their own but agreed-upon strategies within the home organization to those that make and implement decisions individually, would suggest that a range of collaborative outcomes is possible. For example, Figure 4.3 on networked collaborative outcomes suggests otherwise, where 19 alternative outcomes are listed. Simply put, networks and other collaboratives do not always make decisions, nor is it appropriate to apply the "some decision" framework classification to such

---

— Mutual understandings regarding rules, processes, long/short aimss
— Process and procedural understandings framing
— Project/issue/strategic processes mutual acceptance by parties
— Network "steering" understandings: strategic, operational
— Interactive "framing" of core issues
— Procedural understandings, agreements related to prospective outcomes
— Broad, non-agreement mutual player consultation
— Knowledge areas to mutually pursue
— Knowledge areas to individually pursue recommended "for relevant participants) on processes, rules, new knowledge-seeking projects
— Understandings to mutually and independently seek interactively pursue mutually identified aims
— Recognition and support of public/community derived aims
— Identification of debatable issue, the potential pursuit of
— Agreed upon collaborative involvement-by independent agents
— Agreed upon collaborative involvement-by the collaborative or the network itself
— Collaborative network policy and/or program decision
— Implementation strategy-by entities involved: strategic or operational
— Implementation strategy-by collaborative/network-itself-strategic or operational
— Partner exit or option out of the agreed course of action
— Partner exit or option out of network, collaboration permanently.

Figure 4.3 Network Collaborative Interactive Outcomes

Source: Robert Agranoff

The Processes of Reaching Agreement 121

behavior. A collaborative effort can often lead to interacting with partners with differing perceptions and potential problem solutions. It becomes procedurally difficult for parties to impose their solutions on other parties. Exit happens often and is a real possibility. Outcomes require some form of multiple-veto support, however informal. Agreements are often woven through the processes and knowledge that reflect the diversity of knowledge and potential/solutions. Outcomes are ideally based on many forces, even sometimes "democratic" votes in the process—but are always interactive, consultative, and respectful of partners.

Conclusion

We conclude this chapter by reexamining the role of government in CP. Today's government agencies cannot be separated from today's governance, no matter the emergent roles of grants, contracting, and NGOs in service delivery. The government may be first and last among what are often proven to be collaborative goals. They are not usually portrayed in serious examinations as if the government is not actively involved. But, as maintained, networks do not replace governments. Instead, in the analytical blend of CP, the primary role of governmental bodies must be understood and "factored in."

Michael Waltzer warns us that the paradox of civil society is to avoid the "antipolitical tendencies that commonly accompany the celebration of civil society which are overstated; the network of associations incorporates, but it cannot dispense with the agencies of state power" (Waltzer, 1998, p. 138). Waltzer continues,

citizenship is one of the many roles members play, but the state itself is unlike all other associations. It both frames civil society and occupies space within, fixing boundary conditions and the basic rules of associational activity, compelling association members to think about the common good.

(p. 138)

In this respect, NGO activists and networking activities of the civil sector have not totally "hollowed out" or replaced the power of the government. In fact, the influence of the NGO sector in this regard still remains an unanswered question in collaborative management.

The role of networks and collaborative action behavior in governance involving the direct involvement of governments cannot be diminished. This is especially the case for networks at local levels. Public sector practitioners resort to them since they can address *wicked* problems (Rittel & Webber, 1973) that are complex, cross-boundary, and interdisciplinary in nature. To solve such problems, the networks utilize various tools such as "looking for adaptable technologies, developing and managing knowledge, engaging in interactive programming and strategies, looking for feasible solutions, and employing their forms of joint programming and policy-making" (Agranoff, 2018, p. 244).

122 *The Processes of Reaching Agreement*

McGuire and Agranoff drew the sensible parameters around the following type of network and related forms of governance.

> Networks, however, have to be evaluated in light of the realities within which they operate. They—and for the for-profit and nonprofit actors comprising them—are limited in role, capacity, and authority relative to their public agency partners. These typically include legal mandates to take action to address the problem(s) targeted by the network, agency organizational and staffing capacity, the financial resources governments control, the legitimacy government participation brings to the network, and the managerial responsibilities that public agencies assume in running them.
>
> Networks lack control over such formal ties as grants, contracts, and service agreements that bind other parties together. The only powers that networks as entities have are those given to them by formal agreements with the government, those exerted by their partners (including government agencies), and some of their own inherent powers (e.g., the ability of partners to withhold expertise that government lacks). Moreover, networks as entities also only rarely implement programs or even the final agreements reached by partners.
>
> (McGuire & Agranoff, 2010, p. 290)

The last point is particularly important for understanding such types of networks. First, it is important to comprehend that most programs and agreements are carried out elsewhere. Network agreements and understandings are traditionally implemented by programs and agencies included in negotiated solutions (Agranoff, 2018). Second, CP should focus simultaneously on network collaboratives and bureaucracy. Both networks and changing governments matter. However, new bureaucracies tend to be more open to collaboration than other governments. As Agranoff (2018, p. 244) argues, "governments have not 'hollowed out' but have become more connective, and some continue to function more or less as standard classical bureaucracies." In fact, combined shared governance with multiactor governance allows governments to endure the changes in the volatile political environment. Such decentralization leads to a bottom-up governance, whereby "product of diverse practices made up of multiple individuals and all sorts of conflicting beliefs which they have reached against the background of several traditions and in response to varied dilemmas" (Bevir & Rhodes, 2007, p. 81). Jocelyne Bourgon argues that "governments need to forge strong partnerships based on shared power, shared responsibilities, and shared accountabilities" (2009, p. 320). They are in a better position to blend the collective and inventive knowledge necessary to innovate with other stakeholders and create the type of supplementary organizational factors (Agranoff, 2018).

One additional and essential feature in formulating a research and practice agenda of CP is to extend existing research to study the "new bureaucracy." As Chapter 11 will reveal, more extensive research needs to focus on the operating roles of bureaucrats in the light of externalization and network involvement. The activities of local officials in action as they interact and transact with other "higher-tier" governments and with parallel governments, along with NGOs, appear to be central. For example, it would involve an extension of what has been called inter-governmental management research (e.g., Agranoff, 2017; Agranoff & McGuire, 2003; Elazar, 1962; Meek & Thurmaier, 2012; Posner, 1998). It expands traditional study on intergovernmental relations into the intricacies of bureaucrats as impor-tant players inside agencies participate in problem-solving, contracting, and net-work-building (Agranoff, 2018).

References

Agranoff, R. (2007). *Managing within networks: Adding value to public organizations.* Georgetown University Press.
Agranoff, R. (2017). *Crossing boundaries for intergovernmental management.* Georgetown University Press.
Agranoff, R. (2018). *Local governments in multilevel governance: The administrative dimension.* Lexington Books.
Agranoff, R., & McGuire, M. (2001). Big questions in public network management research. *Journal of Public Administration Research and Theory, 11*(3), 295–326.
Agranoff, R., & McGuire, M. (2003). *Collaborative public management: New strategies for public management: New strategies for local governments.* Georgetown University Press.
Agranoff, R., & Pattakos, A. (1979). *Dimensions of services integration: Service delivery, program linkages, policy management, organizational structure, human service monograph series 13, project share.* U.S. Government Printing Office.
Amsler, L. B., & O'Leary, R. (2017). Collaborative public management and systems think-ing. *International Journal of Public Sector Management, 30*(6–7), 626–639. DOI:10.1108/IJPSM-07-2017-0187
Austin, J. E. (2010). *The collaboration challenge: How nonprofits and businesses succeed through strategic alliances.* John Wiley & Sons.
Bevir, M., & Rhodes, R. A. (2007). Decentred theory, change, and network governance. In E. Sørensen & J. Torfing (Eds.), *Theories of democratic network governance* (pp. 77–91). Palgrave Macmillan.
Bourgon, J. (2009). New directions in public administration: Serving beyond the predictable. *Public Policy and Administration, 24*(3), 309–330.
Brown, T. L., Potoski, M., & Slyke, D. V. (2008). The challenge of contracting for large complex projects: A case study of the coast guard's deepwater program. *IBM Center for the Business of Government, 26.*
Brown, T. L., Potoski, M., & Slyke, D. V. (2013). *Complex contracting.* Cambridge University Press.
Brown, T. L., Potoski, M., & Slyke, D. V. (2016). Managing complex contracts: A theoretical approach. *Journal of Public Administration Research and Theory, 26*(2), 294–308.
Brown, T. L., Potoski, M., & Slyke, D. V. (2018). Complex contracting: Management chal-lenges and solutions. *Public Administration Review, 78*(5), 739–747.
DeNardis, L. (Ed.). (2011). *Opening standards: The global politics of interoperability.* MIT Press.
DeNardis, L. (2014). *The global war for internet governance.* Yale University Press.
Eberlein, B., & Grande, E. (2005). Beyond delegation: Transnational regulatory regimes and the E.U. regulatory state. *Journal of European Public Policy, 12*(1), 89–112.
Elazar, D. J. (1962). *The American partnership: Intergovernmental co-operation in the nineteenth-century United States.* University of Chicago Press.

124 *The Processes of Reaching Agreement*

Fernandez, S. (2009). Understanding contracting performance: An empirical analysis. *Administration & Society, 41*(1), 67–100.

Freeman, J. (1997). Collaborative governance in the administrative state. *UCLA Law Review, 45*, 1.

Frey, B. B., Lohmeier, J. H., Lee, S. W., & Tollefson, N. (2006). Measuring collaboration among grant partners. *American Journal of Evaluation, 27*(3), 383–392.

Gajda, R., & Koliba, C. (2007). Evaluating the imperative of intraorganizational collaboration: A school improvement perspective. *American Journal of Evaluation, 28*(1), 26–44.

Girth, A. M., & Lopez, L. E. (2019). Contract design, complexity, and incentives: Evidence from U.S. federal agencies. *The American Review of Public Administration, 49*(3), 325–337.

Goldsmith, S., & Eggers, W. D. (2004). *Governing by network: The new shape of the public sector.* Brookings Institution Press.

Harpst, G. (2008). *Six disciplines execution revolution.* Six Disciplines.

Hislop, D. (2003). Linking human resource management and knowledge management via commitment: A review and research agenda. *Employee Relations, 25*, 182–202.

Kolpakov, A., Agranoff, R., & McGuire, M. (2016). Understanding interoperability in collaborative network management: The case of Metro High School. *Journal of Health Science, 4*(10), 318–332.

Lubell, M. (2013). Governing institutional complexity: The ecology of games framework. *Policy Studies Journal, 41*(3), 537–559.

McGuire, M. (2002). Managing networks: Propositions on what managers do and why they do it. *Public Administration Review, 62*(5), 599–609.

McGuire, M., & Agranoff, R. (2010). Networking in the shadow of bureaucracy. In R. F. Durant (Ed.), *The Oxford handbook of American bureaucracy* (pp. 272–295). Oxford University Press.

McGuire, M., & Silvia, C. (2009). Does leadership in networks matter? Examining the effect of leadership behaviors on managers' perceptions of network effectiveness. *Public Performance & Management Review, 33*(1), 34–62.

Meek, J. W., & Thurmaier, K. (Eds.). (2012). *Networked governance.* Sage.

Morris, J. B. (2011). Injecting the public interest into internet Standards. In L. DeNardis (Eds.), *Opening standards: The global politics of interoperability* (pp. 3–12). MIT Press.

Moseley, C. (2010). *Strategies for supporting frontline collaboration: Lessons from stewardship contracting.* IBM Center for the Business of Government.

Posner, P. L. (1998). *The politics of unfunded mandates: Whither federalism?* Georgetown University Press.

Radin, B. A., Agranoff, R., Bowman, A. O. M., Buntz, G. C., Ott, C. J., Romzek, B. S., & Wilson, R. H. (1996). *New governance for rural America: Creating intergovernmental partnerships.* University Press of Kansas.

Rittel, H. W., & Webber, M. M. (1973). Dilemmas in a general theory of planning. *Policy Sciences, 4*(2), 155–169.

Saz-Carranza, A. (2012). *Uniting diverse organizations: Managing goal-oriented advocacy networks.* Routledge.

Stone, C. N. (2005). Looking back to look forward: Reflections on urban regime analysis. *Urban Affairs Review, 40*(3), 309–341.

U.S. Department of Homeland Security. (2014). *National network of fusion centers.* Final report.

U.S. Government Accountability Office (GAO). (2004). *Project SAFECOM: Key cross-agency emergency communications effort requires stronger collaboration,* Government Printing Office, GAO-04-494, Washington, DC.

U.S. Government Accountability Office (GAO). (2006). *Results-oriented government: Practices that can help enhance and sustain collaboration among federal agencies*, Government Printing Office, GAO-06–15, Washington, DC.

Voets, J., Van Dooren, W., & De Rynck, F. (2008). A framework for assessing the performance of policy networks. *Public Management Review, 10*(6), 773–790.

Waltzer, M. (1998). The ideal of civil society: The path to social reconstruction. In E. J. Dionne (Eds.), *Community works: The revival of civil society in America*. Brookings Institution Press.

Watkins, M. (1994). Negotiating in a complex world. *Negotiation Journal, 15*(3), 245–269.

Wenger, E. (2000). Communities of practice: The key to knowledge strategy. In E. Lesser, M. Fontaine, & J. Slusher (Eds.), *Knowledge and communities* (pp. 3–21). Routledge.

5 On Power and Operations in Collaboration

How does one determine the exercise of power in collaboration without the traditional organization-based hierarchical authority? For example, how do collaborative management operations emerge, and how do relevant administrative processes emerge? As Gordon Tullock maintains in *The Politics of Bureaucracy* (1965, p. 32), administrative relationships become more complex as one "moves down the hierarchy."

Power as related to government and its various manifestations involves what Michael Foucault terms as governmentality and its associated components: (1) institutions, procedures, analyses, and reflections, the calculations and tactics that allow for exercise over a population; (2) pre-eminence over all other forms, e.g., sovereignty, discipline, etc.; and (3) the transformation of the "state by justice" into the administrative state, to eventually becoming "governmentalized." As a result, the institutions of the state have been through the processes of governmentalization (Foucault, 1994). As a result, the "governmentality" view addresses the process of governing as a more or (often) less coherent set of calculations and reflections about how best to govern a wide range of issues (Triantafillou, 2016, p. 379).

Normal power is more fluid as people other than key decision-makers are involved in governmentality, particularly routine transactions. Indeed, in collaboration, such fluidity with persons at different levels of multiple cooperating organizations engaging in cross-organizational transactions, commitments, and decisions is more often quite complex. On the one hand, relationships in CP are far more involved and multiorganizationally intertwined. Yet, despite the appearance of cooperation in these protracted processes, there is no way that political considerations and the exertion of power are absent from these cross-organization transactions. On the other hand, as much as CP involves organizations working across their boundaries and government programs are involved, politics may be hidden "beneath the obvious" in transactions. Still, they are present, sometimes overt, often covert—or to put it another way, on the scene but often behind the scenes and beneath the more obvious surface.

Interagency deliberative power is normally exerted in a less visible form and is multifaceted. It involves the interactive "chemistry" of many different humans whose backgrounds, knowledge, interests, skills, and resource bases vary (Rose &

DOI: 10.4324/9781003385769-5

Miller, 1992; Fung, 2003; Bobker, 2009). Power bases of the collaborating representatives exist in many places but are almost not directly or immediately transferred from a position in the home organization hierarchy to multiorganization deliberative processes. The home agency or one's own organizational power is "suggestive" of relative power but not automatically or even necessarily transferred in collaboration. Indeed, several different power bases are normally brought to any and virtually all collaborative undertakings, manifesting themselves in different ways. In fact, with the operation of power, the undertaking falls in a broad range somewhere between forms of dictatorship and forms of open democracy. Power among institutions and interests constitutes the basis of governing more so than transferred authority from the home organization, even from the lead agency government. It is highly deliberative and structured differently—i.e., interactively— with the exercise of different forms of power.

On Collaborarchy

To look for power within collaborating entities, one must look beyond formal authority and established procedures for what might be characterized as "working structures" that guide decisions. The rhetoric and literature somewhat cloud this issue on networking efforts, where the focus has been on perceived equity in participation-based joint decisions. They are often characterized as "coequal, interdependent, patterned relationships" (Klijn, 1996, p. 93). On the other hand, Ronald Burt (1992) finds that in networks, some people sit in positions of extensive opportunity contexts—filling "structural holes," for example—and creating unequal opportunity, while other players are less able or willing to play power games. Organizational representatives also differ concerning the resources they bring to a collaborative network; thus, different resource dependencies and power differences exist (Rhodes, 1997). Clegg and Hardy (1996, p. 679) suggest that "[we] cannot ignore that power can be hidden behind the façade of 'trust' and the rhetoric of 'collaboration,' and used to promote vested interests through the manipulation and capitulation of weaker partners." The analysis, therefore, turns to concerns of collaborative structure and power in our exploration of management in CP.

Considerable light can be shed on this question by examining one of the author's prior network studies (Agranoff, 2003, 2007). Four operating phenomena emerged as revealed by detailed coding of field discussions across this array of 14 networks: (1) the presence of network champions; (2) internal staffing patterns; (3) the evolved bases of internal political influence; and (4) the varied bases of internal technical influence. The characterization of internal power and authority in each studied network suggests that networks possess discernible power structures and that such structures are of a differentiated nature. They include the presence or absence of a network champion: a person, or, in a few cases, two people most responsible for establishing, moving, and orchestrating the network. During the research period, all but two networks—Indiana Economic Development and Iowa Enterprise—had

128   On Power and Operations in Collaboration

at least one such person and four experienced two champions. The two networks with no identifiable champion struggled the most and were reconstituted after dormancy periods during the timeframe of the study. This undoubtedly contributed to their struggles, a view their participants confirmed during one-on-one discussions. The other networks depended on a leader or champion who carried the structure "heart and soul," as identified in Box 5.1.

Box 5.1   Collaborative Leadership

A series of studies of 52 organizations' successful collaborative leadership studies was undertaken by Chrislip and Larson. who studied involved strong process leadership. They found the primary role of collaborative leaders was to promote and safeguard the process. A pattern of behavior emerges similar to what others have called transforming or facilitative leadership.

Four principles are featured:

1. Inspire commitment and action.
2. Lead as peer problem solver.
3. Build broad-based involvement.
4. Sustain hope and participation.

The results of effective collaborative leadership are transformative, as stakeholders work together as peers, and when collaboration is successful, participants are empowered and a new sense of efficacy and community emerges

Source: Chrislip and Larson (1994, pp. 138–141)

A state program head of a federal agency in one rural development network mentioned that every network should be led by a passionate and a catalytic leader (Agranoff, 2007). Another state official stated that "We need an overall champion, and each subcommittee project needs a mini champion!" (p. 93). Although expertise-based power is equally distributed among network members, networks need leaders who can assist in developing a vision, running an implementation plan, communicating with main stakeholders, and organizing meetings. Usually, this is representative of a key organization in the network holding an upper-level administrative position who can manage necessary in-house professional staff and program resources, can command potential donated home-based administrative personnel and communication assets, and has the other team members' respect in their field. These are key internal political resources. Together, they normally help to form the core of the collaborarchy.

In CP, a network champion cannot always be the collective's convener or chairperson. Often it is the executive of one of the "heavyweight" participating agencies who emails the network leaders regularly through dedicated and designated staff time, "holds the modest network records, operates the listserv and maintains the website" (Agranoff, 2007, p. 93). "In other cases, it is a volunteer who has the capacity to do the work within the home organization; for example, a federal or state agency/program or unit of a college or university" (p. 93). The group chair, who is meant to be a "temporary" chairperson, is occasionally alternated with the network champion in other situations. The problem with this arrangement is that the chair becomes inactive, and the group produces minimal—if any—results annually. In fact, the productivity of such organizational arrangements heavily relies on a "visible, energetic, and dedicated leader," as in case of many voluntary organizations (p. 93). Behind most long-term collaborative undertakings lies the energy and work of a champion and steady activist. In larger networks, such as transportation metropolitan planning organizations (MPOs), the champion and core officership is filled by paid executive staff.

Collaborating bodies also need persons with political influence to help sustain them. Because these bodies are not organizations but are composed of representatives of organizations, they depend on donated dedicated efforts that can be transformed into political power: people who are identified by others as promoters, whose presence, participation, and resource commitment send a message that "this (project) is important and that is why I am here," so to speak. While CP influence is said to flow from role and expertise rather than from position, many participants think that assumption is not completely true, as some of the positions that sustaining participants hold normally put them in a more powerful and influential place than others.

Within these contexts, CP is sustained by power sustainers and promoters who support their champion's role. CP endeavors appear to need these sustaining influentials around their champions. One promoter, for example, described himself and others like him as "vision keepers." These are the people who work in the center or on the front lines of federal and state agencies, agency officials, and significant external contractors. Members who work with programs regularly have expertise that they may share with others. They give champions the program and the organizing energy they need to keep the process rolling. They participate in creating joint information events and activities, share a lot of information, go to meetings to get information and learn about new technologies, and voice the collaborative issues to their home agencies.

For example, CP projects often need from three to six promoters representing a range of different collaborating agencies, many of whom are involved in collaboration and have related that it would be difficult to be a successful champion or even think of sustaining a viable network without the complementary and essential work of several of their fellow promoters and/or vision keepers.

In collaborative undertakings, actors normally are in the business of information and knowledge exchange, and most are also in the business of discovering, adapting, and applying extant technologies. Many come together to

130 *On Power and Operations in Collaboration*

share information/knowledge and learn about emergent technology. Others even pool and sometimes adapt technology to local needs. For example, Iowa Geographic is a prime example in the 2007 study of one of the authors of this volume. It interactively uncovered and changed geographic information systems (GIS) technology from their very complex ortho-infrared project to assist in developing a local community map for economic growth (Agranoff, 2007). In another network, MPO transportation network, there were core and key players, including engineers and planners and others from the technical committee, working very closely with the staff members. Even though the core represents a laid foundation, real operations take place in a technical subgroup led by core members. In addition, MPOs rely on technical activists' expertise, including transportation/highway experts and state and federal officials.

It is necessary to note that the previously mentioned small community research networks (Iowa Geographic and MPO networks) include the core players, who are usually the key funders and volunteer university-based researchers. For example, one development collaborative depends on outside consultants and participants. Iowa Geographic relies "on the head of the Iowa State University GIS Facility, Department of Natural Resources (DNR), Department of Transportation (DOT) GIS specialists, and one or two heavy GIS users from local governments" (Agranoff, 2007, p. 95). Importantly, these professionals—program heads and specialists—advise on business matters and establish the political and technical core of shared power within their collaborative arrangement.

In technically based collaborative undertakings, power could not flow in any other way. It involves seeking adaptable solutions to intractable problems, only some very small portion of which can be solved by simple voting, if at all, while invoking financing packages and exerting raw political leverage through deliberation. New technology unites university-based and agency-based engineers in the search for scale-based solutions. If technically possible, a growing number of legal, regulatory, and financial experts may become involved and become the center of influence in the network (Agranoff, 2007). As one participant put it:

> We can only help a large number of small communities if engineers and technology people step forward and find a way. Then the rest of you can work on dollars and the permitting. Success depends a lot on what I would call "technical activism."
>
> (p. 95)

Although an Iowa Enterprise group has struggled to attract home-based businesses, its core of small business consultants, U.S. Small Business Development Center (SBDC) specialists, USDA loan experts, and university–community development people "provide the very expertise that those home-based businesspeople do not have" (Agranoff, 2007, p. 95).

On Power and Operations in Collaboration   131

Another member claimed that the project would fail if those people and their one webmaster did not contribute their time and effort (Agranoff, 2007, p. 95):

> Iowa Enterprise would have fallen under the lack of inertia that busy home-business people brought to the group. It was not so much lack of enthusiasm, but the ability to know what to do was not there for our members. Some of us just had to use our expertise and experience to do it for them.

Many groups appear to become immersed in technological issues and need to be supported by the collaborative efforts of such a technical core.

Some staffing level in collaborative projects also appears to be part of the power equation (Agranoff, 2003, 2007). Many networks use their scant resources, but external funding undoubtedly allows for the staff to carry out their mandated missions. As a result, the role of the workforce is more significant than the number of employees. Although it differs between collaboratives, staff members sometimes have a sizable amount of network power. For example, as work becomes more coordinated, the political and technical power bases are affected, in addition to the support system. Agranoff (2018) argues that staff labor is equally as important in a non-hierarchical, shared body whereby the activist core primarily works in the home agency, as is common in a volunteer organization. The following statements of participants in his study on 14 networks suggest that staffing should be in the equation for the network power: "Without [name of staff director], despite his need for control, we would not be moving along the way we are, and no doubt there would be more nonproductive confrontations," said one active networker. "Our [staff person] does more than preparing things," another explained, "she ensures that the proper individuals are present for the correct decisions and that the program is moving on the right path." A participant observed, "[Name of former staff member] was so enthusiastic and committed in the collaborative that it appeared to be 'her baby' rather than ours [name of group]. To get anything done, you had to go through her" (p. 100).

Except for the work of Milward and Provan (1998), very little research has been done on operations involving collaborative power (Agranoff, 2003, 2007). Milward and Provan found that network effectiveness was connected to stakeholders' wielding power control among mental health centers at the community level. To be real, power can originate from within the network, but it has to disperse among network champions, promoters, technical influencers, and personnel of different agencies (Agranoff, 2003, 2007). As Chapter 4 explains, decisions are brokered within the context of this shared, interactive non-hierarchical power among network members. In summary, the important building blocks of collaborarchy involve at least five role components of power: champions, promoters, volunteer and paid experts, staff members, and hired consultants. Together, they form the collaborarchy.

132　*On Power and Operations in Collaboration*

Power Within the Network Collaborarchy

Importantly, this five-part component collaborarchy only identifies the normal working sources of collaborarchy-based power, not the ratio or balance between each party/representative element. The mix will depend on the dynamics of the situation. Here, one can only observe and speculate. "Beyond the façade of consensus and collaborative management, stronger partners *take advantage* of weaker partners" (Agranoff, 2007, p. 100). For example, some organization representatives occupy network positions whereby their knowledge, financial resources, organizational status, or legal authority accumulates power within the collective (Agranoff & McGuire, 2001). This power is usually utilized to shape general agreements or influence consensus in decision-making. Power of this nature is sometimes described as "power to" in Clarence Stone's (1989) urban work on collaboratives.

Like many modern organizations, today's collaborative undertakings rely heavily on technical power. For example, some rural development networks—the USDA/RD plus university extension and state economic development departments—happen to be powerful and committed actors such that potential funding resources and technical questions are regarded as coequal with programming and policy issues. On the one hand, by persuading others to make the adjustments required for crucial consensus, their partner members accomplish much of the persuasion and, ultimately, the technical adjustment work required to support the common mission (Agranoff, 2003, 2007). On the other hand, if any of the key players—the USDA/RD plus university extension and state economic development departments—render no support to the network, it eventually slows down these networks' work (Agranoff, 2007; Radin et al., 1996).

Within these definitions, networks and other collaborative enterprises can take many and varied forms. As Box 5.2 suggests, they can be self-developed or mandated. For example, they might be dominated by loose/informal contacts or take the form of tight, formalized networks. They are usually interorganizational, are sector-specific or broader, and could be short-term or cover broad periods of time (Sørenson & Torfing, 2005, p. 197).

Box 5.2　Governance Networks in Operation

- A relatively stable horizontal articulation of *interdependent*, but operationally *autonomous* actors.
- Who interact through *negotiations* that involve bargaining, deliberation and intense power struggles.
- Which take place within a *relatively institutionalized framework* of contingently articulated rules, norms, knowledge and social imaginaries.
- That is, *self-regulating* within limits set by external agencies.
- Which contribute to the production of *public purpose* in the broad sense of visions, ideas, plans and regulations.

Source: Sørenson & Torfing, 2005, p. 195, emphasis in original)

On Power and Operations in Collaboration   133

As an introduction to network management, a straightforward overview of the collaborative process of network management has already been provided in Chapter 4, specifically: activating, framing, facilitating, and mobilizing. These joint actions sum up what normally occurs within deliberations in CP. However, it will be further demonstrated that these actions do not always take place in that sequence. They can be disjunctive. Network actors attach their missions within the collaborative in the order they are challenged without regard to sequence (McGuire & Agranoff, 2014).

When nonprofit organizations and government agencies come to terms with working collaboratively, their first order of business is to understand each organization's mission clearly (Agranoff, 2018). However, the collaboration process can break down if all network members do not have a clear understanding about each organization's capacities and compatibility or incompatibility in the network.

The second and primary premise is for parties to understand government agencies' core or lead roles. An excellent overview of all the potential roles that government agencies play in collaboration—e.g., a provider of various human, technical, and financial resources—can be found in Amsler (2016). Foremost is the "sweeping influence that governmental institutions leave their mark on how issues are defined, what resources are used or are available, the structure of the collaborative process and outcomes that these endeavors produce" Koontz et al. (2004, p. 170). Most involved parties come to terms with the institutional requirements in statutes and regulations, but more critically, only a select few groups are granted broad "policy authority" (Agranoff, 2018). Indeed, the latest research on the coproduction of public/NGO services indicates a more or less minor role for NGOs in the organization of services. The NGO's role proved to be quite limited in making program decisions versus delivering actual services (Cheng, 2009, p. 209). Larger roles are played by government actors in collaboration. Despite the limitations of official representation in the collaboration, government actors also have the opportunity to act in ways that can foster collaborative group efforts. However, agencies may fail to accomplish this, refusing to support others' advocacy or, at the very least, failing to confirm some issues and challenges which prevent productive collaboration (Agranoff, 2018).

A related note on the daunting challenges in dealing with government is the failure to understand that policy and program decisions can also engage communities "governed by decision-making bodies (e.g., city councils, county commissions, metropolitan planning organizations, natural resources-management districts, etc.)" (Agranoff, 2018, p. 91). Unfortunately, the local decision-makers are often not included in the interactive process of collaboration and deliberation, which presents a high risk for collaboration to fail (Edelenbos, 2005).

The interactive process must also come to grips with important statutory-based rules potentially impeding serious attempts beyond mere coordination. For example, since the early 1980s, the Medicaid program (medical payments for low-income persons) has featured a wavier program for HCBS to support eligible clients who would otherwise be institutionalized. HCBS is a federal–state initiative that procures a wide range of externally delivered services, mostly provided by NGOs. In addition, HCBS used to restrict payment for room and board while also prohibiting

134 *On Power and Operations in Collaboration*

other services before eventually allowing them (e.g., day hospitalization, ventilator-dependent services). The "cold bed rule," which obliged governments to reduce institutional beds in an equal ratio to the number of incoming HCBS clients, was eventually repealed. The most recent significant modification, implemented in 2011, allowed previously prohibited family home care providers to be reimbursed under specific conditions. Each of these principles establishes criteria for directing the bounds of states in relation to HCBS and, as a result, specifies some key characteristics of how any collaborative endeavor can function.

These rules are elaborated and contextualized in the work of Bevir and Rhodes (2007) in Box 5.3.

Box 5.3   Bevir and Rhodes's Decentered Theory of Governance

1. A decentered theory of collaborative governance offers more diverse view of state authority and its exercise. Patterns of rule arise as the contingent products of diverse actions and political struggles by the varied beliefs of situated agents.
2. The state is never monolithic and it always negotiates with others. Policy always arises from the interactions within networks of organizations of individuals. Patterns of rule always traverse the public, private, and voluntary sectors.
3. A decentered approach changes our conception of governance. It encourages us to examine the ways in which patterns of rule, including institutions and policies, are created, sustained and redefined by individuals.
4. A decentered theory highlights the importance of beliefs, traditions, and dilemmas for the study of governance that are constructed from interpretations of experience infused with traditions.
5. All governing contests take place in the context of laws and norms that frame governance, most often within local practices of governing. Therefore, what occurs is a complex and continuous process of interpretation, conflict, and activity that produces over changing patterns of rule.
6. A decentered theory implies that network governance arises from the bottom up. Any pattern of governance is a product of diverse practices made up of multiple individuals acting on all sorts of conflicting beliefs.
7. A decentered theory of network or other forms of collaborative governing entails a shift of topos from institutions to meanings in action. Positivist approaches reduce the diversity to a logic of modernization, institutional norms, or correlations across policy networks.
8. The road to understanding change in network governance lies in decentered accounts focusing on the political ethnography of networks to generate narratives that give due recognition to creative individual. In effect, it involves a story telling as an alternative to the mainstream tool kit for many in networks.

Source: Bevir and Rhodes (2007, pp. 77–90)

Processing Barriers

The transaction costs are among the most familiar barriers or impediments to the collaborative agreement. They have been borrowed from economics and are regularly applied to collaborative rulemaking and regulation (Agranoff, 2018). Transaction costs are "the costs of operating by a public organization through contractor/grantee/lessee or other institutional arrangements, including collaborative engagement" (p. 100). Edward Weber (1998) points out that three substantial transaction costs can be distinguished in the area of collaborative environmental rulemaking. They also appear to apply broadly to other collaborative efforts. The first is the process costs or resources such as finance, time, money, and other task disbursement used for collecting information, identifying needs, and negotiating. Information asymmetries and informing others what that organization needs to know in the course of conversation and negotiations exacerbate work across agency and organization boundaries (Agranoff, 2018).

The second set of costs is the implementation costs, which include the time and effort required to meet mandates, adaptations, monitoring technologies, and, most importantly, any program adaptability costs in network activities (Agranoff, 2018). The latter relates to changes in engaged organizations' response capacity to others' concerns and requirements and exogenous factors such as technological advancements and scientific knowledge base changes.

Third are the costs associated with participant behavior, which include numerous challenges such as accounting for non-participants; considering various levels of those who might react negatively, including the threat of litigation; addressing information asymmetries; controlling critical information by parties; delays on the part of agency or organizational executives; and the potential for "wheel spinning" caused by heavy investments in processing (Agranoff, 2018).

One often misunderstood processing barrier that is rarely dealt with involves the clash of different network actors over coproduction of agreements that do not recognize differences in the perception among network actors (Agranoff, 2016). For example, R. P. Lejano and Helen Ingram's (2009) research on CAL-FED indicates that construction of meaning by different parties, similar to that of CP, can result in processing barriers unless new jointly derived constructions emerge of their differences. Specifically, their case studies indicate that fish and wildlife officials, who focus on preserving and maintaining ecosystems, view the world differently from water supply engineers and executives, who perceive water as goods. As a result, the two interests rarely share the same perspective on water matters. For example, if new knowledge is not socially constructed during the network interactions, forging new relationships is very likely to lead to "a continuation of path dependency with only modest adjustments rather than a meaningful move toward transformation" (Lejano & Ingram, 2009, p. 661). Thus, an ameliorative tactic of networks/collaboratives is to lay these differences on the table, publicly explore the depths of a problem, look for solid knowledge to apply, and use this knowledge as a synthesis that can lead to new approaches that satisfy varying interests (O'Toole, 1997, 2015).

The Dynamics of Operational Localism

Most collaborative agreements and related decisions ultimately constitute *potential* actions. These actions are later executed by agencies operating at the project or program levels, representing local governments or NGOs at the community and local levels. This is especially true for programs with a national reach but also a local impact. Regardless of how a federal, central, or intermediate government decides on policies and program directives, they are typically carried out by local governments or some local NGO, or a group of them, who are tied not only to external program goals but also to internal operations, local power structures, and local regimes that must inevitably balance "closer to home" demands/expectations geared to local constellations of interests within local political contexts (Agranoff, 2016). In reality, this localist imperative works in combination with the higher-level objectives associated with comprehensive programs. For example, environmental protection framework laws and regulations may operate differently from a local program because "it all happens locally." Local action or program meets activity as a product in the end analysis of program implementation, which is some type of structured reconciliation between national/regional government objectives and local regime demands (Reed, 2014).

This is an often forgotten and key imperative of power in collaboration. As such, operational localism is understood in general terms from the policy implementation perspective (Williams, 1980). In short, "policy" can be modified as it works its way along the implementation line into a program (Agranoff, 2016, p. 96). These are "collaborative costs" or operational barriers that almost always lie outside the government-enabling policy process. They usually occur at the end of preparation and during the implementation stages. Nevertheless, local adaptations are real and potential power forces, a part of the power equation.

If we look at the local agency level, "a series of internal costs must be balanced against the expectation of opportunity to implement any cooperative agreement" (Agranoff, 2016, p. 96). According to one of the authors of this volume who studied 14 networks, managers and professionals in delivery organizations repeatedly indicated six locally based pre-existing "costs" that dampened external, network, or collaborative derived expectations: (1) time and opportunity costs incurred by the home agency as a result of network involvement; (2) time and energy costs incurred by the lengthy decision-making process based on non-hierarchical, multiorganizational, multicultural human relations processes; (3) agreements not reached as a result of organization power (or veto) or power withholding, including other forms of local political resistance; (4) a network's tendency to gravitate toward consensus-based, risk-averse decision-making agendas, especially in order to avoid offending powerful groups; (5) resource "hoarding," or agencies' failure or refusal to provide critical resources; and (6) legislative policy hurdles, coupled with legislators' and/or senior administrators' unwillingness to make necessary reforms, which frustrated network decisions (Agranoff, 2007). All of these happened to be potential or actual

On Power and Operations in Collaboration   137

barriers reinforcing operational localism to some degree and are potential barriers that stop progress within networks. In CP, most importantly, they open up opportunities for wide on-the-ground interpretation and possible displacement.

Operational localism in these forms, in effect, is based on the empirical implementation studies that "separate policy fact from policy fiction" (Brodkin, 2003, p. 151) or what Anat Gofen's (2014) Israeli research highlights as "street-level divergence" that leads to policy and program changes initiated by policy implementation managers or staff. Such change in policy directives and rules is not always self-serving by operational professionals, according to his research of teachers, nurses, social workers, and other street-level bureaucrats (Agranoff, 2018). Street-level bureaucrats are motivated to serve others and prefer relationships over policies promoting collective action and divergence. Furthermore, such "deviation" may occur due to concealed or transparent behaviors. Programs on the ground must be viewed subtly due to these heterogeneous and various motivations. Divergence, according to Gofen, is a feature of policy change that becomes legitimized as the practice spreads to the actual program in use. At the very least, it highlights the fact that regardless of what networks agree on, operational localism is a key venue for some forms of displacement as implementers deal with their beliefs and motivations, social and work pressures, and a slew of unknowns (see, for example, Lipsky, 1980; Maynard-Moody & Musheno, 2000, 2003).

Network or other collaborative action at the administrative and/or the NGO board level also "has to account for how such 'agreements' are carried into action as the key leaders place 'meaning(s)' that 'shape actions' that are not just representations of people's beliefs and sentiments but fashion actions" (Wagenaar, 2011, p. 3). Administrators are engaged in practices that are inherently dialogical/end-interactive in nature. As Hendrik Wagenaar (2004, p. 651) concludes from his earlier studies of mental health programs:

> To be effective in practice implies that administrators must be willing to understand and be influenced by the point of view of other members of their community, be they clients or colleagues. In this way, practice theory transcends the dichotomy between individual and community. Good administrative practice is not just an individual achievement or a particular faculty of mind. The categories, norms, and standards are in everyone's possession and available for others as grounds for assessing the rightness or reasonableness of the administrator's actions. In fact, productive interactions with clients and colleagues are made possible through this practical judgment transparency. Administrative judgement is not the sum of a vast series of judgments of individual administrators, who each act on the situation at hand. Instead, administrative practice expresses a community of standards, the commonality, and the integrity of an administrative collective.

Wagenaar states in his research that administrators (and agency boards) are under pressure to "concretize abstract statements into concrete objects and acts,"

138 *On Power and Operations in Collaboration*

resulting in practical judgments regarding common circumstances (Wagenaar, 2004, p. 651). Concerning the various CALFED studies, interorganizational agreement can sometimes entail more than a lack of authority to act; it can also entail administrators working to preserve the status quo (on water consumption) in the face of divergent and opposing interests (Hanemann & Dyckman, 2009). In effect, considering how networks and other collaboratives reach agreements, these "other steps" in implementation are always there and almost always locally manifested.

Operational Power Within Collaborative Processes

A necessary condition in collaboration is often the presence of unequal power (Agranoff & McGuire, 2001). Power dynamics usually occur within the collective of collaborating organizations and are based on power dependence. Roderick Rhodes (1997, p. 9) argues that "organizations depend on each other for resources and therefore enter into exchange relationships where they maneuver between one another." Power dependence can explain the interaction of different entities and differentials in power distribution among collaborating actors (Agranoff, 2012). Rhodes (1997, pp. 36–37) says that "such entities are usually controlled by dominant coalitions, which employ strategies within the game's rules to regulate the processes of exchange." From this perspective, power can be used both to facilitate and hinder collaboration processes. Organizational power of an agency can be a "very real barrier when lead organizations serve to keep certain problems off agendas, withhold support for key network strategies or decisions, or withhold required agency-controlled resources" (Agranoff, 2012, p. 164). These actions can be very serious barriers to achieving results. Meanwhile, different types of collaborative power were defined by Stone as the "power to achieve positive outcomes." We have to look at collaborative power as a negative force and as power of getting things done in a collaborative.

Based on his studies of 14 networks, one of the authors of this volume (Agranoff, 2007) distinguishes four different types of interactive power that can positively and negatively affect the outcomes of collaboration. The first is agency power, or the ability to impede or enhance results by playing the power-dependence game: "We cannot disregard the facade of trust and the rhetoric of collaboration employed to promote vested interests through manipulation and submission of weaker partners" (Clegg & Hardy, 1996, p. 679). The second type is the collaborative enterprise's operational power and how it is structured and followed. This dimension is defined by Klijn (2001, p. 139) as generalizable processes that are used, as well as "arena rules" that govern the nature of the power game and "interaction rules" that define internal behavior in the construction of games. Knowledge-based power is the third form, which occurs when technical actors collaborate to discover and solve problems they are originally unsure about. Technical experts combine "framed experiences, values, contextual information, and expert insight that gives a framework for evaluating and absorbing new experiences and information" to

On Power and Operations in Collaboration 139

gain power (Davenport & Prusak, 2000, p. 7). On the other hand, deliberative power is utilized as fresh technical information is infused and new possibilities arise from debates, technical applications, and multiparty interaction. Finally, based on the concept of collaboration as involving real-world power sharing (Gray, 1989; Agranoff, 2012), it entails obtaining "excellent answers through the process" (Innes & Booher, 1999, p. 5).

This fourth type of power—deliberative power—is "perhaps the least understood but most central to engaging in collaborative management" (Agranoff, 2012, p. 165). In many ways, deliberative power is most closely related to the previously mentioned Stone's (1989) "social production" model oriented on community power and community development which was later improved by she and her colleagues (Stone et al., 1999). It is based on the urban regime theory (Stoker & Mossberger, 1994), which holds that society is defined by a lack of coherence rather than a single system of dominance or coordination (i.e., power over some form). Instead, social systems are made up of possible linkages or a loose network of institutional arrangements, with many autonomous actions and preceding midterm agreements: "The question is how to achieve enough cooperation among various community parts to get things done" (Stone, 1989, p. 227). Preferences are another aspect of the social production model. For example, suppose one thinks they are not fixed but may be updated when situations change and new options emerge due to the process. In that case, power is no longer defined by the terms on which fixed preferences prevail but rather by the terms on which fixed preferences are adjusted to one another (Agranoff, 2012). Thus, "opening up new possibilities" in the sense of "a wider understanding of what is conceivable" might be a means of bringing about new sets of optimal configurations through social production (Stone et al., 1999, pp. 354–355).

Box 5.4 illustrates hypothetically deliberative power using hypothetical environmental improvement situations. They show how power is "exercised" in order to facilitate the formation of various forms of joint agreements inside various collaborative agreements (Agranoff, 2012).

Box 5.4   Possible Dimensions of the "Power To" (P2): The Enabling Dimensions in Collaborative Settings

Following are hypothetical illustrations of "power to" that flows from the synergistic operation of environmental networks.

P2a = Power of Discovery of New Ideas: the synergy of solution—collectively, a task group or agency finds a new way to research, propose, and develop a comparative environmental risk program for the community.

P2b = Power of Technical Solutions: brought to the fore that a partnership can use; e.g., an intergovernmental estuary partnership learns about a new way of mitigating fertilizer runoff.

140 *On Power and Operations in Collaboration*

P2c = Power of Feasibility: e.g., the U.S. Environmental Protection Agency and/or a state environmental protection agency agrees that a proposed watershed mitigation proposal, using waivers and statutory relief, jointly proposed by a network is agreed to in principle, and now the details are to be negotiated.

P2d = Power of Willingness to Accommodate: e.g., two influential and large manufacturers, DuPont and General Motors, and the City of Cleveland agree that they are potentially responsible parties in a contaminated land-fill, and are willing to discuss mitigation costs and measures with the Cuyahoga County Brownfields Task Force.

P2e = Power Rebalancing: newly introduced network partners change the formula; e.g., the Iowa sustainable Agriculture Strategic Network (state agencies, agribusiness, producer organizations, farm organizations, universities) adds the Sierra Club, Citizens Environmental Council, and three other environmental advocacy groups to its membership.

P2f = Resource Dependency Change: e.g., a power shift due to the expansion of an interagency coordinating council beyond the U.S. Environmental Protection Agency brings in the U.S. Army Corps of Engineers, Soil Conservation Service, Agricultural Research Service, Federal-State Extension Service, Rural Development Administration, and Economic Development Administration as other federal agencies that can legally, politically, and financially support joint research and operations.

Source: Agranoff (2012 p. 166). Reprinted with permission.

Box 5.4 illustrates how both a "power over" and a "power to" coexist in collaborative management practices and conceptually complement each other. One of the most important conclusions is that collaborating network actors contribute much more than mere positive or negative powers to the negotiation table (Agranoff, 2012). Power in CP is more nuanced. For example, the power of new ideas, new technology, or extant formulaic problem solutions approaches presents great opportunities to reach decisions collaboratively. Thus, the power dimension needs to be expanded to include the power dynamics inside the collaborative undertaking, a principle requiring a widely broadened understanding.

In collaborative activity, the four nuanced power dimensions can be analytically distinguished but are more often intertwined in practice: (1) the familiar power (including established solutions) that the partner brings from the home agency; (2) the internal operational power originating from agency inputs and interactive processes which are necessary for maintaining collaborative processes and achieving outcomes; (3) knowledge-based power necessary for operating technical core of each collaborating organization (e.g., how they process information) (Agranoff,

2012); and (4) the deliberative power of developing new agreement possibilities generated by the search for technical solutions and outcomes that address multiorganization and interagency problems (p. 166). Power exercising is a dynamic and complex process. As a result, power can be a considerably complex and protracted undertaking.

Because these CP power dimensions are likely to be analytically present in various forms, they can and have served as positive forces to facilitate the counteraction of negative synergies of internal agency powers utilized "in resisting joint agreements or action" (Agranoff, 2012, p. 167). These processes can be understood to initiate and maintain agreement on power needs in collaboration. In the absence of hierarchical authority and/or legal power, these more interactive forces "substitute" or work instead of hierarchy. Nevertheless, they are important distinctions in collaborative management.

More on Power in Collaboration

As a core focus of collaboration, management power obviously needs to operate in a shared fashion at the center of understanding (Bryson, Crosby, & Stone, 2006). Ran and Qi (2018) developed a contingency-based framework to look at power sharing in collaboration in an interesting analysis of collaborative power. Their model is based on six contingency factors from three perspectives: contextual (institutional environment), network (different agency missions), and model (power-sharing experience). Their analysis then adds the following six contingency factors.

1. In the institutional environment, the stronger the institutions' environment is in cultivating collaboration, the more beneficial power sharing is for the effectiveness of collaborative governance.
2. Different missions, the less exigent the mission accomplished by collaborative governance is, the more power sharing is for the effectiveness of collaborative governance.
3. The more voluntary (as opposed to hierarchical mandating) the type of collaborative governance is, the more beneficial power sharing is for the effectiveness of collaborative governance.
4. The less power-sharing experience participants have, the less beneficial power sharing is for the effectiveness of collaborative governance.
5. The more widely diffused power sources are, the more beneficial power sharing is for the effectiveness of collaborative governance.
6. The more acceptable the cost-benefit calculation is for participants, the more beneficial power sharing is for the effectiveness of collaborative governance.

Their contingency framework is based on two familiar approaches to studying organizations: institutional theory and resource dependency. The core institutional theory is based on the idea that organizations conform to a framework of social

142   *On Power and Operations in Collaboration*

norms, values, and taken-for-granted assumptions within their operating context. Resource dependency theory is based on the notion that organizational survival relies on an organization's ability to secure critical resources from the external environment. The interorganizational interdependencies are created by the needs of an organization to secure resources from the external environment. In effect, the model, which covers an extensive literature survey, focuses on the balance between power sharing, a core issue in collaborative management.

Finally, Ran and Qi (2018) offer a source of practical suggestions for operating in this collaboration environment. They are identified in Box 5.5 and emphasize guidance for practitioners when working with partners from other organizations.

Box 5.5   Practical Suggestions on Power Sharing

1. When participating in a collaboration, it is necessary for participants to evaluate the institutional environment outside the collaboration, such as the rigidity of regulations and rules that can control the participants' behaviors.
2. Understanding both individual organizational goals and common missions of the collaboration is necessary when sharing power between partners.
3. Improving the internal consent or legitimacy of the mandated collaborative network is significant for power sharing.
4. Choosing the partners who have positive previous experiences in power sharing with others is beneficial for an effective collaboration.
5. Be cautious about participating in a collaboration in which the partners' power sources are extremely asymmetric if you are willing to share more power with your partners.
6. Promoting the "outcome justice" and improving the participants' satisfaction with their benefits gained in collaboration are significant for promoting power sharing. As Huxham (2003, p. 420) indicated, practitioners need to apply any theoretical analysis contingently to guide their efforts in collaboration because "particular approaches to resolving issues are not necessarily transferable to other situations."

Source: Ran and Qi (2018, pp. 836–851)

Practitioners must tend to look at applying these guidelines "contingently" to guide their efforts because "particular approaches to resolving issues are not necessarily transferrable to other situations" (Huxham, 2003, p. 420; Bryson, Crosby, & Stone, 2006).

Seven Common Collaborative Barriers

There are interagency forces that operate "less naturally" to forge collaborative outcomes that emanate not from the nature of programs that are designed to encourage collaboration (professionalism, isolated public agencies, departmental separation, and low resource effort), but rather from the collaborative interactions themselves. Among them are an agency's turf protection, risk aversion, lost time and opportunity costs, human relations costs, the exertion of power by agencies and public resources hoarding, and public policy barriers.

When in a collaborative mode, agencies must simultaneously think of their own organizational concerns and those related to collaboration. For example, if the balance is entirely or too much in favor of the former, protection of agency turf can be a barrier. Bardach (1998, p. 164) defines turf as "the domain of problems, opportunities, and actions over which an agency exercises legitimate authority." Agencies can try to protect their turf by fashioning distinctive competencies, or managers may resist collaboration to protect their autonomy (Bardach, 1998; Orren & Skowronek, 2004). Thomas (2003, p. 35) suggests that

> agency managers (1) may be convinced that they know best, and therefore decide how to carry out agency tasks; (2) may seek to control one's own space to avert loss (or failure) in the new territory if it involves perceived loss of control; and (3) because autonomy reduces uncertainty, managers must be careful not to encourage too many threats to their hierarchy-based organizational environments. Turf can clearly block action.

In this way, the other seven common barriers identified in Box 5.6 are extended manifestations of turf maintenance in many ways.

Box 5.6   Seven Common Barriers to Collaboration

1. Agency turf protection: a collaborating agency's desire for risk aversion, lost internal time and financial resources, displacement of human resources, fear of the unknown, unwillingness to experiment.
2. Risk aversion: consensus-based actions lead to less than desirable results, avoiding sensitive political and costly solutions.
3. Lost time and opportunity costs: lost work and resources in the home organization, solution of human resources, lost time to organization and joint management.

144   *On Power and Operations in Collaboration*

4. Human relations cost: "pull" of time away from home organization, unfinished work at home, time involved in CP meetings and committees, unfinished work at home agency.
5. Power exertion/resistance: resistance to potential solutions, expanded resource commitments, norms and practices of other organizations to integrate, expand, and often waste administrative time.
6. Resource protection: long-term human relations, processing costs, and rare resources.
7. Policy and/or legal barriers: power exertion, prohibitions in the law, executive resistance, reluctance to commit resources upon negative interpretations, prosecution in law, service prohibitions, legally prosecuted activities and services.

Source: Robert Agranoff

Playing the political game involves more than the usual agency boundary questions. It combines extensive human interaction skills, technical knowledge, and interpersonal comfort in dealing with people. It can be learned somewhat, but is usually acquired with the various experiences of wins, losses, and standoffs. Box 5.7 tries a few author-inspired experience-based tips on playing the politics of collaborative management. Again, it is important to highlight that hierarchical and collaborative power are almost always distinct, although co-players need to make these distinctions in action. In CP, different aspects of power—especially knowledge-based and deliberative—are particularly relevant. Also, No. 7 in Box 5.7 is very important.

People approach politics differently, often from long-standing personal experiences and disputes, some of which are unrelated to the issue at hand. For example, one of the authors once found himself at an impasse over an agreement associated with a small-town 30-bed hospital where he worked part-time. It was a power struggle, then more than 30 years old, between local medical doctors and osteopathic physicians. Both had legally based hospital access rights and privileges, but they refused to collaborate. The unproductive result followed a deep dispute that carried over to local politics and the running of the city hospital. To a great degree, city politics were hospital politics—to such a degree that only one of the two town pharmacies filled their prescriptions. Local political party disputes took a backseat to hospital politics in the small town, although they were not "surface visible" but obvious in real action and to many townspeople. So bring your prescription to the "wrong" pharmacy, and one was "told" many times (despite it being in stock) that it had to be ordered for next-day delivery. The right pharmacy seemed to have the right stock for the right physician. So when it comes to politics, expect anything in the real world!

On Power and Operations in Collaboration 145

Box 5.7   Ten Tips on Playing the Political Game

1. There is no way that the politics part of CP can be transmitted to participants by operating manuals. Political sense is mostly intuitive and experience-based. The first step is to avoid mentally shutting off politics. They are present, and must be accounted for! One must sense them and be prepared to act in the face of political concerns, power moves, threats, opportunities, and deliberations. They are ignored at your peril.
2. Be conscious of the fact that home agency hierarchical power is not automatically transferable to collaborative situations in deliberations. Bosses in home organizations wield power but are not always bosses in collaborative processes.
3. Be aware of at least four types of power: agency, operational, knowledge-based, and deliberative. They are often the "core" of CP and will be conceptually and operationally manifested.
4. Power can be a facilitator or resistive force; in many ways, CP supports the "power to."
5. The common collaborative barriers to effective collaboration need to be understood as political and managerial forces.
6. Power is a neutral term regularly regarded as an inherently negative force, but it can be positive.
7. Expect anything! Politics comes at the process from any angle. For example, once in a serious set of interactive negotiations about the client process, a participant brought up the organization's need for used computers. That is completely out of context! The deliberators carefully sidetracked that discussion and got back to the main issue.
8. Be alert for longer-standing differences between agencies' and individuals' personal agendas and/or concerns brought into the deliberations. It may take work to deflect or channel them into a productive discussion.
9. Thus far, nothing has been said regarding partisan issues. A Republican or Democratic issue, whether national or local, may be part of the mix, even though it should not be. Normally, these issues are formally off the table, but they may have to be confronted, or a consensus will need to be reached to deflect or modify such issues.
10. Most CP issues and political concerns are beneath the surface or not formal, or not as obvious. But they are alive and real, often "behind the processing" between agencies and organizations.

Source: Robert Agranoff

Conclusion

This chapter offers a beginning—not an end—to understand the hidden and overt forms of power in CP. To work together, people from different entities are working out programs and services that cross 'agency/organization lines and dealing with the politics of the complexities of multiagency multiprogram involvement. Chapter 6 will offer suggestions for negotiation based on interactive multiagency processes that are rarely on the surface but are nonetheless there and quite real. Box 5.7 provides a useful summary of some ten experience tips for operating politically *within* collaboration across agencies and programs. In many ways, they are preludes to the process of negotiation among parties. Structure and process without hierarchy must find working substitutes, identified here as the core dimensions of collaborarchy with alternative bases of power: agency, operational, knowledge, and deliberation that can be potentially positive or negative CP forces. Subsequent analyses deal with specific situations from the field: stories of politics, barriers to solutions, and key political experiments and experiences. Together, these foci will hopefully extend an understanding of the power bases identified in this chapter.

References

Agranoff, R. (2003). *Leveraging networks: A guide for public managers working across organizations.* IBM Endowment for the Business of Government.

Agranoff, R. (2007). *Managing within networks: Adding value to public organizations.* Georgetown University Press.

Agranoff, R. (2012). *Collaborating to manage: A primer for the public sector.* Georgetown University Press.

Agranoff, R. (2016). The other side of managing in networks. In R. D. Margerum & C. J. Robinson (Eds.), *The challenges of collaboration in environmental governance: Barriers and responses* (pp. 81–107). Edward Elgar Publishing.

Agranoff, R. (2018). *Local governments in multilevel governance: The administrative dimension.* Lexington Books.

Agranoff, R., & McGuire, M. (2001). Big questions in public network management research. *Journal of Public Administration Research and Theory, 11*(3), 295–326.

Amsler, L. B. (2016). Collaborative governance: Integrating management, politics, and law. *Public Administration Review, 76*(5), 700–711.

Bardach, E. (1998). *Getting agencies to work together: The practice and theory of managerial craftsmanship.* Brookings Institution Press.

Bevir, M., & Rhodes, R. A. (2007). Decentred theory, change, and network governance. In E. Sørensen & J. Torfing (Eds.), *Theories of democratic network governance* (pp. 77–91). Palgrave Macmillan.

Bobker, G. (2009). The means do not justify the ends: A comment on CALFED. *Environmental Science & Policy, 12*(6), 726–728.

Bryson, J. M., Crosby, B. C., & Stone, M. M. (2006). The design and implementation of cross-sector collaborations: Propositions from the literature. *Public Administration Review, 66*, 44–55.

On Power and Operations in Collaboration   147

Burt, R. S. (1992). *Structural holes*. Harvard University Press.

Cheng, Y. (2009). Exploring the role of nonprofits in public service provision: Moving from coproduction to cogovernance. *Public Administration Review*, *79*(2), 203–214.

Chrislip, D. D., & Larson, C. E. (1994). *Collaborative leadership: How citizens and civic leaders can make a difference* (Vol. 24). Jossey-Bass.

Clegg, S. R., & Hardy, C. (1996). Conclusion: Representations. In S. R. Clegg, S. Clegg, & C. Hardy (Eds.), *Studying organization: Theory and method* (pp. 676–708). Sage.

Davenport, T. H., & Prusak, L. (2000). *Working knowledge: How organizations manage what they know*. Harvard Business School Press.

Edelenbos, J. (2005). Institutional implications of interactive governance: Insights from Dutch practice. *Governance*, *18*(1), 111–134.

Foucault, M. (1994). *Power*, edited by James D. Faubion. The Free Press.

Fung, A. (2003). Thinking about empowered participatory governance Archon Fung and Erik Olin Wright: *Deepening democracy. Institutional Innovations in Empowered Participatory Governance*, *4*(3).

Gofen, A. (2014). Mind the gap: Dimensions and influence of street-level divergence. *Journal of Public Administration Research and Theory*, *24*(2), 473–493.

Gray, B. (1989). *Collaborating: Finding common ground for multiparty problems*. Jossey Bass.

Hanemann, M., & Dyckman, C. (2009). The San Francisco bay delta: A failure of decision-making capacity. *Environmental Science & Policy*, *12*(6), 710–725.

Huxham, C. (2003). Theorizing collaboration practice. *Public Management Review*, *5*(3), 401–423.

Innes, J. E., & Booher, D. E. (1999). Consensus building and complex adaptive systems: A framework for evaluating collaborative planning. *Journal of the American Planning Association*, *65*(4), 412–423.

Klijn, E. H. (1996). Analyzing and managing policy processes in complex networks: A theoretical examination of the concept policy network and its problems. *Administration & Society*, 28(1), 90–119.

Klijn, E. H. (2001). Rules as institutional context for decision making in networks: The approach to postwar housing districts in two cities. *Administration & Society*, *33*(2), 133–164.

Koontz, T. M., Steelman, T. A., Carmin, J., Korfmacher, K. S., Moseley, C., & Thomas, C. W. (2004). *Collaborative environmental management: What roles for Government*. Washington, DC: Resources for Future.

Lejano, R. P., & Ingram, H. (2009). Collaborative networks and new ways of knowing. *Environmental Science & Policy*, *12*(6), 653–662.

Lipsky, M. (1980). *Street level bureaucracy: Dilemmas of the individual in public services*. Russell Sage Foundation.

Maynard-Moody, S. W., & Musheno, M. (2000). State agent or citizen agent: Two narratives of discretion. *Journal of Public Administration Research and Theory*, *10*(2), 329–358.

Maynard-Moody, S. W., & Musheno, M. (2003). *Cops, teachers, counselors: Stories from the front lines of public service*. University of Michigan Press.

McGuire, M., & Agranoff, R. (2014). Network management behaviors: Closing the theoretical gap. In R. Keast, M. P. Mandell, & R. Agranoff (Eds.), *Network theory in the public sector: Building new theoretical frameworks* (pp. 137–156). Routledge.,

Milward, H. B., & Provan, K. G. (1998). Principles for controlling agents: The political economy of network structure. *Journal of Public Administration Research and Theory*, *8*(2), 203–222.

Orren, K., & Skowronek, S. (2004). *The search for American political development*. Cambridge University Press.

O'Toole, Jr., L. J. (1997). Treating networks seriously: Practical and research-based agendas in public administration. *Public Administration Review*, *57*(1), 45–52.

148 *On Power and Operations in Collaboration*

O'Toole, Jr., L. J. (2015). Networks and networking: The public administrative agendas. *Public Administration Review, 75*(3), 361–371.

Radin, B. A., Agranoff, R., Bowman, A. O. M., Buntz, G. C., Ott, C. J., Romzek, B. S., & Wilson, R. H. (1996). *New governance for rural America: Creating intergovernmental partnerships.* University Press of Kansas.

Ran, B., & Qi, H. (2018). Contingencies of power sharing in collaborative governance. *The American Review of Public Administration, 48*(8), 836–851.

Reed, D. S. (2014). *Building the federal schoolhouse: Localism and the American education state.* Oxford University Press.

Rhodes, R. A. (1997). *Understanding governance: Policy networks, governance, reflexivity, and accountability.* Open University.

Rose, N., & Miller, P. (1992). Political power beyond the state: Problematics of government. *British Journal of Sociology,* 173–205.

Sørenson, E., & Torfing, J. (2005). The democratic anchorage of network governance. *Scandinavian Political Studies, 28*(3), 195–218.

Stoker, G., & Mossberger, K. (1994). Urban regime theory in comparative perspective. *Environment and Planning C: Government and Policy, 12*(2), 195–212.

Stone, C. (1989). *Regime politics.* University Press of Kansas.

Stone, C., Doherty, K., Jones, C., & Ross, T. (1999). Schools and disadvantaged. In C. Stone, K. Doherty, C. Jones, & T. Ross. *Urban problems and community development.* Washington, DC: Brooking Institute Press.

Thomas, C. W. (2003). *Bureaucratic landscapes: Interagency cooperation and the preservation of biodiversity.* MIT Press.

Triantafillou, P. (2016). Governmentality. In C. Ansell & J. Torfing (Eds.), *Handbook on theories of governance.* Edward Elgar.

Tullock, G. (1965). *The politics of bureaucracy.* Public Affairs Press.

Wagenaar, H. (2004). "Knowing" the rules: Administrative work as practice. *Public Administration Review, 64*(6), 643–656.

Wagenaar, H. (2011). *Meaning in action: Interpretation and dialogue in policy analysis.* ME Sharpe.

Weber, E. P. (1998). Successful collaboration: Negotiating effective regulations. *Environment: Science and Policy for Sustainable Development, 40*(9), 10–15.

Williams, W. (1980). *The implementation perspective: A guide for managing social service delivery programs.* University of California Press.

6 The Politics of It All

While not always visible, politics' "hidden hand" proves to be virtually everywhere in social connections. In many ways, the mechanisms of collaboration analyzed in this volume represent an operationalization of more or less formal means of coordination; they are mechanisms through which organizational connection may occur and exhibit "norms that bound the behavior of the actors involved" (Chisholm, 1992, p. 19). In CP, they involve the ultimate "coordination without hierarchy"; that is, politics and administration in collaborating.

Take the example of an agency that serves I/DD persons that wants to convert a large house to a small group home (6–8 persons) in an established neighborhood. In addition to considerable construction/remodeling, a key obstacle is almost always permitting and licensing. Sounds easy if the advocates follow a prescribed licensing procedure format and pay the required fees. Not so fast! Local zoning ordinances, neighborhood covenants, and neighborhood organizations whose members may well voice opposition are laden with politics opposed to any proposed "zoning variance." Some people normally express their concerns regarding the impact of noise, parking congestion, general appearance, and, most importantly, the fear of declining property values. Despite federal and state codes that prohibit various types of discrimination based on disability—e.g., those involved in the Americans with Disabilities Act (ADA) of 1990—there could very well be intense political opposition, despite the federal banning of such discrimination. The ADA of 1990 is a law that permeates through all government levels and impacts local and neighborhood actions. The impacts and actions related to ADA are characterized as "big P" politics, whereas focused city/neighborhood action is considered "small p" politics. ADA-related actions are politically alive at both levels, as in many CP situations.

While often buried in concerns related to governance, politics perpetually pervades collaborative processes as they unfold in the real world. The core issue is that politics are not as transparent as legal provisions, written standards, and regulations which are documented and easy to see. But they are there, too, regularly injected into the process but considerably less visible. For persons involved in collaborative administration, recognizing and confronting political moves or implicit political processes is part of the tacit knowledge that one needs to blend with our

DOI: 10.4324/9781003385769-6

150　*The Politics of It All*

other experiential knowledge, in this situation, applied to interagency collaboration. Indeed, politics of this nature are hard to teach: the best way to learn is from life experiences (van Meerkerk, Edelenbos, & Klijn, 2015; Nicholson-Crotty, 2005, 2009; Klijn & Skelcher, 2007).

This chapter focuses on the broader policy/program politics alive within collaboration. The heart of CP in this chapter will focus on institutions, combined with a "primer" on cooperative roles in politics, situations whereby power is highly dispersed. A discussion of agency building then leads to consideration of agency autonomy, and administrators' protection of "turf" is then raised. This is followed by more direct analysis of the politics of the more powerful or "big P" players, followed by the role of power as it unfolds within collaboration; that is, how "small p" politics are usually played out. Next, this process discussion carries to "interaction politics" as the chapter-opening example of zoning use situation depicts. These issues are very common concerns in engendering concerted actions that are as political as they are administrative.

Politics at the Core: Government

To understand the nature of CP and its varied actors, the involved parties in the collaboration process must grasp public agencies' core, active, or even leading role. Agranoff (2018, p. 90) provides the following overview of these roles.

> An overview of the potential roles that government agencies play in environmental management, for example, [is] as providers of various human, technical, and financial resources. At the core is the politics of government, meaning that the "sweeping influence that governmental institutions do leave their mark on how issues are defined, what resources are used or are available, the structure of collaborative process, and the outcomes that these endeavors produce" (Koontz et al., 2004, p. 170).

It is necessary to note that in terms of carrying out programs, very few groups or agencies are granted completely open "policy authority." However, most statutory issues and regulations cannot be easily avoided, so the politics of government follow along.

One CP study involving heavy doses of politics (see Chapter 1) is the California-based water quality network CALFED, which showed, in repeated situations, that the inherent or uneasy "interdependent" coexistence of informal approaches to CP results in political tensions. While the CALFED informal systems could progress on several dimensions, "the formal system retained the funding, the legal authority, and the perspective to intervene, provide approval, or simply allow the program to continue" (Innes, Connick, & Booher, 2007, p. 170). Therefore, even though government network partners represent their organizations in the collaboration and are responsible for enforcing rules, regulations, and guidelines, they may actually be

The Politics of It All   151

politically constrained in their opportunities to be flexible, which in turn may inhibit the collaborative processes (Agranoff, 2018). But achieving successful collaboration in some cases means that "agencies do not always give in to proactive opposition proposals, resist the advocacy of others, or at least fail to confirm problems and/or recognize certain issues that can block meaningful joint efforts" (p. 90). In collaboration, governmental actors' roles are often key, and "their influence in determining group structure and decision-making processes suggest that these individuals can largely determine the character of the collaboration" (Innes, Connick, & Booher, 2007, pp. 170–171). Such situations are normally "big P" political as well as legal-administrative.

At the local level, where CP really unfolds on concrete issues, it is important to come to the understanding that "policy and program decisions involve *communities* governed by various decision-making bodies (e.g., city councils, county commissions, metropolitan planning organizations, natural resources management districts, etc.)" (Agranoff, 2018, p. 91). However, in the final analysis, official policy decision-makers who are necessarily not collaborative participants make most of the applied "real government" decisions. For example, Jurian Edelenbos's (2005) study of "interactive governance" in five Dutch municipalities warns us to take into consideration the political realities of decision-making at the local level. He discovered that such projects frequently disregard the involvement and participation of local decision-makers who are impacted. Among the summary descriptions for council members were: "mostly ritual coordination," "politicians at a distance from the interactive process," "attention to procedure more than policy content," "no ties with the administrative system," and "politicians remained at a distance" (p. 127). As a result, in these local contexts, little attention was paid to existing institutions that clashed with local politics, i.e., the ordinary deliberative democracy that takes place at this level. "In this new kind of institutionalized action," Edelenbos adds, "collaborative initiatives must be in line with as many current decision points as possible; otherwise, a missing institutional link between the interactive process and the official decision-making process will emerge" (p. 127). Because so many decisions have intrinsically political undertones, failing to engage such ties in the collaborative process might result in high-risk political endeavors if essential decision-makers are effectively excluded from the process.

In addition, no matter how partisan or other power politics are involved, the administrator must also come to grips with important statutory-based rules that potentially impede serious attempts going beyond token coordination. Local zoning, as identified earlier, is a case in point. While some intensive political pressure could be exerted to change the zoning at stake, change then takes on political and economic overtones, as well as any citizen service concerns.

In the environmental arena, the EPA promulgated new rules in 2012 mandating that carbon dioxide (CO_2) levels fall below 2005 amounts by 2030, placing new constraints on states and localities. Some state agencies are being challenged in federal courts, while other states are writing their own standards, moving toward

152 *The Politics of It All*

these goals despite federal indifference. This has led to intense resistance, particularly in states led by Republican governors who have challenged (legally and politically) the right of the federal government to take such direct action that impacts states. That is why states currently act independently in the more open U.S. political system. In the end, a great deal of federal–state collaboration negotiation will be necessary to meet agreed targets. The process will undoubtedly be highly political yet respect the rules in some form (Kardish, 2014, p. 48). Ultimately, at local levels, collaborative rules need to be politically agreed to, and involved stakeholders are expected to abide by those rules, particularly in those common situations when the regulated have been involved in the cooperative processes that lead to rule adjustments (Weber, 2007).

Agency Politics

The practice of leaders improving the territory of the public organization they represent in agency building can also be regarded as a less visible political force to be understood. For example, the EPA has operated in several areas to bring down uncertainty and improve trust in rulemaking activities (Agranoff, 2018). Edward Weber describes the efforts for clean air by its assistant administrator, Bill Rosenberg, who balanced politics with principle, finding the sweet spot of compromise (Weber, 2007). Such actions, however, do not always come out as positive and thus cannot always be relied upon.

A related political dimension is the turf-protecting behavior of many agency managers. For example, Craig Thomas (2003) defined agency turf as the protection of one's own territory or domain in his study of interagency cooperation in biodiversity. Turf imperialism can easily impede collaboration. More turf can be better (Bardach, 1998, p. 177) when embarking on CP from the manager's perspective. For example, in his study of cooperation in biodiversity, "line managers often are convinced that they know best and therefore should decide how to carry out agency tasks, develop programs, and achieve missions" (Thomas, 2003, p. 35). Similarly, Sean Nicholson-Crotty emphasizes that "the role played by bureaucratic competition" demonstrates how administrators attempt to influence policy. Turf protection is considered a dark side of the collaboration phenomenon in that interaction-based results can be resisted and hindered, even by top-level administrations.

Multistakeholder process agreements are autonomous government agencies' adaptation for collaboration between turf protection and building. According to Daniel Carpenter's historical study of bureaucratic autonomy, this is not an easy task to engage in. He defines autonomy as acting according to the wishes of agency administrators, to which politicians and organized interests defer. Carpenter believes that agencies can achieve political legitimacy, knowledge, efficiency, and moral protection by establishing a reputation for competence, efficiency, and moral protection. In these circumstances, elected officials give administrators more leeway while deferring to the agency's wishes (Carpenter, 2001).

The Politics of It All 153

Cross-case research by Thomas Koontz and his team suggests that government officials take leadership positions at the core of collaboration, "helping participants be innovative, providing information, securing resources, or carrying forward implementation plans" (Koontz et al, 2004, pp. 160–161). On the negative side, agency structures established to encourage more traditional methods without high-level government forums or requirements to collaborate, as well as ambiguous federal regulations, might be limiting political considerations (Agranoff, 2018). As a result, they act as special political forces "hidden behind the administration and limit outcomes favorable to cooperation" (p. 93).

The case of the Darby Partnership in central Ohio, examined by the Koontz group, also belongs to 14 network studies of one of the authors of this volume (Agranoff, 2007, pp. 52–55). The Darby Partnership represents an example of a network that is quite constrained in collaborative scope, with "a limited agenda of actions, all primarily geared to listening to partner reports at quarterly meetings" (p. 53). In essence, it is a primary information and dissemination organizational structure, clerically supported by the Nature Conservancy of Central Ohio. In operational circumstances like these, the autonomy of bureaucracies, agency domains, and agency implementation are not particularly threatened by collaborative management activities (Agranoff, 2018).

There is another political consideration related to managing any collaborative governance project. For example, over a decade ago, Michael McGuire framed the important question for collaborative governance scholarship, "Do the actions of a manager contribute to the effectiveness of multiorganizational arrangements, and if so, how?" (McGuire, 2002, p. 600). This touches on some political and administrative aspects of collaboration (Agranoff, 2012, 2018). Based on existing research, we know that governing networks do not just suddenly become "self-sufficient, automated entities" (p. 93); "There is both an operational and strategic character to networks that depend largely on the political and managerial actions of managers" (McGuire, 2002, p. 600). He identified the four types of previously mentioned collaborative interaction: activation, mobilization, framing, and synthesizing. They can prove to be as political as managerial and occur at any process stage. They touch on the many differences in what managers do, from simple organizational goal achievement to nettlesome political process concerns. In many ways, these operational forces all inevitably become enmeshed in politics.

For example, a study by the authors of this volume and Michael McGuire (Kolpakov, Agranoff, & McGuire, 2016) of the STEM Metro School network, comprising 16 school districts in central Ohio (see Chapter 3), was originally planned to admit the most gifted and talented from the region. However, initial school board/superintendent political resistance over "creaming" and removing these students from their home school district scoring base led to near-unanimous political resistance to including only the most gifted. Politically, this led to a more random potential student draw. It clearly was a purely political settlement (see Chapter 8). Moreover, Milward and Provan (1998) have demonstrated that collaborative endeavors like

154   *The Politics of It All*

networks have different perspectives that can be political and managerial. Their "costs" may bear the need to satisfy various concerns, goals, and success expectations. They can be modest, as in the case of the previously menitoned Darby Partnership in central Ohio, or more direct and highly operational like those of Metro School. They both suggest that politics might be both facilitators and constraining forces; clearly, they are political and managerial in nature.

In a very interesting article on administrative politics, Feldman and Khademian (2007) encourage participation by practicing the politics of encouraging inclusion by promoting information with political, technical, and local perspectives in order to create "communities of participation."

Box 6.1   Public Managers' Role in Collaborative Inclusion

1. Public managers incorporate all of those who manage people and programs who need to encourage inclusion as a part of governance.
2. Three foundational perspectives are all important in the formulation, adaptation, and implementation of plans and programs for promoting inclusion: political, scientific, or technical, and the local or experience-based. All are core perspectives.
3. The goal is to create commonalities of participation among different interests in solving problems, based on informational work that identifies and disseminates information about different ways of understanding policy problems.
4. In this process (of multiple contacts), relational work creates connections between people in ways that legitimize perspectives and creates empathy for participants.
5. The primary role of the public manager is engaging the public impacted by policy by exacting opportunities for participation, as well as facilitating public deliberation and decision-making.
6. Inclusive managers need to engage participants in ways that enable them to learn new ways that enable people to work together.
7. In an inclusive community of participation representatives of the political, technical, and local domains (and groups that represent them) will all be seen as having a legitimate role to play as participants in a joint effort to address a problem effectively.
8. In this process, managers will be undertaking two types of work: *informational*, relating to understanding policy issues, and *relational*, creating connections between people who need to work together.

Source: Feldman and Khademian (2007, pp. 305–324)

The Politics of It All   155

As Box 6.1 indicates, in this process are boundary collaborating experiences among different persons engaging in joint activities that create a sense of community. It also promotes working across interests and positions, encouraging people to feel connected. While challenging even diverse interests and resources, "public managers, however, have the ability to make communities of participation more inclusive" (Feldman & Khademian, 2007, p. 319).

The Biggest Politics: Ideas and Big Money

Somewhat outside the realm of topics discussed here and in the most typical undergraduate college classes is to go beyond the mere mention of the role of big money in politics. One journalistic treatment of this area is Jane Mayer's *Dark Money* (2017), a book on the influence led by the wealthy Koch brothers. The "energy wealthy" Kansas brothers spawned an emergent conservative political donor/operatives network. Mayer describes their overall approach:

> the Kochs waged a long and remarkable battle of ideas. They subsidized networks of seemingly unconnected think tanks and academic programs and spawned advocacy groups to make their arguments in the national political debate. They hired lobbyists to push their interests in Congress and operatives to create synthetic grassroots groups to give their movement political momentum on the ground. In addition, they financed legal groups and judicial junkets to press their cases in the courts. Eventually, they added to this a private political machine that rivaled and threatened to subsume, the Republican Party. Much of this activism was cloaked in secrecy and presented as philanthropy, leaving almost no money trail that the public could trace. But cumulatively it formed as one of their operatives boasted in 2015, a *"fully integrated network."*
>
> (p. 6, emphasis added)

Taking advantage of the Supreme Court's *Citizens United vs. Federal Elections Commission* decision in 2010, a ruling that overturned nearly 100 years of restrictions on union and corporate spending on election campaigns, big money moved in. The big politics of ideas flourished with the network of wealthy donors who could now use outside groups as donation conduits technically outside of donor organizations. In many cases, wealthy activists chose philanthropy as their preferred attack mode. The rich, according to Mayer, create a new generation of hyper-political private foundations. Their aim, she concludes, is to invest in ideology like venture capitalists, leveraging their fortunes for "maximum strategic impact" (p. 462). Given the *Citizens United* decision, most of these efforts are largely invisible to the public.

"Big money" can influence politics on both sides of the partisan or issue fences. There are also wealthy progressives on the other side. Examples include George Soros and Thomas Steyer, who spend large sums on liberal causes. These concerns are not normally on the front lines of CP on both sides, but their existence and

156 *The Politics of It All*

roles need to be recognized. Also, there are wealthy "benefactors" of politics at the state and sometimes local levels of various geographic locations of certain issues. For example, a prominent Minnesota family that became wealthy through a state-franchised wholesale liquor business contributed generously and regularly to the coffers of the Democratic–Farmer–Labor Party (the state's affiliate of the Democratic Party), partially out of ideological beliefs and holding on to protective state legislation of liquor sales in the state of Minnesota. Over the years, supporting the family's liquor interests became "the price" of financing progressive issues, most important for the DFL operation. On many sides of cases, these increasingly notable political actors are usually present somewhere in political equations, locally, state, and nationally.

The "Big P" of Politics

In CP, it must be seen that "engagement of public and political world as one essential dimension to build collaborative capacity," a frequently overlooked but virtually ever-present premise (Weber & Khademian, 2008, p. 447). Engagement among the tiers and in the government sphere is set against the empirical reality of the most complex decision-making premises: the importance of politics at the core as decisions are made in many different places. Koppenjan, Koppenjan, and Klijn (2004) identify the role of elected political office holders, who first see the need to weigh interests and confront conflicting values and whose judgments most often ultimately prevail and are ultimately accountable. Despite key collaborative and/or network deliberations, they are at the forefront of normal political decisions. Decision-making capacity—or the lack thereof—is part of the larger stakes of politics that pervade attempts to forge or hinder collaboration.

Another consideration for policy observers is that political networking is necessary for collaboration, although it is not typically linked to political parties, government offices, or administration (Agranoff, 2012, 2018). "A political network needs the agency to coordinate activities and allow the resources as well as provide network support functions" and also to follow with implementing activities (Margerum, 2011, pp. 299–300; see also Fullerton, 2009). Failure or inability to address these larger political concerns—as in the previously mentioned case of a Dutch study of the need to involve local decision-makers (Edelenbos, 2005)—are indeed the big political forces that can facilitate or inhibit real action, as in the CAL-FED network introduced in Chapter 1.

"Big P" politics includes not only understanding the positions of elected officials, taking those positions into consideration, and attempting to address their concerns. It also requires acknowledging that some positions are so entrenched that it would be nearly impossible to bring certain interests to the table (Agranoff, 2018). For example, suppose states struggle to meet EPA-mandated vehicle and large-building emission regulations. In that case, some coal and utility interests will simply refuse to participate in processes that result in a significant compromise to their

The Politics of It All   157

fundamental interests. Instead, they are more inclined to shun institutionalized discussion and issue solving in favor of "playing outside" in lobbying and/or litigation.

As one can see, in these "big P" situations, most interests prove to not be interested in working together or among themselves. This is really "big P" politics, as opposed to "small p" politics, in collaboration by adjusting more minor program adjustments that involve all of the working organizations and interests involved in—or potentially affected by—any decision at all. For example, in baseball parlance, they apply major league versus minor league politics. "Big P" politics" is introduced in Box 6.2.

Box 6.2   About "big P" Politics

1. Recognize and discuss the larger issues of political progress that drive the need for collaboration but realize that a collaborative group of non-power wielding operatives are not usually able to use CP to solve the problem. It may well be in the scope of decision of higher-level government officials.
2. To the extent possible, it will be essential to inform and involve local and regional decision-makers in the collaborative processes that you and your colleagues may be involved. Their support down the line could be critical.
3. Allow the power dynamics of the involved organizations and interests to help guide the degree or depth with which your collaborative operates. The range of potential solution-seeking is considerable, from simply meeting to exchange actions taken by each participating organization to legally authorized planning and decision-making.
4. Avoid "tilting at windmills" by your local collaborative taking on big-picture problems that are to be solved only by nationwide or state government processes. Recognizing these "big P" "key changes" may probably be enough at local levels.
5. Avoid "power plays" with the most powerful whereby the chances of success are minimal. Your group will most often lose and drain away collaborative energy.
6. Unless a particular collaborative body wishes to be informed about larger picture issues, do not waste critical time-based resources on the larger policy/administrative changes. To do so may drive away active problem-solvers.
7. Find reliable informants on how the larger related issues impact your group and use their expertise to maintain a base of data/information/knowledge.
8. Wherever possible, use briefs or short "fact sheets" from people or groups with areas of expertise to keep the other members of the collaborative and public officials informed.

Source: Robert Agranoff

158   *The Politics of It All*

"Big P" politics attracts other known and powerful actors, defined by Agranoff (2018) as "heavy hitters" who exert their influence in respective areas. For example, in the case of rural development, high-level political actions incorporate far more than the usual working interests: soil conservation boards and districts, land grant extension services, and federal and state agricultural agencies. Core agricultural interest groups (e.g., Farm Bureau), farm supply cooperatives, conservation district board members, associated groups, and involved community leaders and farmers are all part of the greater political battle. These forces can—and do—play "big P" politics in rural development. As a result, because of their primary interest, the great forces' interests and the situation are inextricably linked (Radin et al., 1996).

When power is viewed as invincible, and things never change, situations operate in favor of those who benefit from the status quo, according to Paul Steinberg's (2015) analysis of environmental rule revisions. Dissenters are discouraged from mobilizing for change by the impression of invincibility. This form of reluctance is part of the power game, in which control is exercised by setting the game's rules or those who become involved in decision-making that augments legitimate interests. Alternatively, power is tangible in a case of a group, shaping the needs, wants, desires, and aspirations of others. This applies to CP transactions since they depend on the type of power and strategic games played by the parties involved.

For example, to Steinberg, "Those of us who assume that power is unassailable are controlled and manipulated with great efficiency because we impose constraints on ourselves, relieving those in power of the burden of responding to a coordinate challenge" (p. 55). He concludes that "the possession of power by any one person or group is potentially temporary, and the possibilities for change are of and of as alternate paths to change as possible" (p. 55).

Gerry Stoker concludes that politics, such as CP, is valued as a tool of social coordination. Specifically, he describes three reasons for valuing CP: (1) it allows people to make choices beyond individualism and recognizes others' concerns; (2) it is based on flexibility and is a way to overcome uncertainty; and (3) politics can be used to move beyond the base distribution of benefits to help establish social production processes (2006, p. 47). Concerns regarding CP are "a natural byproduct of balancing governability with multiple tiers and horizontal complexity through multi-organization collaborative action and all of their own external accountability" (Kallis, Kiparsky, & Norgaard, 2009, p. 638).

"Small p" Politics: Advocacy and Political Moves

The most direct force in "small p" politics is to regard it as part of the work of CP in the real world. Instead of dealing within the hierarchy, it works within and across organizational boundaries (Agranoff, 2017). For example, as mentioned in Chapter 1, the Medicaid HCBS waiver prohibited federal reimbursement for family-based care in clients' homes for decades. The reason was quite clear: the federal agency and the states were afraid of the massive opportunities for a "rip off" of funds for

The Politics of It All   159

services that were hard to substantiate. Years of local to state to federal complaints and resolutions ultimately led to a relaxation of the home/family care reimbursement under certain defined conditions and restraints. (Actually, a small proportion of HCBS clients are part of this home care waiver program.) It ultimately came to life as a result of literally thousands of "small" political concerns and issues, that is, *"small p" politics at work*, particularly by family members' observations, complaints, and mini lobbying. Agencies and state organization delegates mobilized families and hammered away thousands of complaints about the rule. It was ultimately allowed under limited conditions as specified and negotiated. In the end, it accommodated "small p" politics that were/are regularly played out in the world of collaboration.

Box 6.3   "Small p" Politics Experiential Tips

1. In collaborative transactions, be aware that the authority pattern is not only non-hierarchical but could well shift from issue to issue and program to program as concerns of discussion change over time.
2. As the old *Saturday Night Live* "Coffee Talk" sketch line used to go, "Talk amongst yourselves" (e.g., "The New Deal was neither new nor a deal!"). In doing so, be respectful of others' mission, outlooks, and power bases.
3. Respect home organization hierarchical and specialist positions, but do not let it dominate your or the group's thinking.
4. Listen with eye contact when old agency lines of resistance are carried forward. You perhaps have heard them many times, but not necessarily in this situation. Respect for position is an important verity for collaboration.
5. Constantly be on the search for information data and, ultimately, knowledge that will facilitate the joint process.
6. Work toward the broadening of collective knowledge related to the problem and potential solution.
7. Ask knowledge-based questions from relevant sources that broaden the knowledge base in non-threatening manner. Expect some to be protected. Recognize that to supply some information may be beyond the ability to deliver under statutory prohibition or agency privacy policies.
8. Work together to broaden the collective knowledge base: what is known, what is not known but can be investigated, and what is impossible to know.
9. If internal organizational confidentiality is raised as a knowledge-building barrier, do not necessarily give up. Ask for a hypothetical situation or at least probe the level at which some kinds of data can be analyzed.
10. Try to avoid contesting every issue that comes to the table. Let some minor concerns pass! There is normally ample opportunity to debate

160 *The Politics of It All*

the more important concerns. Moreover, group good will is fueled by participants letting some go.

11. Practice consensus building, group identity-building and feelings of success by recognizing and celebrating small accomplishments.
12. Later challenges—particularly the big ones—may have to be set off until the collaborative has some "small wins" under their collective belts.
13. Do your agreed and expected between-meetings "homework." To not produce in time lets down colleagues, slows processes, and detracts from your home organization's reputation.
14. Where participating and deciding in a small work group, bear in mind that agreement/proposal may not be the final word. There is often more to come.
15. Constantly brief the proceedings of your collaborative "external" work with the home organization, not on details but on general direction. You are the conduit from the collaborative to your organization.
16. Expect failures, as well as victories, and perhaps move factors onto launch, proceed, agree, etc.
17. Respect confidences shared by other participants.
18. If the discussion/process pushes into larger political issues and are raised to another decision level, they may have to be deferred or raised at a higher executive/elected official level.

Source: Robert Agranoff

To begin, most CP efforts are at the core of collaboration in some large or small way in every behavioral-operational direction. Whereas there is no extant formula for political success, a number of the experiential touchpoints in Box 6.3 may become important to keep in mind. In many ways, the "small p" represents the political dimensions of working personally and politically. One or more of these issues may be confronted. Most important, it reflects the collective work of many organizational delegates. It is much more than "grind it out" committee work. CP involves working politically and often on an interactive basis for given purposes while representing a common interest of an organization/members or public agency involved in joint problem-solving. In this game, one is both a delegate of one's own organization and an agent of agreement or some form of collective change. Power flows are dual: from the organization represented and within the individually linked collaboration resulting from the process. It is thus a more complex but "dually realistic" form of power sharing arising out of organizational and operational power.

Cultural theory (CT) is one interesting way to understand "small p" collaborative relationships and their politics. It is based on the idea that the paradox of collaboration is that it is basically people—not organizations—engaged in CP.

The Politics of It All 161

"Collaboration is viewed largely as an institutional phenomenon in public sector research, even though individual actors make it happen" (Gazley, 2010, p. 275). One guide for action in CT suggests that the clash of cultures, based on traditions brought into the mix of interactions from participating agencies/organizations, can be important facilitating or limiting factors. For example, the previously mentioned CALFED studies revealed the huge differences between representatives of large water users and those of conservation interests. Christopher Weare, Paul Lichterman, and Nicole Esparza (2014) analyze CT from a collaborative perspective, concluding that divergent perspectives are manifested by the expression of actors' cultural biases or deep core beliefs that cannot be otherwise explained by instrumental rationality (p. 611). The authors conclude:

Cultural theory builds on a simple but powerful insights: The social relationships within which individuals are embedded generate predictable cultural biases, perspectives on how the world does and should operate, and their preferences for how to live in that world, and these biases, in turn, tend to support and sustain their extant set of social relationships.

(p. 612)

According to Weare, Lichterman, and Esparza, CT has not been widely used as a powerful theoretical concept and can be applied for analyzing the processes of collaboration. However, it is one way to explain how politics are at the core of collaboration. Clearly, it reminds us that people within organizations actually do the work to collaborate. To the extent that cultural differences and the clash of cultures impede the interactive process, they must be considered. CP can then be thought of as a potential and/or actual political force.

Concerns about "small p" go considerably deeper than interagency power dynamics or personal dealings. It clearly goes beyond what is sometimes called "petty politics." Rather, they are related to political dimensions intertwined with the identified "big" issues of power, process, and operational barriers (Agranoff, 2018). For example, Brower and Abolafia (1997) once concluded that lower-level bureaucrats engaged in political moves related to their pursuits of identity improvisational actions. In these situations, "individual identity, self-esteem, and career orientation became the stakes for political action" (p. 307). Whereas most collaboration literature extols the merits of cooperative action as a power leveler, power is plainly unequal in practice, in various real-world settings, raising not just concerns about power as a force in governance. Failure to recognize its impact on collaborative efforts— let alone any constraints of legal authority, resource differentials, and interdependence—may be a detriment to those involved. According to Roderick Rhodes, these forces are a component of the real world of power differentials (1981). Power is "exercised by stronger partners over others who have less power under the facade of confidence and language of cooperation" (Clegg & Hardy, 1996, p. 679). Beyond partner power, power processing within CP includes a multifaceted image, a sort of

162 *The Politics of It All*

three-dimensional power of choice-making, non-decision-making, and meaning-creation. As actors balance what Angel Saz-Carranza refers to as "the paradox of balancing unity and diversity," network-building "power" to influence deliberative progress or establish a collective policy as actors balance what Saz-Carranza refers to as "the paradox of balancing unity diversity" (2012, pp. 100–101).

Collaboration overall must often deal with one or more mostly "small p" power–related disincentives to collaborate. One of the best such accountings is by Barbara Gray (1989), who identifies six different types of power-related CP deterrents:

> (1) institutional disincentives, for example, the concerns of certain organizations, particularly by voluntary NGOs, that mediated negotiation will dilute their core missions; (2) long-standing or historical issues that hark back to past bitter adversarial interactive interactions; (3) concerns for loss of powerbase in a partnership, particularly those in the mix with minority or less powerful positions; (4) differing risk perceptions, such as over the stakes involved in yielding hard-fought interests and positions; (5) technical complexity issues, for example in environmental management having to work within incomplete ecosystem knowledge and/or disagreement over scientific findings; and (6) resistant political and institutional cultures, for example, the previously mentioned relevance of agencies to see negotiated agreements as not feasible and desirable alternatives.
>
> (1989, pp. 247–254)

If these power issues are successfully recognized and managed, "there may be more "at the table" points of convincing interests in engaging a power-related discourse" (Agranoff, 2018, p. 99). As subsequent chapters illustrate, they might include establishing shared tasks, initial agreements on ground rules, self-organizing as opposed to externally imposed structures, use of high-quality research and information, and continuous trust-building (Bryson, Crosby, & Stone, 2006). All are useful tools in the "small p" of CP.

Network studies in collaborative processes have identified distinctive power dimensions, as introduced in Chapter 5. They also manifest "small p" politics. As specified, four different types of operational power emerged in one of the authors' network studies (Agranoff, 2018). Agency power is first defined as "playing the power dependence game using collaborative processes, utilizing an organization's legal responsibilities and mission-related resources" (p. 100). Second, operational power, "games," and internal roles performed by organizations define internal behaviors within the collaborative endeavor. The third type of power is knowledge-based power, in which technical professionals combine their expertise, experiences, and investigations to give frameworks of understanding that can lead to the following steps. Fourth, deliberative power is developed as new technical information is offered and new opportunities emerge from talks, discussions, meetings, and multiparty interactions (Agranoff, 2018).

These "small p" power bases help to define and understand collaborative processing. The fourth, or deliberative, power dimension is perhaps the least understood but is essential to comprehending the complexity of power relations in the process of collaboration. It is key to understanding the political potential in collaboration. Conceptually, it originates from the urban regime theory or the social production or power of deliberation model of Clarence Stone (1989), which was mentioned in Chapter 5. This model is further modified by Stone and his associates (1999) to include the concept of an urban political order as a cluster of evolving relationships (Stone, 2010). Also, it involves recent work on collaborative policy innovation, whereby policy-makers interact with organizations that will potentially implement these policies, when problem searching takes place at later stages. These deliberative interactions demonstrate interactive power in action, as the parties involve advanced searches for solutions on a joint basis. Finally, some deliberative interactions address the most intractable problems—e.g., natural resource use versus conservation, agricultural chemicals versus their non-use—and are approached through these means. These experiments have particularly been undertaken in Denmark (Ansell, Sørensen, & Torfing, 2017).

The types of internal power of these mentioned collaborative operations can be considered part of understanding "small p" politics as core potential facilitators or inhibitors of most activity. Once the actors sit down to participate in the collaborative processes, it is evident that the lack of agency support for specific outcomes: supporting their rules and games, adequate technical information, carelessly managed strategies, and breakdowns in debates are process inhibitors of a "small p" political nature (Agranoff, 2018). The lack of one or more "power to" in the urban regime conceptual framework—for example, the inability to combine knowledge into proposed and workable collaborative solutions, the inability to identify the most practical course(s) of action, or the inability to deal with emerging power rebalancing or significant changes in the configuration of resource dependency—can all be notable political process inhibitors (Agranoff, 2018). On the contrary, the opposite process/interactive conditions can be facilitators. Either direction, they are part of the political process dynamics.

As the dynamics of intercollaborative politics become overwhelming, the experience-based suggestions relayed in Box 6.3 extend the understanding of these important processes to many real-world experiences. They suggest that process is key, as is listening and mutual understanding or mutual agreement based on shared knowledge and possible interest-based neutral discovery.

Conclusion

This is hardly all there is to say about how politics pervades collaboration, but it encompasses some of the core of a broad and often hidden dimension. The practitioner of collaboration obviously cannot go at it alone. Joint concerns mean that others must be deeply involved in the management and with other organizations, technologies, ideologies, and approaches. They should be at the table, and their political side must be seen. They must also be brought in a way that simply or

164 *The Politics of It All*

together somehow they help reach a form of consensus without resorting to raw voting, majority rule, or another form of raw force. Collaboration is force-avoiding. It brings together different people, occupations, delegated specialists, ideas, interests, professional approaches, and much more. Somehow, their contributions must be sorted out legally, interpersonally, technically, and in many other ways. One way is to acknowledge and try to understand and deal with its politics in all forms. Chapter 7 will continue illustrating politics as experience or what can be learned about politics from collaborative research from the field.

References

Agranoff, R. (2007). *Managing within networks: Adding value to public organizations.* Georgetown University Press.

Agranoff, R. (2012). *Collaborating to manage: A primer for the public sector.* Georgetown University Press.

Agranoff, R. (2017). *Crossing boundaries for intergovernmental management.* Georgetown University Press.

Agranoff, R. (2018). *Local governments in multilevel governance: The administrative dimension.* Lexington Books.

Ansell, C., Sørensen, E., & Torfing, J. (2017). Improving policy implementation through collaborative policymaking. *Policy & Politics, 45*(3), 467–486.

Bardach, E. (1998). *Getting agencies to work together: The practice and theory of managerial craftsmanship.* Brookings Institution Press.

Brower, R. S., & Abolafia, M. Y. (1997). Bureaucratic politics: The view from below. *Journal of Public Administration Research and Theory, 7*(2), 305–331.

Bryson, J. M., Crosby, B. C., & Stone, M. M. (2006). The design and implementation of cross-sector collaborations: Propositions from the literature. *Public Administration Review, 66*, 44–55.

Carpenter, D. (2001). *The forging of bureaucratic autonomy: Reputations, networks, and policy innovation in executive agencies, 1862–1928* (Vol. 173). Princeton University Press.

Chisholm, D. (1992). *Coordination without hierarchy: Informal structures in multiorganizational systems.* University of California Press.

Clegg, S. R., & Hardy, C. (1996). Conclusion: Representations. In S. R. Clegg, S. Clegg, & C. Hardy (Eds.), *Studying organization: Theory and method* (pp. 676–708). Sage.

Edelenbos, J. (2005). Institutional implications of interactive governance: Insights from Dutch practice. *Governance, 18*(1), 111–134.

Feldman, M. S., & Khademian, A. M. (2007). The role of the public manager in inclusion: Creating communities of participation. *Governance, 20*(2), 305–324.

Fullerton, D. (2009). CALFED: Tinkering at the edges. *Environmental Science & Policy, 12*(6), 733–736.

Gazley, B. (2010). Improving collaboration research by emphasizing the role of the public manager. In E. O'Leary, D. M. Van Slyke, & S. Kim (Eds.), *The future of public administration around the world: The Minnowbrook perspective.* Georgetown University Press.

Gray, B. (1989). *Collaborating: Finding common ground for multiparty problems.* Jossey Bass.

Innes, J. E., Connick, S., & Booher, D. (2007). Informality as a planning strategy: Collaborative water management in the CALFED Bay-Delta Program. *Journal of the American Planning Association, 73*(2), 195–210.

The Politics of It All   165

Kallis, G., Kiparsky, M., & Norgaard, R. (2009). Collaborative governance and adaptive management: Lessons from California's CALFED Water Program. *Environmental Science & Policy, 12*(6), 631–643.

Kardish, C. (2014). The carbon rebellion. *Governing, 28*(1), 44–48.

Klijn, E. H., & Skelcher, C. (2007). Democracy and governance networks: Compatible or not? *Public Administration, 85*(3), 587–608.

Kolpakov, A., Agranoff, R., & McGuire, M. (2016). Understanding interoperability in collaborative network management: The case of Metro High School. *Journal of Health Science, 4*(10), 318–332.

Koontz, T. M., Steelman, T. A., Carmin, J., Korfmacher, K. S., Moseley, C., & Thomas, C. W. (2004). *Collaborative environmental management: What roles for Government. Washington,* DC: Resources for Future.

Koppenjan, J. F. M., Koppenjan, J., & Klijn, E. H. (2004). *Managing uncertainties in networks: A network approach to problem-solving and decision making.* Psychology Press.

Margerum, R. D. (2011). *Beyond consensus: Improving collaborative planning and management.* MIT Press.

Mayer, J. (2017). *Dark money: The hidden history of the billionaires behind the rise of the radical right.* Anchor Books.

McGuire, M. (2002). Managing networks: Propositions on what managers do and why they do it. *Public Administration Review, 62*(5), 599–609.

Milward, H. B., & Provan, K. G. (1998). Principles for controlling agents: The political economy of network structure. *Journal of Public Administration Research and Theory, 8*(2), 203–222.

Nicholson-Crotty, J. (2009). The stages and strategies of advocacy among nonprofit reproductive health providers. *Nonprofit and Voluntary Sector Quarterly, 38*(6), 1044–1053.

Nicholson-Crotty, S. (2005). Bureaucratic competition in the policy process. *Policy Studies Journal, 33*(3), 341–361.

Radin, B. A., Agranoff, R., Bowman, A. O. M., Buntz, G. C., Ott, C. J., Romzek, B. S., & Wilson, R. H. (1996). *New governance for rural America: Creating intergovernmental partnerships.* University Press of Kansas.

Rhodes, R. A. W. (1981). *Control and power in central-local government relations.* Routledge.

Saz-Carranza, A. (2012). The quest for public value. *Public Administration Review, 72*(1), 152–153.

Steinberg, P. F. (2015). *Who rules the Earth?: How social rules shape our planet and our lives.* Oxford University Press.

Stoker, G. (2006). Public value management: A new narrative for networked governance. *The American Review of Public Administration, 36*(1), 41–57.

Stone, C. N. (1989). *Regime politics.* University Press of Kansas.

Stone, C. N. (2010). *Critical urban studies: New directions.* SUNY Press.

Stone, C. N., Doherty, K., Jones, C., & Ross, T. (1999). Schools and disadvantaged. In C. Stone, K. Doherty, C. Jones, & T. Ross. *Urban problems and community development.* Brooking Institute Press.

Thomas, C. W. (2003). *Bureaucratic landscapes: Interagency cooperation and the preservation of biodiversity.* MIT Press.

Van Meerkerk, I., Edelenbos, J., & Klijn, E. H. (2015). Connective management and governance network performance: The mediating role of throughput legitimacy: Findings from survey research on complex water projects in the Netherlands. *Environment and Planning C: Government and Policy, 33*(4), 746–764.

Weare, C., Lichterman, P., & Esparza, N. (2014). Collaboration and culture: Organizational culture and the dynamics of collaborative policy networks. *Policy Studies Journal, 42*(4), 590–619.

Weber, E. P. (2007). *Pluralism by the rules: Conflict and cooperation in environmental regulation.* Georgetown University Press.

Weber, E. P., & Khademian, A. M. (2008). Wicked problems, knowledge challenges, and collaborative capacity builders in network settings. *Public Administration Review, 68*(2), 334–349.

7 Academic Studies of Collaborative Politics and Management

Effective operation in collaborative politics and management now includes more than reliance on reaction, instinct, and experience related to program-to-program or agency-to-agency interaction. To the extent possible, it also consists of applying research knowledge in ways similar to studies in other areas, which can blend previous outlooks and experiences to solve problems in the field. Increasingly, that involves the transformation of "facts," findings, and experiences into informed political, technical, and strategic decisions. For example, this is clearly the case regarding research on cooperative federalism, as policy research on the long program implementation chains found in these studies provides much insight into the stages of politics within multiple collaborative interactions (Agranoff, 2017; Wright, 1988). This chapter highlights some of this research knowledge describing management challenges faced by public and nonprofit organizations involved in these forms of collaboration. For example, in the United States, cooperative federalism study has broadened over the years to include intergovernmental relations that include the patterns, strategies, programs, and other means of linking programs across levels in a system of overlapping rather than compartmentalized powers (Agranoff & Radin, 2015), in what is known now as an "inclusive" model of federalism.

The complexities of CP operating among so many programs, participating government agencies, and NGOs has led to the need for management of those programs that often work in a networked area of service delivery by federal–state regulatory bodies, bringing on the emergence of intergovernmental management (IGM), which has become the routine operations of modern government. While this chapter is by no means a complete account of IGM, this aspect of federal analysis is aimed at helping collaborating actors navigate the "thickets" of federalism, agencies, and politics.

The Legacy of Intergovernmental Relations

Much of what is known about collaborative management stems from political science research related to operations and interactions by actors—politicians and administrators working within the U.S. federal system. They include statistical and

DOI: 10.4324/9781003385769-7

168 *Academic Studies of Collaborative Politics and Management*

information gathering and studies of program cooperation in federal–state and federal–state–local interactions. For the majority of the 20th century, extensive program cooperation existed within the U.S. federal system. For example, connections in law enforcement in the form of police training, criminal identification, and joint drug enforcement with the U.S. Postal Service (USPS) and state agencies inspecting agricultural products and dangerous materials are based on collaboration among different levels of government. Extensive program cooperation can be found in agricultural and conservation programs and, of course, on "militia"-related matters with state National Guard units and the U.S. armed forces. Although this active cooperation was part of the bureaucratic landscape in the early 20th century, it especially began to increase after the 1950s federal expansion. Scholars of intergovernmental relations commonly refer to this as the period of cooperative federalism, when "complementary and supportive relationships were most prominent and had high significance" (Wright, 1988, p. 71). As a result, cooperative federalism has left an administrative legacy that U.S. administrators engage in regularly.

Administration initially followed a style whereby state and local agencies were asked to implement "federal program funding rules, standards, and financial practices in federal and state law" (Agranoff, 2017, p. 70). However, it was a period of shared administration, with "a tendency for passive reviewing, concern for legal integrity, and encouragement of legal compliance, rather than any tight and comprehensive oversight" (Walker David, 2000). Following a few basic rules, each jurisdiction had significant freedom in making programs work and generally within the different state and local traditions. During that period, program management tended to be pushed down the line, so to speak, with minimum specific supervision or monitoring, before the lead-up to massive expansions of intergovernmental projects. It was clearly less political, or at least it appeared that way.

Jane Perry Clark (1938) was one of the first scholars to recognize and define this cooperative management style. Cooperation between the federal and state governments was particularly experiential, and she found it to be very routine. However, Clark's assessment of disparities among officials and their ability to resolve programs appeared overly optimistic at the time, probably disregarding fundamental political distinctions based on jurisdictional interests and resource restrictions—not to mention comparable administrative competence.

A more focused examination of IGM took place with the academic studies of the federal grants programs during the Great Depression in the 1930s. Although these programs supported cooperation in principle, studies were not always confident about their success (Agranoff, 2017). For example, V.O. Key Jr. (1937, p. 228) identified a "gap between policy determination and the task of administration" because spending money and performance management had been under the control of state agencies "operating in a sphere of and tradition of freedom from central control." In a similar fashion, George Benson (1942) pointed out the Achilles

Academic Studies of Collaborative Politics and Management   169

heel in the performance of state governments as operating partners. While they need to be located at the top of the entire operational system, he wrote, "at times there seems discouraging evidence the core is rotting" (p. 157).

No doubt, the top-down restrictions and procedures were modified in practice. Compliance became one of the early indications of policy implementation concerns. Edward Weidner's study of federal programs (1944, p. 233) concluded that "state supervision of local programs was determined by a meeting of the minds of state and local officials." However, the goal of management was cooperation. This cooperation was explored by David Lilienthal (1939), who found in his work on the Tennessee Valley Authority (TNA) that managerial expertise required such a non-centralized cooperative approach. According to Lilienthal, the essence of field coordination included operatives making the greatest number of decisions, affected residents actively participating and cooperating with state and local agencies, and state and local governments' work "coordinating" as they worked toward common goals.

Dwight Waldo (1948, p. 149) also noted this tendency as the cooperative approach was also observed at the state level. In this regard, John Vieg (1941) studied the cooperation of federal, state, local, and private organizations in Iowa's agricultural programs in four different areas: planning, education, programming, and research. He states that various interests operate "physically side by side" while forging "a rational division of labor and clear understanding of authority and responsibility all the way around; there must be close agreement on all questions" (p. 142).

During World War II, extensive program coordination was particularly necessary for defense production. Having consulted with all levels of government and non-government officials, the President's Committee for Congested Production Areas was instrumental in facilitating all types of local public services. Corrington Gill (1945) stated that the Committee provided a common ground platform for "across the table discussion of common problems" (p. 32).

Politics in the Legacy of Collaborative Federalism

The field-based academic research studies of William Anderson and his associates during the 1950s ultimately produced ten volumes describing the state of collaborative intergovernmental relations between Minnesota government and the federal government. The essence of management under cooperative federalism was captured in Anderson's *Intergovernmental Relations in Review* (1960) and earlier in *The Nation and the States, Rivals or Partners?* (1955). According to Anderson, the federal government's job is to provide money to state and local governments to fund specific initiatives, set certain criteria, and conduct minimal oversight over state and local planning and performance of these functions. The states are in charge of most programs; the state runs some programs by proxy through local governments. Grants encourage federal–state collaboration (for example, in public welfare policies) (Anderson, 1960, pp. 37–38). Anderson also concludes that "complexity,

170   *Academic Studies of Collaborative Politics and Management*

the failure in some cases of the states to act, and political forces motivated by the desire to improve standards of living" inevitably resulted in some degree of national involvement and interest in domestic policy arenas that were previously considered state-centered (p. 14). His investigation of 81 cooperative programs (grants, shared administration, and contracts) between Minnesota and the federal government was said to have resulted in numerous administrative changes in state governments, including the creation of new state agencies and the expansion of existing ones, the establishment of new state merit systems, a greater emphasis on state service planning, and more opportunities for interstate administrative cooperation (1960, p. 62).

The University of Chicago's research group led by Morton Grodzins known as the Federalism Workshop also contributed to studying the cooperative federalism process. Of course, one landmark developmental work from this series is Daniel Elazar's *The American Partnership* (1962). Grodzins compendium based on the studies produced by the Federalism Workshop, particularly his volume *The American System* (1966), was then "the *magnum opus* of cooperative federalism" (Agranoff, 2017, p. 72). His famous "marble cake" metaphor was a device for diverting attention from the federal "layer cake" idea of two different levels of government: federal and state. His basic intergovernmental characterization was several overlapping functions, with administration sharing in many areas beyond grants. National oversight was achieved through a combination of state and local discretion, mutual accommodation, and participation of state and municipal officials in the agenda-setting process (Agranoff & Radin, 2015). Even in the absence of shared funding, collaboration between the federal government, states, and local governments was the norm. Despite considerable animosity and opposition to federal and state control over local programs, productive engagement was stated to have continued (Grodzins, 1966, p. 373). Grodzins work, notably in recreation management, led him to believe that interactions with federal and state governments resulted in significant variance down the line, providing ample room for administrative discretion. The opportunity is open to all; nevertheless, not everyone makes use of it. "When free enterprise is extended to local-federal interactions, some towns profit handsomely while others receive less than an equitable share" (p. 189). Cooperative federalism combines federal aid with the ability of other governments to "constructively participate in the great public service functions" (p. 381).

These changes in the 20th century and the reported processes resulted in cooperative federalism studies—but not until long after the democratization of the electorate and the rise of large industrial organizations, did the U.S. federal, state, and local governments make recognized managerial progress in the professional bureaucratization of their agencies (Shefter, 1978; Skowronek, 1982). These federalism interaction studies brought out the *politics and the administration* of federal programs at operational levels. Indeed, during the early 20th century, the greatest administrative changes actually came first at the municipal and state levels, where policy mostly unfolded. Administrative practices such as formal reports and fiscal audits appeared later, largely as a byproduct of political reform movements, and gradually moved up the line, reaching state and federal agencies as reports, processes, and analyses documenting federal program proliferation during the last half of the 20th century.

This later period highlighted particularly important byproducts of its politics as the federal government passed hundreds of new laws with supporting legal guidelines that were "parachuted" into state and municipal governments at the time (Agranoff, 2017):

> In many ways, the transformation from a system known as "federalism" to "intergovernmental relations" began and laid the foundations for dedicated concern for the "management" of programs that crossed jurisdictions in ways well beyond the formal transactions of earlier times.
>
> (p. 73)

One of the authors of this volume argues that the development of these parachuted programs heralded the emergence of the new era of federalism—IGM—which was "seasoned by politics—managing these programs involved much more than filling out a form or submitting a final report" (Agranoff, 2017, p. 73). Transactions that went above and beyond the ordinary required situational interpretation and mutual understanding of how to apply governing laws and principles (such as norms and standards) to actual conditions faced by participating governments. More regular working interactions were thus subsequently both political and managerial (Agranoff, 2017; O'Toole, 1986; Fountain, 1998; O'Toole, 2010).

U.S. Federalism Means State-by-State Variety

One of the most obvious products of the emergent federal system was that laws and programs are the same yet different. Federal law does not often differ generally and is relegated to the states and local governments—with the exemption of the federal government regulating and impacting interstate commerce, in which exclusively federal and subnational governments play important roles. However, this does not mean that the states or municipal governments cannot also enter these same arenas in other ways beyond transactions across state lines. For example, states usually have their own commercial codes regulating occupations entering commercial fields, and municipalities issue licenses and govern how entry into certain businesses and trades operate locally. In addition, there are numerous subnational differences across municipalities and states in these cases, and the U.S. federal system is generally respectful by abstaining from regulation in these areas.

One clear arena of contemporary interest is that of gun control. Although it has been difficult for the U.S. Congress to enact gun control legislation, the states and some municipalities have filled this "policy vacuum." For example, some state and local governments have increased the screening of gun buyers. Federal law does

172 *Academic Studies of Collaborative Politics and Management*

not regulate private gun transactions, a loophole in gun sales whereby almost half of the purchasers can acquire a gun privately with no background check. While no one knows what proportion of these purchasers would not pass a background test, clearly some would not. Nineteen states and Washington, DC now require background checks for private gun purchases. Twelve states and Washington, DC require gun buyers to pass safety training and undergo a pre-permit process. Some states have enacted "red flag" or extreme risk protection laws that allow police to thwart potential suspected killers. Washington, California, Oregon, Connecticut, Indiana, and Florida have "extreme risk protection order" laws. In addition, courts can be petitioned to permit impoundment from possessing and/or purchasing firearms. Orders in most of these states can be extended for up to one year in some states. Extreme risk protection orders are now being considered in several other states.

Some states have also strengthened gun storage regulations, as surveys have indicated that half or more gun owners do not properly store their weapons. Accidental shootings amounted to about 1,800 per year between 1999 and 2013 (*Economist*, 2018, March 24). Before the 2018 mass school shooting in Parkland, Florida, legislators in 30 states had introduced extreme risk protection orders. Finally, three states—California, Connecticut, and New York—require guns to be securely stored if they are in any way near persons barred from possessing them, with severe fines for violations.

Finally, our purpose is to remind readers that federal systems normally display considerable variance in some important policy/program areas. For example, federalism means multiple tools and joint and overlapping authority. Although it is sometimes depicted as "hyperbolic" in operation, it more resembles a "marble cake" than a layer cake in a theoretical and practical approach, as overlapping intergovernmental problems and solutions are often intertwined.

Development of Intergovernmental Management

As federal programming has expanded its reach to involve a myriad of programs that extend across and through national, state, and local programs that increasingly involve more constituent governments—states, local governments (city, county, and special districts), and the nonprofit and for-profit sectors, the problem becomes one of public management. Its challenge is vertical (e.g., federal–state–local) and horizontal (state–local–NGO) delivery organization. A classic example is Medicaid federal assistance for health and developmental services for low-income, older low-income, physically disabled, and intellectually disabled. In some states, Medicaid is organized by the states and counties. The federal government largely funds it through local public health and social service agencies or health programs sponsored by hospitals and rehabilitation programs, for-profit and nonprofit organizations, and a host of often private NGO vendors. In general, Medicaid is one keystone program that has contributed greatly to what is now known professionally as IGM.

Academic Studies of Collaborative Politics and Management   173

As the U.S. federal system developed in programs like Medicaid, it has also been wrapped in politics that have led to an increased focus on the role of managers in the system. For example, program continuity relied on managerial oversight as programs were enacted and "co-delegated" to other jurisdictions and organizations. As a result, intergovernmental complexity has led to the need for managers—elected and appointed—to try to weave through the technicalities and the politics to make things work. Consequently, development occurred in four operational IGM phases (Agranoff, 2017).

The first phase of IGM, *law and politics*, began building the integral nation-state, primarily in the 19th century,

> when legal distinctions of government were initially defined. The most prominent feature was perhaps the old dual federalism doctrine that held that the national government and the states each were sovereign in their respective spheres and that between them existed areas of activity into which the other could enter.
>
> (Agranoff & Radin, 2015, p. 142)

The second phase of IGM, *welfare state development*, occurred from the early 20th century to roughly the 1960s. "It marked a time of a growing and more professional national government that also included a growing interdependency that linked subnational and state/federal governments" (Agranoff & Radin, 2015, p. 142). In particular, the welfare state in the United States was very much "a federal-state and state-local top-down effort (similar to developments across the globe) that enhanced the fiscal and program strength of national governments" (Loughlin, 2007, p. 389; Watts, 1999). However, in the United States, implementation was largely delegated to subnational governments with varying action requirements, giving rise to IGM.

The third phase of IGM, *working with agents and partners of the government*, emphasized the involvement of organized actors outside the government, such as NGOs, in public programming. "Through some grants but predominantly through contracts, government extensively linked with nonprofit service agencies and for-profit vendors of services" (Smith & Lipsky, 1993, p. 5). In addition, Agranoff and Radin (2015, p. 142) argue:

> both the direct service and support sectors led to new sets of alliances between governments at all levels and public and private entities, including service delivery nonprofits and private businesses, law firms, finance management firms, banks, and insurance companies as issues faced by government agencies became cross-bounder.
>
> (Salamon, 1995)

The fourth IGM phase, *networking*, originated from the expanding welfare state and NGO partnerships. It became fully acknowledged in the first decade of the

174 *Academic Studies of Collaborative Politics and Management*

21st century. "Public agencies and NGOs network to exchange information, enhance one another's capabilities, smooth services interactions and solve policy/program problems" (Agranoff & Radin, 2015, p. 142). In a way, intergovernmental networking became parallel to contracting when networks emerged based on previous contractor-government relations (Brown, Potoski, & Van Slyke, 2008; Zeemering, 2018). Also,

> networks comprising local governments, business associations, and economic development agents have worked among themselves at the community level for four or five decades, and these entities have had extensive links with higher-level governments to secure support to promote local economies (Agranoff & McGuire, 2003; McGuire, 2002).
>
> (Agranoff & Radin, 2015, p. 142)

IGM networking presently includes "officials from the federal government, state governments, local governments, public and private universities, and NGOs representing the nonprofit sectors sitting down with one another 'at the same table' to discuss, explore, negotiate, and solve issues interactively" (Agranoff & Radin, 2015, pp. 142–143). The IGM network phase is multilateral and collaborative and deals with issues beyond traditional bilateral intergovernmental relations (Fowler, 2018). Presently, IGM has become a matter of "contingent collaboration"; that is, Deil Wright's (1988) overlapping authority model extended "beyond governments to include NGOs and other third parties" (Agranoff & Radin, 2015, p. 143).

IGM concerns range from legal and political encounters—for example, between city/state governments with the EPA over automotive emission levels—as they are required to assess costs and health risks to seemingly minor issues like settling managerial differences over the number of keys issued to those that involved key distribution to locked gates that cross highways on interstate highway construction sites. In this sense, IGM involves the very largest macro and very smallest micro concerns confronting managers, with many engineering and technical concerns—e.g., on bridge construction—wedged in.

Essentially, IGM involves the four major dimensions that form the "craft" of managing across boundaries. These four themes allow us to understand IGM as an important key to collaborative management and politics. First is the centrality of legal and political forces in framing and reframing policy issues like air quality and automobile emissions. Second, "the increased interdependencies caused by an expanded welfare state, which has gone far beyond income support to include social protection and support for a number of public concerns including clean air" (Agranoff, 2017). Third, governments at all levels have externalized their policy-making and policy implementation to include a variety of NGO actors—even citizen groups (Gofen, 2015)—that partner with governments. Fourth, the countless state and local governments, NGOs, and interest groups were involved in many administrative and policy arenas of governmental programs. For example,

Academic Studies of Collaborative Politics and Management 175

programs on controlling mercury emissions operate based on networks representing public, profit, and nonprofit organizations performing different program tasks (Agranoff, 2017). Thus, existing federal, state, and private auto emission controls now include "the active mixtures of law and politics, the protective aims of an interdependent state, and the complexity of multilevel governments and NGOs, all working in some networked fashion" (p. 2). As a result, intergovernmental management is now considerably more than governments at the operational level and usually a lot more than federal–state concerns.

The process of IGM that has emerged signifies that the tradition of jurisdictional autonomy has led to government strategies at all independent and interdependent levels, particularly at the management level. The actions of managers representing various governments have become increasingly differentiated and wide-ranging, from program design to post-auditing, prompting the need for management across boundaries and sectors. Moreover, as respective governments have expanded in functions, an increasing number of non-governmental actors have become part of the intergovernmental mix, particularly reaching beyond procurement to include interdependent direct service delivery and agencies. Finally, multiple programs, many levels, and recognition of problem complexity ultimately led to networked "governance" among disparate actors, levels, and auspices, mixing sociopolitical actors in different modes and orders (Saz-Carranza & Serra, 2009; Raab & Kenis, 2009; Maynard-Moody, Musheno, & Palumbo, 1990; Koliba, Mills, & Zia, 2011).

Knowledge: Abstract to Real

What is knowledge, and how is it used in collaborative management? The transformation from data to information to knowledge for interactive CP is at the core of "collaborative existence." Data refers to a "set of discrete, objective facts about events" (Davenport & Prusak, 2000, p. 2). Information is defined as "a message, usually in the form of a document or an audible or visible communication" (p. 3). Information flows around organized bodies via hard networks, including cables, satellite dishes, servers, and soft networks such as written notes, conversations, and speeches (Davenport, 2005).

Knowledge tends to be "broader, deeper, and richer than data or information" (Agranoff, 2007, p. 126). It is highly variable and depends on context, but it is more applicable. Thomas Davenport and Laurence Prusak define it as,

> Knowledge is a fluid mix of framed experience, values, contextual information, and expert insight that provides a framework for evaluating and incorporating new experience and information. It originates and is applied in the minds of knowers. In organizations, it often becomes embedded not only in documents or repositories but also in organizational routines, processes, practices, and norms.

> (2000, pp. 5–6)

176 *Academic Studies of Collaborative Politics and Management*

Knowledge is located within people; it is a part of the human capital assets important in contemporary activities like collaboration. According to Davenport and Prusak, it is deeply human: "Knowledge derives from information as information derives from data. If information is to become knowledge, humans must do all the work" (pp. 5–6). In fact, knowledge is considered both a process and an outcome (Agranoff, 2007).

Knowledge is important in collaborative ventures because of the prevalence of so many technical and interorganizational uncertainties. Jorg Sydow, Gordon Müller-Seitz, and Keith Provan identify them as "effects uncertainty due to forces like unconventional impacts and internal tasks uncertainty" (Sydow et al., 2013, pp. 26–27). In public endeavors, including CP, one would utilize knowledge for problem-solving, ultimately adding public value (Moore, 1995). For example, local agencies and partners working within interagency networks represent knowledge management vehicles. Collaboration, or "connectivity," is a term social network analysts use to describe how knowledge is created. Dynamic interactions among people, particularly at crucial locations in social networks, are essential for problem-solving and creative discovery (Cross et al., 2004). Michael Schrage describes knowledge collaboration as "shared creation" or "people working together on a process, product, or event in a collaborative manner" (1995, p. 33). "Work groups on various technical challenges are the way we learn and evolve; integrate new people into our process," one local government public official told the author, "and while we don't codify method, we rely on the institutional knowledge of a lot of individuals" (quoted in Agranoff, 2007, p. 138). It is also crucial to remember that each participating organization is a distributed knowledge system that must be "assembled" or brought together in real-time (Tsoukas, 1996).

In CP, knowledge blends what can be documented or formalized with the intuitive knowledge of how to do a task. Michael Polanyi concludes that knowledge is "formulae which have a bearing on experience", in the sense that knowledge is personal knowledge, from knowing how to communicate on the internet to playing piano, from riding a bicycle to writing a scientific article. This requires skillful action based on "personal knowing" (1962, p. 49).

Knowledge management is understood to have two analytical components, *explicit* and *tacit* knowledge. First, explicit knowledge can be easily encoded by signs, words, numbers, or pictures (Agranoff, 2018). It "can be expressed in formal and systematic language and shared in the form of data, scientific formulae, specifications, manuals and such like" (Nonaka, Toyama, & Konno, 2000, p. 7). Most people are familiar with this form of knowledge. On the other hand, tacit knowledge is very important for the CP because it is contextual and "embedded in the senses, individual perceptions, physical experiences, intuition, and rules of thumb" (p. 115). It is almost never documented but is "frequently communicated through conversations with the use of metaphors" (Polanyi, 1962, p. 49). Different forms of tacit knowledge include implicit understanding, mental frameworks, hunches, and discipline-based principles (Agranoff, 2018; Saint-Onge & Armstrong, 2004;

Academic Studies of Collaborative Politics and Management   177

Nicolini, 2011). Donald Moynihan (2008) lists different forms of tacit knowledge in his study of network learning, including learning from previous experience, existing information systems, virtual learning, learning forums, and learning from collaborative experience.

The tools utilized in knowledge management are not necessarily highly complex but are techniques often known under different names, such as information, communication, and human resource practices. Table 7.1 and Table 7.2 provide

Table 7.1 Explicit Knowledge Management Activities

Type of Activity	Example/Use
Intranet	State agency communication system; allows field offices and state headquarters to be in interactive electronic contact and builds selected bodies of management information.
Listservs of discussion groups	Quadrennial plan regional groups; broken down by areas of economic development interest (manufacturing, value-added agriculture, services), first step in plan development.
Databases	Accident frequency and location within the metropolitan area; one input into project/plan development.
Corporate (network) libraries	Catalogs of independent economic/business listings and how to access them; library provides access by web links to virtually any business ranking service, related studies, and plans.
Virtual organizations	Value-added agricultural partnership is a non-formally organized group of funders/researchers/entrepreneurs that explores data and information and tries to produce new knowledge.
Information portals	Access by internet to various web uses by non-governmental organizations and state agencies for planning and decision-making.
Electronic archiving	Ortho-infrared mapping of the state to 1 meter square, a variable for public agency use; for example, in transportation, natural resource, agriculture, and other planning/programming.
Knowledge maps	Ideational targeting of existing freight terminals, public transport stops, green trails, handicapped access, and so on, for planning purposes.
Decision-support systems	Travel demand forecasting model; use of current measurable travel habits with projected employment/population estimates for needs-based decisions.
Chief knowledge officer	Head of program also serves as chief information/knowledge officer for state department of administration; uses state agency interactively generated data and information to develop usable knowledge.

Source: Agranoff (2012, p. 237). Copyright 2012 by Georgetown University Press. Reprinted with permission.

178 *Academic Studies of Collaborative Politics and Management*

Table 7.2 Tacit Knowledge Management Activities

Type of Activity	Example/Use
Sharing best practices	Biannual/state geographic information system (GIS) conference; sharing among three GIS tiers: (1) expert, technically involved; (2) administrator/manager; and (3) novices, contemplating GIS use.
Informal mentoring	Field-based watershed coordinators work with landowners, local government officials, and others to disseminate degradation and conservation knowledge, including river basin studies.
Formal mentoring	Community visitation teams work with small towns on their community development challenges to write a formal plan together.
Task force/work group	Special study of the problem of "business succession" in rural small towns—that is, the closing of local businesses when the current entrepreneur retires or otherwise closes the business; for planning and policy purposes.
Electronic decision-support group work	Using university electronic work laboratory to develop proposed program revisions.
Discussion groups	Organized focus groups to prepare state rural economic development strategy.
Expert interviews	Presentations/questions of vendor-experts at meetings to demonstrate latest GIS technology.
Apprenticeships	A series of plan coordinators are university interns or new graduates who primarily fund and blend research and plan programs from a variety of federal and state resources.
Training programs	Operational, conservation, and regulatory compliance workshops for small water company managers and technicians.
Cultural change	Cooperative development center tries to create natural atmosphere of sharing of informational staff.
Fostering collaboration	Rather than petitioner and petitioned, the state division works together with two state-level peak interest groups and a host of non-governmental organization providers to share information, create program knowledge, and guide the program's future.

Source: Agranoff (2012, p. 238). Copyright 2012 by Georgetown University Press. Reprinted with permission.

examples of typically used explicit and tacit knowledge activities during the process of collaboration. For example, suppose one examines the examples given in Table 7.1. In that case, collaborative organizations frequently use information portals, intranets, information databases, unified libraries, e-archives, and group decision-support systems emerging beyond organizational boundaries (Agranoff, 2018). In addition, practices such as listservs, discussion groups, virtual organizations,

Academic Studies of Collaborative Politics and Management 179

knowledge maps, and chief knowledge officer designations are less known in information management or human resource management. Still, they are known in collaborative management (Agranoff, 2018).

Similarly, implicit approaches described in Table 7.2 are almost equivalent to activities occurring in single organizations, particularly apprenticeships, mentoring, sharing best practices, workgroups, coaching, training, and promoting collaboration. For example, Agranoff (2008, 2012) argues that collaborative entities in the public sector widely use them. Traditionally they differ to some degree from "the expert systems, artificial intelligence, case-based reasoning, and broad knowledge systems employed by so-called high-flying corporations (Davenport & Prusak, 2000; Koliba et al., 2016)" (Agranoff, 2018, p. 116).

One of the authors of this volume identified a five-step knowledge development process during the collaborative process. The first step in the sequence is to look at each agency and partner to see their information bases, then convert these data into formats that the collective body may use. Following this, there is a close look to see if there are any less evident tacit knowledge-based methods for the core to use. Then, as needed by the group, expand on the preceding and apply it to specific challenges. Finally, knowledge is returned to component organizations to expand its application (Agranoff, 2018).

Inventories, map libraries, workshops, best-practices books, working manuals, workgroups, communities of practice, decision models, cross-agency transactions, and any new individual partner data sources could all be generated as part of this extensive and interorganizationally interactive journey. As a result, cross-organizational knowledge tends to concentrate on mutually agreed upon and negotiated concerns, issues, and difficulties (Agranoff, 2018).

Collaborative partners can only solve interactive problems by stepping back from their agency position and trying to address problems collectively and rationally. The kind of knowledge base that partners can build jointly to fashion prospective solutions is often critical in mutually based problems (Agranoff, 2018). Like business alliances, partnerships, and networks in the private sector, public management networks also need "the ability to integrate and utilize scientific advances and the creation of an impression of relative successes" (Black, 2014, p. 410).

Communities of practice, for example, can be seen of as vehicles for social learning since they use the communicative styles, discourses, and repertories of the people involved (Agranoff, 2018). According to Jacob Torfing (2016), they can produce three outcomes. First, by redefining their identities and altering the conditions of their interaction, they establish and maintain the mutual engagement of those affected. Second, through coordinating efforts, establishing shared responsibility, and reconciling contradictory perspectives, these communities of communities contribute to a shared understanding and practical fine-tuning of their joint venture. Third, these practices transfigure "the participants' repertoire, discourses, and styles" (Agranoff, 2018, p. 119).

180   *Academic Studies of Collaborative Politics and Management*

Jacob Torfing (2016, p. 54) argues that "learning alters the identities, interaction, discourse, and activities of a community of practice in ways that improve its performance." These practices are particularly necessary for horizontal leadership with followers from different backgrounds, methods, and experiences to collaborate in solving wicked policy problems using innovative approaches.

Tacit and explicit knowledge do not oppose each other. In fact, they are two sides of the same coin. In the real world of CP, they are joined together (Agranoff, 2012). Knowledge Management requires *skillful action*, and the knower "necessarily participates in all acts of understanding" (Polanyi & Prosch, 1975, p. 44). However, for Hardimus Tsoukas, explicit knowledge always remains uncertain without the presence of tacit knowledge: "It is vectoral, we know the particulars by relying on our awareness of them for the for attending to someone else" (2005, p. 158). Knowledge is a key social-political experience that involves processes that must break through administrative and organizational processes that require applied (resolute) political wisdom, risk-taking tolerance for differences, organizational responsiveness, and adaptability (Vigoda-Gadot et al., 2005).

Rules/Practices of Engagement

Several multidimensional facets of network power were identified earlier, including network "champions, the key agency-based administrator core, the internal operational core, and the technical core" (Agranoff, 2012, p. 152). Each type of "power" can facilitate or inhibit the collaboration process.

One of these types is "power to" new possibilities in collaboration which originate from the research of civic engagement scholars like Innes, Connick, and Booher (2007), who propose the following rules of engagement:

1. Including the full range of stakeholders.
2. Dividing meaningful tasks.
3. Entailing participants to set their own ground rules.
4. Developing mutual understanding and avoidance of positional bargaining.
5. Following self-organizing processes.
6. Exchanging information that is accessible and fully shared.
7. Reaching a consensus that is agreed when all interests are explored.
8. Following explicit and transparent implementation steps.
9. There is ample opportunity for public review of a draft agreement by stakeholders and the public.

(Agranoff, 2012, p. 152)

Building on this research, David Booher (2008) suggested the following six fundamental features of deliberation in collaboration.

1. Structures have to be dynamic; they undergo changes over time.
2. System information is transformed into data that can recognize the dynamics of interactive patterns.

Academic Studies of Collaborative Politics and Management   181

3. Agents' interactions gravitate toward various potential responses, whereas various possible activities can be explored and potentially strengthened.
4. The collaborative system carries out a fine-tuned, parallel quest for potential options.
5. The system is based on a perpetual interaction of bottom-up and top-down processes.
6. The deep uncertainty in the world constantly pressures the collaboratives to enrich internal diversity.

These rules of engagement heavily rely on social networking—give and take as participants look for other possibilities for solving wicked problems.

It is also clear that the managers representing agencies can exhibit specific behaviors promoting the process of deliberation (Agranoff, 2012). They include well-known rules of collaborative management/engagement: cogoverning, structuring lateral processes, information, knowledge orientation, etc. These rules

> involve activity promoting collaborating activity geared toward forging new possibilities, ranging from promoting inclusiveness to measuring and monitoring collaborative activity. The process factors in deliberative power identified here underscore the importance of mutual learning, advancing knowledge, building communities, and employing interactive processes.
>
> (p. 153)

Along with the rules of engagement, they comprise the important behaviors that managers can exhibit in building collaboratives and networks.

Collaborative Fatigue: A Political Process

One familiar process barrier that occurs "within the group" is the process dimension identified by Chris Huxham and Siv Vangen as "partnership fatigue" (2005, p. 72). It is a core matter of the internal politics of collaboration or "small p" politics. Still, it is nevertheless a core component of CP. In collaborative management, intergovernmental and interlocal processes are extensive and time-consuming. It thus presents a potential risk of a different type of political stripe. It is often coupled with a lack of clarity about the one with whom one is collaborating.

Therefore, the challenge of managing ambiguity and complexity often proves to be an exhausting force (Agranoff, 2018). Constant change can also lead to relationship inertia between partners. They can become increasingly fluid. A shift from expected group-oriented, task-focused give-and-take relationships to a new situation such as one or a few leaders perform most of the work, for example, can take the collaboration process and "move [it] out of the control of their membership" (Huxham & Vangen, 2005, p. 78). Finally, leadership activities are perpetually overcoming obstacles, not in a collaborative way (like forcing partners out or excluding agencies), a sort of "collaborative thuggery," as Huxham and Vangen (2005, p. 78)

182 *Academic Studies of Collaborative Politics and Management*

label it, as a substitute for "grind-it-out" process facilitation. Together, these fatigue issues raise real CP process obstacles.

Huxham and Vangen (2005) list seven important fatigue-related or inertia-related views on collaborative management:

1. We must have common aims, but we cannot agree on them.
2. Sharing power is important, but people behave as if it is all in the purse strings.
3. Trust is necessary for successful collaboration, but we are suspicious of each other.
4. We are partnership-fatigued and tired of being pulled in all directions.
5. Everything keeps changing.
6. Leadership is not always in the hands of the members.
7. Leadership activities continually meet with dilemmas and difficulties.

(p. 75)

Subsequently, these mentioned challenges pose a serious risk to collaboration. They all constitute "small p" politics that easily exhaust the parties involved in a collaboration. Therefore, they "need to be recognized, avoided, and somehow overcome by managing the engagement game" (Agranoff, 2018, p. 103).

Is it possible to overcome these challenges to successful collaboration? If confronted, can they indeed lead to successful outcomes? Julia Wondolleck and Steven Yaffee (2000) suggest eight solutions to make the interaction process meaningful and legitimate:

1. Substantive process involvement as opposed to token participation.
2. While agencies each delegate decision-making aspects on a limited basis, in-group collaborative recommendations need to be taken seriously.
3. Early and often public (official, citizen) involvement.
4. The importance of decision-making by consensus process leads to inclusiveness, involving many different interests and guidance by persons who are effective at facilitating the group process.
5. Managing productive and efficient meetings.
6. Use of efficient, organized structures that incorporate designated workgroups and task forces.
7. An ability to incorporate agreements/recommendations from technical support.
8. Finding ways to make these processes endure over time.

(pp. 101–110)

Wondolleck and Yaffee (2000) conclude that "These investments in the interactive process as opposed to focusing entirely on products means that involved partners fail to see the process as meaningful and legitimate" (p. 110). "Clearly, [in CP], without these process investments, it is not always clear that commitments

Academic Studies of Collaborative Politics and Management 183

are upheld and relationships blended into taking core process toward improving interpersonal dynamics and can lead to better on-the-ground management of natural resources and communities" (p. 101). Investments in these forces can facilitate action on the one hand and "blunt some of the sharper edges of politics" (Agranoff, 2018, p. 104) on the other hand.

Purposing in Collaboration

Why is all this collaborative effort undertaken? What does the research literature tell us about collaboration? Seven broad types of collaborative efforts appear to be the most formidable: problem identification and information exchange, finding and understanding existing technologies, the adaptation of technologies, broadening of knowledge infrastructures, capacity building, making program adjustments, and joint policy-making (Agranoff, 2007).

The first type of collaborative efforts is problem identification and information exchange. This is the most basic information function in collaboration with any operation because several parties must come together to discuss a problem's multiple facets, learn about the technologies utilized to address each facet, and eventually discover how the various agencies want to proceed with technical solutions. Thus, the key to the collaborative information process is bringing in those stakeholders who are directly or indirectly affected by an issue (Agranoff, 2018). A collective group can pool the information and decide that the problem has been extensively studied, which will allow looking more deeply into an issue. For example, I/DD networks can explore the advantages and disadvantages of different kinds of development approaches, ranging from residential service to home-based care. They can also take the next step of seeing how similar actors in other service areas have attempted to address similar issues. It is possible to compile a list of prospective solutions, and seminars and meetings can be utilized to learn more about feasible alternatives. For example, one watershed network, the Darby Partnership in Ohio, has undertaken all these means (Agranoff, 2007). Finally, one can educate stakeholders about implementing a particular solution and how any possible action can be affected by the actions of other stakeholders (Agranoff, 2018).

The second broad category involves finding and understanding existing technologies (Agranoff, 2018). How is extant technology found and revealed? This stream of information is constructed "within the technical expertise that is within reach of network participants, or it is sought outside, such as from university or commercial researchers and vendors" (p. 145). This has been the primary function of the Iowa Geographic Information Council. Various knowledge transfer vehicles exist in collaborative arrangements: roundtable presentations; regional, national, and international conferences; and invited guest speakers, blogs, vlogs, and webinars. In addition, several collaboratives have technology committees responsible for identifying and sharing new developments with the entire group. Some have full-time technical staff (contracted staff members, in some cases) who are subject matter experts responsible for identifying and presenting solutions. Many collaboration networks operate on such an exchange of technical knowledge daily. As needs are exchanged and programs are adjusted within, "valuable expertise is accessed and exchanged. Whether formal or informal, technical knowledge is accessed and enhanced by transactional contacts within the network" (Agranoff, 2007, p. 224).

Adaptation of technologies is the third broad category. In most cases, it requires some form of application of technology findings. However, there can be situations in the collaboration process when technology brought outside cannot be adapted, and the network cannot incrementally adjust this technology to the current situation (Agranoff, 2012). In order to tackle the difficulties of information societies in an increasingly chaotic, volatile, and complicated environment, analytical thinking must be reinforced with "greater creativity and vision, more mental flexibility, and more intuition" (Franz & Pattakos, 1996, p. 638). The network must effectively cooperate in order to transfer or build a technical solution based on recent research and technological advancements (Agranoff, 2018). For example, one state's small-town water aid network was the first to create and fund a wastewater reuse technology. The network looked at how a small community may set up cluster permits to install, operate, and comply with EPA requirements for a group of surrounding villages. The network technology committee has already studied existing technology and established its own strategy for building such a creative system. A team of network hydrologists and engineers went through a lengthy research and development procedure to achieve this. Their network finance committee was then tasked to research the expenses and funding options for such a system and report back to the network steering committee. Environmental experts from the state were tasked with speaking with the EPA about the process of acquiring operational permits for cluster systems (Agranoff, 2012). Finally, the entire process—construction, finance, and obtaining permits—was implemented, and the project was piloted. The task of changing and enhancing existing technological knowledge through collaborative efforts is not unusual.

Broadening of knowledge infrastructures is the fourth category, since disseminating knowledge is necessary for collaboration. Collaboratives lack the hierarchical channels for transmitting knowledge found in single organizations, which is also exacerbated by irregular in-person meetings (Agranoff, 2018). Actors are frequently in direct contact with one another and/or the clientele or populations they serve. Therefore, electronic communication channels—including e-mail, websites, and electronic bulletin boards—often supplement in-person meetings and phone calls. Since administrators and program managers in different organizations do not have time to exchange information in person, many networks and collaboratives are pressured to adopt ICT approaches to transform information into usable knowledge. For example, rural development networks are often aware that many of the people they are trying to help live in remote areas, so they try to determine the degree of the lack of internet connectivity, including generational and income-based hurdles. As a result, they are working harder to extend electronic communication to rural

Academic Studies of Collaborative Politics and Management 185

residents' informal outreach networks, such as county extension offices, higher education rural institutes, community colleges, high schools, local libraries, state agency offices at the county level, chambers of commerce, and other voluntary associations. They also collaborate with community leaders in these institutions to convey tacit or experiential knowledge. Similarly, transportation metropolitan planning organizations (MPOs) rely on information-rich databases, data repositories, research models, and other tacit and explicit knowledge forms to make decisions.

The fifth category, capacity building, involves the ability to assist network actors such as agencies or organizations and their representatives of members in CP "to anticipate and influence change; make informed and intelligent policy decisions; attract, absorb, manage resources: and evaluate current activities to guide future action (Honadle, 1981)" (Agranoff, 2012, p. 150). Many collaborative bodies and networks are heavily engaged in capacity building "particularly to develop and transmit knowledge architectures for subsequent solution-based activity and adaptation by its partners and clients, a form of knowledge management" (p. 150). This is the essential function of some public management networks. For example, let us look at the public policy and information-based study developed by the Lower Platte River Corridor Alliance watershed network. Members of this network were interested in creating, disseminating, and utilizing knowledge by its participants and within their respective organizations (Agranoff, 2018), but they lacked capacity. As a result, they resorted to cross-organizational training, annual meetings, technical assistance services, and technology seminars for effective knowledge acquisition and utilization. In short, many networks and collaborative bodies develop various capacities for integrating knowledge into internal action.

The sixth category is making program adjustments, called "blueprinting interactive strategies," used by agencies and/or organizations participating in collaborative projects (Agranoff, 2012). This type of "networking" is traditionally utilized by metropolitan- or interlocal-level human services offered on an interagency basis (Agranoff, 1986). These networks include a variety of agencies and programs which jointly chart coordinated action plans executed somewhere else by one or more of the major partners (Agranoff, 2012). "These strategic and programmatic approaches can be institutionalized or blueprinted, such as with common interagency funding application form" (p. 151), or suited to a specific situation, such as attracting a firm. These strategies can be implemented ad hoc, like when a network assists a town in obtaining funds to rehabilitate a central business area. They can also be strategic policy-oriented, such as efforts taken by a state-level multiagency/ organization plan to keep the developmentally disabled out of major facilities. For example, reciprocal programming for strategy development might thus be a formal or informal activity for some network collaboratives (Agranoff, 2018). These mutually agreed-upon strategic methods are significant collaborative outcomes for numerous networks that do not have "final decision authority to act on behalf of participating stakeholders but can act by mutual understanding" (Agranoff, 2012, p. 151).

186   *Academic Studies of Collaborative Politics and Management*

The seventh and final category, joint policy-making, is frequently associated with comprehensive planning bodies, program councils, and networks (e.g., Koppenjan, Koppenjan, & Klijn, 2004; Sørensen & Torfing, 2009). In reality, it is a poorly understood conclusion that only a few collaboratives—for example, the transportation MPOs—have the legal authority needed to act in such policy decision capacities (Agranoff, 2012). For instance, in the United States, "they hold either federal and/or state authorization to make decisions in their charters, and in the case of the MPOs, both levels authorize such decisions" (p. 151). Moreover, even when these bodies have such powers, "they differ from representative bodies of elected officials where formal votes are taken, the majority rules, and political considerations are paramount" (p. 151). Moreover, these decision-making bodies within the policy network differ from rigid hierarchies, where one person is ultimately in charge of making legally binding decisions.

In these collaborative decision bodies, like MPOs, deliberations are likely to be both technical and political since there is a major emphasis on study and technical expertise, and voting is more of an enabling formality after a negotiated agreement is reached (Gray, 1989; Forester, 2009). In fact, most of these decision-making organizations must respect network members while also taking the required technological and quasi- (or pseudo-)legislative steps to enable them to combine information with a shared policy or activity (Agranoff, 2012). Having extended discussions within the network, many of these bodies constantly return agency proposals back until the decision-makers reach some agreement. As representatives of various government, quasi-government, and non-governmental organizations, these component administrators and executives come together to collaborate—but with home organization missions and agendas, with all their attendant aims, legal mandates and rules, and internal operating procedures. They typically represent their organizations' demands, corporate cultures, and political aspirations. These component administrators and executives must decide, but they cannot do so using the same position or legal authority they have in their organizations. As a result, they are involved in the process of reciprocal adjustment while applying existing knowledge, while the partners go through an interactive learning process simultaneously (Agranoff, 2012). They are also open to deliberate strategic and/or decision-making processes that are not hierarchical.

Conclusion

While often disparaged as a barrier to cooperation and joint problem-solving, political forces are, on the surface, inherently neutral. Box 7.1 offers some more central findings ranging from federalism to program management. They can be either supportive or resistive forces—or even sometimes neutral. Political issues in any situation likely bring together potentially differing aims, resources, and ideas; however, they cannot be avoided. Few CP-related situations are "neutral" or "apolitical" in practice. As a result, it is better to recognize them and understand and deal with them, no matter how much they contribute to the process or any other kind of fatigue. Hopefully, the academic research-based findings on federalism and intergovernmental management, knowledge management, collaborative engagement politics, process engagement politics, and the processes of collaboration undertakings will help better understand the often hidden politics in and of interactive collaboration processes. Its nettlesome processes are procedural, technical, interpersonal, political, and non-hierarchical.

Box 7.1   From Federalism to Local Problem Resolution

- Systematic concern for the growth, impact, cost, and effectiveness in the federal system led to the study of cooperative federalism by academia and governmental entities to help understand politics.
- The rise of cooperative agreements—particularly in the regulatory arena—underscores the importance of the broadened knowledge needed to approach complex problems in such arenas as environmental protection.
- Research on the federal system over time has revealed both cooperation and conflict, although top-down program analyses far exceed extensive research on bottom-up program examination. It clearly brought out political dimensions.
- Only recently have observers and researchers begun to recognize the daunting CP challenges, and interest in mutual interdependence and networks and networking has prompted the beginning of sorting out the complexities.
- Problem-solving induces the integration of data, information, and knowledge into knowledge that can be employed to different situations.
- Knowledge needs to be developed in both of its main components: explicit or formal, and less formal tacit or experiential.
- Explicit and tacit knowledge must be processed as knowledge management and applied to specific situations. Explicit and tacit knowledge are complimentary. Both are critical to tackle CP.
- CP brings on interactive costs as well as benefits. It is important to become cognizant of both.
- It is important to understand that programs are adjusted as they go down the line from enactment to "street-level" application.

Source: Robert Agranoff

188 *Academic Studies of Collaborative Politics and Management*

References

Agranoff, R. (1986). *Intergovernmental management: Human services problem-solving in six metropolitan areas.* SUNY Press.

Agranoff, R. (2007). *Managing within networks: Adding value to public organizations.* Georgetown University Press.

Agranoff, R. (2008). Collaborating for knowledge: Learning from public management networks In L. B. Bingham (Eds.), *Big ideas in collaborative public management.* ME Sharpe.

Agranoff, R. (2012). *Collaborating to manage: A primer for the public sector.* Georgetown University Press.

Agranoff, R. (2017). *Crossing boundaries for intergovernmental management.* Georgetown University Press.

Agranoff, R. (2018). *Local governments in multilevel governance: The administrative dimension.* Lexington Books.

Agranoff, R., & McGuire, M. (2003). *Collaborative public management: New strategies for local governments.* Georgetown University Press.

Agranoff, R., & Radin, B. A. (2015). Deil Wright's overlapping model of intergovernmental relations: The basis for contemporary intergovernmental relationships. *Publius: The Journal of Federalism, 45*(1), 139–159.

Anderson, W. (1955). *The Nation and the states, rivals or partners?* University of Minnesota Press.

Anderson, W. (1960). Intergovernmental relations in review (No. 10). *Intergovernmental Relations Series.*

Benson, G. S. (1942). *New centralization.* Rinehart.

Black, J. (2014). *The power of knowledge: How information and technology made the modern world.* Yale University Press.

Booher, D. E. (2008). Civic engagement as collaborative complex adaptive networks. In E. Bergrud, & K. Yang (Eds.) *Civic engagement in a network society* (pp. 111–148). Information Age Pub.

Brown, T. L., Potoski, M., & Van Slyke, D. M. (2008). *The challenge of contracting for large complex projects: A case study of the coast guard's deepwater program.* IBM Center for the Business of Government, 26.

Clark, J. P. (1938). *The rise of a new federalism.* Columbia University Press.

Cross, R., Parker, A., Prusak, L., & Borgatti, S. P. (2004). Knowing what we know: Supporting knowledge creation and sharing in social networks. In E. L. Lesser & L. Prusak (Eds.), *Creating value with knowledge: Insights from the IBM Institute for business value.* Oxford University Press on Demand.

Davenport, T. H. (2005). *Thinking for a living: How to get better performances and results from knowledge workers.* Harvard Business Press.

Davenport, T. H., & Prusak, L. (2000). *Working knowledge: How organizations manage what they know.* Harvard Business School Press.

Economist. (2018, March 22). What works to reduce gun deaths. Vol 426 #9084. https://www.economist.com/united-states/2018/03/22/what-works-to-reduce-gun-deaths

Elazar, D. J. (1962). *The American partnership: Intergovernmental cooperation in the nineteenth-century United States.* University of Chicago Press.

Forester, J. (2009). *Dealing with differences: Dramas of mediating public disputes.* Oxford University Press.

Fountain, J. E. (1998). Social capital: Its relationship to innovation in science and technology. *Science and Public Policy, 25*(2), 103–115.

Fowler, L. (2018). Intergovernmental relations and energy policy: What we know and what we still need to learn. *State and Local Government Review, 50*(3), 203–212.

Academic Studies of Collaborative Politics and Management   189

Franz, R., & Pattakos, A. N. (1996). *Economic growth and evolution: The intuitive connection.* Intuition at Work.

Gill, C. (1945). Federal-state-city cooperation in congested production areas. *Public Administration Review, 5*(1), 28–33.

Gofen, A. (2015). Citizens' entrepreneurial role in public service provision. *Public Management Review, 17*(3), 404–424.

Gray, B. (1989). *Collaborating: Finding common ground for multiparty problems.* Jossey Bass.

Grodzins, M. (1966). *The American system: A new view of government in the United States.* Transaction Publishers.

Honadle, B. W. (1981). A capacity-building framework: A search for concept and purpose. *Public Administration Review, 41*(5), 575–580.

Huxham, C., & Vangen, S. (2005). *Managing to collaborate: The theory and practice of collaborative advantage.* Routledge.

Innes, J. E., Connick, S., & Booher, D. (2007). Informality as a planning strategy: Collaborative water management in the CALFED Bay-Delta Program. *Journal of the American Planning Association, 73*(2), 195–210.

Key, V. O., Jr. (1937). *The administration of federal grants to states.* Public Disputes.

Koliba, C. J., Gerrits, L., Rhodes, M. L., & Meek, J. W. (2016). Complexity theory, networks, and systems analysis. In C. Ansell & J. Torfing (Eds.), *Handbook on theories of governance.* Edward Elgar Publishing.

Koliba, C. J., Mills, R. M., & Zia, A. (2011). Accountability in governance networks: An assessment of public, private, and nonprofit emergency management practices following Hurricane Katrina. *Public Administration Review, 71*(2), 210–220.

Koppenjan, J. F. M., Koppenjan, J., & Klijn, E. H. (2004). *Managing uncertainties in networks: A network approach to problem solving and decision making.* Psychology Press.

Lilienthal, D. E. (1939). Electricity: The people's business. *The ANNALS of the American Academy of Political and Social Science, 201*(1), 58–63.

Loughlin, J. (2007). Reconfiguring the state: Trends in territorial governance in European states. *Regional and Federal Studies, 17*(4), 385–403.

Maynard-Moody, S., Musheno, M., & Palumbo, D. (1990). Street-wise social policy: Resolving the dilemma of street-level influence and successful implementation. *Western Political Quarterly, 43*(4), 833–848.

McGuire, M. (2002). Managing networks: Propositions on what managers do and why they do it. *Public Administration Review, 62*(5), 599–609.

Moore, M. H. (1995). *Creating public value: Strategic management in government.* Harvard University Press.

Moynihan, D. P. (2008). Learning under uncertainty: Networks in crisis management. *Public Administration Review, 68*(2), 350–365.

Nicolini, D. (2011). Practice as the site of knowing: Insights from the field of telemedicine. *Organization Science, 22*(3), 602–620.

Nonaka, I., Toyama, R., & Konno, N. (2000). SECI, Ba and leadership: A unified model of dynamic knowledge creation. *Long Range Planning, 33*(1), 5–34.

O'Toole, Jr., L. J. (1986). Policy recommendations for multi-actor implementation: An assessment of the field. *Journal of Public Policy,* 181–210.

O'Toole, L. J. (2010). The ties that bind? Networks, public administration, and political science. *P.S.: Political Science and Politics, 43*(1), 7–14.

Polanyi, M. (1962). Tacit knowing: Its bearing on some problems of philosophy. *Reviews of Modern Physics, 34*(4), 601.

190 *Academic Studies of Collaborative Politics and Management*

Polanyi, M., & Prosch, H. (1975). *Meaning.* University of Chicago Press.

Raab, J., & Kenis, P. (2009). Heading toward a society of networks: Empirical developments and theoretical challenges. *Journal of Management Inquiry, 18*(3), 198–210.

Saint-Onge, H., & Armstrong, C. (2004). *The conductive organization.* Elsevier.

Salamon, L. M. (1995). *Partners in public service: Government-nonprofit relations in the modern welfare state.* John Hopkins University Press.

Saz-Carranza, A., & Serra, A. (2009). Institutional sources of distrust in government contracting: A comparison between home-based and residential social services in Spain. *Public Management Review, 11*(3), 263–279.

Schrage, M. (1995). *No more teams! Mastering the dynamics of creative collaboration.* Doubleday.

Shefter, M. (1978). Party, bureaucracy, and political change in the United States. In L. Maisel & J. Cooper (Eds.), *Political parties: Development and decay.* Sage.

Skowronek, S. (1982). *Building a new American state: The expansion of national administrative capacities, 1877–1920.* Cambridge University Press.

Smith, S. R., & Lipsky, M. (1993). *Nonprofits for hire.* Harvard University Press.

Sørensen, E., & Torfing, J. (2009). Making governance networks effective and democratic through metagovernance. *Public Administration, 87*(2), 234–258.

Sydow, J., Müller-Seitz, G., & Provan, K. G. (2013). Managing uncertainty in alliances and networks: From governance to practice. In T. K. Das (Ed.), *Managing knowledge in strategic alliances* (pp. 1–43). Information Age Publishing.

Torfing, J. (2016). *Collaborative innovation in the public sector.* Georgetown University Press.

Tsoukas, H. (1996). The firm as a distributed knowledge system: A constructionist approach. *Strategic Management Journal, 17*(S2), 11–25.

Tsoukas, H. (2005). *Complex knowledge: Studies in organizational epistemology.* Oxford University Press.

Vieg, J. A. (1941). Working relationships in governmental agricultural programs. *Public Administration Review, 1*(2), 141–148.

Vigoda-Gadot, E., Shoham, A., Schwabsky, N., & Ruvio, A. (2005). Public sector innovation for the managerial and the post-managerial era: Promises and realities in a globalizing public administration. *International Public Management Journal, 8*(1), 57–81.

Waldo, D. (1948). *The administrative state: Conclusion* (pp. 150–154). Classics of Public Administration, Thomson Wadsworth Publication.

Walker David, B. (2000). *The rebirth of federalism* (2nd ed.). Chatam House.

Watts, R. L. (1999). *Comparing federal systems.* Mc Gill-Queen's University Press.

Weidner, E. W. (1944). State supervision of local government in Minnesota. *Public Administration Review, 4*(3), 226–233.

Wondolleck, J. M., & Yaffee, S. L. (2000). *Making collaboration work: Lessons from innovation in natural resource management.* Island Press.

Wright, D. S. (1988). *Understanding intergovernmental relations.* Brooks.

Zeemering, E. S. (2018). Sustainability management, strategy and reform in local government. *Public Management Review, 20*(1), 136–153.

8 Stories in Collaborative Politics

Clifford Geertz, the well-known anthropologist, defines culture as a collective act of interpretation, the stories we tell one another about ourselves in an attempt to make ongoing sense of why we do what we do (Geertz, 1973). This chapter is an extended analysis of stories related to CP. Following Geertz's traditions, field-based conversations with managers, as Ralph Hummel (1991, p. 32) suggests, "show that they are quite capable of defining their reality, judging what kind of knowledge is useful to them, and developing validity standards relevant to their world." Moreover, Sandfort (1999) argues:

> If the actual social processes that occur at the front lines are examined, we discover that frontline staff in both the public bureaucracy and small contractors draw on the same sources of evidence—past relations, daily experiences, clients' stories—when assessing the organizations with which they are mandated to collaborate.
>
> (p. 315)

As a result, narrative aspects such as field-based stories can also "draw inspiration, concepts, and research information from many sources" (McSwite, 2002, p. 89; see also Agranoff, 2018).

With stories, essential disclosures emanate from such conceptualized simple interactions as communication, dialogue, and idea sharing among the purveyors of academic disciplines (Baracskay, 2011). It also brings imagination and wisdom to the discourse. As Rowland Egger (1959, pp. 451–452) concluded decades ago concerning the novel, "The recognition of the novel as a lengthy source of wisdom about administrative phenomena is an important reassertion of the fact that administration was, is, and will always remain, in the considerable degree an artistic performance." So is the situation of related stories, from which we can also learn much. Over the five decades of research and action plus observation, one of the authors, Dr. Robert Agranoff, has demonstrated that getting out into the field doing research lets you know what is happening below the surface, particularly "below the survey." It also puts "meat on the bones" of the real world.

DOI: 10.4324/9781003385769-8

192   *Stories in Collaborative Politics*

A Story About Medicaid Waivers in North Carolina

The North Carolina waivers story in Box 8.1 that occurred early in the research career of one of the authors of this volume, Dr. Agranoff, raised his antennae regarding federal–state regulation and particularly the need to learn about the real world in practice. Apparently, not everybody follows the rules, at least not all the time and in the same way. Practitioners in the field operated differently than printed Medicaid waiver procedures manuals assumed. This study subsequently emerged among the eight states under our study, ranging from no formal waiver seeking (the ideal process for permission) to those states that virtually always followed the rules (followed then sought proper prior permission). Furthermore, it drove home that there are not only 50 states, but there are many more interpretations and variations in the "real world." Many look somewhat different from proscriptions in the *Federal Register*, where rules are published. Why? The answer is mainly in the nexus between government and politics. Moreover, it illustrated that the world of practice is clearly bound up with the world of theory, in this case, any "political practice."

Box 8.1   Waiver of the Rules in North Carolina

One memorable story from North Carolina is distinctive, introduced in Chapter 1. It occurred in a federal study of health departments in the North Carolina umbrella (combined) human services department, part of a study in the 1970s. A week in the field taught Dr. Agranoff a great deal.

Here is a prime example. A state planning director reported and described some eight or ten administrative actions in the Medicaid statutes that at the time were only allowable with formal Medicaid 1915C written waivers (official, approved permission to circumvent legal intent or regulations).

Several were explained in considerable detail, particularly on who were involved as the operating partners. One missing partner was the federal government, which was legally required to review and approve the waivers. Dr. Agranoff reacted with a follow-up question related to intergovernmental management in action on how the waiver process proceeded and the degrees of federal, state, and local/nonprofit administrative involvement/ site approval of state actions.

A state planning director responded, "We do not apply for waivers. We just do it." Dr. Agranoff followed up with probes about federal audits. He kept the conversation going and raised concern about penalties by remarking, "You must spend a lot of time negotiating waivers." The planning director responded, "That is not an issue" [pause]. I asked, "Why is that the case? They are required." The planning director responded, "You see, Bob, I am a Roman Catholic, and we Catholics believe it is better to ask for forgiveness later instead of permission before. We do not seek preapproval for waivers. We just do it!"

Source: Robert Agranoff

Stories in Collaborative Politics 193

A Story About Budgeting Politics in Indiana

Box 8.2 is a story about an exemplary small town that was foremost in forging connections with other potential partners in the community, particularly in economic and community development. It was the "ultimate" in networked linkages via collaboration. But Salem was different, at least in one unique way:

Box 8.2   The Budget: Salem, Indiana, 1998

After being ushered in by a secretary-receptionist, Dr. Robert Agranoff entered the Mayor's office (there was no other evidence of mayoral staff offices around the city hall). It was an austere office with piles of papers everywhere. The office contained a desk and two wooden chairs placed in front: no conference table or working table. A sign on his desk said, "Frank Newkirk Senior, Mayor."

Frank Newkirk, Sr., 86 years old, came from behind his desk, shook hands, and said, "I'm Frank Newkirk; how are things up in Bloomington?" He invited Dr. Agranoff to sit down. A two-way speaker on his desk was currently being amplified from the police dispatchers' office. Before Dr. Agranoff was able to speak, Newkirk looked at the big brown amplifying box (an ancient intercom system) and listened. A call reporting a lost cat came in after a few moments. He switched the channel, and the public works office was on the line. The director of public works was dispatching a pothole repair team to one of the city's arterial streets. Newkirk reminded the director of a pothole on a nearby street that a constituent had called into the Mayor. After giving that directive, Newkirk shut the squawk box off. He turned to Dr. Agranoff and said, "I find that I can learn a lot about the city and how to run it with this little machine."

He paused and looked at Dr. Agranoff. It was his time. Dr. Agranoff explained the purpose of the study and that Salem was one of six out of 237 cities to be featured. He beamed and said, "we do our best here to have good working relations with everybody in Indianapolis and their field people. Sometimes with the feds, too!" Dr. Agranoff asked his first question about the city's economic development strategy. As Newkirk answered, it was clear that although he may not appear to be the world's most sophisticated executive, he was no mere figurehead or country bumpkin mayor. Newkirk understood and articulated a coherent development strategy that demonstrated his direct involvement. When the entire discussion was near completion, his knowledge of detail made it clear he had some direct role in all grants, loans, revolving funds, tax abatements, and intergovernmental transaction instruments.

194 *Stories in Collaborative Politics*

After the last question, Dr. Agranoff asked if he could see a member of the city council who has taken a lead role in economic development. Dr. Agranoff said: "Give me his number, and I will schedule him." Newkirk replied, "He is waiting now, outside my office, if you can see him now." Not having another appointment for an hour, Dr. Agranoff said yes.

Finally, Dr. Agranoff asked for a series of documents: a table of organization, a list of grant reports, recent development projects, the city budget, and an exchange of letters regarding the city's out-of-compliance water supply with the state department of environment. Newkirk balked at the budget only, saying, "I think the budget will be impossible." Dr. Agranoff thought, "is he trying to hide something?" Newkirk then buzzed his secretary on the intercom and gave her the list of documents requested. She immediately came through the door and said she could put her hands on everything but the budget. Dr. Agranoff would have to return later because some would have to be photocopied. Dr. Agranoff should come back that afternoon to pick up the documents. He said goodbye to the Mayor and reminded him of our "Exit discussion" in 2.5 days. It was already on Newkirk's calendar. Dr. Agranoff glanced at the page: only one other entry for that entire day.

When Dr. Agranoff returned to the Mayor's office the following late afternoon to retrieve the documents about Salem's budget, the secretary handed him a stack of papers and said, "I got you the budget. We called the newspaper, and they looked it up, photocopied it, and delivered it to us earlier this afternoon."

Source: Robert Agranoff

This story about the "politics of budgeting" was part of the field study portion of the Drs. Agranoff and McGuire book *Collaborative Public Management* (2003). In addition to the 237-city survey, Drs. Agranoff and McGuire selected six cities of various population sizes "high and deep" in intergovernmental activity. In addition to Salem, they included Cincinnati, Ohio; Garfield Heights, Ohio; Beloit, Wisconsin; Ithaca, Michigan; and Woodstock, Illinois, where about five working days each were expended with guided conversations to elaborate on the detailed close-ended questionnaire that followed an International City Management Association (ICMA) national economic development survey. In addition to the topic-based material on collaborative management, they learned much about public management "out there" in general. The story regarding Salem is just one such incident of literally hundreds we heard about in the field.

"The Budget" indeed suggested a great deal about the arena of study by Drs. Agranoff and McGuire. First and foremost, "high-flying" intergovernmental management is not only conducted by professionally trained managers in the ICMA mold, but by the "common touch" of a small-town mayor, politics and all, who travels far on their intuitive ability, to see the large picture and to work to put together the pieces in a less formal way than professional planners/economic development specialists might produce. It also indicated that some small towns could play the intergovernmental grants

Stories in Collaborative Politics   195

and regulation adjustment games quite well without the highly paid and trained staff and/or consultants used by many big cities. For example, Mayor Newkirk and his partners (county, development district) could work "between the lines" across jurisdictions. They seemed aware of the need "to network" like the big cities are said to do and to "move between the agency/organization silos," so to speak.

The subsequent conversations with that active council member opened the research team's eyes to some four dozen steps and eight jurisdictions and private entities involved in expanding their industrial park. One of the authors of this volume, Dr. Agranoff, and Dr. McGuire could map the complicated picture from discussions about the process. It was a real lesson in crossing boundaries (Agranoff, 2007, 2017) and ultimately became a good teaching tool. Indeed, it taught them much about what goes on between horizontal and vertical intergovernmental program lines. Finally, what about the budget or the "punch line" of the story, so to speak? Salem appeared to have no working picture of a total or any compiled budget. Instead, it just seemed to move full steam ahead incrementally.

A Story About Low-Tech Solutions in River Falls, Wisconsin

A story in Box 8.3 about the potential—or lack thereof—for alternative service delivery. In River Falls, it was a simple struggle between contracting out a police two-way radio to a third party or in-house delivery for after-hours emergencies. During Dr. Agranoff's (one of the authors of this volume) first two years in River Falls (his undergraduate days), there was a unique way to call the police (fire used a telephone chain to alert volunteers).

Box 8.3   The "Bat Signal" in River Falls, Wisconsin, Until 1960

It seems that after 5 p.m., the only city employee of River Falls, Wisconsin (a population of 5,000 people) other than the police patrol car officers was the operator of the municipal power plant, which was some three-quarters of a mile from the main street near the Kinnikinnic Riverbed. To call the police after 5 p.m., you called the power plant operator on duty. He recorded the call and activated a light switch that lit a bare light bulb hanging over a bank in the middle of Main Street. When the officers in the one-night police patrol car happened to notice the bulb on, e.g., after coffee, they would activate their patrol car red lights and dash down to the power plant, pick up a call write-up slip and then dash back to town to answer the call. Great response time in emergencies! In 1960, a weekly paper headline story relayed that "Federal Revenue Sharing Brings Police Two-Way Radio System." So the "bat signal"—a quaint way to call the police after hours—ended. Presumably, response time was considerably improved after 1960.

Source: Robert Agranoff

---

196 *Stories in Collaborative Politics*

The "bat signal" story is illustrative, particularly to younger people, of what the world was like a bit before contemporary communication devices like smartphones. The River Falls City Council refused to spend the money on a two-way radio system. That would include another staff person or police officer on duty 24 hours a day, which meant it would be a political decision. Another alternative could have been to contract out (i.e., pay for) dispatching or to agree with the two River Falls county sheriff's departments (River Falls is split into two counties). As in the case of other entities, it indicates that government could be "low-tech"—in this case, thanks to local politics.

In the same way that one of Dr. Agranoff's high-school-age part-time jobs was as a manual pinsetter in a bowling alley (yes, there were), at least the bat signal arrangement gave the government a human touch and, in one tiny way, linked the small town with the feds through revenue sharing. However, after 1960, no longer was the "bat signal" employed. As River Falls faced a decision between in-house delivery dispatching or contracting out or entering into a mutual service agreement, the city chose not to collaborate further, saving funds by not using the bat signal. As a result, the power plant night operator was no longer part of the call "system."

A Story About Collaborative Devolution in Ukraine

Box 8.4 is a story about "collaborative devolution." As a local government consultant for a USAID project, one of the authors, Dr. Robert Agranoff, presented a state–local collaborative model in the United States that works in most states: home rule or delegating authority downward to let communities decide many issues for themselves. Dr. Agranoff spent a few years advising the post-Soviet Union Parliament of Ukraine on regional and local government concerns. When asked, "What was the Ukraine experience like?" in his visit more than a decade before Ukraine became war-torn during the early 2020s, Dr. Robert Agranoff always began with this story. It virtually captures the entire experience.

Box 8.4   Home Rule in Ukraine, 2010

Dr. Robert Agranoff was asked to present about U.S. local government at a workshop session to parliamentary deputies and two justices on the Ukraine Constitutional Court. He chose local "Home Rule," whereby—to varying degrees—U.S. state legislatures grant broad powers to cities and some urban counties: government discretion in areas such as taxation, regulation, organization, and service operations. It took about 20 minutes to develop the issues and a two-page handout translated into Ukrainian and Russian. When he finished his talk, Dr. Agranoff was asked questions and provided comments.

Stories in Collaborative Politics 197

The first was from an academic, law Prof. Nikolay Kornienko, then a justice of the Constitutional Court. He made a statement to this effect: "If Ukraine adopted any form of home rule, there would be total chaos." End of home rule/autonomy discussion.

Source: Robert Agranoff

The response of Justice Kornienko captured Dr. Agranoff's several years of frustrating exposure to democratic subnational governments in this non-Western world. Discretion or subnational rule always seemed to hit a political brick wall. Dr. Agranoff admitted to a possibly naïve overreach using the example of home rule in the audience's minds; local decision-making and the potential for collaboration were really at issue here. The idea of either inherent or delegated regional powers working with others proved to be outside Soviet- and subsequently Russian-conditioned thinking. Local government was understood to be at the end of a hierarchical organizational and political chain of some sort. The localities were where people lived but were not particularly self-governed. In short, Dr. Agranoff came a long way and expended many USAID resources to be told in one sentence that it would not work, particularly politically, even with the fall of the Soviet Union and an independent Ukraine. This government concern was simply a matter of political thinking carried over from the Soviet era. Any potential for national–local collaboration by decentralization seemed to be out of the question. In effect, Dr. Agranoff came a long way to be told it would not work in a very short time. So much for home rule in Ukraine.

A Story About the "Big Boys" of Politics

This exemplifies what Dr. Agranoff has termed "Big P" politics. It demonstrates the existence of heavy political overtones and the politics of collaboration/noncollaboration related to administrative reform. This story was provided in detail in Box 1.3. The report described how Indiana Gov. Evan Bayh's chief of staff asked Dr. Agranoff to chair a task force to integrate the various state government health and human services agencies into a "comprehensive department" of human health services. The task force included cabinet-level human service agency program heads, peak lobby association executive directors/lobbyists, academics, civic association leaders, and professionals representing in-home support, social welfare, public health, vocational rehabilitation, mental health, and developmental and physical disabilities. When the group finally introduced the working plan to interested parties, the Indiana State Medical Association (ISMA) dropped a "political bomb" of sorts, refusing to be part of the new "umbrella" department, which required removing the Public Health Department from the new structure. Dr. Agranoff tried to

198 *Stories in Collaborative Politics*

reason with the ISMA, arguing that it had virtually no public health involvement and cross-programming was essential under many circumstances. Unfortunately, the task force could not successfully fight the powerful ISMA. However, with lukewarm support from some others, the ISMA had no real stake in the game. So, Dr. Agranoff brought the news to the task force. They collectively blew off steam and ultimately removed Public Health from the proposal but left Medicaid assistance payments and some smaller programs in the new structure. That critical battle was won. Medicaid and a few other small health programs would remain in the combined Department of Family and Social Services Administration (FSSA).

Thus, this is the political nature of reorganization. The new structure bill passed. Indeed, the rest is history, so to speak, as the FSSA was created and stands today with some 5,000 employees. But, to most of us on the task force, it became part of our "pragmatic ontology of experience" (Clandinin & Rosiek, 2007, p. 41). The "big hand of politics" was at work. We clearly could not—not with a new governor—take on one of the significant forces of politics on some "reorganization turf." The politics of administrative reform was clearly at work, as often happens in the real world of government.

A Personal Journey Story of Dr. Agranoff

Stories of politics and administration have always played some essential role in the author's (Dr. Robert Agranoff) personal understanding, even his becoming an academic. Life seemed to set off consciousness about how governing was organized and carried out, particularly among collaborating partners. Dr. Agranoff's pre-college experience in the U.S. Navy drove home some levels of political and organizational sensitivity to the nature, operation, and influences related to politics in bureaucracy. He was certain that he had been among the few enlisted sailors stationed at the Naval Operating Base in Norfolk, Virginia that regularly read the *New York Times* at the base library. Moreover, Dr. Agranoff was able to "touch and feel" public administration at the basic or "street" level in the small, 12-person pediatric clinic (for dependents). He worked as a hematology technician. For example, Roy, his career Navy Chief, who administered the clinic, was then a 24-year man who had served a total of only 18 months at sea, the rest being shore duty entirely in the Norfolk area, despite supposed career person sea duty rotation requirements. Dr. Agranoff asked him why he never again went to sea after his first voyage. He answered. "You see, I have a ship buddy from his one sea rotation in Navy Personnel in Washington. When it is sea duty rotation time, I call him. He moves my file (before electronic records) to the amphibious base slot at Little Creek, Virginia, a few miles away, which also counts as sea duty on my record. So far, it has worked." It can be counted as involving what has been defined as "small p" bureaucratic politics.

Where did the *New York Times* come in? In an obscure news item before the end of his service time, a news story said that it was to be shortened in time to support a federal budget reduction. It mentioned early discharge for some draftees like Dr.

Agranoff. He told chief Roy, who immediately called his buddy in Navy Personnel. When he hung up the phone, he said to Dr. Agranoff, "It's a good thing I called. It started your paperwork; otherwise, there might have been 3–4 weeks of delay. So you are now in the first group to be mustered out!" It suggested to Dr. Agranoff that a lot was going on in the politics of government between what the *New York Times* reported and what was happening in the world of politics ("small p") at the "street-level" operation of bureaucracy.

Another personal experience story revealed to Dr. Agranoff how communication unfolded earlier. He was amidst his Ph.D. dissertation research at the Minnesota Democratic–Farmer–Labor Party headquarters in Minneapolis. Dr. Agranoff was given research access to all party records and correspondence through the support of the state chairman and executive director. One letter from the early 1960s came from a newly appointed postmaster from Oak Island, which is as remote as one could be in Minnesota. Oak Island is in the middle of Lake of the Woods, which juts north into Ontario, Canada. It could only be reached by water (usually by boat) or by small plane, and the island had no telephone landlines (before cell coverage). The only way to connect with the mainland was by airplane with landing/takeoff floats.

The letter of Dr. Agranoff, as reconstructed, went as follows:

Dear State Chairman Farr:

I am sorry we were unable to meet by phone last Tuesday. It was foggy. The plane to Warroad [a small town on the mainland] was fogged out, so I could not get to the pay phone at the general store. My next planned air flight into Warroad will be on Tuesday next in 10 days. If the payphone is available, I plan to call you then. Sorry about the missed meeting, but the weather was out of control. That is life in Lake of the Woods.

Clearly, even in the early 1960s, with modern communications as they then existed, Dr. Agranoff had never encountered anyone who had to charter a plane to make a phone call. Instead, one might call it "life in the slower lane." Meanwhile, the U.S. postal station on Oak Island remains open as of 2023 for three days per week. Clearly, communication with the mainland has improved.

Constructing Experience-Based Stories of Collaboration

Over the years, both in politics and in studying public administration in the field, a series of observations regarding administrative politics can be shared. Space limits only identification, but they are elaborated elsewhere (Agranoff, 2017). First and foremost, always be on the lookout for the formal *and* the informal. The story in Box 8.2 regarding the Salem budget initially led to suspect a combination of the locals hiding something, fiscally or politically. But it turned out to be more

200 *Stories in Collaborative Politics*

a matter of "disorganization" or some unconventional clerical or organizational style. Otherwise, the examination of Salem's broad networking program demonstrated considerable political astuteness, combined with a keen use of intergovernmental contracting.

Second, one must be aware of "big P" and "small p" politics repeated in any living story. The Indiana FSSA task force on reorganization brought home both as the various groups manifested their interests while the ISMA weighed in heavily on its big issue. Both are at work quite often. For example, an aborted attempt at municipal annexation to the city of Bloomington, Indiana, recently brought opposition from its largest employer, located just outside of the town. Substantially increased property taxes were among the publicly stated concerns. The Indiana legislature passed a special state legislative bill that blocked such annexation for five years. Again, it was the "big boys" at work.

Third, today's complex organizations (hierarchies) and interacting interest associations and agencies can lead to an emergent sort of "network politics." It involves a set of connective interests, potential information, and resource interactions. As a result, a politics of interaction occurs, including turf protection, mission incompatibility, resource hoarding, and many moves between that are identified in this book. But, like the North Carolina waivers in action, do not write off these "administrative" questions and issues as non-political. In truth, many political negotiations with the feds regarding details no doubt followed in North Carolina that they did not choose to tell us about.

Fourth and related, anyone who has practiced public management is aware of turf protection. Turf is the territory or domain of an organization and its programs. Aside from the potential of mission incompatibility, any administrator can draw a "moat" around their organization and/or programs. This is politics *and* management, so always be aware of the smell of smoldering or burning turf, even if there is no apparent fire. An anticipated turf protection is always there, but not always as direct as was the ISMA in the Indiana FSSA situation.

Fifth, in the era of collaborative management and involvement in networks, be aware of different types of power. At least four are identified in this volume in Chapter 7 as a sort of politics of interaction: agency power (including finance and other resource issues), operational power, knowledge-based power, and deliberative power. All have political power, as well as management undertones and/or overtones. Thus, keeping one's political antennae out is always important while involved in interactive processing.

Sixth, an emergent political issue is what can be called "mission sensitivity," as agencies and interests work together. For example, the ISMA clearly demonstrated how the mission could be a concern. Each entity has its unique mission. Some are bound to be more "in sync" than others. The point is that some who are incompatible with other agencies will resist collaborative moves; for example, resource sharing or serving different clients. These mission challenges can be at work as inevitable moves are, and are as political as they are administrative. Stories of resource scarcity or inability to service new clients will often be told. The more

Stories in Collaborative Politics   201

incompatible the mission of these agencies, the more likely there are also political stories to be told.

Seventh, it is likely that process politics—as in the story of home rule in Ukraine—are at work. The learning experience here was that a post-Soviet country had not developed and was not ready for forms of delegated power like home rule or delegation of most types of autonomy. Do not assume that to be what seems a "logical democracy" to most of us does not generate some political opposition. Justice Kornienko's frame of reference undoubtedly involved his conception of top-down democracy. But, as actors often do so, it is essential to always keep one's political antennae up.

Eighth, a given set of political-administrative norms is generally assumed to reflect everyone's preferences, but in reality, it is the case. Once, when working for a farm organization, one of the authors of this volume, Dr. Agranoff, spoke to a local group about an impending federal bill relating to price support and production quotas. When the question period opened, the first response was from a farmer who vociferously objected to recent local store openings on Friday night instead of the previous Saturday practice. Dr. Agranoff distinctly remembered him saying, "It used to be we could take a bath once on Saturday evening for both shopping and church. Now we have to take two baths." The discussion caused a deflection of interest in the farm program. It turns out, at least to this farmer, this was a local political issue that outweighed any federal farm bill talk. Indeed, in politics, expect anything!

Ninth, always be sensitive to the street-level activity that is clothed in personal "small p" politics. The stated experiences with Dr. Agranoff's chief in the Navy opened his eyes to transactions between bureaucrats and clients at the basic level. He watched him face and solve patient problems among literally hundreds of service "accommodations" of a political nature at "low levels," so to speak. They may not always be able to be overcome or eliminated, but these street-level accommodations are both administrative and political. It is one important reason why public work is not always for the faint-hearted.

Tenth, and finally, like in the North Carolina waiver and bat signal stories, the long chain of program implementation means many political opportunities for political adjustment or even displacement that can happen along the line. Two key areas that are political and administrative are operational localism, like in North Carolina, where implementers have an opportunity to put their stamp on programs (Reed, 2014), and street-level divergence, like the bat signal in River Falls, as direct contact staff further shape policy as it meets clients (Gofen, 2014). As a result, of course, political and managerial stories emerge.

Making Better Stories

How are stories developed? To corporate executive David Armstrong (1992), in his short book, *Managing By Storying Around*, storytelling helps managers establish less rule-bound agendas, reinforce policy manuals, render organization charts less

202   *Stories in Collaborative Politics*

important, reinforce decentralized decision-making, and help recognize and articulate patterns. Armstrong employs a suggestive checklist for story writing. He suggests short, personalized themes, using words that form a mental picture, e.g., the bat signal or the week's paper budget. Also, he urges verification and—where possible—uses those involved. To Armstrong, making storytelling part of the management approach can serve many needs. They help give recognition, reinforce the organizational vision, contribute to goal-focus, reinforce extant organizational culture, foster friendly communication, increase involvement across the organization, and support training by setting expectations (pp. 244–245).

Conclusion

We learn about politics in many ways. The events and situations in North Carolina, River Falls, Ukraine, Salem, and the "big boys" in Indiana politics demonstrate the pervasive aspects of politics. To be sure, not every administrative move on every collaborative management project or effort is political, but more often, politics are there but not always easy to see. In collaborating with other organizations, we must constantly look for politics, however invisible or obscure they may be. Stories allow us to encompass their historical and temporal dynamic. Dawoody (2007, p. 14) concludes that "Reality is revealed to the complex administrator, through an active construction in which he participates," opening up the world as an open system with a capacity to respond to change. This includes politics in an administration typically outside of a direct political party nature; for example, in most collaborative efforts.

To David M. Boje (1991), storytelling offers many organizational advantages. First, their meaning unfolds through the storytelling event because they are contextually embedded. Next, using the story format in context will reveal other related stories, as researchers can also "unpack" very brief enactments in dialogue to discover the reality underlying the linguistic enactments; e.g., political change, changing relationships, and the impact of turbulent events. That clearly proved to be the case embedded in Salem's economic development efforts. Sometimes, storytelling can be helpful for managers trying to cope with rapid change or some unique position. For example, one can see "story text and performance as two sides of the same coin and gives us insight into the complex and varied ways organization members use storytelling in their work world" (p. 125).

Another research arena lies in the potential use of stories in collaboration research. For example, regarding organizational change like experiences related to collaboration (e.g., North Carolina and Salem), Reissner's (2011) analysis of stories can better understand how new interpretive schemes are constructed and negotiated and which additional factors influence processes like those of collaboration. Also, stories can be aligned with the external political and social environment processes in a program's functioning. Most importantly, some work on stories can lead to a richer understanding of change as it occurs, solving as they are "filtered through a thicket of stories and perceptions that are re-framed and re-interpreted" (p. 606).

Reflecting on the influence of Shakespeare, Wachhaus (2017, pp. 6–7) points out the thematic contributions derived from his "stories." First is recognizing that the human element profoundly impacts the operation of the government machinery. The second is acknowledging that multiple perspectives are necessary to fully view drives, goals, and procedures in complex social webs. Third, Shakespeare points to the required multilevel stories and essential details, the complex problems embedded in the larger picture. In this sense, it provides a broader and deeper view. In a similar respect, Farmer (2016, p. 16) concludes that "Shakespeare offers at least four clues: leadership/entrepreneurship, policy leadership, heroes and archvillains, and the role of insights and reflections." In this respect, one can learn much from the experiential stories of politics like those indicated.

Finally, one is reminded of McSwite's (2002) admonition that overcoming just the appearance of success is to use literature and stories to "sufficiently acknowledge the extent to which our political process is inconsistent with the goals of enterprises" (p. 95). Overcoming this barrier also "involves producing and beginning to tell each other stories of the world of public administration, and using whatever stories we can find that relate to our world to inspire our studies of it and reach our students" (p. 96). Dr. Agranoff's years of work in the field and personal political experience while observing have opened many windows to the world of conducting CP research. Many of these notable collaborative openings and insights have been through stories told and/or observed in the field, deeply enriching our understanding of the political and operational aspects of collaborative public management and related endeavors.

References

Agranoff, R. (2007). *Managing within networks: Adding value to public organizations*. Georgetown University Press.

Agranoff, R. (2017). *Crossing boundaries for intergovernmental management*. Georgetown University Press.

Agranoff, R. (2018). *Local governments in multilevel governance: The administrative dimension*. Lexington Books.

Agranoff, R., & McGuire, M. (2003). *Collaborative public management: New strategies for public management: New strategies for local governments*. Georgetown University Press.

Armstrong, D. M. (1992). *Managing by storying around a new method of leadership*. David M. Armstrong.

Baracskay, D. (2011). *The Palestine liberation organization: Terrorism and prospects for peace in the holy land*. ABC-CLIO.

Boje, D. M. (1991). The storytelling organization: A study of story performance in an office-supply firm. *Administrative Science Quarterly, 36*(1), 106–126.

Clandinin, D. J., & Rosiek, J. (2007). Mapping a landscape of narrative inquiry: Borderland spaces and tensions. In D. J. Clandinin (Ed.), *Handbook of narrative inquiry: Mapping a methodology* (pp. 35–76). Sage Publications.

Dawoody, A. (2007). *The war on terror between islamophobia and reconstructing reality* (No. 228). Academic Public Administration Studies Archive-APAS.

204 *Stories in Collaborative Politics*

Egger, R. (1959). The administrative novel. *The American Political Science Review, 53*(2), 448–455.

Farmer, D. J. (2016). Out of the fly-bottle? A post-script on post-traditional public administration. *International Journal of Organization Theory and Behavior, 19*(1), 90–102.

Geertz, C. (1973). *The interpretation of cultures.* Basic Books.

Gofen, A. (2014). Mind the gap: Dimensions and influence of street-level divergence. *Journal of Public Administration Research and Theory, 24*(2), 473–493.

Hummel, R. P. (1991). Stories managers tell: Why they are as valid as science. *Public Administration Review, 51*(1), 31–41.

McSwite, O. C. (2002). Moving on (legitimacy is over): Millennial consciousness and its potential. In *Rethinking administrative theory: The challenge of the new century* (pp. 3–22). Praeger.

Reed, D. S. (2014). *Building the federal schoolhouse: Localism and the American education state.* Oxford University Press.

Reissner, S. C. (2011). Patterns of stories of organisational change. *Journal of Organizational Change Management, 24*(5), 593–609. DOI:10.1108/09534811111158877

Sandfort, J. (1999). The structural impediments to human service collaboration: Examining welfare reform at the front lines. *Social Service Review, 73*(3), 314–339.

Wachhaus, A. (2017). Platform governance: Developing collaborative democracy. *Administrative Theory & Praxis, 39*(3), 206–221.

9 The Process Challenges and Struggles of Joint Undertakings

Many collaborative efforts prove to be relatively simple to reach an agreement and execute. In these situations, the level of disagreement is relatively mild, almost too easy. However, issues between agencies are easily resolved with minimal disruption to participating agencies. As illustrated in Table 9.1, many require minimal two-party or multiparty engagement, even despite regular interaction; e.g., concerning client referrals, grant applications and execution, actions of councils of agencies, and exchanges of information. But what about those more extensively involved, "big-picture" engagements? Moves like these, identified in this volume, bring out more protracted and intense CP. These could include networks that organize strategies that involve the commitment of many agencies, joint ventures, public–private operating partnerships, networks that involve joint agreements and strategies, technical workgroups operating jointly or with multiple agency operations, and so on (see Chapter 3). These collaborative activities—the third and fourth columns in Table 9.1, not only require more intense involvement in the process but are subject to *heavier forms of politics*: big-picture political items, with less guarantee of success and considerably more involvement, plus the greater likelihood of success and lots more of what we will identify here as the *heavy politics of collaborative management*. This chapter focuses on the perils and pitfalls, plus the opportunities of these more extensive forms of engagement and agreement.

In these big-picture moves, CP is rarely simply attending joint meetings and using parliamentary procedure to "vote" on issues. More likely, extended discussions and bringing out various parties' concerns proceeds by protracted "invested actions and agreements." Voting is often not—even sometimes never—part of such processes. "Winners"—or at least the prevailing facts of contented parties and the non-losers—are "accommodated" and hopefully emerge out of extended processes. Usually, the situation involves discussion and seeking avenues of potential agreement, avoiding frequent "vetoes" or "pullouts" of potential partners before the agreement. Lots of processes and little voting are usually the name of the game here, where lots of CP are played, and sometimes a resolution is reached and sometimes not. Indeed, it is common for parties to end in a stalemate or non-decision instead of agreement in CP.

DOI: 10.4324/9781003385769-9

206 *The Process Challenges and Struggles of Joint Undertakings*

Table 9.1 Challenges of Collaborative Governance

Governance Tool	Formal Modes of Transaction	Types of Information	Modes of Transaction	Networking
Social/ Economic Regulation	Legislated controls, rules	Hearings, pricing practices, reporting	Reports on practices/ participation rates, networking	Performance standards, negotiation, territories
Contracting	Structure business arrangement, selecting administration, written contracts, renewal, termination	Specify requirements, reporting, performance monitoring, informal conversations	Monitoring cost/ performance, discussions, period of review	Contracting agencies and businesses, trade associations
Grant	Cash award based on promised activity application, renewal, termination	Annual reports, monitoring	Informal contact, information, discretion seeking	Periodic meetings
Direct Loan	Loan application/ review	Fiscal capacity to repay	Repayment schedule, audit	Post-audit discussions, meetings with recipients
Loan Guarantee	Loan application/ review	Fiscal capacity to repay	Payment schedule, audit	Discussions about use of loan
Tax Expenditure	Enactment of formal application/ forms, compliance	Benefits, tax outlay	Audit	Informal discussions, proof of use
Fees and Charges	Legislative authorization, administration levy	Costs, scheduled payments	Monitor, audit, and compliance assurance	Fee payer/user meetings, reports on cost, usage
Vouchers	Eligibility, distribution mechanics, degree of choice	Expenditure reports on suppliers, consumer knowledge, finding buyers	Audit, performance evaluation	Open meetings, interactions with suppliers

Source: Agranoff (2012, p. 118). Copyright 2012 by Georgetown University Press. Reprinted with permission.

The Process Challenges and Struggles of Joint Undertakings 207

Perhaps the most crucial feature of this process, in addition to heavy CP, is that the absence of hierarchical power is real in collaborative management. Agreement by mutual or multiple accommodations replaces hierarchical decision-making and voting, although voting may be present within individual agencies as their representatives agree to "play." In other words, with CP, by nature, one is facing non-hierarchical, non–position-based agreement-reaching. However, as much as an agency brings its "political baggage" to any joint effort, new sets of CP interpartner dynamics and politics are also introduced into the process. Indeed, internal agency dynamics must be factored into external interagency dynamics. As a result, some of the core ins and outs of these processes become our orientation.

The Challenge

Policy and administration in this dispersed power world have highlighted the importance of collaboration and multiparty implementation, mainly through the many processes illustrated in this volume. Today's public programs, such as transportation, environmental management, and human services, require the interactive participation of multiple levels of government, nonprofit and for-profit NGOs, and increasing doses of citizen and client-based involvement (Agranoff, 2016). This overlapping authority and shared involvement at the operational level stems from the complexity of operating multiple programs in the 21st century (Agranoff & Radin, 2015). At the operational level, programming becomes both increasingly external and internal, conductive in its nature (e.g., Amsler & O'Leary, 2017; Saint-Onge & Armstrong, 2004; O'Leary & Bingham, 2009; Vandeventer & Mandell, 2007; Agranoff, 2012). Collaborative management and networking have become the usual answer for solving program and policy problems caused by the challenges of increased complexity (Agranoff, 2016). However, collaboration and network governance also have distinct disadvantages that may pose potential managerial barriers to effective joint program implementation. These issues are critical to comprehending and implementing collaborative management. These concerns must also be addressed in collaborative program management in this shared-power world, particularly regarding the expanding number of multiorganizational process management scenarios; hence, our continued interest in CP's process challenges.

Collaborative structures matter in contemporary governance, but participants face resolution barriers in solving problems and issues among organizations. Take the example of a multisector policy task force that comes up with a creative, feasible, and fundable model program for integrating recent immigrants in a medium-sized city. However, the proposal faces a lack of state legislative support and federal backing for enabling such a program. That is a real-life barrier. As Scharpf (1994) concludes, "while network structures will reach across organizational boundaries, their effectiveness will be equally or even more selective, depending on the pre-existing distribution of strong and weak ties among formally independent individual and organizational actors" (p. 49). The concept of embedded negotiations,

208 *The Process Challenges and Struggles of Joint Undertakings*

in other words, provides no promise of optimality under real-world conditions. For example, in the real world of local networks that were charged with developing Agenda 21 plans in the towns surrounding Barcelona, under the encouragement of the European Union (EU), Blanco and Gomá (2002) found relatively varying levels of success in citizen organizing for these environmental challenges. In several cases, the program networks confronted hostile local power structures, overemphasizing process versus actual outcomes, frustration concerning the low prospects of the ultimate enactment of regional and national policies, and use of such other governance tools as court orders and consent decrees to resolve local environmental problems. In the CP literature, there is less discussion of these core obstacles as compared to considerably stronger literature about how networks and other joint efforts can be successfully managed (Klijn & Koppenjan, 2000; Rhodes, 2000; Agranoff & McGuire, 2001; Thompson, 2003; Klijn, 2008; Agranoff, 2017).

Concern for managing this type of issue agreement-reaching stems from the growing complexity and interdependence that has transformed public programs over the past several decades. One significant contributor, as mentioned, is the growth of intergovernmental programs. In the United States, federal financing and regulatory programs now reach "down" deeply into state and local governments for co-design and decentralized implementation. Moreover, NGOs' applied operations or joint programming bring added managerial demands (Agranoff, 2017). For instance, one of the authors of this volume studied one program involving financing and programming by the federal government, the design of programs at the state level, and substantial NGO operations by literally hundreds of programs operating in each state on a contractual basis (Agranoff, 2016). Indeed, the HCBS waiver of federal requirements reaches not only from federal–state to NGOs but to I/DD families and clients as self-advocates (Agranoff, 2013; Thompson, 2012). The multiplicity of programs and services like this are also found in the transportation, environmental, and other policy areas, which brings on the need for deeply involved collaboration and forms of networking. As a result, interactions caused by complexity focus on ways to increase interdependence. In Chapter 3, as well as in this chapter, "to collaborate" refers to one of the most involved aspects of interorganizational contact—beyond informal and serendipitous administrative process actions, while connecting agencies, programs, and interests in structured, regular, and usually formal ways (Agranoff & Radin, 2015).

As a result, this chapter aims to draw some parameters on "collaborative limits" as a form of collaborative management by looking deeper into agencies' internal operational processes. Hopefully, it will extend the dialogue on the more limiting aspects involving networking and other forms of extensive collaboration, perhaps improving its practice as a result. For example, early in the systemic assessment of interagency collaboration, Barbara Gray (1989) identified several interorganizational collaborative disincentives, such as experiential and ideological preventive theories, technical shortcomings and increasing complexity, power disparities, cultural norms that emphasize individualism, "differing perceptions of risk, and

The Process Challenges and Struggles of Joint Undertakings   209

getting public agencies to understand and come to grips with the need for working together" (Agranoff, 2016, p. 96). These appeared to emerge as core obstacles. Here we go deeper into some of these earlier identified operational challenges, going beyond the usual superficial "heralding of the importance of 'shared aims', leading to 'working together' to look inside network operations and how they might provide process barriers" (Agranoff, 2016, p. 83).

Asymmetrical Power

It is initially important to return to the analysis of power, which under most circumstances is likely to be asymmetrical in most big-picture process challenges. An initial conceptualization of this collaborative challenge recognized that power may not only be unequal (Agranoff & McGuire, 2001) but that an array of organizations exists concerning one another in a power-dependence relationship. Rhodes's study of government transformation in the United Kingdom (UK) argues that organizations become dependent on each other for resources and subsequently engage in exchange-based relationships with constant negotiations and bargaining (Rhodes, 1997a). Power dependence, therefore, "explains why different entities interact and explains some variations in power distribution within networks" (McGuire & Agranoff, 2011, p. 267). For example, according to Rhodes, dominant coalitions typically maintain control over these entities by utilizing game rules to regulate the exchange processes. Similarly, Klijn and Skelcher (2007, p. 598) define it as the "instrumental conjecture," whereby "powerful governmental actors increase their capacity to shape and deliver public policy in a complex world through the instrumental use of networks" (McGuire & Agranoff, 2011, p. 267).

However, other conjectures demonstrate that power can be seen as a force to facilitate or inhibit network processes. As a blocking force, agency/organization power is authentic when lead organizations tend to remove certain problems from a discussion agenda, do not provide support for crucial network strategies or administration's decisions, or do not supply necessary agency-controlled resources. These forces represent a sort of negative social energy that is sometimes overlooked. Newman's (2005) interviews with higher-level UK civil servants engaged in network processes demonstrated that "the Labour Party centralizing control mechanisms (for example, inspection and audit) hindered and distracted from their roles in visionary leadership, creating contradictions between centralization and decentralization" (McGuire & Agranoff, 2011, p. 267). These are some of the actual power-dependence barriers to achieving collaboration.

There are different ways to overcome these power-dependence barriers. Bargaining can be used to address such hurdles to collaboration (Rhodes, 1997b; Agranoff & McGuire, 2003, 2004, McGuire & Agranoff, 2011). There are also internal sources of power once a network is activated. For example, Agranoff (2007, 2017) found power within the network to be distributed among agency managers, technical experts or professionals, and staff members. "These individuals bring to the networks their agency's resource-based power and their willingness to make a process succeed in solving complex problems" (McGuire & Agranoff, 2011, p. 267). Technical expertise based on human capital and the vital internal resources for completing necessary program tasks is also instrumental in overcoming authentic agency power in such procedures.

Similarly, Thomas (2003), embracing the literature on professionalism (Wilensky, 1964, for example), believes that "interagency working specialists receive many of their incentives from external groups and fellow practitioners outside of the agency" (McGuire & Agranoff, 2011, p. 267). Thomas (2003) argues that many knowledge-based communities are organized around some particular ideas. In the same fashion, Newman (2005) found some specific interactions changing agency power: "Patterns of relationship and hierarchies of knowledge were being reshaped, and new spaces and sites of action that could not be controlled from the center were opening up" (2005, p. 730). Therefore, working together continuously to solve similarly defined challenges can help reduce the agencies' influence on the collaborative process. (See Wondolleck & Yaffee, 2000 for details).

A closely related issue to resource bases is the well-known force of agency turf. As identified earlier, Bardach (1998) defines turf as "the domain of problems, opportunities, and actions over which an agency exercises legitimate authority" (p. 164). Agencies can try to protect their turf by "fashioning distinctive competencies, and/or managers may resist collaboration to protect their autonomy" (McGuire & Agranoff, 2011, p. 267). According to Thomas (2003), agency managers should be aware that they might be convinced that they are the best people to carry out agency tasks, that they may seek to control their own space to avoid failure (or loss) in unfamiliar territory, that they may seek autonomy to lessen the uncertainty, and that they should be cautious not to facilitate the emergence of too many threats to these conditions. Turf can undoubtedly prevent collaboration.

Various strategies can be used to counteract turf battles among the network partners. Mandell and Steelman (2003) recommend joint ventures, cooperative agreements, contractual relationships, and coordinating councils to prevent agencies' fears regarding turf protection. To overcome turf problems, Agranoff (2007) suggests delegating the management of programs to partner agency services in the networks. Koppenjan, Koppenjan, and Klijn (2004) recommend three vital managerial strategies for removing barriers like turf wars by searching for common ground:

1. avoidance of early fixations, which furthers awareness of the plurality of perceptions and preferences;
2. furthering substantive variety and favorable conditions for learning and intermediate adoptions; and
3. joint image-building and a search for common ground for mutual interactions despite recognition of enduring differences.

(p. 162)

The Process Challenges and Struggles of Joint Undertakings   211

Obviously, there is no unique and guaranteed solution to mitigate turf-protecting behaviors' impact. However, applying the previously mentioned techniques and strategies can somewhat reduce the negative effects of turf-protecting behaviors. After all, one of the benefits of networking/collaboration is opening new "action possibilities" by open systems (Agranoff, 2017; Johanson & Mattson, 1987, p. 48).

Government Is Usually First Among "Equals"

In the nature of CP, the government cannot easily be pushed aside or relegated to minor status. In many situations, it may be more than "just another organization" that has come to the table. Alison Gash (2017, p. 462) concludes that participants in collaborative governance must avoid reifying state control or privilege and being perceived as merely some superficial or symbolic exercise in participation: "Although the collaborative cannot be a puppet of the state, it cannot ignore the state" (p. 462). A collaborative body cannot marginalize government from a collaborative policy's power base. To overlook or discount this impact is at the participants' peril.

Foremost in the public sphere is for parties to come to grips with the core or lead role that government agencies often play. An excellent overview of all the potential roles that government agencies play in environmental management (for example, contributing various human, technical and financial resources) is provided by Koontz and his colleagues (2004). One of the most profound findings is the "sweeping influence that governmental institutions do leave their mark on how issues are defined, what resources are used or are available, the structure of the collaborative process and the outcomes that these endeavors produce" (p. 170). The institutional provisions in laws and regulations are where most involved parties come to a conclusion, as few groups are rarely given complete "policy authority."

Parties engaged in communication should also consider the statutory-based rules that potentially hinder the collaboration process. For example, since the early 1980s, the Medicaid program (medical payments for low-income adults) has featured the HCBS waiver program to support qualified clients who would otherwise be institutionalized. HCBS is a federal–state program that purchases a wide range of externally supplied services, the majority of which are provided by nonprofit organizations. In addition, HCBS used to restrict payment for room and board while prohibiting other services before eventually allowing them (e.g., day hospitalization, ventilator-dependent services). The most notable was the "cold bed rule," which compelled states to reduce institutional beds in proportion to incoming HCBS clients; it was eventually repealed. The most recent significant modification, made in 2011, allowed previously prohibited family home care providers to be reimbursed under specific conditions. Each of these guidelines established parameters for state HCBS regulations and outlined certain essential characteristics of properly operating network of providers (Agranoff, 2016).

212   *The Process Challenges and Struggles of Joint Undertakings*

In the environmental arena, the EPA developed new rules in 2012 requiring CO_2 levels to drop by 2030, which posed new legal constraints on the U.S. states (Agranoff, 2016). Some state agencies were challenged before federal courts, while others wrote their own standards. Regardless of the path taken by states, collaboration between federal government and states was necessary for reaching agreed objectives. As a result, the affected parties were finally following the rules in one form or another (Kardish, 2014). Meanwhile, EPA resisted these rules under the administration of former U.S. President Donald J. Trump, but jurisdictions must comply until the courts rule differently. Rules were accepted as a result of the collaboration process, and all stakeholders must follow them, especially if the regulated were participating in any cooperative processes that resulted in rule revisions (Weber, 1998).

Enhancing the territory of public organizations used by its leaders can be considered a positive or negative force in collaborative management. An example of the positive side can be found in practices by the EPA to reduce uncertainty and increase trust in rulemaking in many areas. Edward Weber (1998, p. 32) describes the efforts of Bill Rosenberg, then the Assistant Administrator for Clean Air:

> During the legislative battles over clean air Rosenberg had earned a reputation as "an obsessive strategist, balancing environmentalists' demands against the realities of a cost-conscious White House. He was . . . an entrepreneur . . . in perpetual search of clean air deals . . . . In meeting after meeting . . . he looked for the sweet spot of compromise: what it would take to fix the problem" and bridge the gap among competing interests. Finally, Rosenberg's reputation as "the pit bull of clean air" earned him the respect of his EPA staff and key leaders of the national environmental lobby, while his business background and evident concern for cost-effectiveness offered assurance to industry.

This kind of action can always be positive and expected. Many agency managers are very protective of their territories. For example, Craig Thomas (2003) defined turf as protecting "one's own territory or domain" (p. 31). Turf imperialism can inhibit cooperation, but as Bardach (1998, p. 177) observes, "from the manager's point of view, all other things equal, more turf is better." Thomas (2003) argues that "line managers often are convinced that they know best, and therefore, should decide on how to carry out agency tasks, develop programs, and achieve agency missions" (p. 31). Turf protection has proved to be one dark side of collaboration.

The multistakeholder process is the "reconstitution" of government agencies for participatory government and non-government management, somewhere between turf protection and building. As Daniel Carpenter's (2001, p. 4) historical study demonstrates, this is not always an easy undertaking. Political and organized interests defer to bureaucratic autonomy, defined as performing acts consistent with administrators' views. Carpenter believes that agencies can achieve political legitimacy by establishing a reputation for knowledge, efficiency, and moral protection.

The Process Challenges and Struggles of Joint Undertakings   213

Politicians award administrators licenses under these circumstances because they defer to the agency's objectives. According to Thomas Koontz et al.'s (2004) cross-case research, governments' leadership position can be at the heart of collaborative activity, assisting participants in becoming innovative, giving information, securing resources, and carrying out implementation plans. On the negative side, agency structures geared to encourage more traditional techniques—such as the lack of high-level government forums or mandates to collaborate or otherwise work together and ambiguous federal standards—are limiting considerations. Finally, the forces mentioned above can impede the collaboration process and limit the positive outcomes of collaboration.

Be Aware of Mission Incompatibility

When agencies' agents come together to work collaboratively, the premise is to understand each organization's mission clearly. For example, process breakdown hinges or is at risk unless the parties clearly understand what each organization is all about and how they might be compatible/incompatible in the network/ collaborative.

Parties involved in collaboration process should understand the core or lead role that government agencies can play. Koontz and his team (2004) provide an excellent overview of the possible roles of government agencies in environmental management, including the provision of different human, informational, technical, and financial resources. But the most critical role is defined as the "sweeping influence that governmental institutions do leave on how their issues are defined, what resources are used or are available, the structure of the collaborative process, and the outcomes that these endeavors produce" (p. 170). Inasmuch as few parties are given broad "policy authority," most involved government agency actors comply with institutional requirements in statutes and regulations (Agranoff, 2016).

It is possible that many efforts are limited or prevented from leading to meaningful action by the role undertaken by participants. In fact, some collaborative endeavors are limited only to raising and discussing problems and reporting on individual activities. For example, some activities may have such a narrow scope or aim that some network actors can even not carry them out while other numerous parties can accomplish them (Agranoff, 2016). The earlier identified Ohio information exchange-only network, Darby, is a case in point. Different scholars attempted to develop the classification of networks based on such activities. For example, Margerum (2011) divides networks into three types: social, interorganizational, and political, concentrating on the critical roles of social and political contacts, agency-based programs and budget components, and working elected officials and interest groups. Keast et al. (2004, p. 368) classify networks as

(1) cooperative, emphasizing participant interactions; (2) coordinative, where interactive learning and problems or solutions are clarified; and (3) collaborative,

214   *The Process Challenges and Struggles of Joint Undertakings*

where the actors are actually doing something, changing policy or program, working toward systems change, often involved through building new collective ventures.

One of the authors of this volume developed a classification of networks based on his 14-network study (Agranoff, 2007) and classified them by their core missions ranging from mutual exchange to actual policy-making and policy implementation. There were two types: those that identified interorganizational strategies solely to be carried out by participating organizations and governmental agencies, and those that identified interorganizational strategies only to be carried out by network members (Agranoff, 2016). In reality, few networks were engaged in such policy/program decisions (for example, the transportation [action] networks). This mission is critical, and collaborative agreement/disagreement can range from clearly limiting or avoiding decisions, to decision-based policy-making in the scope of purpose.

Overprocessing Barriers

On the contrary, like with fashion, "too much of a good thing" is possible by extended sessions of coming together and talking through various mission-related concerns, potential strategies, potential resource exchanges, and so on, which can be limiting, so to speak. Related, there can also be too much action or overprocessing of collaborative work, leading to both suboptimal collaborative outcomes and collaborative inertia. Climbing the "hurdles of process" is often crucial to achieving actual results, as described in the common intake process from Chapter 3. However, this process can exhaust collaborative efforts (McGuire & Agranof, 2011). Sometimes, it can also "make it difficult to cope with the power of external forces, such as key power agencies, or to overcome policy barriers" (p. 268). In addition, changes in governing structures and reorganization of one or more agencies may also directly affect process changes. Finally, how successful networks overcome these collaborative obstacles becomes a crucial point to collaborative action (Mandell & Keast, 2007).

Extensive processing involves trade-off costs that hinder successful results in collaboration. Research by Huxham and Vangen (2005) on collaboration in Scotland discovered the phenomenon of collaborative inertia as a lack of collaborative advantage. When collaboration is characterized by slow progress, painful experiences, a lack of accomplishments, and even network breakdown, there is a lack of collaborative advantage (McGuire & Agranoff, 2011). They discovered a variety of social dynamics that contribute to *"collaborative inertia."* One has mixed objectives or intentions when partners get together to figure out the intricacies between apparent, assumed, and hidden goals. These can be divided into collaboration, partner organizations, and individual actor goals. Another source of domination and power is the partners who control the purse strings. Finally, there is skepticism, which might arise due to a lack of collaborative trust-building.

The Process Challenges and Struggles of Joint Undertakings   215

Other related process dimensions are terms coined by Huxham and Vangen: "partnership fatigue" and "a lack of clarity about with whom one is collaborating" (2005, p. 72). However, constant change can result in inertia as "relationships between partners become increasingly fluid" (Agranoff, 2012, p. 183). In addition, "[l]eadership activities are continually facing obstacles to success and removing them in a less than collegial fashion (for example, pushing partners out, isolating agencies) in a sort of collaborative thuggery as a substitute for process facilitation" (McGuire & Agranoff, 2011, p. 269). According to Huxham and Vangen (2005), network leadership is responsible for finding solutions to address collaborative inertia by adjusting work styles to move agendas forward at all costs, even putting other partners in charge of the process.

The "Costs" of Processing

Once participants are in the throes of moving the collaboration agenda, "process costs" need to be considered; for example, Agranoff (2007) found that network participants are very serious about the time and opportunity costs of being taken away from their organization's managerial and operational activities. Similarly, Chen (2008) and Graddy and Chen (2006) point to the weight of transaction costs resulting from the collaboration. Joint operation "clearly takes a toll on partner organizations' ability to achieve collaborative outcomes" (Chen, 2008, p. 358). In addition, many person-hours can be spent in task forces, ad hoc groups, or workgroups in addition to more formal partner meetings (McGuire & Agranoff, 2011).

Even when collaborative inertia is overcome, it still results in prolonged/extended human relations processing as participants attempt to respect the multicultural nature of collaborative endeavors (McGuire & Agranoff, 2011). Consensus—the primary aim of collaborative decision-making—means allowing "everyone to put their agenda on the table as 'joint efforts' to unpack complex political, financial, technical, and regulatory issues" (p. 269). Problem-solving might limit the scope of work due to the need for consensus and the discipline of respecting partners' risk-averse agendas. Similarly, Scharpf concludes that German joint "policy-making is constrained by high consensus requirements among governments representing diverse constituencies" (1996, p. 366). Coglianese (1999) also finds that collaboratives with many competing or possibly conflicting stakeholders tend to be more sensitive and risk-averse regarding the problem agenda, frequently leading to the lowest common denominator types of decisions.

Process costs can be real obstacles to reaching consensus, especially when combined with the barriers to collaboration we identified earlier. To overcome the costs, network leadership should set realistic agendas, respect agency expectations, and focus on common goals (McGuire & Agranoff, 2011). For example, Edelenbos and Klijn view the collaboration process as an evolving state of flux that is a "constant interplay between process design and process management" (2006, p. 426). Nevertheless, to Koliba et al. (2018, p. 369), it places a significant burden on governing

216 *The Process Challenges and Struggles of Joint Undertakings*

through these barriers, "to govern is to guide, steer and shape the operating functions of some whole . . . through complex networks of individuals, groups, organizations, and institutions."

Policy Barriers and Policy Energy

Collaborative agendas and policies pose perhaps some of the most significant barriers to achieving collaborative results (McGuire & Agranoff, 2011). Among the most critical issues concerning the development of interactive results is the process of transforming a collaborative-generated, multiagency solution through the application of policy energy. Collaborative bodies often find reasonable solutions but then run into political, financial, or legal barriers preventing the next step. Despite being poorly understood, policy barriers to success prove to be logical and powerful. Networks or other collaboratives may attempt to modify existing public policy provisions in an effort to get around them, but this is frequently a complicated and protracted process. A few viable solutions have been proposed to address this problem in the United States, including representative policy-makers such as state legislators in the process, which will improve the efficacy of knowledge-based appeals and increase lobbying on behalf of the group. As a result, knowledge generated by networks gets transformed into brokered consensus and becomes incorporated into the policy process, which may evolve over relatively long periods (Koppenjan, Koppenjan, & Klijn, 2004).

A collaborative's scope may be so constrained or limited that solution-focused actions are also generally limited. For example, O'Toole (1997) was one of the first to acknowledge the fact that administrators working within networks "should not assume that they possess authority" (p. 48). As identified, one of the authors of this volume's typology of networks indicates that some networks possess no operational authority, particularly to joint programs (Agranoff, 2007). They merely exchange information. Other networks engage in information exchanges and attempt to "build partner knowledge-related and problem-solving capabilities," whereas activity is only within participating agencies (McGuire & Agranoff, 2011). A third network type focuses on problem-solving approaches, albeit indirectly, since they blueprint strategies that client agencies and service clients follow. The fourth network type possesses power to make critical network-related decisions and uses consensus-based processes to implement these decisions (Agranoff, 2007).

Nevertheless, their legally ascribed powers can often be relatively narrow in scope for the fourth type of network (McGuire & Agranoff, 2011). Their "policy adjusting ability is narrowly defined compared to the partner agencies' retention of the major powers, particularly in the case of government agency partners" (p. 270). Moreover, any deliberative results usually are long-term for the other three types of networks and depend on the decisions of different government organizations, NGOs, and commissions. Even then, such networks can only influence a given policy adjustment or program direction, not decide on it. For example, "[O]nly

The Process Challenges and Struggles of Joint Undertakings   217

under limited conditions and situations do networks have the ability to compel compliance" (p. 270).

The lack of a technical solution to a public issue that a collaborative may be addressing can create additional and different obstacles (McGuire & Agranoff, 2011). A technical barrier, in this case, refers "to the knowledge base or previously established solution to a presenting problem" (p. 270). There may be no apparent solution; "to be sure, administrators and specialists often come to the collaborative enterprise to brainstorm and deliberate on potential solutions, a process known in European circles as policy transfer, the exchange of knowledge and information through networks" (De Jong & Edelenbos, 2007, p. 270). One of the advantages of networks is that they combine bits and pieces of less structured knowledge into workable solutions (Davenport, 2005). However, McGuire and Agranoff (2011) warn us that there are some situations when a group of brilliant people can not figure out a solution:

> In pre-Katrina New Orleans, the failure to plan for evacuation of inner-city and immobile citizens was in part a failure of collaboration among local organizations but also because the jurisdictions working together could not figure out how to come up with a workable plan of evacuation that was testable by prior exercise (Kiefer & Montjoy, 2006). In another example, for decades, rural wastewater specialists in the U.S. networking with legal and financial state bureaucrats ran into the lack of viable systems for clusters of 8–12 houses as an alternative to septic systems. Some technical developments emerged in the late 1990s and early 2000s, such as peat bio filter drainage combined with lift stations, that then had to be made economically feasible and legally acceptable to the environmental and health organizations (Fallah, 2004, 2006). And to give a further example, when the spectrum of autism disorders was broadened in the late 1980s and early 1990s to include such previously excluded conditions as Asperger's Syndrome, networks of social service providers, school officials, and health professionals were at a loss as to how to plan for services for this group. No one really knew what types of interventions worked, and, as a result, either no services or services that were only offered to more severely handicapped individuals were available (Castellani, 2000). Until providers could discover what might work, professionals hit a technical wall, something that is a frequent barrier to network activity.
>
> (p. 270)

Policy barriers can turn out to be among the highest and strongest stone walls of collaborative management (McGuire & Agranoff, 2011). Börzel (1998) argues that these barriers emerge when partner organization bargaining serves as the basis for horizontal cooperation across organizations, and the representatives are not fully autonomous since they have to follow the rules and mandates of their respective organizations. Joint network action cannot easily overcome these substantive policy barriers in the path of network solutions, regardless of their nature, if they

218 *The Process Challenges and Struggles of Joint Undertakings*

are financial or programmatic (McGuire & Agranoff, 2011). Klijn and Koppenjan (2000) recommend we avoid the theoretical presumption that "governments are like other actors. Governments have unique resources at their disposal and work to achieve unique goals. They occupy a special position" (p. 151). These are legal and decision authority, budgets, personnel, and democratic legitimization (Agranoff, 2017). A collaborative usually deals with (not overcomes) these policy barriers by "involving the real decision-makers or their representatives in the negotiating mix of the network and reaching early-stage reconciliation of interests" (McGuire & Agranoff, 2011, p. 271). Klijn and Edelenbos (2007, p. 203) recommend several management strategies that can also be used to remove policy barriers:

1. activation of actors and resources: selective activation, coalition building, building common ground, resource mobilization;
2. creation of organizational arrangements: realizing ad hoc cooperation structures, like sounding boards, project groups, consultation groups, etc.;
3. guidance of interaction: mediation, brokerage, conflict resolution, etc.;
4. goal-achieving strategies: creating divergence and convergence in the perceptions of problems and solutions;
5. joint knowledge production: the strategy of searching collaboratively for information questions and ways to answer them; and
6. trust creation: the strategy of developing a relationship of trust with other interested actors in the network.

Conclusion

Ultimately, the process of collaborative management must be understood, as is the case concerning governance in general, as a "distributed process engaging many stakeholders from different sectors and governing levels" (Ansell & Torfing, 2017, p. 8). The practice and theory of collaborative management have to come to grips with is the process of accommodation and adjustment by acknowledging the weak scope of some collaborative and network authority, the existence of power asymmetries, and the reality of who actually makes the decisions in an agreement through joint efforts. Researchers must recognize that many collaborative decisions and recommendations are nothing more than proposals and they do not necessarily set or decide policy. Many collaborative entities are, in essence, limited in their ability to make things happen. We must learn more about the previously unstudied barriers to action, such as how and when agreements become implemented, who implements them, the power imbalances during the implementation process, and the efficacy of collaborative alternatives to formal networks. Most critical is that more also needs to be known about collaborative results. For example, when is an outcome an actual decision or a brokered agreement that is potentially successful and measurable? Finally, how are results generated? These are among the ongoing challenges suggested by the analysis of barriers and opportunities. Two decades

The Process Challenges and Struggles of Joint Undertakings   219

ago, the organization guru Phillip Selznick (1996) concluded that the intention to develop context-focused theoretical models of organizing

> should guard against a disposition to overlook, for the sake of the paradigm, the limited partial, highly contingent nature of the truths discovered . . . . Although we have learned a great deal about unintended effects, the so-called law of unintended consequences—one does not suppose we are ready to abandon the quest for more effective and humane cooperative systems.
>
> (p. 276)

Moreover, Selznik mirrors the advice of John Dewey in his *Logic: The Theory of Inquiry* (1935) that "social science should be guided by life and practice rather than intellectually self-generated conceptions that grow out of social tensions, needs, and troubles that lead to the core values at stake in the social experience" (Agranoff, 2016, p. 103). In this regard, a more thorough, more neutral diagnostic reconstruction and problem-solving approach must be used to examine collaborative behavior. Indeed, as will be suggested in Chapter 12, there is a long way to go in this regard.

Laurence O'Toole, a public management scholar who wrote a ground-breaking article in 1997 on the importance of public management networks, attempted to define networks as one feature of collaborative management in his updated version of the original article (2015). He argues that they appealed to both academics and practitioners greatly. However, O'Toole warns us that the real variation in networks suggests that managers should be wary of "any general and precise injunctions for practice" and that "networks can also produce unattractive or even destructive outcomes" that work within collaborative. Collaboration is accompanied by "varying levels of commitment and clashes of organizational cultures" (Agranoff, 2016, p. 103). Public management, in general, involves emergent tasks and skills of interaction within the hierarchy and the collaborative arrangement, and, finally, some networks also operate, in effect, for "dark purposes," e.g., the exclusion of some interest to protect agency monopolies, or to limit the scope of the action. To reap the benefits of networks, "we need to know much more about how networks and networking behavior can shape performance and affect the most salient values in our governance systems" (O'Toole, 2015, p. 8). Besides knowing networks' dark or limited sides, we should seriously assess "other sides" of collaborative structures (Agranoff, 2016).

References

Agranoff, R. (2007). *Managing within networks: Adding value to public organizations.* Georgetown University Press.

Agranoff, R. (2012). *Collaborating to manage: A primer for the public sector.* Georgetown University Press.

Agranoff, R. (2013). The transformation of public sector intellectual/developmental disabilities programming. *Public Administration Review, 73*(1), 127–138.

220 The Process Challenges and Struggles of Joint Undertakings

Agranoff, R. (2016). The other side of managing in networks. In R. D. Margerum & C. J. Robinson (Eds.), *The challenges of collaboration in environmental governance: Barriers and responses* (pp. 81–107). Edward Elgar Publishing.

Agranoff, R. (2017). *Crossing boundaries for intergovernmental management*. Georgetown University Press.

Agranoff, R., & McGuire, M. (2001). Big questions in public network management research. *Journal of Public Administration Research and Theory, 11*(3), 295–326.

Agranoff, R., & McGuire, M. (2003). *Collaborative public management: New strategies for public management: New strategies for local governments*. Georgetown University Press.

Agranoff, R., & McGuire, M. (2004). Another look at bargaining and negotiating in intergovernmental management. *Journal of Public Administration Research and Theory, 14*(4), 495–512.

Agranoff, R., & Radin, B. A. (2015). Deil Wright's overlapping model of intergovernmental relations: The basis for contemporary intergovernmental relationships. *Publius: The Journal of Federalism, 45*(1), 139–159.

Amsler, L. B., & O'Leary, R. (2017). Collaborative public management and systems thinking. *International Journal of Public Sector Management, 30*(6–7), 626–639.

Ansell, C., & Torfing, J. (2016). Introduction: theories of governance. In C. Ansell & J. Torfing (Eds.) *Handbook on theories of governance* (pp. 1–18). Edward Elgar Publishing.

Bardach, E. (1998). *Getting agencies to work together: The practice and theory of managerial craftsmanship*. Brookings Institution Press.

Blanco, I., & Gomá, R. (2002). *Governance y Territorio: La Política de Proximidad en el Nuevo Contexto de Redes*. I. Blanco y R. Gomá: Gobiernos locales y Redes participativas, Ariel, Barcelona.

Börzel, T. A. (1998). Organizing babylon-on the different conceptions of policy networks. *Public Administration, 76*(2), 253–273.

Carpenter, D. (2001). *The forging of bureaucratic autonomy: Reputations, networks, and policy innovation in executive agencies, 1862–1928* (Vol. 173). Princeton University Press.

Castellani, P. J. (2000). The administration of developmental disabilities services in state government. In J. J. Gargan (Ed.), *Handbook of state government administration*. Marcel Dekker.

Chen, B. (2008). Assessing interorganizational networks for public service delivery: A process-perceived effectiveness framework. *Public Performance & Management Review, 31*(3), 348–363.

Coglianese, C. (1999). The limits of consensus: The environmental protection system in transition: Toward a more desirable future. *Environment: Science and Policy for Sustainable Development, 41*(3), 28–33.

Davenport, T. H. (2005). *Thinking for a living: How to get better performances and results from knowledge workers*. Harvard Business Press.

De Jong, M., & Edelenbos, J. (2007). An insider's look into policy transfer in transnational expert networks. *European Planning Studies, 15*(5), 687–706.

Dewey, J. (1935). *Logic: The theory of inquiry*. Holt.

Edelenbos, J., & Klijn, E. H. (2006). Managing stakeholder involvement in decision making: A comparative analysis of six interactive processes in the Netherlands. *Journal of Public Administration Research and Theory, 16*(3), 417–446.

Fallah, P. (2004). *Dr. Michael Mcguire's interview at Ohio Environmental Protection Agency*, Columbus, OH.

Fallah, P. (2006). *Dr. Michael Mcguire's interview at Ohio Environmental Protection Agency*, Columbus, OH.

Gash, A. (2017). Collaborative governance. In C. Ansell & J. Torfing (Eds.), *Handbook on theories of governance* (pp. 254–267). Edward Elgar Publishing.

The Process Challenges and Struggles of Joint Undertakings 221

Graddy, E. A., & Chen, B. (2006). Influences on the size and scope of networks for social service delivery. *Journal of Public Administration Research and Theory, 16*(4), 533–552.

Gray, B. (1989). *Collaborating: Finding common ground for multiparty problems.* Jossey Bass.

Huxham, C., & Vangen, S. (2005). *Managing to collaborate: The theory and practice of collaborative advantage.* Routledge.

Johanson, J., & Mattson, L. G. (1987). *Interorganisational relations in industrial systems: A network approach compared with a transaction cost approach.* International Studies of Management Organisation, 63–74.

Kardish, C. (2014). The carbon rebellion. *Governing, 28*(1), 44–48.

Keast, R., Mandell, M. P., Brown, K., & Woolcock, G. (2004). Network structures: Working differently and changing expectations. *Public Administration Review, 64*(3), 363–371.

Kiefer, J. J., & Montjoy, R. S. (2006). Incrementalism before the storm: Network performance for the evacuation of New Orleans. *Public Administration Review, 66,* 122–130.

Klijn, E. H. (2008). Governance and governance networks in Europe: An assessment of ten years of research on the theme. *Public Management Review, 10*(4), 505–525.

Klijn, E. H., & Edelenbos, J. (2007). Meta-governance as network management. In E. Sørensen & J. Torfing (Eds.), *Theories of democratic network governance.* Palgrave Macmillan.

Klijn, E. H., & Koppenjan, J. F. (2000). Public management and policy networks: Foundations of a network approach to governance. *Public Management an International Journal of Research and Theory, 2*(2), 135–158.

Klijn, E. H., & Skelcher, C. (2007). Democracy and governance networks: Compatible or not? *Public Administration, 85*(3), 587–608.

Koliba, C. J., Meek, J. W., Zia, A., & Mills, R. M. (2018). *Governance networks in public administration and public policy.* Routledge.

Koontz, T. M., Steelman, T. A., Carmin, J., Korfmacher, K. S., Moseley, C., & Thomas, C. W. (2004). *Collaborative environmental management: What roles for Government.* Washington, DC: Resources for Future.

Koppenjan, J. F. M., Koppenjan, J., & Klijn, E. H. (2004). *Managing uncertainties in networks: A network approach to problem solving and decision making.* Psychology Press.

Mandell, M., & Keast, R. (2007). Evaluating network arrangements: Toward revised performance measures. *Public Performance & Management Review, 30*(4), 574–597.

Mandell, M., & Steelman, T. (2003). Understanding what can be accomplished through interorganizational innovations: The importance of typologies, context and management strategies. *Public Management Review, 5*(2), 197–224.

Margerum, R. D. (2011). *Beyond consensus: Improving collaborative planning and management.* MIT Press.

McGuire, M., & Agranoff, R. (2011). The limitations of public management networks. *Public Administration, 89*(2), 265–284.

Newman, J. (2005). Enter the transformational leader: Network governance and the micropolitics of modernization. *Sociology, 39*(4), 717–734.

O'Leary, R., & Bingham, L. B. (Eds.). (2009). *The collaborative public manager: New ideas for the twenty-first century.* Georgetown University Press.

Orren, K., Skowronek, S., & Karen, O. (2004). *The search for American political development.* Cambridge University Press.

O'Toole, Jr., L. J. (1997). Treating networks seriously: Practical and research-based agendas in public administration. *Public Administration Review, 57*(1), 45–52.

222 The Process Challenges and Struggles of Joint Undertakings

O'Toole, Jr., L. J. (2015). Networks and networking: The public administrative agendas. *Public Administration Review, 75*(3), 361–371.

Rhodes, R. A. W. (1997a). "Shackling the leader?": Coherence, capacity and the hollow crown. In *The hollow crown* (pp. 198–223). Palgrave Macmillan.

Rhodes, R. A. W. (1997b). *Understanding governance: Policy networks, governance, reflexivity and accountability.* Open University.

Rhodes, R. A. W. (2000). The governance narrative: Key findings and lessons from the ERC's Whitehall Programme. *Public Administration, 78*(2), 345–363.

Saint-Onge, H., & Armstrong, C. (2004). *The conductive organization.* Elsevier.

Scharpf, F.W. 1996. 'Can there be a Stable Federal Balance in Europe?', in J.J. Hesse and V. Wright (Eds), *Federalizing Europe?* (pp. 361–373). Oxford: Oxford University Press.

Selznick, P. (1996). Institutionalism "old" and "new". *Administrative Science Quarterly*, 270–277.

Thomas, C. W. (2003). *Bureaucratic landscapes: Interagency cooperation and the preservation of biodiversity.* MIT Press.

Thompson, F. J. (2012). *Medicaid politics: Federalism, policy durability, and health reform.* Georgetown University Press.

Thompson, G. (2003). *Between hierarchies and markets: The logic and limits of network forms of organization.* Oxford University Press on Demand.

Vandeventer, P., & Mandell, M. P. (2007). *Networks that work: A practitioner's guide to managing networked action.* Community Partners.

Weber, E. P. (1998). Successful collaboration: Negotiating effective regulations. *Environment: Science and Policy for Sustainable Development, 40*(9), 10–15.

Wilensky, H. L. (1964). The professionalization of everyone? *American Journal of Sociology, 70*(2), 137–158.

Wondolleck, J. M., & Yaffee, S. L. (2000). *Making collaboration work: Lessons from innovation in natural resource management.* Island Press.

10 Assessing and Improving Collaborative Performance

How does one assess the ability of collaborative efforts to improve performance? The primary purpose of this chapter is to focus on management for performance, not necessarily measuring it. The key to understanding and improving collaborative performance management is rooted in mission orientation. The fundamental goal of collaborative action is the creation of public value, or an increase in the value of processes and outcomes, as Mark Moore has defined *public value* (Agranoff, 2021). Moore said that "public managers are seen as explorers who, with others, seek to discover, define, and produce public value . . . . They look out to the value of what they are producing as well as *down* to the efficacy and propriety of their means" (1995, p. 20, emphasis in original).

One of the prominent collaboration management scholars, Russell Linden, explains the importance of collaborative performance management: "Today's enlightened leaders in both public and private sectors understand the value chains of which they are a part of, and they know that most of their pressing problems can be solved by collaborative actions with others" (2010, p. xvi). In his groundbreaking study of collaborative management, Eugene Bardach defines it as "any joint activity by two or more agencies that are intended to increase public value by their working together rather than separately" (1998, p. 8). He identifies the main challenge of collaborative performance management as a necessity to overcome political and institutional barriers while collaborating partners find integrative solutions. Therefore, collaborative performance management encompasses those management activities aimed at increasing public value (May & Winter, 2007; Ysa, Sierra, & Esteve, 2014).

As maintained throughout this volume, the emerging roles of public managers in collaborative management are continually evolving and extending the reach of the state to a variety of NGO partners (Agranoff, 2021). This poses a significant problem in assessing and improving collaborative performance. Moreover, it is not clear that government oversight in its more traditional operations is entirely functional in a collaborative atmosphere. Also, it remains an open question whether governments' actions are thus, as has been maintained, since "governmental organizations are no longer the central steering actor in policy processes and managerial activities"

DOI: 10.4324/9781003385769-10

224 *Assessing and Improving Collaborative Performance*

(Klijn, 1997, p. 33). Nevertheless, collaborative actions and network actions do have an impact. But "how much" and to what extent these actions are "changing behavior" in the public sphere still remains a matter of assessment (Rhodes, 1997).

This chapter thoroughly examines managerial roles and actions related to understanding and improving collaborative performance. The focus is on three aspects of performance understanding and improvement. First is an in-depth look at continuous improvement practices specifically applicable to collaborative management. Second, the chapter moves to revisit interoperability in greater detail than occurred in its introduction in Chapter 4, inasmuch as it primarily focuses on a core feature of making collaboration work at a level that brings together the working parts of multiple public, private, and nonprofit organizations in the finite details in the world of practice, that of implementation across organizations. Third, eight emergent performance-related managerial roles in collaborative management are examined. In general, the focus shifts from more traditional "public operations" to those that John Loughlin (2000) defines as public service/operation to partnerships involving public agencies and NGOs.

Continuous Improvement (CI) in Practice

Few dedicated collaborative operations or networks make an effort to engage in the kind of continuous improvement (CI) functions needed to understand the multijurisdictional, multiorganizational process efforts they necessarily participate in. CI operationally differs from the more traditional studies of network performance in public management (e.g., Koliba, Campbell, & Zia, 2011; Koliba, Meek, & Zia, 2010). CI connects *process* assessment to a type of results orientation in understanding the inner workings that lead to potential process redesigns that serve the self-interests of the network/collaborative managers and their component participants because "re-engineering works" in dispersed collaborative systems such as networks. This has been a critical theme around healthcare reforms in the UK (Halvorson, 2013, p. 217). Because network strategies utilize highly complex interactive systems, CI "entails a complexity perspective that includes advanced nonlinear dynamics with continuously changing performance landscapes, that is, systems that depend on beneficial outcomes" (Agranoff, 2021, p. 382). CI explanations must go beyond outcomes to include standards that arise from the agents' interactions, along with the patterns and feedback mechanisms, allowing for adaptive management based on system dynamics that contribute to outcomes (Kolpakov, Agranoff, & McGuire, 2016; Koppenjan & Klijn, 2014, p. 159). Why is CI relevant to understanding collaborative governance? The answer is simple. Being part of collaborative processes, CI provides better knowledge of the bottlenecks in the collaboration process and identifying ways to overcome them.

Warren Bennis (1967) suggested in his essay titled "The Coming Death of Bureaucracy" that organization revitalization is critical for embracing the social dynamics that stagnate and regenerate along with process cycles. The revitalization includes "the ability to learn from experience, the ability to 'learn how to learn' by acquiring and using feedback mechanisms on performance, and the ability to direct one's destiny" (Agranoff, 2021, p. 382). He foresaw the need for bureaucratic structures to control and adapt to the essence of significant human conditions: integration, power distribution, adaptation, and revitalization. Networks and other forms of collaboration are instrumental in such adaptive behaviors.

One of the best examples of operational adaptation is Julianne Mahler's analysis of organizational learning at the National Aeronautics and Space Administration (NASA) (2009) based on the Challenger and Columbia space shuttle accidents. She describes it as a sequence of seven steps: (1) emphasis on work processes accompanied by outputs and outcomes; (2) establishment of real or virtual forms for information integration and event comparison; (3) balance between professional standards and technologies; (4) strengthening institutional memory of organization to remember event/crises/workaround/unsolved problems; (5) maintenance of professional standards; (6) dissemination of new conclusions related to operations and performance; and (7) knowledge preservation while reviewing established procedures and routines.

Operations Analysis and CI

One way to begin considering CI—an aspect of collaborative management that has only recently attracted attention—is to expand current quantitative and qualitative process analysis to more directly address expected operations process obstacles and look for improvements. First of all, to integrate operations involving two or more organizations, CI efforts must address interoperability requirements (Agranoff, 2021). Interoperable management entails coordinated efforts by several agencies and groups working on the same project (Agranoff, 2016). The interoperability difficulty associated with CI is the degree of links at the working levels based on understood, agreed-upon, and performed operational processes that present substantial obstacles to network participants.

On the other hand, interoperability management is defined as regularized programming involving two or more entities for which operating policies and processes have been interactively stated and are carried out by numerous organizations. For example, McGuire and Agranoff (2014) found that process analysis is central to understanding interoperability in public management networks. Process interoperability is not an end in itself. Instead, it "is a means to achieve the ability to respond when coordinated actions go the next step, and reciprocal interaction is deeper" (Agranoff, 2021, p. 384). As will be detailed later in this chapter, it relies on shared and agreed-upon goals and objectives, planning, operational data, role distinction, and an integrated operating system that facilitates communication.

Process Flows and CI

Analysis of the CALFED process, a collaborative environmental science program discussed in Chapter 1, sheds light on very important successes in overcoming formidable obstacles in measuring and managing collaborative performance. One unique CI strategy, for example, utilized a record of decision (ROD) to determine the rationale used when deciding between options or when confronted with future decision-based tasks (Innes, Connick, & Booher, 2007). Furthermore, Norgaard, Kallis, and Kiparsky (2009) reported that problem explanations were provided within the dispersed governance lacuna. This allowed for a broader view of problems and supported efforts to blur the lines between policy-makers and managers on the one hand, and scientists on the other hand, bringing out different perspectives as managers demand the "right answer" while scientists are faced with "real-time" problems that require decisions. "Science advisors cannot and should not dictate policy goals," one involved practitioner concludes, "but they can help translate those goals into clear, measurable outcomes; characterize the level of certainty and effort associated with achieving specific goals; and identify tradeoffs between goals for decision-makers" (Bobker, 2009, p. 727). Finally, the value of the scientific program in assisting policy-makers in analyzing the underlying assumptions of various management options is demonstrated through process analysis.

The presence of multiple leaders in the network also facilitates the process of CI in collaborative management. According to Angel Saz-Carranza and Sonia Ospina (2011), leadership should be regarded as a "collective achievement rather than the property of individuals" (p. 406). Their study found that the network did not just evolve to the implementation stage. Instead, "simultaneous management appeared and reappeared through concept formulation, collaboration, build-out, and operations" (Agranoff, 2021, p. 384). This implies the potential importance of CI at all stages of development. Furthermore, the process analysis revealed that each participating network component (i.e., participant) needed to pay attention to the input from the lead or core public agency or NGO, not as a hierarchical replacement, but because of the need to work within the boundaries of the process nexus of networking activity, adjusting structures and operations to the process nexus of networking activity (Agranoff, 2016). Other studies in collaborative management also emphasize the importance of process analysis for analyzing collaborative performance (Koliba, Meek, & Zia, 2010; Agranoff, 2014; Cepiku, 2014; Keast & Mandell, 2014).

Process flows and analysis of the process by elements can also be instrumental for CI by looking for potential problems and areas for improvement. Using descriptive measures of social network analysis, the second author of this volume, Kolpakov (2013), examines structural changes of networks over time in his study of Metro School, a STEM school in Columbus, Ohio. Specifically, he looked at: (1) network homophily or interactions based on sector, gender, and collaboration experience similarity; (2) degree centrality, identification of actors with many ties; (3) betweenness centrality, analysis of network brokers connecting different parts of a network; (4) density or number of existing ties in a network; (5) reciprocity/ mutuality, the number of symmetric ties among network actors; and (6) the transitivity index, i.e., the ratio of the number of potentially transitive triads, indicating hierarchy and exchange of resources in a network (Wasserman & Faust, 1994; Contractor, Wasserman, & Faust, 2006). His analysis investigated prevailing processes leading to formation, development, and maturation of networks over time, combined with an analysis of the structural configurations at actor, dyadic, triadic, and whole-network levels—changing through the network evolution and the effect of individual characteristics of network actors on the structure of a network over time. This developmental analysis serves the CI knowledge base by looking theoretically at how networks and other collaboratives evolve and move through various developmental and operational stages. From an instrumental or policy/program perspective, the study helps explain how networks respond to complex problems involving multiagency and multisector processes. In a sense, this robust approach to network modeling can clearly contribute to the process of CI analysis.

In their comprehensive survey-based study of a disaster relief network in Haiti, Isabella Nolte and her associates (Nolte, Martin, & Boenigk, 2012) examined collaborative outcomes and outputs at three network levels: individual organizations, the partnership/network, and the community. Quality, regular forces like regular meetings, shared feedback on agendas, progress, and learning from each organization's experience were key collaborative outcomes and outputs identified by Nolte and her colleagues. They found that while most organization representatives tend to focus more on the costs of collaboration involvement, the research revealed that the benefits of participation are both tangible and intangible. In addition, Nolte and her associates claim that "Pursuing joint goals in a collaborative setting provides organizations with the opportunity to gain insights into the partners' way of working and enables the acquisition of scarce resources such as expected knowledge" (p. 653). Nolte concludes that:

> Well-performing partnerships can also gain the attention of politicians and funders, and organizations might be able to acquire resources more easily if they participated in well-performing disaster responses. Finally, organizations that work together with others during disaster response can focus on the tasks they conduct best and address shared problems more efficiently. Concerning organizational outcomes, one respondent noted, reflecting on the collaborative: "We could do more with less resources; we could do better what we used to do."
>
> (p. 653)

Developments in CI

In the future, CI and collaborative performance research will gravitate toward using complexity and big data analysis. For example, real-time performance data that has been adapted to both planning and operations anchored in shared network and language, built from industry standards and metrics test modeling, systems planning, and economic

228 *Assessing and Improving Collaborative Performance*

and environmental impact assessments were included in Koliba, Campbell, and Zia's (2011) analysis of four traffic congestion management networks. Related to this, Koliba (2014) notes that relationships between network variables are usually considered linear, but this may not be the case. Specifically, he discusses the impact of "multiplier effects" (p. 99) that can bring both negative and positive feedback lags. These process elements could potentially identify critical CI results leading to changes in performance. This type of analysis seems promising for examining network performance data (network structures and functions, performance knowledge, and complex system evolution, adaptation, and performance) (Innes & Booher, 1999).

Based on their research, Joop Koppenjan and Erik-Hans Klijn (2014) identified four other process-related approaches to management that can be useful for CI. The first approach is the use of adaptive management, continually evolving and sensitive to the content of ideas and the creation of interactive processes and regulations (Agranoff, 2021). As difficulties are resolved, the second approach is to reduce any positive feedback that may distort existing equilibria. The third approach is negative feedback mobilizing interactions that support the existing equilibrium to establish long-term support. The fourth approach is to improve more constructive positive feedback, which is especially important when changing operational decisions necessitates opening relatively closed collaboratives. Overall, they suggest that combining complexity theory with governance theory will help simplify the complex web of organizations, players, and interests that interact in interactive networks and other collaboratives. Finally, complexity theory may raise the awareness and sensitivity of actors to the numerous and diverse concerns emanating from the ever-changing environments of public and nonprofit organizations. Simply put, we need to understand the complex practices leading to the effectiveness of collaborative networks in different contexts.

Koliba (2014) argues that as new data-mining programs allow large volumes of verbal and numerical data to be analyzed for patterns, theory-building in CI will be supported in future years by the type of analyses that align performance with system dynamics, capturing theory-building with computer simulation modeling with techniques such as system dynamics, agent-based modeling, social network analysis, and qualitative comparative analysis. They will, without a doubt, contribute to a better understanding of collaborative performance. Other emerging techniques include augmented mapping, which can be used alone or in combination with public participatory or collaborative GIS programming to provide fresh insights into how network members cluster around spatially connected problems and the cleavages that exist between them (Nielson, 2012).

Assessing Interoperability in Collaborative Performance Management

The history of interoperability (IOp) includes mapping practices that originated in the business sector, specifically in supply chain management and assembly-operations management, whereby two or more organizations assemble separately produced parts into one product. Indeed, interoperations are at the heart of "implementation," when planning and operations are brought together by developing and strengthening their connections (Agranoff, 2021). To facilitate a process of working together, IOp is "a focused internal-external effort to enhance collaborated organizational learning (McFarland, 2008)" (Kolpakov, Agranoff, & McGuire, 2016, p. 319).

IOp can be demonstrated using the public sector example of the National Incident Fire Command's wildland fire program, first described in U.S. Government Accountability Office (2006). This program includes five federal agencies, numerous state governments, and state-based NGOs, with varying involvement depending on each forest area. The program is based on ten broad overlapping steps (Kolpakov, Agranoff, & McGuire, 2016):

1. Joining together separate resources and organizations.
2. Recording of agency/organization rules and procedures.
3. Designing a command-and-control structure.
4. Developing a management strategy based on mutual agreement.
5. Exploring a resource utilization sequence.
6. Developing an agency "donated" staffing procedure.
7. Agreeing and developing common standards, rules, norms, policies, and procedures.
8. Setting incident response policies and procedures.
9. Developing and maintaining a "council" or networked organized structure.
10. Negotiating and developing interagency policies and procedures.

To people outside of the National Incident Fire Command's wildland fire program, IOp may be primarily found in step 10, dealing with policies and procedures. In practice, IOp is much more. In fact, IOp is an active learning community in which people share a common repeatable approach focused on the use of similar language and techniques based on shared experiences (Glazer, 2012).

As introduced earlier (Chapter 3), interoperable management can be conceptually distinguished from its closely related administrative counterparts (Kolpakov, Agranoff, & McGuire, 2016): (1) *interoperational consultation*, which includes the search for information or advice across organizational lines about a particular practice; (2) *interoperational transactions*, found in grants or contracts between two or more organizations; and (3) *interoperational coordination*, when two or more organizations regularly exchange information or refer clients without operating internally on an interactive basis (Agranoff & McGuire, 2003a). In contrast, IOp refers "to regularized programming involving two or more entities for which operating policies and processes have been articulated and are executed interactively to measurable degrees" (Kolpakov, Agranoff, & McGuire, 2016, p. 319).

According to the U.S. Government Accountability Office (GAO) report for homeland security, the most frequent challenge in developing effective IOp-based

230 *Assessing and Improving Collaborative Performance*

communications is not technical in nature—it is predominantly cultural and organizational. The three principal challenges for the U.S. Department of Homeland Security include (1) clearly identifying and defining the problem; (2) establishing national interoperability performance goals and standards that balance nationwide standards with the flexibility to address differences in state, regional, and local needs and conditions; and (3) defining the roles of federal, state, and local governments and other entities in addressing interoperable needs (U.S. Department of Homeland Security, 2005). All these issues are interorganizational in nature, requiring some form of collaborative management (Kolpakov, Agranoff, & McGuire, 2016).

Authors of this volume and their longtime collaborator (Kolpakov, Agranoff, & McGuire, 2016). conducted an empirical study of interoperability in Metro School, a networked STEM school in Columbus, Ohio, and identified the core elements of IOp. The technical elements were identified from one case as the ten steps of the National Incident Fire Command Program from a U.S. Government Accountability Office report (2006). The cultural and organizational elements of IOp were derived from a homeland security study by Charles Wise (2006), who concludes that homeland security IOp requires a networked model instead of a hierarchical model, "a challenge of interagency and intergovernmental affairs" (p. 302). The organizational elements of IOp include: defining and articulating common outcomes, establishing reinforcing or joint strategies, identifying needs and leveraging resources, agreeing on agency roles and responsibilities, establishing compatible policies and procedures, developing cross-agency monitoring mechanisms, reinforcing agency and individual accountability, and involving an array of intergovernmental and NGO actors (Wise, 2006).

Wise (2006) concludes that this type of adaptive management involves "putting into place a formal framework that facilitates interpersonal interaction across agencies and levels" (p. 315). Using Wise's conclusions, Jenkins (2006, p. 321) points to contemporary organizations' difficulties implementing such behavior changes. Therefore, he recommends establishing structures and processes "that provide incentives and rewards for collaboration, consultation, and support for implementing key goals" (p. 321). Similarly, Jenkins recommends clear problem identification, establishing IOp goals, and defining governmental roles and roles of government collaborating entities.

The application of IOp goes well beyond emergency management and disaster response recovery (Kolpakov, Agranoff, & McGuire, 2016). The Denver area Metropolitan Planning Organization (MPO) has emphasized transportation planning for addressing land use, growth control, and local use of space coordination using a consensus-based IOp approach (Margerum, 2005). Thompson (2012) found that with few exceptions, Medicaid-funded programs are run by the states through a variety of contracts and purchase of services arrangements. These range from externalized/contracted case management to several medically related direct services (such as dental, vision, and physical therapy) by subcontracts that support the work of primary private healthcare agencies and practitioners centered around the

Assessing and Improving Collaborative Performance   231

patient. Also, in the mid-1990s, CALFED, a federal–state partnership, had evolved into an operating multisectoral endeavor improving water quality based on science-based standards. It integrated the conservation measures in the Sacramento and San Joaquin river basins, solving operating problems and working with large water suppliers (Kallis, Kiparsky, & Norgaard, 2009).

IOp encompasses both process and technical aspects of systems to be integrated so all components of systems would work together (Agranoff, 1991, 2013; Agranoff & Pattakos, 1979). Glazer (2012, p. 119) states, "an operation must first be organized . . . and is fueled by effective decision-making and effective decision-making is driven by data." Regarding operations, it "is made possible by a long chain of enablers, working backward to define the work system" (p. 119). IOp entails far more cross-border managerial actions than simply creating the organizational design (Agranoff, 2021). It is also evident that functioning numerous organizational structures in separate (analytical or real-time) networks/networking as distinct entities are necessary (Kolpakov, Agranoff, & McGuire, 2016).

For the effective functioning of IOp systems, related decision-making, structural, and information components should be identified. For example, four essential functions are considered core in the Incident Command System (ICS) fire control system. First, they go beyond that of command and interactive decision-making by managing: (1) operations to manage all tactical activities; (2) planning, gathering, and evaluating current and forecasting information; (3) logistics to provide ongoing support for network participants; and (4) financing administration to track money and time in handling situations (Howitt & Leonard, 2009; Varley, 2009).

Large, complex systems and single-agency directives have different functions. In IOp processing, they are widely dispersed among network actors. In either case, these systems share several characteristics, such as gathering and analyzing information about a system, making predictions about how things will change, developing and deciding on options, and formulating plans (Kolpakov, Agranoff, & McGuire, 2016). The hallmarks of ICS in action include regular briefings and planning cycles (Varley, 2009). Furthermore, many studies of emergency management networks emphasize the importance of implementing mechanisms that foster trust, assembling and developing timely information and communications technology, and working toward mutual goal adjustment among interorganizational actors with divergent objectives (Kapucu, Garayev, & Wang, 2013).

The Kolpakov, Agranoff, and McGuire (2016) study of Metro School, an experimental STEM school network in Columbus, Ohio, produced several empirical findings regarding IOp. They discovered that while defining discrete interoperability components can seem daunting, the study's exploratory social network analysis results point to distinct elements of this complex concept. The first is that separating the governance or planning core from the operational core is critical for a properly situated interoperability system. The well-placed governance planning body structures, such as the policy-oriented Metro Partnership Group and the policy-steering more technical Educational Council, enabled the planning, gathering,

232 *Assessing and Improving Collaborative Performance*

and evaluating of current and forecasted data. The operational core develops, oversees, and manages all tactical operations during the implementation stage. It is represented structurally by a small number of Metro network centers responsible for programming across agencies. Second, another component of interoperability evaluated by reciprocity is agreeing on the roles and duties of participating agencies. IOp can explain the increasing level of reciprocity during the network creation stage. Kolpakov, Agranoff, and McGuire (2016, pp. 328) argue that "[a]t the beginning of the collaboration, network members need to agree on roles and responsibilities and establish compatible policies and procedures" and "[t]his requires a great deal of two-way communication and interaction to set rules, norms, and values for the effective future functioning of the network (Rank, Robins, & Pattison 2010)." Finally, another procedural element of IOp that may be assessed by betweenness centrality is control of information and the level of negotiations in the network. A high level of betweenness indicates consistent negotiation patterns with different agencies' representatives for optimal resource use (Wasserman & Faust, 1994).

Kolpakov, Agranoff, and McGuire (2016) argue that as organizational/program paradigms change to interorganizational domains, IOp will become increasingly relevant to many other designations. IOp is definitely an extension of postmodern dedifferentiation across agency lines, even though its need has existed for a long time (Clegg, 1990). Newer organized forms will require "management" by IOp procedures as more networked operations emerge, such as Metro School and CALFED.

Future Research in IOp

When it comes to establishing numerous expectations and links at different levels, the notion of IOp holistically includes the realities of multiple stakeholders who constantly work with or modify different expectations. There is undoubtedly a need for more study in the field of IOp. Line contact activities, for example, dropped out of the IOp network as operational interactions became prevalent in the Metro network. In addition, a planning network was clearly distinguishable from a core implementation network (Kolpakov, Agranoff, & McGuire, 2016). However, the transformation of network learning across many organizational domains has emerged as lessons learned from the Metro study. This is in line with the conclusions of Bruns's (2013) study on scientific research coordination. In her research, IOp type coordination was achieved by combining and arranging three different types of practices: (1) expert practice, which generates unique contributions; (2) coordination practice, which coordinates contributions across domain boundaries; and (3) collaborative practice, which amends expert practices. As a result of these practices, separate scientific contributions become "interworkable" and compatible. These findings suggest that IOp will need to "chunk down" these processes even more. For example, important policy concerns like planning and execution will require numerous actors representing many public and non-public entities with diverse missions and knowledge bases (Kolpakov, Agranoff, & McGuire, 2016).

Assessing and Improving Collaborative Performance   233

Whereas the New Public Management (NPM) approach, popular in the early 2000s, has emphasized more market-based approaches, its contrasts with hierarchical management are unclear. NPM also underscores the interactive basis of non–command-and-control regulation of competition and choice. To some degree, market-based approaches can substitute for a standard public management orientation, although the connective tenets need to continue. As a result, government under NPM increases its prevalence in connecting its agencies with NGOs and clients.

Barbara Romzek and Jocelyn Johnston (2002) identified many major NPM-related obstacles in contracting for services, including the availability of competition, the contractor's capacities, the funder's ability to make appropriate evaluations, and the theoretical basis for contracting. Box 10.1 summarizes contract management connections that matter in human services.

Box 10.1   Contract Management Connections in Human Service Do Matter

1. Healthy levels of provider competition provide market incentives for strong performance at the lowest possible cost. It may mean the potential loss of a contract to more cost-effective competitors.
2. Resource adequacy reflects the capacity of the funder to fund staff and other expenses related to its accurate cost projections, analysis of contractor capacity, and training for new contract staff.
3. In-depth planning for measuring contractor performance facilitates the evaluation of the provider's performance and cost-effectiveness.
4. Intensive training for contract management staff often requires retooling and reinvesting in converting staff from service delivery to service oversight duties.
5. In evaluating the contractor's staff capacity, funders must ensure that the contractor has the capability to staff up adequately and in a timely fashion so as not to compromise performance.
6. Funders must access the contractors' potential to manage the financial side of service delivery.
7. In addressing the theoretical integrity of the rationale for contracting, one must ask: does the undertaking meet the social problem or program need? Other than economic and efficiency reasons, a policy reform based on a flawed rationale is probably doomed.
8. The political strength of the client advocacy groups—that is, their influence with officials such as legislators—can lead to situations in which the enforcement authority of contract managers is undercut.
9. Subcontractor relationships are complex. Effective implementation in human services arenas normally requires cooperation—if not the integration of services—among separate contractors, thus making accountability more difficult.

234 *Assessing and Improving Collaborative Performance*

> 10. Funders will shift risks downward to the contractor. In programs such as managed care, whereby prepaid or capitated payments are involved, the contractors are exposed to losses that cannot be covered by agreed payments; consequently, the contractors resist expensive clients or cut back on higher-paid staff.
>
> *Source:* Summarized from Romzek and Johnston (2002, pp. 423–453)

As suggested in points 7–10 (Box 10.1), the most critical problems and issues are related to the need for cooperation in complex relationship systems. They reinforce the old notion that contracting is basically a relational process.

Another issue is that in the competitive marketplaces for government contracts, only a small number of providers have been scrutinized (Agranoff, 2017). The research of Jocelyn Johnston and Amanda Girth (2012) highlighted issues in various domains and at several levels of government. When government employees are required to participate in competitiveness improvement methods, their time and energy are expended, and transaction costs rise. As a result, in-house expertise is lost when programs, contract design, and monitoring are contracted out. "Contractors are now overseeing other contractors with growing frequency, and the role of government in public service provision is shrinking" (Johnston & Girth, 2012, p. 19).

When comparing performance in the public, private, and nonprofit sectors, it is also apparent—contrary to some people's perceptions—that the private and nonprofit sectors are more effective. As a result, competition should not be viewed as a panacea or a guarantee of improved performance. Furthermore, competition might jeopardize other government goals relating to service quality and program effectiveness, such as service continuity in many social welfare programs (Fernandez, 2009). By stimulating competition, "managing markets" drains administrative resources in many circumstances. Most significantly, it implies actual costs that must be considered (Johnston & Girth, 2012). Moreover, the public sector's administrative capacity for contract control has been a long-standing challenge (Girth, 2014; Romzek & Johnston, 2005; Van Slyke, 2003).

Improving Collaborative Performance: New Roles of Public Managers

The job of modern public managers includes leading and guiding the public agency and facing newer challenges to collaborate with other public agencies and NGOs (Agranoff, 2017). Managing organizational boundaries did not remove traditional organizational responsibilities such as managing human and financial resources, operations, planning, etc. Except for the usual responsibilities of full-time coordinators, the new collaborative roles are limited in scope and centered around a slight but critical edge of a manager's time (Agranoff, 2021). They are, however, critical in this brave new world of public management. Public administration has been "repositioned" in this regard, as George Frederickson (1999) observed more than 20 years ago, emphasizing knowledge and information development through cooperation.

Specifically, eight collaborative improvement functions have become prominent at the management level: "leadership mobilization, network promotion, brokering collaborative activity, collaborative capacity development, making strategic public investments, providing new forms of technical assistance, assessing the value-adding of collaboration, and facilitating automatic feedback and learning" (Agranoff, 2021, p. 393). Each of these functions—each elaborated on in the following subsections—poses emergent challenges that add to public managers' internal and operational roles in different contexts: local economic and community development, human services, transportation, planning, environmental management, emergency management, and many others.

Leadership Mobilization

This involves people from different organizations participating in policy and entrepreneurial leadership. In fact, this is both internal and external mobilization (Agranoff, 2005). Therefore, collaborative managers must receive top management guidance and support. For example, former Michigan Gov. Arthur Engler played a key role in fostering high-tech economic growth. Also notable is former Indianapolis Mayor Steven Goldsmith's enthusiasm for implementing managed competition initiatives, documented in Osborne and Gaebler's (1992) *Reinventing Government*. Natural bureaucratic resistance and turf protection—there are many—can flourish without such backing. Top agency executives, like department heads, would also provide leadership support. The importance of empowerment cannot be overstated. "Leaders must go beyond lip service to create an internal environment that fosters participation, information sharing, shared learning, and participatory decision-making" (Agranoff, 2005, p. 34). This empowerment approach is, in many ways, a continuation of more traditional executive leadership roles (Klijn, Steijn, & Edelenbos, 2010).

Public managers must engage key external stakeholders. They should start by inviting managers from different agencies but at the same level of government. They will later engage potential cooperating executive agencies, elected executive officials, and legislative body representatives. Other agencies will need to be persuaded through various means, as they are not always happy to share missions, physical facilities, staff, or resources, nor are they always eager to change their agendas (Agranoff, 2005). Legislators are fierce guardians of their turfs, which they incorporate into executive branch-created networks. Katz and Nowak (2017) recommend identifying one or more network champions among legislators and regular communication with them early.

It is equally important to reach organizations outside the government, such as alternative service deliverers, competing businesses, and advocacy groups, to be

236 *Assessing and Improving Collaborative Performance*

part of the collaboration. As a result, it is recommended that top managers/administrators of these firms be contacted in order for them to designate technical and management people who will eventually engage in the collaboration and negotiating processes. These are more unusual jobs, such as persuading groups of external parties to form new working partnerships with the government (Agranoff, 2005).

Network Promotion

This is why members of the public must remake themselves by supporting the creation and flow of information among government departments and beyond (Agranoff, 2005). Generating partnerships, networks, challenge grants, venture capital pools, business incubator programs, and electronic information networks is the responsibility of today's public managers. Because it is evident that any party involved in collaboration does not have all of the answers to their challenges, management must prioritize the development of networks. Because knowledge-producing and -commercializing sectors are limited to a small number of regions worldwide, the current economy is hastening this trend. Several state and municipal governments in the United States are well-positioned to bring together research, technology, investment, and marketing. The various partners may be able to develop channels that get resources to solutions by working jointly, which is the primary goal of advanced manufacturing networks like Cleveland Advanced Manufacturing Partnership (CAMP) in Ohio. These partners do not naturally join forces, but external forces aid them. Public managers are in a unique position to participate in such gatherings. As a result, today's bureaucrats cannot wait for the phone to ring or for an e-mail message to arrive. Instead, they should seek out and incorporate potential partners who can help transform human capital into live problem identification and solution systems (Crosby & Bryson, 1992; Katz & Nowak, 2017).

Brokering Collaborative Activity

This collaborative improvement function is related to government intervention. Contemporary public managers must uncover and generate future possibilities for action, combining finite public resources with external resources, initiatives, and investments, rather than waiting for ideas to come from outside government (Agranoff, 2005). They must act as brokers by bringing the interested parties together and seeking timely public investments. In the new economy, public managers must allocate resources strategically in business incubators and industry clustering. The most crucial is information technology, as governments must make significant expenditures on information infrastructure access and development in collaboration with the private sector. Adaptable investments are required in the telecommunications industry since entrepreneurs always constantly seek the latest technology. In addition, global communication promotes scientific collaboration at the international level (Toft & Audretsch, 2000).

However, more actions are needed. Today, the public manager does not have the luxury of observing how these programs develop (Agranoff, 2005). Bringing different actors to the table and facilitating differs from just distributing grants or monitoring contracts. Brokering necessitates a diverse range of negotiation abilities and the development of a collaborative problem-solving culture that prioritizes equality, adaptability, discretion, and a focus on outcomes (Agranoff & McGuire, 2003b; Bardach, 1998; Stone et al., 1999). Perhaps, this kind of team building is not entirely new, but collaborating across organizations is possibly different from managing within a hierarchical organization (Agranoff & McGuire, 2001; Agranoff, 2012, 2017).

Collaborative Capacity Development

Developing the capabilities of local communities and locally based groups is another collaborative improvement. This function has a far-reaching objective of mobilizing resources and funds to address wicked policy problems (Rittel & Webber, 1973) at the community level. According to Agranoff (2005), the objective of self-sufficiency is an exceptionally essential aspect of the modern economy because regional clusters and agglomerations of industries in which knowledge and information combine to create growth in supportive settings are critical. Similarly, Toft and Audretsch state, "Economic activity based on new ideas and tacit knowledge is not easily copied by competitors far from the original source nor easily transferred to lower-cost countries by multinational corporations" (2000, p. 8). Local governments must now have a collaborative capacity that includes the creation of a friendly regulatory structure (e.g., permit assistance), business assistance activities (e.g., site selection), the location of needed support business services (e.g., finance and subcontractors), and promotion of the community's social and environmental infrastructure (e.g., education improvement) (Agranoff, 2005). This collaborative capacity requires capability at the local level, although it can be easily underwritten and promoted by state governments and private investors.

The collaborative management competencies of contemporary public managers go beyond just teamwork. These days, they should also be skilled in capacity building. For example, the state economic development official becomes an active team member, according to one of the volume's authors (Agranoff, 2005), by bringing expertise in the technical operation of programs and regulatory infrastructures, legal rules, and procedures regarding program involvement, and external potential resources (e.g., federal funding). In addition, public managers actively participate in teams' activities seeking and implementing collaborative solutions. Public organizations are no longer passive program participants in substantive policy areas such as local economic development since the times of entrepreneurial states are long gone. They are no longer passive observers or spectators in the game of collaboration. Instead, they are truly active players and "coboundary spanners" in this game (Provan & Kenis, 2008).

Making Strategic Public Investments

Public managers have been transformed into strategic investors because of the increasing necessity to create incentives to work with other public agencies. It is no longer a game of waiting for appropriation and allocating resources among competing agencies. Instead, the public agency must respond to resource requests differently, just as it did with endogenous policies. The tiny amounts of seed funding, grant monies, tax modifications, or regulatory relief that are available are increasingly requiring some promise of return on investment, a bigger private match, or an in-kind donation that is soundly rooted in a predetermined strategic or priority judgment. This is the model used by the most successful company incubation programs. For example, offering incubation spaces is not enough; they must be strategically based on solid policies and programs (Agranoff, 2005).

The current economic state of affairs has exacerbated this situation. Developmental economists argue that many entrepreneurial firms in markets using the innovation strategy leave and enter industries (Toft & Audretsch, 2000; Katz & Nowak, 2017). Because the possible number of enterprises that a state agency or municipal economic development department will have to deal with is potentially overwhelming, this situation has significant consequences for collaboration at the state and local levels (Agranoff, 2005). This places an additional heavy burden on the public manager who makes decisions to allocate limited resources to work with business organizations. Which industries should be selected since they look like winners, and which ones should be dropped? Given government organizations' political and administrative nature, picking winners has always been challenging for authorities.

To perform this collaborative improvement function successfully, public managers should first add the most public value through some form of a priori strategic direction setting, usually with external agents, and then deploy limited public resources to leverage external investments by matching the right applicants with the right strategy (Agranoff, 2005). As a result of this process, public managers will need to be familiar with human capital requirements, credit availability, regional economies, possible markets, and miscellaneous investment-related issues. For example, O'Toole (1997) claims that these activities are not part of standard legal and technical program procedures which public managers perform.

Providing New Forms of Technical Assistance

Public managers' increased technical assistance role in developing connections based on available human capital is often ignored in collaborative improvement functions (Reich, 1991). For example, economic development personnel should cooperate with persons with experience in the four pillars of the present economy: globalization, knowledge, regionalism, and fluid entrepreneurship. Internal–external technical support vehicles—such as the Michigan Economic Development

Corporation and its interdisciplinary account teams, Cleveland Tomorrow, and the Central Indiana Corporate Partnership—will become increasingly popular as human capital becomes increasingly important (Agranoff, 2005).

Human capital is more critical than education and training when it comes to programming based on collaboration. This can be illustrated in the CAMP example. Cleveland Tomorrow, a public–private economic development organization dedicated to reviving the area's failing industrial economy, started this program in 1983 (Agranoff, 2005). Because sophisticated industrial technology-based needs clearly require a well-educated and skilled workforce, this PPP originally featured university partners such as Case Western Reserve and Cleveland State universities. CAMP later established ties with community institutions and school districts. "Great walls" between public school systems and other government agencies are crumbling as state and local government officials reach out to communicate educational needs and expectations, and schools respond by developing programs that eventually lead to the human capital needed to meet collaborative challenges. The school-work relationship is an example of the required links that present daunting challenges to today's governmental agencies tackling society's most complex policy issues (O'Toole, 1997).

Today, public managers inform collaborating partners about other participants' existing technologies and human capital to address wicked policy problems (Rittel & Webber, 1973). Similarly, they must make networks and collaboratives aware of the potential of other collaborative bodies such as networks, partnerships, alliances, and consortia (Agranoff, 2005). Again, this specific form of technical assistance is very different from standard bureaucratic awarding and grant procedures, program and fundraising oversight, and program information, rules, and financial requirements.

Assessing the Value-Adding of Collaboration

Eugene Bardach suggests that public managers "should not be impressed by the idea of collaboration per se, but only if it produces better organizational performance or lower costs than its alternatives" (1998, p. 17). The reason for collaborative investment usually includes more than a hazily defined common public purpose but also the benefits collaboration can offer to each partner's mission and operations and the experts and managers as professionals (Agranoff, 2005). As a result, value-adding can be assessed from the perspectives of: (1) the administrator/specialist; (2) the participating organization; (3) the network process; and (4) the network outcomes. By shifting the emphasis to intermediate outputs, this value-adding helps bridge the gap between difficult-to-measure results (Wye, 2002, p. 27).

Public managers and specialists often do not understand the benefit of network participation and collaboration from the value-added perspective. The exception is Craig Thomas's study of biodiversity preservation collaboration among different public, private, and nonprofit organizations where program

240 *Assessing and Improving Collaborative Performance*

specialists interact naturally without being forced into collaboration. They "have similar values, believe in the same causal relationships, and have a common methodology for validating knowledge, all of which shape their formulation of best management practices" (2003, p. 41). Professional managers view the process of collaboration across organizations as expanding possibilities in terms of technological and synergistic development. The benefits of networks and collaboratives, according to existing business management literature, include expanding information and access to other organizations' expertise, pooling and accessing financial and other resources, sharing risks and innovation investments, managing uncertainty, meeting the need for operational flexibility and response time, and accessing other adaptive efficiencies (Alter & Hage, 1993; Perrow, 1992; Powell, 1990). These functions are potentially channeled via critical problem-solving or program-adjusting processes, which add value to one's organization/collaboration.

The network/collaborative itself provides potential value in both processes and outcomes. Even though networks require considerable time and effort, the relationships they generate can be "important conduits to improved outcomes" (Keast, 2016, p. 449). From a process perspective, collective rather than individual organization-based processes of organizing, decision-making, and programming are predominant, with group dynamics typical for individual organizations (Agranoff, 2003b; McGuire, 2002; Agranoff, 2012). According to Kickert and Koppenjan (1997, p. 47), managing a collaborative entity entails "formal or informal benchmarking of shared steering" of interaction processes that include activation, guided mediation, strategic consensus, joint problem-solving, and maintenance-implementation-adjustment activities. These activities ultimately lead to collaborative performance outputs and outcomes. The results of networks vary, but the collaborative performance output of specific networks can include: client referrals, websites, service agreements, grants, proposals, mutual referrals, and joint investments (Agranoff, 2005). Collaborative outcomes usually end stages of collaborative processes such as "adapted policies, joint or collaborative databases, exchanged resources, new program interfaces, mutually adapted technologies, and enhanced interagency knowledge infrastructures (Agranoff & McGuire, 2001; Kickert & Koppenjan, 1997; O'Toole, 1997, 2015)" (Agranoff, 2005, p. 39). Collaborative performance management can be along these dimensions. Finally, we should hold collaborative activity accountable to the standards of performance that cannot be achieved by efforts of a single organization or simple contracting but measured by criteria jointly developed by all collaborating actors (Klijn & Koppenjan, 2000).

Facilitating Automatic Feedback and Learning

While assessing collaborative performance, collaborative partners can utilize two additional value-adding performance management approaches. The first approach uses automatic feedback as a possible "alternative" to political battles over comprehensive program reviews or program "compliance" procedures. Bureaucratic agencies can become more customer-driven or market-oriented as they become more collaboratively involved (Agranoff, 2005). According to Ross and Friedman (1990), if the customer defines the need and chooses to co-invest, one line of responsibility is drawn: the customer's use of the service and subsequent decisions to reinvest will establish or disprove the program's suitability. Although this does not guarantee complete accountability, it does produce actual demand and the market "values" such as public spending.

A second approach includes developing collaborative learning structures similar to Peter Senge's learning organizations "where people continually expand their capacity to create the results they truly desire, where new and expansive patterns of thinking are nurtured, where collective aspiration is set free, and where people are continually learning how to learn together" (1990, p. 3). At least four types of learning have been distinguished: (1) reflective or social, from the external environment; (2) instrumental, from evidence and experience; (3) political, based on policy experiences and processes; and (4) symbolic, based on the extant challenges and experiences (Gilardi & Radaelli, 2014, pp. 156–159). Collective learning has been defined as bringing diverse aspects of a community together through social production by increasing the variety of alternatives through interactive processes (Agranoff, 2005). "Social production can be a matter of bringing about a fresh configuration of preferences through opening up new possibilities . . . bringing together sufficient resources to pursue a broadly defined purpose" (Stone et al., 1999, pp. 354–355).

Mark Imperial's (2004) study of environmental performance management systems in networked processes led to some critical characteristics of collaborative improvement systems. First, performance management raises concerns regarding conflicting positions, interests, and values. Second, collaborative performance management systems tend to be quite complex and increase costs and problem identification among participating organizations. Third, these systems can facilitate and motivate collaborative action, primarily through discussions. Fourth, performance management can improve collaborative processes through communication and interaction. Fifth, performance management can bring tensions between organizational autonomy, performance, accountability, harmony, and diversity (Saz-Carranza, 2012). Sixth and related, given the political nature of such processes, leadership is crucial in managing differences attributed to the diverse goals of participating organizations.

MarkImperial (2004, p. 36) provides a series of valuable recommendations for developing collaborative performance management systems in his study of watershed governance, which are summarized in Box 10.2. According to Imperial (2004), collaborative performance management can broaden public value, stimulate interorganizational partnerships, benefit active network participants, and generally enhance collaborative process outcomes.

242 *Assessing and Improving Collaborative Performance*

Box 10.2   Building Collaboration Into Performance Management

- Structure goals and measures that create a shared sense of purpose and motivate network partners toward a specific set of actions.
- Ensure that measures are understandable and easy to communicate to the public.
- Ensure that performance management systems create regular and repeated opportunities for interaction and information exchange to foster peer pressure and develop trust. These interactive processes should be designed to promote learning, adaptation, and change.
- Use performance management systems to steer and coordinate the activities of network participants by improving communication, coordinating actions, and integrating policies so that each organization advances the network's shared goals or objectives.
- Use performance management to celebrate success by marking milestones and accomplishments in ways that promote programmatic accomplishments to politicians, journalists, stakeholders, and the public.
- Use performance management to sustain momentum for collaborative efforts and keep the "bandwagon" rolling by demonstrating that collaborative activities are making progress toward shared goals.
- Use performance management to reduce "random acts of kindness" by moving from pursuing a series of isolated projects to addressing specific problems systematically over a prolonged period of time by focusing action on specific goals or measures.

Source: Imperial (2004, p. 36)

Conclusion

It is not yet clear that the role of government in its traditional function is completely changing to more passive roles. So even though collaboratives and policy networks are essential, strengthening political participation, redefining the connecting roles of public actors while influencing policy objectives, influencing actor behavior, and changing the nature of accountability are all still important (Rhodes, 1997). It is too early to conclude that "governmental organizations are no longer the central steering actor in policy processes and management activities" (Klijn, 1997, p. 33). The degree to which collaborative activity minimizes the traditional role of "the state" remains an open question in an interconnected world (Agranoff 2005; McGuire & Agranoff, 2010).

Collaborative management appears to have some minimal potential to weaken the traditional government role, but it is not absent in important respects (Agranoff,

Assessing and Improving Collaborative Performance

2021). For example, the domain of the public agency may be impacted by the participation of managers in public management networks, although it is uncertain to what degree. To be sure, compromises are made, decisions are swayed, plans are changed, resources are directed, intense groups wield political power, and public blame is shared directly or indirectly. But, as external groups exert agency influence, all of these could be more indirect activities that have been ongoing for some time. In many circumstances, for example, network activities may have just a little impact on the operations of public organizations engaging in the network.

Studies on network behavior by Agranoff and McGuire (Agranoff, 2003, 2017, 2021; Agranoff & McGuire, 2003b) suggest that public managers use between 10% and 20% of their work time for collaborative activities (network involvement). More traditional or everyday within-organization management (Lipnack & Stamps, 1994) and some level of government substitution are better seen as an overlay atop collaborative network activity. Given the context of intergovernmental relations, every public organization is bound inside a certain jurisdiction, which retains day-to-day operational authority over any prospective collaborative network moves involving its activities (Agranoff, 2017; Agranoff & McGuire, 2003a). Craig Thomas (2003) found that line managers in public organizations do not usually go beyond controlling their own organizations in the network. However, public officials' turf-protecting behavior should never be underestimated. They make little tweaks to encourage "nettlesome difficulties" on occasion. Thomas also discovered that program specialists seek technological expertise and an understanding of interdependency rather than control over each other's programs. This leads to situations in which collaborative networks are pressured to substitute programs they manage (Agranoff, 2003). Finally, Cristofoli and Markovic (2016) believe that the function of the enabling state may be more slightly modified at the periphery than at the center in the era of collaborative management.

References

Agranoff, R. (1991). Human services integration: Past and present challenges in public administration. *Public Administration Review, 51*(6), 426–436.

Agranoff, R. (2003). *Leveraging networks: A guide for public managers working across organizations.* IBM Endowment for the Business of Government.

Agranoff, R. (2005). Managing collaborative performance: Changing the boundaries of the state? *Public Performance & Management Review, 29*(1), 18–45.

Agranoff, R. (2012). *Collaborating to manage: A primer for the public sector.* Georgetown University Press.

Agranoff, R. (2013). The transformation of public sector intellectual/developmental disabilities programming. *Public Administration Review, 73*(Special Issue on Health Care), 5127–5138.

Agranoff, R. (2014). Bridging the theoretical gap and uncovering the missing holes. In R. Keast, M. P. Mandell, & R. Agranoff (Eds.), *Network theory in the public sector: Building new theoretical frameworks* (pp. 193–210). Routledge.

Agranoff, R. (2016). The other side of managing in networks. In R. D. Margerum & C. J. Robinson (Eds.), *The challenges of collaboration in environmental governance: Barriers and responses* (pp. 81–107). Edward Elgar Publishing.

Agranoff, R. (2017). *Crossing boundaries for intergovernmental management*. Georgetown University Press.

Agranoff, R. (2021). Continuous improvement in collaboration management. In J. W. Meek (Ed.), *Handbook of collaborative public management* (pp. 373–401). Edward Elgar Publishing.

Agranoff, R., & McGuire, M. (2001). Big questions in public network management research. *Journal of Public Administration Research and Theory, 11*(3), 295–326.

Agranoff, R., & McGuire, M. (2003a). *Collaborative public management: New strategies for public management*. Georgetown University Press.

Agranoff, R., & McGuire, M. (2003b). Inside the matrix: Integrating the paradigms of intergovernmental and network management. *International Journal of Public Administration, 26*(12), 1401–1422.

Agranoff, R., & Pattakos, A. N. (1979). *Dimensions of services integration*, Project SHARE, Rockville, MD.

Alter, C., & Hage, J. (1993). *Organizations working together* (Vol. 191). SAGE Publications, Incorporated.

Bardach, E. (1998). *Getting agencies to work together: The practice and theory of managerial craftsmanship*. Brookings Institution Press.

Bennis, W. G. (1967). The coming death of bureaucracy. *Journal of Occupational and Environmental Medicine, 9*(7), 380.

Bobker, G. (2009). The means do not justify the ends: A comment on CALFED. *Environmental Science & Policy, 12*(6), 726–728.

Bruns, H. C. (2013). Working alone together: Coordination in collaboration across domains of expertise. *Academy of Management Journal, 56*(1), 62–83.

Cepiku, D. (2014). Network performance: Towards a dynamic multidimensional model. In R. Keast, M. P. Mandell, & R. Agranoff (Eds.), *Network theory in the public sector: Building new theoretical frameworks* (pp. 174–192). Routledge.

Clegg, S. (1990). *Modern organizations: Organization studies in the post-modern world*. Sage.

Contractor, N. S., Wasserman, S., & Faust, K. (2006). Testing multitheoretical, multilevel hypotheses about organizational networks: An analytic framework and empirical example. *Academy of Management Review, 31*(3), 681–703.

Cristofoli, D., & Markovic, J. (2016). How to make public networks really work: A qualitative comparative analysis. *Public Administration, 94*(1), 89–110.

Crosby, B. C., & Bryson, J. M. (1992). *Leadership for the common good: Tackling public problems in a shared-power world*. John Wiley & Sons.

Fernandez, S. (2009). Understanding contracting performance: An empirical analysis. *Administration & Society, 41*(1), 67–100.

Frederickson, H. G. (1999). The repositioning of American public administration. *Political Science and Politics, 32*(4), 701–711.

Gilardi, F., & Radaelli, C. (2014). Governance and learning. In D. Levi-Faur (Ed.), *The Oxford handbook of governance* (pp. 155–168). Oxford University Press.

Girth, A. M. (2014). A closer look at contract accountability: Exploring the determinants of sanctions for unsatisfactory contract performance. *Journal of Public Administration Research and Theory, 24*(2), 317–348.

Glazer, H. (2012). *High performance operations.* Pearson Education.

Halvorson, G. C. (2013). *Don't let health care bankrupt America: Strategies for financial survival.* CreateSpace Independent Publishing Platform.

Howitt, A. M., & Leonard, H. B. (2009). Structuring crisis response. In A. M. Howitt & H. B. Leonard (Eds.), *Managing crises: Responses to large-scale emergencies,* Congressional Quarterly Press.

Imperial, M. T. (2004). *Collaboration and performance management in network settings: Lessons from three watershed governance efforts.* IBM Center for the Business of Government.

Innes, J. E., & Booher, D. E. (1999). Consensus building and complex adaptive systems: A framework for evaluating collaborative planning. *Journal of the American Planning Association,* 65(4), 412–423.

Innes, J. E., Connick, S., & Booher, D. (2007). Informality as a planning strategy: Collaborative water management in the CALFED Bay-Delta Program. *Journal of the American Planning Association, 73*(2), 195–210.

Jenkins, W. O. (2006). Collaboration over adaptation: The case for interoperable communications in homeland security. *Public Administration Review, 66*(3), 319–321.

Johnston, J. M., & Girth, A. M. (2012). Government contracts and "managing the market" exploring the costs of strategic management responses to weak vendor competition. *Administration & Society, 44*(1), 3–29.

Kallis, G., Kiparsky, M., & Norgaard, R. (2009). Collaborative governance and adaptive management: Lessons from California's CALFED Water Program. *Environmental Science & Policy, 12*(6), 631–643.

Kapucu, N., Garayev, V., & Wang, X. (2013). Sustaining networks in emergency management: A study of counties in the United States. *Public Performance & Management Review, 37*(1), 104–133.

Katz, B., & Nowak, J. (2017). *The new localism: How cities can thrive in the age of populism.* Brookings Institution Press.

Keast, R. (2016). Network governance. In C. Ansell & J. Torfing (Eds.) *Handbook on theories of governance* (pp. 442–453). Edward Elgar Publishing.

Keast, R., & Mandell, M. P. (2014). A composite theory of leadership and management: Process catalyst and strategic leveraging: Theory of deliberate action in collaborative networks. In R. Keast, M. P. Mandell, & R. Agranoff (Eds.), *Network theory in the public sector: Building new theoretical frameworks* (pp. 33–50). Routledge.

Kickert, W. J. M., & Koppenjan, J. F. (1997). Public management and network nanagement. In W. J. Kickert, E. H. Klijn, & J. F. Koppenjan (Eds.), *Managing complex networks: Strategies for the public sector* (pp. 35–61). Sage.

Klijn, E. H. (1997). Policy networks: An overview. In W. J. Kickert, E. H. Klijn, & J. F. Koppenjan (Eds.), *Managing complex networks: Strategies for the public sector* (pp. 14–32). Sage.

Klijn, E. H., & Koppenjan, J. F. (2000). Public management and policy networks: Foundations of a network approach to governance. *Public Management and International Journal of Research and Theory, 2*(2), 135–158.

Klijn, E. H., Steijn, B., & Edelenbos, J. (2010). The impact of network management on outcomes in governance networks. *Public Administration, 88*(4), 1063–1082.

Koliba, C. J. (2014). Governance network performance: A complex adaptive systems approach. In R. Keast, M. P. Mandell, & R. Agranoff (Eds.), *Network theory in the public sector: Building new theoretical frameworks* (pp. 84–102). Routledge.

246   *Assessing and Improving Collaborative Performance*

Koliba, C. J., Campbell, E., & Zia, A. (2011). Performance management systems of congestion management networks: Evidence from four cases. *Public Performance & Management Review*, *34*(4), 520–548.

Koliba, C. J., Meek, J. W., & Zia, A. (2010). *Governance networks in public administration and public policy*. CRC Press.

Kolpakov, A. (2013). *Structural development of public management networks over time: Where process meets structure*. Ph.D. Dissertation. SPEA. Indiana University, Bloomington, Indiana.

Kolpakov, A., Agranoff, R., & McGuire, M. (2016). Understanding interoperability in collaborative network management: The case of Metro High School. *Journal of Health Science*, *4*(10), 318–332.

Koppenjan, J., & Klijn, E. H. (2014). What can governance network theory learn from complexity theory? Mirroring two perspectives on complexity. In R. Keast, M. P. Mandell, & R. Agranoff (Eds.), *Network theory in the public sector: Building new theoretical frameworks* (pp. 157–173). Routledge.

Linden, R. M. (2010). *Leading across boundaries: Creating collaborative agencies in a networked world*. John Wiley & Sons.

Lipnack, J., & Stamps, J. (1994). *The age of the network: Organizing principles for the 21st century*. Jeffrey Stamps.

Loughlin, J. (2000). Regional autonomy and state paradigm shifts in Western Europe. *Regional & Federal Studies*, *10*(2), 10–34.

Mahler, J. G. (2009). *Organizational learning at NASA: The Challenger and Columbia accidents*. Georgetown University Press.

Margerum, R. D. (2005). Collaborative growth management in metropolitan Denver: "Fig leaf or valiant effort?". *Land Use Policy*, *22*(4), 373–386.

May, P. J., & Winter, S. C. (2007). Collaborative service arrangements: Patterns, bases, and perceived consequences. *Public Management Review*, *9*(4), 479–502.

McFarland, K. R. (2008). *The break through company*. Crown Business.

McGuire, M. (2002). Managing networks: Propositions on what managers do and why they do it. *Public Administration Review*, *62*(5), 599–609.

McGuire, M., & Agranoff, R. (2010). Networking in the shadow of bureaucracy. In R. F. Durant (Ed.), *The Oxford handbook of American bureaucracy* (pp. 372–395). Oxford University Press.

McGuire, M., & Agranoff, R. (2014). Network management behaviors: Closing the theoretical Ga. In R. Keast, M. P. Mandell, & R. Agranoff (Eds.), *Network theory in the public sector: Building new theoretical frameworks* (pp. 127–156). Routledge.

Moore, M. H. (1995). *Creating public value: Strategic management in government*. Harvard University Press.

Nielson, M. (2012). *Reinventing discovery: The new era of networked science*. Princeton University Press.

Nolte, I. M., Martin, E. C., & Boenigk, S. (2012). Cross-sectoral coordination of disaster relief. *Public Management Review*, *14*(6), 707–730.

Norgaard, R. B., Kallis, G., & Kiparsky, M. (2009). Collectively engaging complex socio-ecological systems: Re-envisioning science, governance, and the California Delta. *Environmental Science & Policy*, *12*(6), 644–652.

Osborne, D., & Gaebler, T. (1992). *Reinventing government: How the entrepreneurial spirit is transforming the public sector*. Addison- Welsey.

O'Toole, Jr., L. J. (1997). Treating networks seriously: Practical and research-based agendas in public administration. *Public Administration Review*, *57*(1), 45–52.

O'Toole, Jr., L. J. (2015). Networks and networking: The public administrative agendas. *Public Administration Review, 75*(3), 361–371.

Perrow, C. (1992). Organisational theorists in a society of organisations. *International Sociology, 7*(3), 371–380.

Powell, W. W. (1990). Neither market nor hierarchy: Network forms of organization. *Research in Organizational Behavior, 12*(1), 295–336.

Provan, K., & Kenis, P. (2008). Modes of network governance: Structure, management, and effectiveness. *Journal of Public Administration Research and Theory, 18*(2), 229–252.

Rank, O. N., Robins, G. L., & Pattison, P. E. (2010). Structural logic of intraorganizational networks. *Organization Science, 21*(3), 745–764.

Reich, R. (1991). *The work of nations: A blueprint for the future.* Vintage.

Rhodes, R. A. W. (1997). *Understanding governance: Policy networks, governance, reflexivity and accountability.* Open University.

Rittel, H. W., & Webber, M. M. (1973). Dilemmas in a general theory of planning. *Policy Sciences, 4*(2), 155–169.

Romzek, B. S., & Johnston, J. M. (2002). Effective contract implementation and management: A preliminary model. *Journal of Public Administration Research and Theory, 12*(3), 423–453.

Romzek, B. S., & Johnston, J. M. (2005). State social services contracting: Exploring the determinants of effective contract accountability. *Public Administration Review, 65*(4), 436–449.

Ross, D., & Friedman, R. E. (1990). The emerging third wave: New economic development strategies. In R. S. Fosler (Ed.), *Local economic development strategies for a changing Economy.* International City Management Association.

Saz-Carranza, A. (2012). The quest for public value. *Public Administration Review, 72*(1), 152–153.

Saz-Carranza, A., & Ospina, S. M. (2011). The behavioral dimension of governing interorganizational goal-directed networks: Managing the unity-diversity tension. *Journal of Public Administration Research and Theory, 21*(2), 327–365.

Senge, P. (1990). *The fifth discipline: The art and practice of the learning organization.* Currency Doubleday.

Stone, C., Doherty, K., Jones, C., & Ross, T. (1999). Schools and disadvantaged. In C. Stone, K. Doherty, C. Jones, & T. Ross. *Urban problems and community development.* Brooking Institute Press.

Thomas, C. W. (2003). *Bureaucratic landscapes: Interagency cooperation and the preservation of biodiversity.* MIT Press.

Thompson, F. J. (2012). *Medicaid politics: Federalism, policy durability, and health reform.* Georgetown University Press.

Toft, G., & Audretsch, D. (2000). *Creating a new Indiana economy.* Indiana University Institute for Development Strategies.

U.S. Department of Homeland Security. (2005). *A comprehensive and sustained approach needed to achieve management integration.* U.S. Government Printing Office, GAO-05-139.

U.S. Government Accountability Office (GAO). (2006). *Results-oriented government: Practices that can help enhance and sustain collaboration among federal agencies.* Government Printing Office, GAO-06-15.

Van Slyke, D. M. (2003). The mythology of privatization in contracting for social services. *Public Administration Review, 63*(3), 296–315.

Varley, P. (2009). The 9/11 pentagon emergency (A). In A. M. Howitt & H. B. Leonard (Eds.), *Managing crises: Responses to large-scale emergencies.* Congressional Quarterly Press.

248 *Assessing and Improving Collaborative Performance*

Wasserman, S., & Faust, K. (1994). *Social network analysis: Methods and applications.* Cambridge University Press.

Wise, C. R. (2006). Organizing for homeland security after Katrina: Is adaptive management what's missing? *Public Administration Review, 66*(3), 302–318.

Wye, C. (2002). *Performance Management: A "start where you are, use what you have" guide.* Center for Improving Government Performance, National Academy of Public Administration.

Ysa, T., Sierra, V., & Esteve, M. (2014). Determinants of network outcomes: The impact of management strategies. *Public Administration, 92*(3), 636–655.

11 The Future Politics of Public Bureaucracy in a Connected Era

Despite the externalization, government remains a formidable force in CP. This chapter focuses on the political and organizational transformations that occur due to newly emerged collaborative management—with and between organizations—as future challenges are met. Public organizations are not disappearing, but they are changing mightily. While these transformations are essential, so too is related *governance* in complex interorganizational relations, multiactor policy-making, and operations in interorganizational connections (Osborne, 2010). Writing in *Governing* magazine, a publication for state and local officials and administrators, William Fulton identifies some of the changes beyond self-driving cars and the decline of retail stores that will lead to the "automated city" as cities continue to take advantage of the efficiency of proximity, "as work is automated and transactions move online, the nature of economic efficiency will be transformed" (2018, p. 23) (See Fulton's case study in the concluding Chapter 12). In this regard, he observes that as jobs become oriented to creativity, empathy, and human connection, virtually all face-to-face skills jobs will be concentrated in cities, albeit in changing forms. Moreover, it is fundamentally changing the nature of work, particularly face-to-face work like collaborative management, that people will increasingly do to keep organized life going.

Work will continue to be organized differently in adaptive entities and managed inward and outward in urbanized areas. Indeed, organized life in the public sector is becoming ever more *relational*, both within to help posture organizations across internal boundaries and across to posture bureaucratic workers to work across the boundaries with other internal units and with external organizations. These are not future but present movements, as they relationally link and thus provide clues for the future. In other words, traditionally and formally, bureaucracy is about divisions and legally charged missions and purposes, and in that sense they remain—but they are in altered form. Many authority lines in a traditional sense still "remain" but are now manifested differently, and—as will be demonstrated—not necessarily because politics and power do remain, as they are shifting *externally*.

This chapter sheds additional light and provides sharp focus on CP in order to recognize this changing bureaucratic trend. It begins by introducing how public organizations are changing to become more relational structures. For discussion

DOI: 10.4324/9781003385769-11

250   *The Future Politics of Public Bureaucracy in a Connected Era*

purposes, they are identified as 1.0, or traditional structuring, and emergent 2.0 bureaucracy as interactive structures. Significantly, 2.0 organizations do not necessarily replace 1.0 organizations, but they now exist side by side, almost like organizational overlays. Next, eight analytically identifiable roles for the future bureaucratic organizational participant are examined: new management duties, playing politics, relational management, network collaborative interactions, operational mapping, governance processing, continuing tasks/roles, and working at interoperable processing. Finally, the politics of collaboration within an emergent organizing 2.0 are identified. Whereas the focus is on emergent managerial processes, their inherently political nature is also part of the "new politics of collaboration," as the previous Chapter 10 and subsequent analysis in this chapter highlight.

Introducing 2.0 Interacting Organizations

What is the organization of the future becoming? While there are no certainties, it is politics of agreement and the possible—politically and operationally—will somehow fall somewhere between the rigid rule-bound hierarchy and loose open structuring that shifts with the need to make missions compatible with political and operational expectations. Both authors' most diverse 2.0 experience (Agranoff, 2012a; Kolpakov, Agranoff, & McGuire, 2016) is detailed in our earlier introduction to the Ohio Metro School network study. Metro is a school carved out of 16 school districts in Central Ohio. It focuses on a STEM advanced high school education for a limited number of students.

The Metro structure has evolved over time. The development and maintenance of Metro are accomplished through the interactive networking of students, parents, teachers, school administrators, partner representatives, learning site representatives, and others. Ideas and practices are filtered into the school and Educational Council (EC) administration, teachers' meetings, student town hall meetings, and, most importantly, through the informal interactive dynamics of the extensive Metro network. These pieces—plus the activities of students, parents, and intermittent learning resources—make it challenging to call Metro an organization in the 1.0 or Weberian sense. Legally, Metro is not even a school. Instead, it is a 2.0 networked entity held together by collaboration.

Metro is thus not an *organization* in the standard, hierarchical, or 1.0 sense. But it nonetheless has an unusual standing as an organized public entity. Metro was initially made possible by the dedicated energies of key community leaders, particularly the former president of The Ohio State University (OSU) and the CEO of Battelle Corporation, whose support and resource commitments moved others to foster the concept of a STEM focus, coupled with a small school approach. Several identifiable levels now combine to constitute Metro as a "hypercollaborative": the Educational Council (EC), the Metro Partnership Group, the KnowledgeWorks firm, the Metro principal, and Battelle. As the school continues operations, layers of teachers, learning site representatives, corporations, and support personnel from OSU have also become network participants. In addition, Metro's operations reach well beyond the school's building and

The Future Politics of Public Bureaucracy in a Connected Era   251

personnel by involving different learning partners across the Columbus metropolitan area. It also provides a demonstration of 2.0 organizing.

Organizational Features: 1.0 and 2.0 Compared

An organizational entity like Metro School has proven to be an alternative to a single organization based on hierarchy. Like any organization, Metro School consists of a governing body, an EC, and a governance and advisory body, Metro Partnership, except its structure is not *divisionalized* or specialized (Agranoff, 2012a). The Metro School represents a network with overlaying connections of students, parents, teaching staff, school administrators, representatives of learning sites, and learning partners. The Metro network features consensus-based decision models instead of a command-and-control model. Its participants experience role differentiation but operate with a fluid, participatory, agreement-seeking orientation. Authority is thus found in many places. Theoretically, this hyperconductive agency is very different from that of a classic hierarchy. An additional series of features, summarized in Table 11.1, appear to be among the hallmarks of Metro relational

Table 11.1 Features of 1.0 and 2.0 Organizations

Feature	1.0 Organizations	2.0 Organizations
Organizational Structure	Divisionalized	Nondivisionalized overlays of collaborating staff working externally
Organizational Governance	Closed hierarchy	Flexible collaborarchies
Operational Enablement	Legal authority	Transfer of partial authority from participating organizations
Professionalization	Specialization in bureaus, disciplinary orientation	Epistemic communities based on shared beliefs
Planning and Organization of Operations	Program- and project-oriented in a single unit	Interactive, discursive, and sequential across units of different organizations
Problem-Solving and Decision-Making	Within the unit, forward-looking	Across units, complex and ad hoc
Strategy/Boundary-Spanning Interactions	Legislative authorization of bureau and program	Sets of joint strategies by multiple agencies
Operations	Executed by divisions and departments	Interoperability
Accountability	Single or limited points, other indirect	Multiple direct points
Legitimacy	Agency strategies and interdepartmental accommodations	Self-built through continuous contact efforts

Source: Agranoff (2012a, p. 192). Copyright 2012 by Georgetown University Press. Reprinted with permission.

252   *The Future Politics of Public Bureaucracy in a Connected Era*

organizing. At the same time, the Metro experience suggests that the applicability in other situations and thus illustrates a postmodern organizing situation.

An increasing number of organizations like Metro are likely to be governed more openly in a nondivisionalized mode to one degree or another, with network-like, highly flexible collaborarchies. For example, one of the authors of this volume in the study of 14 networks (Agranoff, 2012a) characterized them as "self-managed bodies of officials who employed self-imposed rules that used consensus-building/ agreement to develop collaborative capacity" (Bardach, 1998, p. 307), encouraging "exchanges and the development of cooperative dispositions and mutual understandings between the individuals trying to work together on common tasks" (pp. 192–193). The Ohio Metro study demonstrates that the principle of "soft guidance" by persons or the multiple focal nodes accurately describes when decisions are made, and actions are taken (Windhoff-Hentier, 1992). Such guidance is the network equivalent of direct supervision in hierarchical organizations (Kolpakov, Agranoff, & McGuire, 2016). This guidance is based on the centrality of two administrators—the Metro principal and CEO of the EC responsible for information flow and planning. Nevertheless, they do not dominate or directly oversee the network's operations, politically and legally. The Metro principal is the center of the Metro universe, but overwhelming evidence from previous network management research suggests that other "hubs" are critical to network success (Meier & O'Toole, 2003; Kolpakov, Agranoff, & McGuire, 2016).

Agranoff (2012a) argues that despite the classical approach in public administration that considers networks in theory to be flat, self-organizing, completely interdependent bodies, the presence of a network center is not an uncommon phenomenon in practice. Research on the effectiveness of community mental health networks suggests that their effectiveness can be partially explained by central coordination based partly on the extent to which the network was coordinated centrally through a core agency (Provan & Milward, 1995). The school principal seems to be that hub at Metro, although other actors have remained part and parcel of Metro's operation.

As summarized in Table 11.1, emergent organizing appears to represent an alternative to hierarchical legal authority by *transferred governance*. To avoid the risk of complete anarchy and insufficient accountability, partnerships, alliances, networks, and related collaborative entities need to have somebody with consensual authority. Legally based executive authority is not really conducive to politics and their interorganizational nature. Instead, these groups are more at ease transferring partial authority (i.e., the ability to accept certain politics) from the hierarchical agencies they represent to more collegial bodies that take political and operational input from below, reach consensus, and make decisions. This is very much how the Metro EC works.

It has some overlapping representation on the Partnership Group, including the key superintendent who sends almost 60 percent of the students to the Metro

The Future Politics of Public Bureaucracy in a Connected Era 253

School, but it listens on most policy issues to the Partnership Group, which in turn overlaps with the administration, which relies on multiple lateral inputs.

(Agranoff, 2012a, p. 193)

In specific ways, governance is predicated on major partners' ability to delegate (small) portions of their hierarchical authority to the collaborative structure.

Metro experience also suggests that specialization is blurred in these network arrangements. For example, a 2.0 organization is communally run and staffed by highly professionalized *epistemic communities* oriented to produce a high level of collaboration (McGuire, 2009). This type of leadership "community" is comprised of "professionals from different disciplines who share common outlooks, possess similar solution orientations, and share normative principles and related beliefs that can provide a value-based rationale for social action" (Haas, 1992, p. 3). In addition, the Metro group embraces K–12 and higher education faculty, industry researchers, potential business employers, and advocates for small schools (Agranoff, 2012a). Having worked together for a while, they gradually evolved into a community of practice. According to Wenger (2000), communities of practice are self-organizing systems capable of creating and utilizing knowledge through informal learning and mutual engagement processes. Indeed, adhering to the ideals of multidisciplinary engagement, learning, and knowledge creation is a characteristic of the emergent organizing experience.

A related 2.0 characteristics is that planning and organizing are less unitized, project-oriented, or problem-focused. Instead, it is typically "flexible and springs from multiparty agreements that are *interactive, discursive,* and *sequential*" (Agranoff, 2011, p. 284, emphasis in original). For example, the Metro network was built piece by piece, not as an externally created structure (e.g., by a consultant) or a "finely tuned machine completely ready to operate from the outset with a five-year plan" (p. 384). Just as it did during its formation, the Metro network meets its challenges as they emerge on a case-by-case basis. For example, it did not have a four-year high school graduation template for its first two years but took on issues as they emerged and required action. As Hunter and Agranoff (2008) comment on the development of Metro curricula:

Physical education was not addressed until almost the third year. Algebra II was taught before Algebra I in the first year because of a need to link students with projects. Social studies teachers were added only in the second year. Metro has operated without a uniform discipline code but relies on the codes of the student's home districts. As needs arise, plans follow to meet a particular need. This non-linear mode appears to be essential in network management.

(p. 82)

Like most 2.0 organizations, Metro's operations are complex and represent a series of interactions and transactions within different networks. At Metro, a cycle of problem emergence, problem delay, and problem resolution highlights how adaptive structures must foresee challenges but often postpone fixing them until they have gathered the multiple agreements and resources required for earlier, more pressing needs (Agranoff, 2012a). One example is the Metro School's lack of space. Metro had to first identify a location by relying on the assistance of Battelle and OSU. Metro had to find learning locations outside the school when the students started attending classes. In the third year of Metro's existence, when the first class was set to enter OSU, a new capacity issue arose: where would classes be held if not at OSU because the existing facility can only have 200 students?

Like many other collaborative entities, "both small and large problems are solved as they need to be faced, by collaborative agreement, not when they are uncovered" (Agranoff, 2012a, p. 194). As time passes, the essential network strategic interactions are regularized or structured into "sets" of joint strategies analogous to bureaucratic interdepartmental operations. Unlike agency strategies, strategic interactions are approached as negotiations, adjustments, accommodations, or working decisions by partners between major key network players. For example, the EC receives information annually and decides on "how much to 'levy' each school district per pupil (it is roughly the amount equal to that of state assistance) for the coming year" p. 195). Also, upon the advice of the Partnership Group, the school districts have agreed to convert student portfolios (individually, not group prepared) to the equivalent of college credits. Because school districts, through their superintendents, have been politically opposed to "paying for low-income school lunches, special education services, and early college tuition, the school has absorbed these costs in the first two situations and received a grant in the third" (p. 195). These major "hot potato issues" gradually became operational policies arising from consensus-based decisions and negotiations between Metro and major learning organizations. Instead of being legally mandated, they constitute a set of collaborative operational "rubrics" essential for Metro School.

Another set of essential organizational concerns involves programming, which constitutes the core of interorganizational conductivity for 2.0 organizations (Agranoff, 2012a). For example, instead of "divisional, departmental execution, high conductivity demands more detailed, articulation-based *interoperability*" (Jenkins, 2006, p. 321). IOp became an integral part of collaborative management by bridging organizations and operations at a more detailed level (Agranoff, 2012a). We defined interoperability in Chapter 4 as "reciprocal communication and accommodation in order to reach interactive operating policy and programming" (Kolpakov, Agranoff, & McGuire, 2016, p. 318). Because the Metro curriculum coordinator, principal, and school district staff member review the student records and portfolios, the Metro procedure of giving each student credit for work completed in the classroom, field, or laboratory matches this process. It includes much more than the typical "bargaining and negotiation" that is frequently overused in the literature, as suggested, including "joint agreement on core principles, interactive planning, exploration of mistakes or a failure to launch, reaching key understandings,

The Future Politics of Public Bureaucracy in a Connected Era   255

program articulation routines, reciprocal operations, and feedback and correction" (Agranoff, 2012a, p. 195). Based on the example of Metro School, one can conclude IOp has become a more and more irreplaceable boundary-spanning activity in the eyes of practitioners and academics as organizations engage in collaboration across sectoral and government-level boundaries.

By making connections to the different stakeholders, network organizations like the Metro School encounter multiple and direct performance accountability expectations from other network actors to external industry and business stakeholders, the academic community, state and local agencies, coalitions, students and the families, and finally to their communities (Agranoff, 2012a). Organizations are expected to have a single level or a limited number of direct accountability points in general management. But to the 2.0 organizations like Metro School, virtually all accountability points are not "department to department," but indirect.

Esmark (2016) identified three fundamental challenges related to network accountability. First, networks and networked agencies should be considered representative forums, which are very inclusive and reach necessary stakeholders beyond the agency's formal membership. Second, these structures need to "institutionalize procedures for publicly assumed responsibility and explain basic communication standards to the stakeholders or moral constituency outside of network" (Agranoff, 2012a, pp. 195–196). Third, internally, a networked agency must give political recognition to various sorts of mandates or sanctions from representative groups while also paying attention to unorganized stakeholders. This can be difficult to achieve for multiorganizational bodies, which complicates the process of collaborative performance. As Robert Behn (2001, p. 77) notes that collaborative operations are defined as those which reflect that "the one-bill, one policy, one organization, one accountability holder principle doesn't work for performance."

Finally, any multiple partner networked body like Metro School is required to develop and maintain its own legitimacy. Agranoff (2012a) argues that using the established legal and legislative authority to build networked entities' legitimacy is impossible. Even in case of the absence of a legal charter, any organization should establish its own credibility. Human and Provan (2000) emphasize the importance of public acceptance of a network or organizational entity. Legitimizing the Metro network as a known identity, particularly for outsiders, is one mechanism for network growth and acceptance. In addition, building legitimacy implies growth in network membership, more available resources, and political support. Over time, the principal partners of Metro School established reciprocal relations for a more robust collaborative capacity. However, the results of social network analysis and the interviews with key stakeholders pointed to a sizable gap in the degree of connectivity with middle-level learning partners (Kolpakov, Agranoff, & McGuire, 2016; Hunter & Agranoff, 2008). Metro is now working to create a method for these potentially powerful organizations to participate in information sharing and planning, so this interconnectivity remains a critical element of Metro's growth, potential adaptation, and enhancement of legitimacy in the long run.

256 *The Future Politics of Public Bureaucracy in a Connected Era*

Therefore, the Metro networked structure represents a 2.0 type of organized body following a new science or so-called quantum approach instead of a Newtonian approach. Many modern organizations are Newtonian because they are boundary units that built their legitimacy as bureaucracies under the rules of legal authority with established divisional structures that developed rules and procedures (Agranoff, 2012a). These organizations are Newtonian in the sense of machine imagery and in the sense of materialism, focusing on what can be understood via our physical senses. Like scientists who concentrate on the matter, contemporary organizations are explained by their structural components, such as functions, units, divisions, line-staff, auxiliary staff, and standards.

On the other hand, the new science concentrates on the whole rather than the parts, emphasizing that systems are the entire entity and that relationships are critical, resulting in a whole new set of linkages that cannot be simply reduced or explained by studying the individual pieces independently (Agranoff, 2012a). The quantum mechanical viewpoint, for example, differs from everyday reality in which "relationship is the essential determinant of everything" (Wheatley, 1999, p. 11). On the other hand, subatomic particles take shape and are only experienced in relation to something else. They simply don't exist as self-contained "objects." As Wheatley argues, "There are no basic 'building blocks'" (p. 11).

Using a quantum analogy, the emergent organized bodies like Metro School can be viewed as "potentially boundaryless, making relational adjustments to their systemic needs, and as highly 'non-machinelike' as they face strategic challenges in a more unconventional way (Clegg, 1990)" (Agranoff, 2012a, p. 197). This type of organizing represents some sort of resistance to traditional control processes by focusing "on the constructed nature of people and reality" (Alvesson & Deetz, 2006, p. 256). This is clearly how to comprehend the network relationships resulting in the emerging and developing Metro School as a quintessential 2.0 organization.

Seven Emergent Political and Managerial Challenges of 2.0 Organizing

Two decades have passed since George Frederickson (1999) reminded the field of public administration that "the essential element of contemporary public administration is the decreasing link between jurisdiction and public management" (p. 702). This is exacerbated by the trend toward externalization and the additional pillars of decentralization and globalization (Keating, 1999). These two concerns play a role in the current challenges, although they are outside the scope of this chapter. As Robert Agranoff and Michael McGuire (2003) established, intergovernmental management (IGM) necessitates collaborative management's best political and managerial skills. So, how does organizing reclaim its place in this maze of intergovernmental and external collaboration? In the network era, how do we manage intergovernmental relations? What kind of political talents are required? What tools and abilities can be used to manage across multiple levels of government and sectors

The Future Politics of Public Bureaucracy in a Connected Era 257

in the 2.0 era? Seven techniques or practice concepts—discussed in the following subsections—can be used to assist managing entities like Metro and other highly networked organizations in achieving these goals.

Organizing Structures to Maximize Connections and Promote Interaction

Internal operations must be positioned for external activities, which is the primary challenge. Fewer government entities, particularly state and municipal governments, provide direct services "in-house" or within the organization. For example, vast state human services bureaucracies with thousands of state institution employees give way to bureaucratic units that primarily manage and oversee facility construction, purchase of Medi care grants, contracts, and/or federal pass-throughs (or matching, in the case of the massive Medicaid program) (Agranoff, 2012b). In addition, external vendors or community-based NGO entities provide the majority of the services. This means that government agencies must be prepared to collaborate with an ever-increasing number of external partners and maintain regular internal operations.

This type of agency is a *conductive organization*. Hubert Saint-Onge and Charles Armstrong (2004) define it as "an organization that continuously generates and renews the capabilities to achieve breakthrough performance by improving the quality and flow of knowledge and by calibrating its strategy, culture, structure, and systems to the needs of customers and the market-place" (p. 213). Even though their work focuses on corporate organizing, Saint-Onge and Armstrong highlight organizational activities such as forging external partnerships, developing alliances and coalitions, forming cross-organizational teams, and actively managing interdependencies:

> The capability to effectively manage complex partnerships is growing in importance as organizations are reconfigured. Organizations are becoming more and more involved in complex value-creation networks, where the boundaries between one organization and another become blurred, and functions become integrated. It's becoming a critical organizational and leadership capability to be able to create and leverage participation in network-designed and delivered solutions.
>
> (2004, p. 191)

Additionally, Saint-Onge and Armstrong (2004) suggest appointing administrators functionally responsible across the organization, establishing the performance program at the organizational level, establishing units specifically promoting flow between organizations, forming client-oriented services units, branding practices of linking internal and external functions, forming knowledge intensive teams, and establishing functional units instead of units based on traditional division of labor.

Public agencies who are strongly involved with the outside world or who must consider these types of organizational changes may find it challenging to organize

258   *The Future Politics of Public Bureaucracy in a Connected Era*

along these lines. Several states, for example, have established Medicaid policy offices, which were initially created to oversee payments processing, but now that Medicaid also funds a broad range of medically related services for the elderly and disabled, the roles of these offices are much broader:

> to work with external providers in creating databases and information systems, to oversee federally mandated performance expectations, to study potential linkage systems, and to network with larger providers and state associations interactively to assess and improve joint managerial concerns expected by Medicaid.
>
> (Agranoff, 2012b, p. 204)

In contract management, for example, the contract document alone is insufficient. Contracting for services requires complex forms of political and operational linkages (Brown, Potoski, & Van Slyke, 2006), which in turn need planning for performance evaluation, staff training, the ability to evaluate contractor staff capability, the ability to evaluate contractor financial management activity, and comprehending contractor/subcontractor relationships, as well as establishing necessary political community standards and policies (Romzek & Johnston, 2002). Quality standards for contracted residential services and outpatient clinics, which are now required of Medicaid and a growing number of other federal programs, and state government public health standards for contracted residential services and outpatient clinics, present another set of interactive challenges for organizing (Agranoff, 2012b). Finally, concerns about quality improvement (evaluating the client's performance of goals against program objectives) and contract data reporting could be included as additional challenges (Bradley & Moseley, 2007). These concerns are about a body/organization that functions in its community on a political and operational level.

As a result of these functions, several common organizing themes emerge. To begin with, cross-border activity is both multiactor and connective. It usually implies the necessity for coordinated federal, state, and sometimes local programs and the involvement of many external providers (Agranoff, 2012b). Second, collaborative public management has a policy/programming component that blends regular federal program input with state administration/regulation; now, the policy must consider the realities of policy execution by new armies of providers/contractors. Third, each connecting step necessitates working understandings and assessments involving at least two levels of government and several NGOs before services are delivered to clients, which must be configured based on extensive political and operational interaction. It is impossible to leave roles and responsibilities to chance. Fourth, the public agency's job now involves a significant amount of shared administration of a services arrangement/assessment, replacing the end-of-program review of the past or specific service delivery's post-oversight role. It requires a shift in audit organization away from command-and-control hierarchical programming. Conducive organizational design increasingly comprises "positioning the

The Future Politics of Public Bureaucracy in a Connected Era   259

agency" to work more outside on shared information, knowledge, and assessment and less inside on top-down program management (Agranoff, 2012b).

Understanding Within Interjurisdictional Politics

Understanding and applying political knowledge has been a part of the collaborative approach for some time. For example, a study of metropolitan human services bodies by one of the authors revealed that "governmental actors appeared to be successful when they recognized the political nature of their task. In the process of working out solutions to problems, politics—both partisan politics and interorganizational politics—must be explicitly acknowledged" (Agranoff, 1986, p. 7). Externalization expands the game of interorganizational politics among power actors to include new service provider agencies and a slew of business representatives that serve as administrative and program advocates for their service providers' members/affiliates (Agranoff, 2012b). Politics in today's games encompasses longstanding federal agencies (such as the regional office), program administrations at the state level, grantees, and much more. As a result, the delivery system has been assimilated into the managerial/political subsystem.

The network of actors in state-level intellectual and developmental disabilities (ID/DD; for example, intellectual impairment, autism, and cerebral palsy) later illustrates the possible countless political points. States are established on similar ID/DD politics patterns, which involve multiple actors/stakeholders in developing financial and service systems (Agranoff, 2012b). To begin with, the federal government has rehabilitation services and Medicaid offices. The majority of state–federal engagement occurs at the regional office level of the federal government.

However, the majority of political action takes place at the state level. The state administrative cabinet in human services and two significant bureaucratic departments, the state Medicaid office and the state intellectual disability office, are the first. In some states, mental health is combined with the last. Second, there may be an overhead agency, such as state budget bureaus or specialized agencies like Indiana's Bureau of Quality Assurance, which oversees and reviews non-Medicaid and state-funded ID/DD programs (Medicaid does its own monitoring). Third, state legislative actors, leaders, and state budget agencies play crucial policy roles (Agranoff, 2012b). For example, Indiana has separate legislative study committees for developmental disability and autism. A governor's council on developmental disabilities, a program-political study, and a federally sponsored advocacy group are all available in each state. Most states have university-based research and service units that the federal government partially supports as part of the Centers for Excellence program. Finally, state and federal courts hear individual and class action lawsuits, profoundly impacting services.

The field of NGOs is likewise diversified. The NGO provider community, for example, is a fourth political dimension that includes therapy-based groups, day programs, nursing homes, case management organizations, and other organizations (Agranoff,

260 *The Future Politics of Public Bureaucracy in a Connected Era*

2012b). Some agencies are pretty large, with tens of thousands of staff and expenditures in the millions of dollars. The majority of the nonprofit organizations in this group have citizen boards representing their communities. For example, state associations of therapy-based organizations and state Association for Retarded Citizens (ARC) organizations are industry trade associations and client advocacy groups. Each state association groups for-profit and nonprofit organizations together and charges dues based on the size of their member agencies' budgets. They are now significantly involved in both administrative and legislative liaisons. The families/guardians/advocates of ID/DD individual clients and programs, in general, are the next group. Many of them are also members of their state's ARC. Finally, each state has a workforce, including a shrinking number of state personnel but a growing army of NGO direct-care workers numbering in the hundreds of thousands. They remain a potential significant political power in many jurisdictions, mainly where they are unionized.

As services proliferate outside of government, state officials, legislative leaders, industry-led associations, and advocacy groups collaborate to lead the network ID/DD initiative at the state level. Other policy areas—such as disaster management, transportation, economic development, environmental activism, and rural development—are likely to have a comparable list of prospective political actors (Agranoff, 2012b).

Although not all of these actors are involved in administrative politics, many of them are. To continue the ID/DD example, the Indiana Association of Rehabilitation Facilities (INARF) and Indiana ARC meet on a regular basis with state agencies such as the Family and Social Services Administration (FSSA); Office of Developmental Disabilities, Aging, and Rehabilitation Services (DDARS); Office of Medicaid Policy; and several other ID/DD representatives drawn from the network (Agranoff, 2012b). They worked together to develop a system to transition clients from state institutions to community settings called "person follows the funding." Over $40 million in state money and applicable Medicaid payments were transferred to the collaborative effort in 1997–1999. The 317 Plan (as it was known) was the first of a series of network-based program adjustments. In 2009, the four authorities (ARC, INARF, DDARS, and Medicaid Policy) collaborated on several administrative improvements, including reviewing and revising the Outcome and Assessment Information Set (OASIS) resource-allocation model produced by the FSSA (developed by a contractor). OASIS was suspended during the negotiations, and a new method of moving potential clients off the waitlist was agreed upon. A new allocation model for day services was agreed upon, behavior management service funding levels were maintained, and adjustments were made to expand funding for individuals who require 24/7 coverage.

Furthermore, the four political bodies agreed that anticipated OASIS rate reduction modifications would be delayed until one full quarter of billing experience had passed. Finally, the OASIS consistent rate methodology was placed on hold indefinitely. After that, one of the key players in this situation stated, "We've completed enough work with our small group to the point where we can start involving more people in the process . . . . Work planned to address the major concerns associated

The Future Politics of Public Bureaucracy in a Connected Era   261

with retooling the model in the next weeks . . . [including] chances for consumer, family, and provider input in numerous critical areas" (INARF, email, August 6, 2009). This is how CP typically plays out in the era of high connectivity when the "devil of the administrative details" is not only at risk, but also at very high resource stakes for providers, industry associations, and advocates, as well as the government agency (Agranoff, 2012b). The ever-expanding CP will continue to work at the forefront of management as long as these sorts of interactive politics exist.

As a result of externalization, the politics of collaboration has opened up to a far more significant number of regular players who do more than "lobby" on behalf of legislation (Agranoff, 2012b). Instead, they work together to manage within agreed-upon political and administrative constraints. For example, knowing the two or three tiers of government agencies and grantees in the early days of grants was sufficient. That is no longer the case. Instead, a wide range of policy actors and organizations are currently involved. In this ID/DD example, a total of eight state-level categories were politically active, representing hundreds of interests and more than 20 key system actors, many of whom regularly interact on most subjects. This creates a significant duty on the collaborative manager to comprehend subsystem politics and administrative operations, two concepts that are becoming increasingly entwined. As administrators engage in such politics, it is critical that they under-stand their network program's specifics and pressure points.

Network-Building

A shift from passively examining different functions to network promotion and involvement is one apparent transformation for the collaborative manager. Exter-nalization brings the 2.0 bureaucrat into the network, building on prior operations such as grant application preparation and review, notifying potential grantees and checking awardees on legal compliance, managing grantee program intent and pro-gram and budgetary auditing, and the like. Previously, it was appropriate for public involvement provisions to unfold at the community level for awarding/compliance officials to evaluate a written report on the process, usually a locally created sum-mary, if there was no dispute. That process now includes delivery agencies, some of which are in direct rivalry with one another, and government inaction is no longer acceptable (Agranoff, 2012b). As our ID/DD example shows, the network is very complex and does more than carry out the funding agency's directives. Actors, especially executants, are involved in operationalization, making political and tech-nical adjustments to policy programs on the fly as difficulties arise. At this point, government "input (legal, political, and other) must be injected, pushed, and other-wise protected" (p. 208). As a result, the government program manager must be an organizer and a party to any agreements made. In their research on environmental collaboration, Julia Wondolleck and Steven Yaffee (2000) discovered that federal and state administrators were consistently, personally, politically, and managerially involved in networks, usually in some joint lead capacity.

262 *The Future Politics of Public Bureaucracy in a Connected Era*

Networks must be held accountable for achieving their objectives. Their leadership's job is to ensure that the mechanisms and structures in place allow network members to collaborate, share knowledge, learn, and carry out their obligations. The network's output is the development of capabilities (Saint-Onge & Armstrong, 2004). Leaders, particularly "champions," who are frequently the leaders of significant government agencies, are crucial. They, together with "alliance managers" (heads of important organizations), maintain organizational commitment by enabling employees to work together efficiently and serving as role models for trust and collaboration (Holbeche, 2005, p. 179). They are frequently the leading political players. Network leaders are in charge of building capacity, fostering knowledge flow inside and between organizations, aligning important organizations, analyzing mutual capabilities, and adjusting organizational structures to meet the requirement of the external environment. Finally, a set of skills for working across boundaries is recommended for staff program managers, including "the ability to deal with ambiguity, an open and flexible attitude toward style, the ability to build on one another's expertise, an experimenting spirit, the ability to create a negotiated and understood means of communication and decision making, and the ability to build trust and take judicious risks" (Agranoff, 2012b, p. 208). These assist in developing a working manager's skill set, including a well-honed repertory for collaborating across organizations and jurisdictions (Holbeche, 2005, pp. 180–181).

However, while the call to coordinated action is straightforward in theory, it is not easy in practice. It requires political maneuvering and operational coordination while administering. It includes the requirement for government agencies and their leaders to reinvent themselves by stimulating the creation and flow of information across government and outside agencies and taking coordinated action. Undoubtedly, this position highlights public managers' modern extensive involvement as alliance managers in developing "partnerships, networks, challenge grants, venture capital pools, contracts for services initiatives, and electronic information networks" (Agranoff, 2012b, p. 209). For example, MPOs have been instrumental in bringing together federal, state, and local officials and local private-sector and citizen participation to develop area-wide long-range multimodal transportation plans for some time.

Furthermore, MPOs have attracted "an entire set of actors," where "expectations were raised very high by the promise of coordinating federal programs and leveraging numerous financing pots" (Edner & McDowell, 2002, p. 22). These groups have collaborated to create innovative transportation models, "identify state-of-the-art community best practices, and promote interactive networking" (Agranoff, 2012b, p. 209). Unfortunately, these MPO partners did not form independently; elected and administrative leaders brought them together. As a result, these government officials are in a critical position to carry out essential convening activities. As a result, today's bureaucrats are excited to read about agency networks in their local newspapers, trade publications and journals, or for NGOs to search for them. Rather than reacting, public officials should seek out and incorporate

The Future Politics of Public Bureaucracy in a Connected Era   263

potential stakeholders who can help transform human capital into live problem-solving systems (Crosby & Bryson, 1992). In addition, public managers must render critical support and participate in relevant political activities as champions and alliance leaders.

Creative Human Resource Bases

Operational staff—program managers and technical specialists—are needed by champions and alliance managers who can move beyond their particular expertise and work across organizational boundaries to explore wicked policy problems (Rittel &Webber, 1973) and find/adapt solutions to those problems. Managers in collaborative roles used to be preoccupied with their technical professional abilities in their own programs (Agranoff, 2012b). Professionals in the fields of psychiatry, psychology, social work, rehabilitation, and special education were crucial in this area. Engineers and planners were in charge of transportation, public works, planning departments, and so forth. This is unlikely to significantly alter the level of staffing-specific programs in the future. However, these positions now encounter new challenges. People interact more and learn from one another, working in a collaborative body using symbolic analytic work, as defined by Robert Reich (1991). He outlines four critical abilities for today's problem-solving: (1) the ability to abstract; (2) the ability to think in systems or perceive reality as a system of causes and effects; (3) the desire to experiment; and (4) the ability to collaborate.

Recruiting, developing, and retaining managers who can uphold their specialty, be true to their jurisdiction's or agency's program, and engage in this type of symbolic analytic work is one of the most challenging managerial issues today. According to Thomas Davenport, it is critical in today's interdependent world because the most recent symbolic analytic phase of managerial work has "an interactive, collaborative approach to work in which patterns (of observation and supervision) are increasingly difficult to perceive." People may dispute that this work has any structure at all; according to Davenport, "every day is different" (2005, p. 65). This component of human resources demands that workers translate accumulated knowledge to be disseminated across organizations. This particular type of knowledge belongs to the "invisible assets" that exist primarily in the minds of humans, requiring less stringent supervision and collaboration between workers and management (Agranoff, 2012b).

For this type of knowledge worker, the supervisory rules are different. For example, Davenport lists the following supervisory rules for managing knowledge workers: (1) managers participating in work rather than overseeing it; (2) organizing communities rather than hierarchies; (3) retaining workers rather than hiring and terminating them; (4) developing knowledge skills rather than manual skills; (5) instead of assessing visible job performance, evaluating invisible knowledge achievements; (6) creating knowledge-friendly cultures rather than ignoring internal culture; (7) discouraging bureaucracy instead of supporting it; and (8) utilizing a

264 *The Future Politics of Public Bureaucracy in a Connected Era*

variety of human resources in different locations, instead of relying only on your personnel. These human resource management principles can apply to public agency employees collaborating with others outside their agency to resolve challenges and difficulties. As a result, the new collaborative manager promotes the home agency's program goals and requirements, strengthens the interagency community, and collaborates with staff members to develop innovative knowledge-based solutions (Agranoff, 2012b). These concepts are also just as likely to be political as they are operational.

Working Toward Joint Knowledge, Knowledge Management

A large part of interactive network activities among collaborating partners entails finding innovative ways to solve the most difficult challenges. It demands the best problem-solving work from managers and specialists from various agencies and the best earlier work in designing and operating different kinds of information. In the field of environmental management, for example, "effective interactive multiparty land use planning and zoning normally follow extensive studies of regulatory policy, current use, environmental threats, agricultural practices, water quality assessments and many other means of information" (Agranoff, 2012b, p. 211).

According to Davenport and Prusak (2000), the crucial role in organizations is played by knowledge which is "a fluid combination of framed experience, values, contextual information, and expert insight that provides a framework for evaluating and assimilating new experiences and information" (p. 5). Knowledge management (KM) is aimed at "identifying, extracting, and capturing 'knowledge assets' to exploit them to accomplish goals to a large extent" (Newell et al., 2002, p. 16). Data and information are not the same as knowledge, since knowledge is broader, more profound, and richer. It is highly fluid and contextual, yet it is more valuable since it considers experience, insight, and context. As a result, knowledge encompasses more than just facts and figures. As part of human capital assets, people have become increasingly significant in recent activities, including all sorts of management (Agranoff, 2012b). It is, after all, fundamentally human. "Knowledge derives from information as information derives from data. If information is to become knowledge, humans must do all the work" (Davenport & Prusak, 2000, p. 6). Knowledge is, in effect, both a process and a result. In the public sector, we apply knowledge to find solutions and thereby add public value (Moore, 1995).

Collaboration between agencies may be and is a critical vehicle for KM collaboration, or what social network experts call connectivity, which is crucial to knowledge (Agranoff, 2012a). Problem-solving and creative discovery depend heavily on dynamic interaction among people, particularly at strategic points in social networks (Cross, Borgatti, & Parker, 2002). That is why so many diverse players are working together to manage knowledge. Michael Schrage (1995, p. 33) defines *collaboration activity* as "shared creation, that is, people

The Future Politics of Public Bureaucracy in a Connected Era   265

working interactively on a process, product, or event." As one network activist notes, "Workgroups on various technical issues [are] the way we learn and grow; integrate new people into our process . . . and while we don't codify process, we rely on the institutional knowledge of a lot of people" (quoted in Agranoff, 2007, p. 173).

In collaborative networks, Agranoff (2007) finds that most of the 14 networks he studied used the following five-step sequence for managing interagency knowledge (Agranoff, 2012b, pp. 211–212).

- Existing (organizational) sources of information and/or external databases are integrated. Networks exist to some degree to share information.
- Existing information is converted that is most essential to those forms of explicit knowledge that are useful to the network: inventories, map libraries, program evaluations, planning studies, fact sheets, practical guides, poll results, conference proceedings, funding studies, market studies, and long-range plans.
- A less systematic look is taken at tacit issues or "what we don't record": issue discussions, consultation report discussions, workshops, best-practices books, and internal task groups (such as communities of practice, project panels, advisory committees, technical presentations, hands-on outreach or how-to sessions, community visitation teams, conferences and workshops, working manuals, circulated committee notes, public hearings and forums, expert roundtables, and information dyadic or small group exchanges).
- Some networks form KM programs, whereas others are less structured, providing a vehicle to share knowledge; facilitating study groups, special committees, and workgroups as communities of practice; promoting peer networking; compiling reports; evaluating network program sessions; organizing joint operations and shared staff; promoting workshops; organizing and operating mapping programs and decision models; and organizing cross-agency analysis of service requests, referrals, and client dispositions. Most importantly, these approaches are rarely codified and are almost always geared to solve particular problems agreed on by the collective actions of the network.
- Knowledge is also fed back into network participant organizations for their internal use: for example: data sets, consultant reports, public forums, educational programs, technical exchange sessions, web postings, legislative decision-making reports, and reports applicable to administrative agencies and fulfilling the data needs and services modeling for small governments with lean or no analytical staff.

Because data and information sources are broadly spread in the networks, all government agencies and NGOs have a political and operational stake in this game. Managerial and political actors in networks and other collaboratives seek innovative ways to identify, organize, and adapt information approaches to their complex problems.

Communities of Practice

Network participants need to translate knowledge into working and real-life inter-organizational solutions, which is a different form of knowledge creation identified in the previous discussion about KM. Establishing interdisciplinary groups of problem-solvers help build high-quality connective relationships. Interacting agencies frequently deliberate by forming communities of practice and utilizing people from various disciplines who share similar perspectives (Agranoff, 2012b). For example, the USDA/RC state program offices have expanded their loan, grant, and housing development programs for small towns to include the participation of state governments and NGOs in several working groups in critical rural problem areas like value-added agriculture/agribusiness, technology adaptation and transfer, and venture capital sourcing for business development.

These groups function as communities of practice to a large extent. According to Etienne Wenger (2000), they are self-organizing systems that share the potential to develop and apply knowledge through informal learning and mutual involvement. Most communities of practice are self-organized, bringing in new knowledge holders from wherever they can be found when they are needed. Participants from all three levels of government and the non-governmental sector are typically involved in joint programs (Agranoff, 2012b). For example, the 30-plus state rural development councils established in the late 1980s operate similarly to communities of practice (Radin et al., 1996). However, maintaining such communities is yet another collaborative challenge since it requires retaining the various types of knowledge carriers by challenging busy individuals to solve critical public problems and utilizing their technical experience and know-how in an interdisciplinary manner.

Using a multiagency group of experts who often come from various organizations and disciplines but share common outlooks and solution orientations might help to foster community. These professionals may not always be top-level administrators but have extensive multidisciplinary knowledge, CP, and program experience (Agranoff, 2012b). For instance, Peter Haas (1992, p. 3) suggests that "these individuals can represent a variety of disciplines and share normative and principles beliefs that provide a value-based rationale for social action." They also have similar causal views, validity ideas, and policy orientations. The goal of such an epistemic community is usually to produce consensus knowledge. Even in the face of weird facts, the community may defer judgment to preserve its scientific validity while preserving its power resources for the time being (Haas, 2000).

Mark Imperial's (2004, p. 17) study of CP in three estuary management programs discovered that each group of interdisciplinary actors, the majority of whom were technical staff, were able to secure jurisdictional commitments, "synthesize monitoring information on threatening conditions and establish joint reporting processes that assessed partners' collective programs in terms of shared goals" (Agranoff, 2012b, p. 213). Because they can disproportionately affect structured learning and behavior, these experiences show that interdisciplinary communities

The Future Politics of Public Bureaucracy in a Connected Era   267

can be crucial knowledge sustainers. Yet, even though these participants may not always be the movers and the shakers, they "are well situated to provide a driving logic for cooperation" (Thomas, 2003, p. 41). Bringing together diverse specialists from the programming community for this form of improved deliberation/collaboration means that today's administrators will almost certainly be partners in one or more of these communities (Agranoff, 2012b).

Citizen Engagement as a Part of CP

In a world where NGO government grantees and/or contractors increasingly deliver direct services, the more or less long-standing traditional public program function requiring evidence of citizen involvement for program approval now extends to various forms of citizen engagement, which goes beyond holding hearings. Furthermore, in today's world of networks, individuals and citizen groups do more than communicate with and petition government agencies; they are integral to the overall program design (Agranoff, 2012b). Moreover, being part of "complex adaptive networks" (Booher, 2008), "citizens and citizen groups place their issues in the public realm everywhere, from the point of program policy choice to the point of service delivery" (Agranoff, 2012b, p. 214). This practice solidified CP as an essential component of the project, particularly in terms of its political elements.

The function of civic involvement in government initiatives as a whole is outside the scope of this book but has been the subject of numerous investigations in the public administration literature (for example, Bryson, Crosby, & Stone, 2006; Cooper, Bryer, & Meek, 2006; Forester, 2009; Fung, 2009; Smith & Ingram, 2002). One key CP point is that—contrary to common assumption—federal programs and/or judicial actions have fostered numerous grassroots citizen initiatives, such as the growth of popularly rooted voluntary groups resulting from a mutually beneficial relationship with federal programs (Agranoff, 2012b). Local grassroots activities, citizen boards, joint administrative private agency executive-citizen efforts, partnerships, and multiagency alliances facilitated the disintegration of "towering bureaucracies of elites and specialists" who had vested interests beyond the individual community (Schambra, 1998, p. 48). As interpreted by federal courts, the Americans with Disabilities Act of 1990 has resulted in stringent enforcement of the rights of disabled individuals and/or their advocates/families "to have a direct role in the disposition of any course of treatment/or residential placement" (Agranoff, 2012b, p. 215). This means that the client/advocate must participate in the action and agree to any set of suggested services at the point of service. As a result, the client—who could be a citizen—becomes a direct participant in the service network and a "political" actor. Subsequently, it has led to a new concern of involvement, according to Pam Solo and Gail Pressberg (1998, p. 83): "How do we achieve citizen empowerment—both individual and group—when the issues have become so nuanced and detailed, yet the problem solving now cannot be left to government alone?"

268   *The Future Politics of Public Bureaucracy in a Connected Era*

In CP, it is a new and relevant force. However, the externalization of services and the engagement of various agencies exacerbate the problem of citizen involvement. Privatization adds more weight to civic engagement. Third-party agencies, such as government-contracting managed care businesses or garbage-collection firms, are not incentivized to involve the citizen and community. Many organizations are part of the significant for-profit corporations that obfuscate the government-citizen relationship (Smith & Ingram, 2002). As a result, citizen engagement and decision-making become more complicated, putting additional demands on citizens' organizations. However, such contracting is supposed to make the public agency more conducive (Agranoff, 2012b).

It is also crucial to understand that nonprofit contracting, voucher programs, and other government–to–community organization links bring new actors to provide public services (Agranoff, 2012b). Smith and Ingram (2002) point out that many nonprofits and community organizations have established a "keen stake in government funding and regulatory policy" (p. 57). As previously stated, this prompted service provider trade associations to organize politically, individually, and collectively to affect the policy process. As a result, providers and their agents are key network players in CP. This is the case, for example, with state associations representing NGO agencies working with ID/DD people. Public managers in these fields are now accustomed to dealing with this type of participation/advocacy.

Empowerment and deliberation are also the rules of the day when it comes to citizens. "The new vigor of the civil society reflects a large increase in the capacity and will of people to take control of their own lives and transform them" (Commission of Global Governance, 1995, p. 35). Empowering people to act beyond voting and engage in various forms of active participation, allowing them to determine their own destinies in their communities, cities, states, regions, and beyond. For example, in the case of MPO in Denver, citizen groups that desire bike trails, hiking paths, and paratransit services, have realized that policy committees are no longer ready to consider their ideas "under advisement." Instead, these groups request a seat at the negotiation table and more direct access to drafting policy proposals based on participation from citizen groups and government agencies.

> Engagement may also include various self-help programs (homeowners' associations and cooperatives), control over local enterprises (community development corporations), neighborhood improvement and business associations, power over credit or retail transactions and practices, self-protection from fraudulent and abusive practices, and building leadership skills (advocacy, group process, and speaking).
>
> (Agranoff, 2012b, p. 216)

Individuals' ability to engage in discourse, lead, and deal with critical policy and political issues improves when they are empowered (Booher, 2005).

The Future Politics of Public Bureaucracy in a Connected Era   269

With more public agencies engaging in CP, there is a growing need for more distributed leadership and pluralized connectedness. Clearly, there are no magic formulas for dealing with the new public sector or new politics for organized interests (Agranoff, 2012b). This entails the most effective collaboration procedures, for which there are numerous essential and venerable public-organizing books and guides (for example, Brody, 1982; Chrislip & Larson, 1994; Forester, 2009). As part of the network of involved program participants, citizens and their groups now do more than provide recommendations. They and their groups contribute to the crucial program and operational decisions. Citizen action thus advances to the forefront of CP activity in the network era, creating another place where politics, policy, and programming intersect.

The Future/Transformation of Bureaucracy

What does the public agency or bureaucracy look like as the present evolves into the future? It has been maintained that public organization is becoming increasingly relational/connective to a great degree. The trends identified in Box 11.1 mark the present as relational bureaucracy, but without eluding its enduring legal and political dimensions. The latter is because if we ever could, one cannot totally separate politics from administration. Collaborative bureaucracy is clearly political as well as operational.

Box 11.1   The Future of Bureaucracy/Transformation

Key Themes

1. Public agencies remain in form and functional operation as standard organizations but also as a more open hierarchical structure.
2. Public agencies operate conductively/relationally with other government agencies plus engage a host of external interlocutors.
3. Public agencies additionally engage in networked or hybrid public–NGO joint structures to solve those challenging problems that exceed didactive or other limited interorganizational engagement.

Emergent Roles and Functions

1. New or reinforced duties for public officials, e.g., maintaining legal sideboards with external parties, explaining external authority limits in collaboration, convening multiparties, process orchestrating, and interentity brokers.
2. Bureaucrats playing politics, plain and simple; for example, dealing with citizen involvement and group representation, working with external association demands, handling client/client advocates, and related matters.

270 *The Future Politics of Public Bureaucracy in a Connected Era*

3. Relational management or human relations crosses the boundaries of working organizations, and people-to-people interactions, some of which are easy and some intractable, along with important trust-building.
4. Network/interaction process involvement and leadership, including convening, information/knowledge management, seeking accommodation and agreement, and allocating tasks across variegated organized entities. Also, working at the core of emergent cross-entity interoperability processes is reciprocal communication and adaptation across agencies and programs.
5. The emerging practice of structuring and operational mapping reflects extant cross-agency planning, articulation, process sequencing, reporting, and redesign.
6. Handling governance processes of information gathering, assessment, and system redesign, including sequenced operations and orchestrating entire interactive system dynamics among entities.
7. Continuing public agency roles while incorporating externally derived information, such as maintaining legal, regulatory, and program guidance; leading interactive operations, financing, and operational policies; and legislative oversight, reporting and liaison, information accrual, and other modes of direct involvement as governmental actors representing administration.

Source: Agranoff (2018, p. 245)

This is summarized in Box 11.1 on the transformation of bureaucracy. It reads by the observation that bureaucratic agencies are not likely to be the same in the light of collaborative administration, but also joint organizational structures are increasingly emerging to solve nettlesome cross-boundary challenges. Seven emergent bureaucratic functions are identified following the previous discussion of collaborative roles. They include traditional functions, politics of programs, human relations management, networks, increasing interactions, operational mapping, governance processing within collaboration, interactive/interoperable public agency roles, and working within cross-entity processes. Together they provide an attempt at blueprinting for the collaborating public agency, which is the emergent process of CP.

Conclusion

Multiple policies, programs, and delivery agencies lead to collaboration and attendant political processes. As Timothy Conlan and the late Paul Posner conclude,

> policy challenges and the resources needed to address them are not the preserve of a single level of government . . . . Accordingly, the programmatic and fiscal

The Future Politics of Public Bureaucracy in a Connected Era 271

fortunes of all levels of government have become more intertwined and inter-dependent than ever before.

(2008, p. 2)

The NGO sector could now be added to the government mix—and prominently, in many cases. Consequently, public management has embarked on a new era in which everything—public and non-public—appears to be linked somehow, and the concept of networking is moving alongside that of hierarchy to support collaboration. Karen Orren and Stephen Skowronek (2017, p. 123) conclude:

Once the public interest in administrative management was hollowed out of the substance and reduced to so many procedures, opportunities for outside intervention in the formulation of policy multiplied, and the capacity to engage the process at its many points of access began to pay a premium. For president, Congress, Court, and agency, administration in the policy state are all about the flexible response, but for their constituents and clients it has become "blood sport." Everyone gets to share in policy's specifications as long as they can power up.

Networks are clearly not the only administrative solution, as Chapter 3 demonstrates. Indeed, many are pretty "limited in scope, mission, and authority to decide, and they are clearly not replacing governmental authority" (Agranoff, 2012b, p. 219). However, they make sense in the few cases when problems and solutions call for collaboration across jurisdictions and boundaries when issues cannot be adequately addressed by the policies, programs, and auspices of a single organization, government agency, or other entity. In these situations, networks like Metro in Ohio can carry the heavy weight of obtaining agreements and solutions, which governments can later enable. Managing across the bureaucratic pathways requires political settlement by collaboration, and networking is crucial for collaboration. Moreover, CP must find a way to move beyond its legal and government-to-government orientations and recognize the necessity for meaningful networking activities in building partnerships. This occurs throughout the system. Finally, the new collaborative, complex dimension has been demonstrated here by looking in some detail at the emerging type of managerial activities currently employed.

A new set of collaborative expectations have been imposed on many public managers. For example, the roles of local government emergency management administrators have been clearly changed given recent hurricanes, floods, and increasing homeland security concerns (McGuire, 2009; McGuire & Agranoff, 2010). Exponential externalization results "in the need for new state administrative capacity, the challenge of flexible online personnel shortages, increased variety in compliance demands, notable knowledge use shortfalls, uneven funding flows, and uneven efforts to encourage networks" or other forms of collaboration at the state level (Agranoff, 2012b, p. 220). These issues must be resolved. In other words, we live in an era when there are different expectations for increasing the interactions among agencies.

272 The Future Politics of Public Bureaucracy in a Connected Era

Meanwhile, the discipline of public management and the training of public administration practitioners must consider 2.0 organizing and the new demands for collaboration identified in this chapter. The new brave world of collaboration requires

> understanding and operating within new frameworks; managing externally and nonhierarchically, dealing with the unique politics/administration mix, promoting and operating within networks, collaborating in knowledge-based management, dealing with continuous interdisciplinary communities, and dealing with the politics of direct citizen involvement in the stages and details of operations.
>
> (Agranoff, 2012b, p. 220)

Traditional public administration problems must be "moved in" alongside these concerns. For example, suppose collaborative actors in earlier IGR eras regarded their job as complex. In that case, they should see what their contemporary colleagues are now facing—such as traffic congestion, massive capital needs, threats of terrorism, environmental deregulation, rampant substance abuse, citizenship and immigration issues, disabling human conditions, and global warming—while wrestling with nettlesome interprogram and interagency expectations.

References

Agranoff, R. (1986). *Intergovernmental management: Human services problem-solving in six metropolitan areas.* SUNY Press.

Agranoff, R. (2007). *Managing within networks: Adding value to public organizations.* Georgetown University Press.

Agranoff, R. (2011). Collaborative public agencies in the network era. In D. C. Menzel & L. H. L. White (Eds.), *The state of public administration: Issues, challenges, and opportunities* (pp. 272–294). Routledge.

Agranoff, R. (2012a). *Collaborating to manage: A primer for the public sector.* Georgetown University Press.

Agranoff, R. (2012b). Managing externalization: New intergovernmental roles for public managers, In J. W. Meek & K. Thurmaier (Eds.), *Networked Governance* (pp. 196–223). Sage.

Agranoff, R., & McGuire, M. (2003). *Collaborative public management: New strategies for public management: New strategies for local governments.* Georgetown University Press.

Alvesson, M., & Deetz, S. (2006). Critical theory and postmodernism approach to organizational studies. In S. R. Clegg, C. Hardy, T. B. Lawrence, & W. R. Nord (Eds.), *The Sage handbook of organization studies* (pp. 255–283). Sage Publications.

Bardach, E. (1998). *Getting agencies to work together: The practice and theory of managerial craftsmanship.* Brookings Institution Press.

Behn, R. D. (2001). *Rethinking democratic accountability.* Brookings Institution Press.

Booher, D. E. (2005). A call to scholars from the collaborative democracy network. *National Civic Review, 94*(3), 64–67.

Booher, D. E. (2008). Civic engagement as collaborative complex adaptive networks. In *Civic engagement in a network society* (pp. 111–148). Information Age Publishing.

Bradley, V. J., & Moseley, C. (2007). National core indicators: Ten years of collaborative performance measurement. *Intellectual and Developmental Disabilities, 45*(5), 354–358.

The Future Politics of Public Bureaucracy in a Connected Era 273

Brody, R. (1982). *Problem solving: Concepts and methods for community organizations.* Human Sciences Press.

Brown, T. L., Potoski, M., & Van Slyke, D. M. (2006). Managing public service contracts: Aligning values, institutions, and markets. *Public Administration Review, 66*(3), 323–331.

Bryson, J. M., Crosby, B. C., & Stone, M. M. (2006). The design and implementation of cross-sector collaborations: Propositions from the literature. Special issue, *Public Administration Review, 66*, 44–55.

Chrislip, D. D., & Larson, C. E. (1994). *Collaborative leadership: How citizens and civic leaders can make a difference* (Vol. 24). Jossey-Bass.

Clegg, S. (1990). *Modern organizations: Organization studies in the postmodern world.* Sage.

Commission of Global Governance. (1995). *Our global neighborhood.* Oxford University Press.

Conlan, T. J., & Posner, P. L. (2008). *Intergovernmental management for the 21st century.* Brookings Institute.

Cooper, T. L., Bryer, T. A., & Meek, J. W. (2006). Citizen-centered collaborative public management. *Public Administration Review, 66*, 76–88.

Crosby, B. C., & Bryson, J. M. (1992). *Leadership for the common good: Tackling public problems in a shared-power world.* John Wiley & Sons.

Cross, R., Borgatti, S. P., & Parker, A. (2002). Making invisible work visible: Using social network analysis to support strategic collaboration. *California Management Review, 44*(2), 25–46.

Davenport, T. H. (2005). *Thinking for a living: How to get better performances and results from knowledge workers.* Harvard Business Press.

Davenport, T. H., & Prusak, L. (2000). *Working knowledge: How organizations manage what they know.* Harvard Business School Press.

Edner, S., & McDowell, B. D. (2002). Surface-transportation funding in a new century: Assessing one slice of the federal marble cake. *Publius: The Journal of Federalism, 32*(1), 7–24.

Esmark, A. (2016). Democratic accountability and network governance: Problems and potentials. In E. Sørensen & J. Torfing (Eds.), *Theories of democratic network governance* (pp. 274–296). Palgrave Macmillan.

Forester, J. (2009). *Dealing with differences: Dramas of mediating public disputes.* Oxford University Press.

Frederickson, H. G. (1999). The repositioning of American public administration. *PS: Political Science and Politics, 32*(4), 701–711.

Fulton, W. (2018, February). Automated city. *Governing, 31*(5), 23.

Fung, A. (2009). *Empowered participation: Reinventing urban democracy.* Princeton University Press.

Haas, P. M. (1992). Introduction: Epistemic communities and international policy coordination. *International Organization*, 1–35.

Haas, P. M. (2000). International institutions and social learning in the management of global environmental risks. *Policy Studies Journal, 28*(3), 558–575.

Holbeche, L. (2005). *The high performance organization: Creating dynamic stability and sustainable success.* Routledge.

Human, S. E., & Provan, K. G. (2000). Legitimacy building in the evolution of small-firm multilateral networks: A comparative study of success and demise. *Administrative Science Quarterly, 45*(2), 327–365.

Hunter, M., & Agranoff, R. (2008). *Metro high school: An emerging STEM school community.* PAST Foundation.

Imperial, M. T. (2004). *Collaboration and performance management in network settings: Lessons from three watershed governance efforts.* IBM Center for the Business of Government.

274   *The Future Politics of Public Bureaucracy in a Connected Era*

Jenkins, W. O. (2006). Collaboration over adaptation: The case for interoperable communications in homeland security. *Public Administration Review, 66*(3), 319–321.

Keating, M. (1999). Asymmetrical government: Multinational states in an integrating Europe. *Publius, 29*(1), 71–86.

Kolpakov, A., Agranoff, R., & McGuire, M. (2016). Understanding interoperability in collaborative network management: The case of Metro High School. *Journal of Health Science, 4*(10), 318–332.

McGuire, M. (2009). The new professionalism and collaborative activity in local emergency management. In R. O'Leary & L. B. Bingham (Eds.), *The collaborative public manager: New ideas for the twenty-first century*. Georgetown University Press.

McGuire, M., & Agranoff, R. (2010). Networking in the shadow of bureaucracy. In R. F. Durant (Ed.), *The Oxford handbook of American bureaucracy* (pp. 372–395). Oxford University Press.

Meier, K. J., & O'Toole, Jr., L. J. (2003). Public management and educational performance: The impact of managerial networking. *Public Administration Review, 63*(6), 689–699.

Moore, M. H. (1995). *Creating public value: Strategic management in government*. Harvard University Press.

Newell, S., Scarbrough, H., Robertson, M., & Swan, J. (2002). *Managing knowledge work*. Palgrave Global Publishing.

Orren, K., & Skowronek, S. (2017). *The policy state*. Harvard University Press.

Osborne, S. P. (2010). Public governance and public services delivery: A research agenda for the future. *The New Public Governance*, 413–428.

Provan, K., & Milward, H. B. (1995). A preliminary theory of interorganizational network effectiveness: A comparative study of four community mental health systems. *Administrative Science Quarterly, 40*(1), 1–33.

Radin, B. A., Agranoff, R., Bowman, A. O. M., Buntz, G. C., Ott, C. J., Romzek, B. S., & Wilson, R. H. (1996). *New governance for rural America: Creating intergovernmental partnerships*. University Press of Kansas.

Reich, R. (1991). *The work of nations: A blueprint for the future*. Vintage.

Rittel, H. W., & Webber, M. M. (1973). Dilemmas in a general theory of planning. *Policy Sciences, 4*(2), 155–169.

Romzek, B. S., & Johnston, J. M. (2002). Effective contract implementation and management: A preliminary model. *Journal of Public Administration Research and Theory, 12*(3), 423–453.

Saint-Onge, H., & Armstrong, C. (2004). *The conductive organization*. Elsevier.

Schambra, W. C. (1998). All community is local: The key to America's civic renewal. In E. J. Dionne (Ed.), *Community works: The revival of civil society in America* (pp. 44–49). Brookings Institution Press.

Schrage, M. (1995). *No more teams! Mastering the dynamics of creative collaboration*. Doubleday.

Smith, S. R., & Ingram, H. (2002). Implications of choice of policy tools for democracy, civic capital and citizenship. In O. V. Elliott & L. M. Salamon (Eds.), *The tools of government: A guide to the new governance*. Oxford University Press.

Solo, P., & Pressberg, G. (1998). Beyond theory: Civil society in action. In E. J. Dionne (Ed.), *Community works: The revival of civil society in America* (pp. 81–87). Brookings Institution Press.

Thomas, C. W. (2003). *Bureaucratic landscapes: Interagency cooperation and the preservation of biodiversity*. MIT Press.

Wenger, E. (2000). Communities of practice: The key to knowledge strategy. In E. Lesser, M. Fontaine, & J. Slusher (Eds.), *Knowledge and communities* (pp. 3–21). Routledge.

Wheatley, M. J. (1999). *Leadership and the new science: Discovering order in a chaotic world.* Berrett-Koehler Publishers.

Windhoff-Hentier, A. (1992). *The internationalization of domestic policy: A motor of decentralization.* European Consortium for Political Research Joint Sessions, Limerick, Ireland.

Wondolleck, J. M., & Yaffee, S. L. (2000). *Making collaboration work: Lessons from innovation in natural resource management.* Island Press.

12 Conclusion

Administering Collaborative Affairs in the Digital Era

The world of dispersed power among various public and public-serving organizations and jurisdictions involves organizations, governments, and NGOs regularly working together. Networks and related collaborative bodies have become important means of carefully structured deliberation that can enable citizens, organizations, and other stakeholders to "transcend initially divergent positions working together to envision joint goals and to design and implement policies and programs" (Page, 2010, p. 262). This has brought on a new form of administration, networking, and other forms of collaborative management, as in the example of CERN in Box 12.1, and its attendant CP, forging a parallel alternative to but not necessarily replacing traditional government hierarchy. One must not forget that new forms of organized collaboration regularly emerge in the era of connection. One example is the adaptations of strategic alliances, which allow for loose connections of different organization platforms to facilitate cross-boundary interactions and access to a partner's technology with limited controls. Also, cross-national "boundary organizations" address complex social and physical phenomena that cross many disciplines and permanent workgroups that work on scientific integration (Franklin et al., 2019). Collaborative management has brought about a new set of concerns, including the political, which is this volume's core focus.

Box 12.1   CERN: The Importance of Connection

Taking advantage of the human connection needed to make use of machine learning is CERN, the European Organization for Nuclear Research (https://home.cern). Established in 1954, CERN provides a range of particle accelerator facilities that enable others' research in fundamental physics. It is designed to unite people from around the world to push the frontiers of science and technology. It is governed by a collaboration of nation-states, and its international relations and industry, procurement, and knowledge transfer

---

DOI: 10.4324/9781003385769-12

departments are particularly active in collaborative outreach and reformation exchange. CERN's collaborative nexus is clearly part of the revolution in biotechnology, as well as new social and political connection models.

Source: Harari (2018)

It is also an electronic world that has changed the nature of today's communication patterns. For example, the late Oliver Sacks (2019, p. 29) concluded in his final column that contemporary communication by current means, like the ever-used smartphone and other electronic devices, has made social interaction to the "subtle, pervasive draining out of meaning, of intimate contact, from our society and culture" (p. 29). He continues by saying

> As a neurologist, I have seen many patients rendered amnesic by destruction of the memory systems in their brains, and I cannot help feeling that these people, having lost any sense of a past or a future and being caught in a flutter of ephemeral, ever-changing sensations, have in some way been reduced from human beings to Humean ones.
>
> (p. 29)

A personal experience, by contrast, came a few years ago with a distinguished federalism colleague, the late Ronald Watts, who was previously president of Queen's University in Kingston, Ontario. One of the authors of this volume, Dr. Robert Agranoff, was forming a research committee and emailed him to request his service on that committee. He emailed the request, to which Watts responded with one word, "No." Dr. Agranoff immediately responded, "Why?" Watts's response was quick: "Born 1926." End of transaction. This seemingly impersonal electronic era response appeared to be draining of meaning. In contrast, it actually reflected years of professional and personal interaction, and given Watts's professional and individual contributions, it was understandable and clever. Indeed, the Watts/Agranoff exchange leads to a good contact story with *meaning*.

Our examination of CP increasingly appears in these electronic contexts. Christopher Pollitt (2009) observes that networks and other forms of collaborative management have materialized simultaneously as rapidly as expanding information transfer and storage. Mobile phones, voicemail, e-mail, and so on have clearly accelerated the speed and variety of communications, along with the current post-bureaucratic concern over what is and is not official or legal, which has compounded our concerns (see the attached case, Box 12.2). Whereas post-bureaucratic influences may be significant, there may be problems when attitudes favor rapid, "real-time" decision-making, greater flexibility, informality, and preference for decision-making in small ad hoc teams (from different entities) rather than stabilized,

278   *Conclusion*

well-ordered hierarchy. Moreover, the role of rapid communication has led to what Pollitt calls "inducing a sense of simultaneity—of everything being connectable in the present, pushing aside other protected sense of time. Moreover, political discourse is growing in which people claim to have made little sense in former historical periods" (p. 209). To Pollitt, this compounds our problems with analyzing and understanding CP, as rapid decisions and changes in the bureaucratic organization lead to compressed decision-making that is "more careless of history and experience than was the norm under traditional bureaucracy" (p. 201).

Box 12.2   Case Study: Civic Level Connecting—The Automated City

There are bigger changes coming than just self-driving cars. Everybody in the business of cities these days is talking about autonomous vehicles and how they will change our urban future: less parking, more continuous traffic, no traffic signals, Uber without drivers. But the truth is that the change we are beginning to see in cities today—probably the biggest change since the introduction of the automobile—is much more profound than just self-driving cars.

Cities are ultimately engines of commerce. They exist primarily because there is economic efficiency in proximity. But as work is automated and transactions move online, the nature of that economic efficiency will be transformed.

The shift to online shopping, for example, holds the potential to be just as revolutionary for cities as the shift to self-driving cars. We're already seeing how brick-and-mortar stores are on the decline, leaving in their wake both urban and suburban blight, as well as new opportunities for real estate development.

But e-commerce is also fundamentally changing the nature of urban congestion, as more and more UPS and FedEx trucks pile up on the streets. In fact, it's altering the very economic basis for cities by eliminating retail jobs but replacing them with jobs at fulfillment centers in desired locations. This has been good for some cities, such as Pennsylvania's Bethlehem and Allentown. Still, the trend will further accelerate the winner-loser pattern among cities: If there's no fulfillment center, there are no retail jobs.

Perhaps the most pervasive transformation will be automation and the impact on jobs. In the 20th century, cities thrived because successful companies needed to have huge workforces in concentrated locations—be it a Ford manufacturing plant in Detroit or a Fortune 500 office building in Manhattan. Today, many of those jobs are being done by robots. That's why manufacturing employment is going down even as manufacturing output is going up.

But that doesn't mean jobs will go away. It means human jobs will be reoriented around human skills such as creativity, empathy and personal connection. And those jobs require face-to-face contact, which means they'll be most successful if they are concentrated in cities.

The work that people do keeps changing over time. But cities don't go away. They simply reinvent themselves to focus on the face-to-face work people must do to keep the economy chugging. And that's the most likely future scenario for urban life in America.

Source: Fulton (2018, p. 23)

In the electronic era of the internet, philosopher Michael Patrick Lynch (2016, p. 187) cautions us that we cannot become captured by our machines and lose our creative selves:

We must be careful not to mistake the "us" on the Internet of us for "everything else." As I've argued, the digital world is a construction and constructions are real enough. But we don't want to let that blind us to the world that is not constructed, to the world that predates our digital selves. And the Internet of us is not only going to affect how we see our world; it will affect our form of life. One aspect of this concerns autonomy. The hyperconnectivity of knowledge can help us become more cognitively autonomous and increase what I called epistemic equality. But I've argued it can also hinder our cognitive autonomy by making our ways of accessing information more vulnerable to the manipulations and desires of others. And it can lead us to overemphasize the importance of receptive knowing—knowing as downloading.

Lynch (2016) reminds us that we are the toolmakers, which ultimately shapes how we understand the world and our role within it. It encourages us to see the natural environment as a platform upon which we operate. Eventually, they become integrated into our lives. We must caution that electronic means of communication must not become the tools of our lives. That would raise the danger that we cease to see our own personhood as an end in itself. "Instead, we begin to see ourselves as devices to be used, as tools to be exploited" (p. 187).

Moreover, as remote work is more possible, technology allows for work from "virtual spaces" in geographically spread areas. Increasingly, location will have less importance for work. Indeed, Pat East (2018) maintains that the most desirable workplaces will feature quality places (e.g., civic culture, arts, entertainment, universities) and "world-class" co-working and incubator places.

280 *Conclusion*

People vs. Machines

In a very profound neuroscientific analysis of the role of person–machine interaction (e.g., Facebook, internet), Susan Greenfield (2015) points to the "vital role of the context in which the mind is operating from one conscious moment to the next" (p. 85). She makes it clear that machines can never take the place of context and human experience, where:

> the intense, ever-changing dynamic (interpersonal) reaction between coalitions of brain neurons is nothing like the rigid electronic circulating of computational devices. Experiences of an interpersonal nature (personal give and take) build in "neural assemblages" in the brain, as all available connections that "feed" or convert sensory takes on the world to more cognitive ones, as the development of particular patterns of responses and skills enable persons to navigate and thrive in one's own environment, reading against pre-existing emotions and ever changing one's connectivity. The more we can relate a phenomenon, action, or fact to other phenomena, facts, or actions, the deeper the "understanding, that is, seeing one thing in terms of another."
>
> (p. 81)

Through the lens of neuroscience, identity is best seen as an activity rather than a state—not as a solid object or property locked away in one's head, but as a specific type of subjective brain state, a feeling that changes from one moment to another to the next. To Greenfield (2015, pp. 82–85), there are five essential criteria that the physical reality must deliver for one to feel that it is a unique entity:

1. One needs to be fully conscious, allowing for the subjectivity of one's experience.
2. The mind must be fully operational, reacting to various objects, people, and events allowing for neural connectivity.
3. One reacts in a particular way determined not just by one's past experiences and the overall context, as the two previous items, but also how those experiences have subsequently shaped one's broader beliefs, linking memory and beliefs.
4. The potential validation or refutation is therein associational beliefs to potentially modify one's behavior and how one might respond differently in subsequent connections, the difference between mind and identity, with the former being passive and the latter—identity—is active and "depends on some kind of societal context" (p. 83). That leads to a context-dependent action-reaction.
5. The specific instances of action and reaction at a particular moment, within a specific context, replete with values and memories, are their incorporated into a still-wider framework—a narrative of your cohesive past, present, and future.

In other words, the process leads to moment-to-moment personal complexity. In a sense, the scenario of a lifetime of memories and beliefs is funneled into a single moment of consciousness. This process constitutes the kind of human activity at the core of CP that computational machine activity like AI cannot become a substitute. To Greenfield (2015, p. 85):

> Everything that happens has its own moment in time but can now be linked to all other events by virtue of either preceding or following them. Your identity is therefore a spatio-temporal phenomenon combining the hardwired, long-term, generalized neuronal network of the mind with momentary consciousness, the fleeting generation of macro- scale coalitions of neurons (assemblies) in less than a second. The long-term generalized network of connectivity is your mind, which can now in turn play its part at any particular moment in time. If consciousness is indeed linked to the fleeting generation of macro-scale coalitions of neurons in less than a second, and if the enduring networks of neuronal connections (the mind) can drive a more extensive coalition (assembly), then the ensuing "deeper" consciousness would be directly related to a deeper understanding of events, people, and objects as you encountered them.

Greenfield (2015) concludes with the importance of connectivity: "It is these connections, the personal association between specific objects and people, that give those objects special significance that contribute to a line as a narrative" (p. 271). However, as in the situations mentioned in Watt's works, this type of connectivity is expected to remain a core interpersonal aspect of CP in the future.

Metagovernance

In the field of CP, connectivity is taking place alongside the broader context of metagovernance, an emergent approach to interactive governance. According to Jacob Torfing et al. (2012), it is based on four theoretical streams. First is interdependence, or interest mediation between interdependent actors with different interests (Rhodes, 1997). Second, it involves governability, which combines rational choice institutionalism with systems approaches to social development (Kooiman, 2003). Third are institutional theories of normative integration, leading to governance networks as interactive behaviors that bring together interdependent actors by emerging rules, norms, values, and perceptions that define the logic of appropriate action that regulates and sustains interaction (Powell & DiMaggio, 1991; March & Olsen, 1996). Fourth is governmentality theory (Foucault, 1991), which offers a post-structure discourse that defines governance networks (and other collaborative devices) as increasingly reflective, governing by mobilizing and shaping the free actions of actors who are connected in and through interactive policy and program areas. Together, these four approaches provide a framework for unpacking the conceptual approaches to collaborative management through metagovernance. Indeed, approaching metagovernance has thoroughly altered the public face of bureaucracy relating to today's bureaucratic politics and public institutions.

282   *Conclusion*

Government institutions nevertheless remain at the core or "hub" of metagovernance. As Michael Walzer warns in discussing the paradox of civil society, the antipolitical tendencies that commonly accompany the celebration of civil society are overstated in metagovernance. Clearly, within the "network of associations governance incorporates, it cannot dispense with, the agencies of state power" (1998, p. 138). In elaborating on this paradox, he writes,

> [C]itizenship is one of the many roles that members play, but the state itself is unlike all other associations. It both frames civil society and occupies space within it, fixing the boundary conditions and the basic rules of associational activity, compelling association members to think about the common good.
>
> (p. 138)

For example, in the network era, metagovernance thus operates within these institutional and organizational parameters. It is also a truism that some networks are clearly more influential than others and more capable of some degree of marginalizing government power. Thus, despite actual legal and operational limits on the ability of many networks and/or collaboratives to push public agencies aside, networks usually can only exert short- and long-term influence. Some networks clearly do make the kinds of policy and program adjustments that proponents of collaborative governance ascribe to them for solving complex social problems, including broadened participation, expanded knowledge bases, enhanced resources, and flexibility to deal with cross-agency, multidisciplinary, and cross-jurisdictional challenges (Agranoff, 2007).

Nonetheless, in the final analysis, metagovernance deliberations and the proposed solutions rarely replace government decisions, thus implying the provocative metaphor of a "hollow" state. Instead, NGOs are more likely to influence the course of action taken by government—or influence new strategies and programs undertaken by government—than to replace government discretion. Practitioners of metagovernance generally agree that the government always makes the final policy call, even if implementation of the decision might be shared (Agranoff, 2007; Agranoff & McGuire, 2003; Cheng, 2019).

A Note on Collaborative Leadership

In their recent book *The New Localism*, Bruce Katz and Jeremy Nowak address the critical nature of success in navigating among the "networked reality" of urban power, bringing together the forces of public, private, and civic institutions that "coproduce the economy and cogovern critical aspects of city life" (2018, p. 230). As this volume also emphasizes, the key is to bring together disparate forces to solve problems that cannot be solved individually.

Conclusion   283

Success requires a series of attributes quite similar to those of most emergent collaborative leadership qualities:

1. Leaders must learn to and be able to cultivate collaboration, connection, and trust among persons who often have vastly different missions and organizational cultures.
2. Leadership comes from the deployment of soft (i.e., indirect) rather than hard power, looking for the less explored (e.g., knowledge), looking for persons who can design, finance, and deliver, while synthesizing disparate forms of information while leaders "sit at the intersection of multiple agencies, nonprofit organizations and specialized disciplines that literally speak different languages while seeking similar if not the same outcomes" (p. 233).
3. Leadership is often exercised by persons who are at the top of some hierarchy or elected to office. "In a world driven by collaborative governance, the people who are often responsible for transformative change are connectors who bridge the gap between major stakeholders, forge consensus solutions and initiatives, and then execute them with firm backing" (p. 234).
4. Leadership depends on the power of affirmative vision. It depends on both the technical skill to craft a version and the emotional intelligence to find one that fits a particular place at a particular time.
5. Leadership depends on grounding affirmative visions in affirmative evidence. The connective thread through most situations involves supplying assets rather than processing aggressive liabilities and designing plans rather than diagnosing problems as the group discovers that information is power.
6. Leadership "depends on being active rather than passive" (overcoming endless searching for "perfect 'evidence-driven' policies and instead exploring common technologies, citizen sourcing (e.g., crowdsourcing) and convening local entrepreneurs, in the process becoming more tech-savvy, working with those who are moving from lab to testing to prototyping to ubiquitous adoption (p. 237).

These leadership attributes are a function of the era of collaboration, as leaders are required to develop new capacities and competencies, build crucial social capital, increase collaboration across many sectoral boundaries, and provide catalysts for collective action and problem-solving. Regarding the cities that Katz and Nowak studied, leadership requires "problem solvers who bring out the hidden potential in communities, mobilizing this new set of intermediaries to help them realize the full potential of the 'New Localism'" (p. 245). Transcending governments, the new metagovernance involves cities that now need to champion leadership that crosses many boundaries and involves many people and organizations at different levels and specialties. For example, we know that many exciting innovations occur locally in critical policy areas like energy. However, we still do not understand how local government collaboratively connects with state and federal programs (Fowler, 2018).

284   *Conclusion*

Complex Adaptive Systems

CP involves quite complex systems. Christopher Koliba, Jack Meek, and Asim Zia (2011) conclude that collaboration in governance networks represents *complex* systems with emergent qualities and the ability to adjust to changing conditions and self-organizing. There are so many parts at play in complex systems that standard linear equations are unable to predict their interactions; the system's overall behavior can only be understood as an emergent consequence of the holistic total of all the behaviors embedded within it (Agranoff, 2017). Koliba and his associates come to the conclusion that researchers, modelers, and practitioners can collaborate together to "develop situational awareness of the governance complexity around them, combining systems thinking, filtering information, and applying descriptive patterning to network adaptation" (p. 234).

The dynamics of complex adaptive systems include the self-organizing processes of collaboration, which allow them to evolve, adjust internal structures, and manage their environment (Teisman & Klijn, 2008). Complex adaptive systems have already been integrated into leadership theory, emphasizing learning and also innovative and flexible capacities of bureaucracies and interorganizational systems (e.g., Lemaire & Provan, 2018; Uhl-Bien & Marion, 2009). The application of this approach in collaborative settings focuses on capacity development, non-linear processes, and the constant process of spontaneous emergence (Koliba, Meek, & Zia, 2011, p. 234). This approach could be the next best alternative to understanding CP and networks. "Software-based" network platforms that integrate multiple partnerships or only include the data that is required collectively and interactively from the agency could be the subsequent development in network platforms as information system technology develops and adapts to the interactive needs of network participants (Agranoff, 2017). These gadgets may also help to speed up the adoption of interoperability.

In the future, AI will enrich the potential of CP. This rapid technology enables machines to perform tasks much faster than humans. Deep learning, a type of AI, offers untapped potential in CP and interoperability since it allows systems to learn and improve by analyzing many examples rather than having the solutions explicitly written (Agranoff, 2017). It is currently used in powering advanced web search engines, blocking spam emails, suggesting reply texts in emails, translating web pages, recognizing voice commands, and recommending movies to watch on Netflix, Amazon, Hulu, and many other applications (*The Economist*, 2016a, p. 5). Deep learning supercharges artificial neural networks and establishes biologically inspired brain networks by utilizing enormous quantities of processing power and data training. The neurons are then given weights that operate as activators. In a neural network, training entails altering the neurons' weights so that a particular input gives the desired output.

As AI has already been used for data mining of numerous reports and official documents as part of the advanced use of the internet, it can be utilized for the

Conclusion 285

interoperable aspect of collaborative management. For example, Agranoff (2017), claims that AI interactive procedures apply to seemingly unique situations in the work of public and nonprofit agencies dealing with disaster response, emergency management, human services integration, and other network applications. However, as the philosopher Michael Lynch concludes,

> The Internet has created an explosion in receptive knowledge. While wonderful, adaptive, and creative in many respects, it isn't enough, we need to exchange reasons and play by shared epistemic rules if we are going to solve the information coordination problems that face all societies.

> (2016, p. 60)

Globalization and CP

Informal and formal values, norms, procedures, and institutions help public sector actors identify, understand, and address transboundary problems to varying degrees and affect collaboration in several ways (Weiss, 2016). In the era of the world of networks, horizontal and vertical linkages operate—to some degree—"outside of the nation-state, below the state, and through the state" (Agranoff, 2017, p. 240). Vertical networks involve links between national and supranational officials to whom authority has been assigned, whereas horizontal networks link counterpart officials across boundaries. "Hierarchy and control lose out to the community, collaboration, and self-organization" (Slaughter, 2009, p. 97). Therefore, global networks tend to be managed and orchestrated instead of directed or administrated. The ability to make the most significant number of valuable connections—based on the knowledge and skills to harness that power and achieve the shared goal—is the source of power in such global networks (Slaughter, 2009, p. 100). These increased supranational influences represent new power configurations, but they are "rearticulated" and "reterritorialized" emerging connections concerning global forces in the same way that domestic networks do not replace government. For example, global city regions and other territorialized matrices have emerged while state-organized territorial power remains (Brenner, 1998).

One of the authors of this volume, Agranoff (2007), identifies the following examples of the global influence on the practices of collaborative management:

(1) the influence of cross-national organizations, such as the International City and County Management Association (ICMA), in connecting local governments;

(2) the within-country trends that originate and spread, for example, the U.S.-developed municipal home-rule movement;

(3) the substantive cross-national influence such as the International Convention on the Rights of Persons with Disabilities;

286   *Conclusion*

(4) the changes from other governments' experiences, such as big data's impact on professionals who have been influenced by international trends and standards, particularly in environmental management; and

(5) the governing influences that are raised by international trends but implemented within subnational governments, for example, citizen involvement in planning horizontal networks that support the elderly in their homes.

(p. 240)

Using appropriate information, knowledge, expertise, and practices, any type of subnational government requires a balance of central policy-making and administration and the so-called "metagovernance" by Guy Peters (2015). He calls it "control over the devolved local delegation and coadministration" (p. 128). These metagovernance conditions are now part of the global environment, including those of collaboration, because of the inescapable reality that no one can "go it alone" when it comes to the challenges of globalization (Lindenberg & Dobel, 1999, p. 22).

According to Manuel Castells (1996), global networks share standard features characterizing cross-national movements. First, they represent multimodal, decentered, maximizing opportunities for parties involved in the collaboration. Second, "whereas they may begin communications connections on Internet social movements, they tend to occupy defined spaces—for example, urban space—making the Internet their core vehicle" (p, 241). Third, they tend to produce "their own form of 'timeless time,' eschewing clock time in anticipation of constant change" (p. 241). Fourth, they tend to contribute to community creation and capacity building. Fifth, these connected movements are virtual since the demonstration effects of several movements spring up in many places. Sixth, "the deliberations that occur, if any, occur in the 'space of autonomy,' particularly when dealing with leaderless movements" (p. 241). Seventh, these "horizontal, multimodal networks create elements of togetherness as a source of empowerment" (p. 241). Eighth, "they are self-reflective networks, not necessarily in 'assemblies,' but through multiple Internet searches, such as blogs and interactive discussions" (p. 241). Finally, they are usually citizen-oriented and use deliberation-based consensus techniques. Even though Castells first developed global criteria for social protest movements, they can be equally applied to subnational governance. Castells concludes, "The digital social networks based on the internet and wireless platforms are decisive tools for organizing" (p. 229; see also Wells, 2015).

When it comes to constituent governments—that is, the actions of regional, provincial, and other similar second-order governments and localities like cities, counties, and city regions—networking collaboration is now primarily viewed as a bottom-up activity that complements national-level legal and economic policy efforts (Agranoff, 2017). As Allen Scott (2001, p. 6, emphasis added) notes,

The local *can* be an important arena of social reconstruction in its own right, as being a conduit through which various national policies are mediated. The *local*

Conclusion 287

is all the more important given the psychic and political distance of the central state from many of the constituencies that make up modern global city regions, compared to the immediacy and relevance of the local community.

Digital Research

The increasing visibility of citizen engagement has highlighted the importance of electronic contacts, which can then refocus attention on public agency NGO contact. For example, Donald Tapscott (2009, p. 257) predicts "tremendous potential for government to create new forms of value by focusing on what it does best by creating partnerships for other activities . . . [using] a Web-based platform . . . and other Web 2.0 technologies." He proposes that governments employ various digital techniques to deal with contractors, similar to how businesses deal with suppliers and consumers. But, of course, this is already in the toolbox of government. As shown by Agranoff and Yildiz (2007, p. 333), it often employs information services contractors to establish digital communications, reporting, record-keeping, assessment, accounting, and other functions that involve the government agency and a grantee/contractor by the following means:

1. Producing and posting information via web pages, emails, and teleconferencing, encouraging contact for activists and non-activists.
2. Easing coordination and overcoming the limits of dyadic and triadic communication through "one-to-many" media: e-mail, teleconferencing, website presence, electronic document transfer, and interactive chatrooms.
3. Initiating interaction among administrators and specialists by electronically arranging meetings, distributing advance materials, organizing exercises and simulations, and otherwise sharing technical, legal, and financial information.
4. Assisting task groups, workgroups, seminars, and conferences to arrange results and findings into usable information and knowledge.
5. Using electronic decision-making software—for example, web-based geographic information systems, groupware, and interoperable solutions—to "broker" feasible processes and decisions.
6. Pooling information and databases from partner agencies and organizations in a problem-oriented format across users to enhance the network knowledge base.
7. Building management information systems and software packages decision-making models using data from several partners for projects such as intelligent transportation demand models, client service flows, stream bank remediation planning, etc.

In this fast-developing digital world, AI assessments and linkages can be easily added to the preceding list (Agarwal, 2018). Governments and nonprofit organizations currently use enhanced data sources for various purposes, from reporting street potholes to efficient public use. For example, Agranoff (2017) provides an

288 *Conclusion*

example of using big data in Boston, Massachusetts. Its "Score Initiative" program was created to improve planning and citizen services and engage citizens in governing locally. Based on learning and results of a thorough analysis of local service databases, this program enhanced cross-departmental connections, broke stuff out of the intraorganizational silos, and improved enforcement of local service regulations; the strategic use of this urban data initiated and promoted collaborative partner advocacy and interoperability of participating organizations. Enhanced data-based knowledge—whether programmed or developed through AI—can, on the other hand, work against a jurisdiction's intergovernmental case or weaken its conclusions when seeking additional funds, authorizing experimental programs, or seeking asymmetrical program avenues not covered by standards or rules. "Municipal governments should become the caretakers of the local data ecosystem, creating a framework that encourages others to share data," one digital government researcher concluded (*The Economist*, 2016b). Clearly, the internet and related information technologies such as smartphones and cloud computing make it inexpensive and straightforward to transmit, collect, store, and analyze increasingly vast amounts of data.

One can easily conclude that collaboration and networking in the era of externalized relations and electronic data make it critical to understand and gauge the digital impact on management across governments and nonprofit and private organizations as they are increasingly engaged in collecting and analyzing enormous amounts of data.

Open-Source Technology and the Roles of AI

In increased use of connective interactive management with system dynamics and the call for capturing theory-building with computer simulation modeling while using such techniques as extensive data analysis, system dynamics, agent-based modeling, social network analysis, and qualitative comparative analysis has become a pressing issue. Constantly improving AI data-mining programs analyze large amounts of qualitative and quantitative data to identify patterns (Koliba, 2014). According to Agranoff (2017), these programs will improve collaborative performance and expand knowledge in various areas. Dragićević and Balram (2004) emphasize using emergent techniques such as augmentative mapping, which can be used alone or together with public participative or collaborative GIS programming. Finally, they propose new ways of clustering different network partners around spatially related problems (Mahmood et al., 2012).

More interesting alternatives to using AI in collaboration appear on the horizon. For example, Michael Nielsen (2011) claims that prolonged engagement can increase collaborative volume in specific fields of study, producing what he refers to as "conversational critical mass" (p. 28). This can be accomplished through collaboration modularization, which divides collaborative tasks into smaller subtasks that can be completed individually. Interoperability in public management networks will also improve as a result of this. Rich and well-structured information commons, for example, can arise as a result of promoting minor contributions, lowering obstacles to the entrance, and extending the breadth of expertise in solving collaboration difficulties, according to Agranoff (2017).

What Works in Collaboration?

The electronic era has led to significant breakthroughs in using AI for a variety of research and practical applications. Today computer-assisted designs can solve several problems, including those related to collaborative management and network operations. AI has the potential to be used in simulating how organizations and other entities can learn to work together. Collaborative approaches and "systems" can be experimented with or simulated. For example, continual "rules" can "predict" or profile projected collaborative structures and possible operations. Repeated scans of formalized and informal potential systems can be "run," and it is likely that interactive results can be scanned and projected. This type of mapping based on machine learning is one of the latest applications.

AI has already proved its value concerning ecology/conservation. Conservation International maintains a spreadsheet that includes more than 200 projects on issues like deforestation rates, species counts, grant sizes, and grant management quality. Moreover, in 2004, a group that is pushing evidence-based conservation launched an online index/repository of relevant peer-reviewed literature, *Conservation Evidence*. which is based on the review of more than 230 ecological journals. It also has a book version, *What Works in Conservation* (Sutherland et al., 2018) that is 662 pages long and has been downloaded more than 35,000 times. There is no reason why an international collaborative entity could not use AI to perform information exchange and program AI simulations.

Open-source information has an untapped potential to augment the deliberate power of interacting parties in networks. For example, open-source information helps shift attention away from information that participants already know and toward knowledge they need to in order to tackle challenges, thereby performing the critical role of "collective insight" (Nielsen, 2011). Since collaboratives and networks operate in open cultures of sharing, "whereas much information is moved out of people's heads . . . and onto the network" (Nielsen, 2011, p. 183), the search for meaning is part and parcel of network processes. AI could be pervasive in these situations.

Moreover, suppose public networks are occupying niches once held by bureaucracies. In that case, it is crucial to build a theory that explains critical aspects of their efficacy and how they are managed differently. Such "testing" calls for the AI application in forms of evaluation and assessment that extend well beyond the small number of studies currently preferred; that is, that moves toward meta-analyses of cases, particularly those that are cross-sectoral and bridge policy and program boundaries (Isett et al., 2011; Berry et al., 2004).

290　*Conclusion*

One important product of the study of network/collaborative processes includes the possibility that it is distinct from hierarchical management in many vital ways. Foremost, it has been suggested that there may be a new sequential management process—that is, a "POSDCORB equivalent"—that in part distinctively sets off-network management, as once empirically proposed and demonstrated by McGuire (2002): activation, mobilization, framing, and synthesizing. The concept of interoperability, or reciprocal communication and operation, has great AI potential as a network management approach. For example, an area of management that is frequently mentioned is leadership in networks, on which studies upon studies have accumulated for some time (Agranoff, 2014). These studies vary from a survey by Bennis and Biederman (1997) on steering groups toward creative collaboration to more empirical studies like the Koppenjan, Koppenjan, and Klijn (2004) study on managerial coping with uncertainty. Finally, collaborative leadership has been subject to many past studies (e.g., Silvia, 2011; Keast & Mandell, 2014; Crosby & Bryson, 2005). All of these have AI potential.

Network management dates back to the earliest wave of public management network studies, particularly the work of Keith Provan and Brinton Milward (1991, 1995) on lead organizations in public networks, along with the work of Provan and Patrick Kenis (2008) on a network administrative organization. Organizational resources provided to the network by collaborating organizations often make up networks as organized structures. These resources include hierarchical positions in organizations, technical staff expertise, dedicated network staff, and information bases (Agranoff, 2014; McGuire, 2009). It is well understood that the power and influence contributed to operations determine organizations' ability to impact networks (Gray, 1989; Schapp & van Twist, 1997). This ability is "blended with or can be modified by the social production of network participants when dealing with new ideas or reaching deliberative solutions (Gray, 1989; Schapp & van Twist, 1997; Stone et al., 1999)" (Agranoff, 2014, p. 203). However, most networks appear to be "self-organizing structures that are generally enabled or chartered, have different nonhierarchical authority structures, use regularized cross-agency communication systems, have separate internal power structures, and set internal arrangements in terms of structure" (Agranoff, 2007. p. 83). Subsequent research concluded that these same networks were structured with

> many organized roles, including network champions, agency administrator steering partners, signatory but less involved copartners, governing structure members (core group, executive committee council), standing committee members, technical and problem-based workgroup participants, other technical staff from agencies, and organizations and network staff (Agranoff, 2012); (see also Holbeche, 2005; Mandell, 2001; Rethemeyer & Hatmaker, 2008).
>
> (Agranoff, 2014, p. 203)

Although network structure research is still in its early phases, it should advance core or internal network knowledge when combined with theory-building on non-hierarchical structuring. It requires indexing and compilation, assisted by AI, like biology, such as *What Works in Conservation* (Sutherland et al., 2018).

Conclusion

The deepening complexity in modern, constantly interacting governing systems—international to local—has led to greater visibility of the role of all governments and connected NGO service delivery agencies. The chain of globally influenced agents from higher-level governments, including cross-organizational operations, down through intermediate regional and state governments, includes various government and externalized service operations. Meanwhile, the current challenge at the government operation level is to

> balance respect for the individual encounter that is at the heart of street-level service provision, and at the same time negotiate the larger questions of . . . serving as witness to the ritual role of these public systems in civic life.
>
> (Lipsky, 2010, p. 237)

Relationships like these, however impersonal, "are necessary to create the 'public' and to separate it from the 'private,'" which is, concludes Steven Conn (2012, p. 306), "so important to build community and to make democracy work." As with this emerged "governance" collaborative management and politics, "is being shaped and reshaped in constellations of public and private actors that include (nation) states, international and regional organizations, professional associations, expert groups, civil society groups, and business corporations" (Kennet, 2010, p. 31). Thus, new political structures and policy spaces have multiplied as new networks and related forms of collaboration lead to innovative layers of governance, organizational strategies, and new public technologies. These actions are based on rules or institutions, or what Paul Steinberg (2015, pp. 1–12) calls "the machinery that makes coordinated social activity possible" and "the big levers that will ultimately decide whether we can reconcile the pursuit of prosperity with thoughtful stewardship." Government and governing are now lateral, horizontal, and vertical in many interactions. Moreover, it cannot all be done in a day, as an astute commentator concludes regarding dealing with California's governing crises (Zacchino, 2016, p. 276), that the states are "no different; the attempt to shape history through bureaucratic and legal means is no pure science."

References

Agarwal, P. K. (2018). Public administration challenges in the world of AI and Bots. *Public Administration Review, 78*(6), 917–921.

Agranoff, R. (2007). *Managing within networks: Adding value to public organizations.* Georgetown University Press.

Agranoff, R. (2012). *Collaborating to manage: A primer for the public sector.* Georgetown University Press.

292 *Conclusion*

Agranoff, R. (2014). Bridging the theoretical gap and uncovering missing holes. In R. Keast, M. P. Mandell, & R. Agranoff (Eds.), *Network theory in the public sector: Building new theoretical frameworks* (pp. 193–210). Routledge.

Agranoff, R. (2017). *Crossing boundaries for intergovernmental management.* Georgetown University Press.

Agranoff, R., & McGuire, M. (2003). *Collaborative public management: New strategies for public management.* Georgetown University Press.

Agranoff, R., & Yildiz, M. (2007). Decision-making in public management networks. In G. Morcol (Ed.), *Handbook of decision-making* (pp. 319–345). Marcel Dekker Publications.

Bennis, W., & Biederman, P. W. (1997). *Organizing genius: The secrets of successful collaboration.* Nicholas Brealey.

Berry, F. S., Brower, R. S., Choi, S. O., Goa, W. X., Jang, H., Kwon, M., & Word, J. (2004). Three traditions of network research: What the public management research agenda can learn from other research communities. *Public Administration Review, 64*(5), 539–552.

Brenner, N. (1998). Global cities, glocal states: global city formation and state territorial restructuring in contemporary Europe. *Review of international political economy,* 5(1), 1–37.

Castells, M. (1996). *The information age* (Vol. 98). Blackwell Publishers.

Cheng, Y. (2019). Exploring the role of nonprofits in public service provision: Moving from coproduction to cogovernance. *Public Administration Review, 79*(2), 203–214.

Conn, S. (Ed.). (2012). *To promote the general welfare: The case for big government.* Oxford University Press.

Crosby, B. C., & Bryson, J. M. (2005). *Leadership for the common good: Tackling public problems in a shared-power world.* John Wiley & Sons.

Dragićević, S., & Balram, S. (2004). A Web GIS collaborative framework to structure and manage distributed planning processes. *Journal of Geographical Systems, 6*(2), 133–153.

East, P. (2018, December 14). The future of work. *Blooming Herold Times,* p. B2.

The Economist. (2016a, June 25). Artificial intelligence: The return of the machinery question. *Special Report,* 1–16. http://www.economist.com/news/special-report/2170076

The Economist. (2016b, March 26). *Special report on technology and politics.* http://www.economist.com/news/special-report/21695198-ever-easier-communications-and-ever-growing-data-mountains-are-transforming-politics

Foucault, M. (1991). *The Foucault effect: Studies in governmentality.* University of Chicago Press.

Fowler, L. (2018). Intergovernmental relations and energy policy: What we know and what we still need to learn. *State and Local Government Review, 50*(3), 203–212.

Franklin, A. L., Grossman, A., Le, J., & Shafer, M. (2019). Creating broader research impacts through boundary organizations. *Public Administration Review, 79*(2), 215–224.

Fulton, W. (2018). Automated city. *Governing, 3*(5), 23.

Gray, B. (1989). *Collaborating: Finding common ground for multiparty problems.* Jossey Bass.

Greenfield, S. (2015). *Mind change: How digital technologies are leaving their mark on our brains.* Random House Incorporated.

Harari, Y. N. (2018). *21 lessons for the 21st century.* Spiegel and Grace.

Holbeche, L. (2005). *The high performance organization: Creating dynamic stability and sustainable success.* Routledge.

Isett, K. R., Mergel, I. A., LeRoux, K., Mischen, P. A., & Rethemeyer, R. K. (2011). Networks in public administration scholarship: Understanding where we are and where we need to go. *Journal of Public Administration Research And Theory, 21*(suppl_1), i157–i173.

Katz, B., & Nowak, J. (2018). *The new localism: How cities can thrive in the age of populism.* Brookings Institution Press.

Keast, R., & Mandell, M. P. (2014). A composite theory of leadership and management: Process catalyst and strategic leveraging: Theory of deliberate action in collaborative networks. In R. Keast, M. P. Mandell, & R. Agranoff (Eds.), *Network theory in the public sector: Building new theoretical frameworks* (pp. 33–50). Routledge.

Kennett, P. (2010). Global perspectives on governance. In S. P. Osborne (Ed.), *The new public governance?* (pp. 35–51). Routledge.

Koliba, C. J. (2014). Governance network performance: A complex adaptive systems approach. In R. Keast, M. P. Mandell, & R. Agranoff (Eds.), *Network theory in the public sector: Building new theoretical frameworks* (pp 84–102). Routledge.

Koliba, C. J., Meek, J. W., & Zia, A. (2011). *Governance networks in public administration and public policy.* CRC Press.

Kooiman, J. (2003). *Governing as governance.* SAGE.

Koppenjan, J. F. M., Koppenjan, J., & Klijn, E. H. (2004). *Managing uncertainties in networks: A network approach to problem solving and decision making.* Psychology Press.

Lemaire, R. H., & Provan, K. G. (2018). Managing collaborative effort: How Simmelian ties advance public sector networks. *The American Review of Public Administration, 48*(5), 379–394.

Lindenberg, M., & Dobel, J. P. (1999). The challenges of globalization for northern international relief and development NGOs. *Nonprofit and Voluntary Sector Quarterly, 28*(1_suppl), 4–24.

Lipsky, M. (2010). *Street-level bureaucracy: Dilemmas of the individual in public service.* Russell Sage Foundation.

Lynch, M. P. (2016). *The internet of us: Knowing more and understanding less in the age of big data.* WW Norton & Company.

Mahmood, M. N., Horita, M., Keast, R., & Brown, K. (2012, October 1–2). *Using argumentative mapping and qualitative probabilistic network in resettlement planning process: A case study of Padma Multi-purpose Bridge Project.* Proceedings of 2012 International Conference on Construction and Real Estate Management, Kansas City, MO.

Mandell, M. (2001). Impact of network structures on community building efforts: The los angelos round table for children community studies. In M. Mandell (Ed.), *Getting results through collaboration: Networks and network structures for public policy and management.* Quarum Books.

March, J. G., & Olsen, J. P. (1996). Institutional perspectives on political institutions. *Governance, 9*(3), 247–264.

McGuire, M. (2002). Managing networks: Propositions on what managers do and why they do it. *Public Administration Review, 62*(5), 599–609.

McGuire, M. (2009). The new professionalism and collaborative activity in local emergency management. In R. O'Leary & L. B. Bingham (Eds.), *The collaborative public manager: New ideas for the twenty-first Century.* Georgetown University Press.

Nielsen, M. (2011). *Reinventing discovery: The new era of networked science.* Princeton University Press.

Page, S. (2010). Integrative leadership for collaborative governance: Civic engagement in Seattle. *The Leadership Quarterly, 21*(2), 246–263.

Peters, B. G. (2015). *Pursuing horizontal management: The politics of public sector coordination.* University Press of Kansas.

294 *Conclusion*

Pollitt, C. (2009). Bureaucracies remember: Post-bureaucratic organizations forget? *Public Administration, 87*(2), 198–218.

Powell, W. W., & DiMaggio, P. J. (Eds.). (1991). *The new institutionalism in organizational analysis.* University of Chicago Press.

Provan, K., & Kenis, P. (2008). Modes of network governance: Structure, management, and effectiveness. *Journal of Public Administration Research and Theory, 18*(2), 229–252.

Provan, K., & Milward, H. B. (1991). Institutional-level norms and organizational involvement in a service-implementation network. *Journal of Public Administration Research and Theory, 1*(4), 391–418.

Provan, K., & Milward, H. B. (1995). A preliminary theory of interorganizational network effectiveness: A comparative study of four community mental health systems. *Administrative Science Quarterly, 40*(1), 1–33.

Rethemeyer, R. K., & Hatmaker, D. M. (2008). Network management reconsidered: An inquiry into management of network structures in public sector service provision. *Journal of Public Administration Research and Theory, 18*(4), 617–646.

Rhodes, R. A. (1997). *Understanding governance: Policy networks, governance, reflexivity and accountability.* Open University.

Sacks, O. (2019, February 4) The machine stops. *New Yorker.*

Schapp, L., & van Twist, M. J. W. (1997). The dynamics of closedness in networks. In W. J. Kickert, E. H. Klijn, & J. F. Koppenjan (Eds.), *Managing complex networks: Strategies for the public sector* (pp. 62–78). Sage.

Scott, A. J. (Ed.). (2001). *Global city-regions: Trends, theory, policy.* OUP.

Silvia, C. (2011). Collaborative governance concepts for successful network leadership. *State and Local Government Review, 43*(1), 66–71.

Slaughter, A. M. (2009). *A new world order.* Princeton University Press.

Steinberg, P. F. (2015). *Who rules the earth?: How social rules shape our planet and our lives.* Oxford University Press.

Stone, C., Doherty, K., Jones, C., & Ross, T. (1999). Schools and disadvantaged. In C. Stone, K. Doherty, C. Jones, & T. Ross. *Urban problems and community development.* Brooking Institute Press.

Sutherland, W. J., Dicks, L. V., Ockendon, N., Petrovan, S. O., & Smith, R. K. (2018). *What works in conservation.* Open Book Publishers.

Tapscott, D. (2009). *Grown up digital: How the net generation is changing.* McGraw-Hill.

Teisman, G. R., & Klijn, E. H. (2008). Complexity theory and public management: An introduction. *Public Management Review, 10*(3), 287–297.

Torfing, J., Peters, B. G., Pierre, J., & Sørensen, E. (2012). *Interactive governance: Advancing the paradigm.* Oxford University Press.

Uhl-Bien, M., & Marion, R. (2009). Complexity leadership in bureaucratic forms of organizing: A meso model. *The Leadership Quarterly, 20*(4), 631–650.

Walzer, M. (1998). The idea of civil society: A path to social reconstruction. In E. J. Dionne (Ed.), *Community works: The revival of civil society in America.* Brookings Institution Press.

Weiss, T. G. (2016). *Global governance: Why? what? whither?* John Wiley & Sons.

Wells, C. (2015). *The civic organization and the digital citizen: Communicating engagement in a networked age.* Oxford University Press.

Zacchino, N. (2016). *California comeback: How a "failed state" became a model for the nation.* Macmillan.

Index

1.0 organizations 250–250, **251**
2.0 organizations **251**, 253–255, 256

accountability **251**; direct 105, 255; external 158; loss of 18; network 255
action networks 86–87, 214
activation 57, 61, 119, 153, 218, 240, 290
Adarand Constructors vs. Pena 16
Administration Procedures Act (APA) 65
administrative state 125
advisory boards *34*
Advisory Commission on Intergovernmental Relations (ACIR) 68
Affordable Care Act (ACA) 92
African Network Information Centre (AfrINIC) 105
agenda 5–6, 58, 67, 70, 75, 85, 138, 153, 186, 201, 215, 227, 235; decision-making 156; discussion 209; personal 245; *see also* agenda-setting; collaborative agenda
agenda-setting 45, 59, 170
agreements: voluntary agreements 10; *see also* interlocal agreements; cooperative agreements
American Partnership 170
Americans with Disabilities Act (ADA) 8, 159, 267
Anderson, W. 169
Ansell, C. 163, 218
apprenticeships **158**, 179
Area Agencies on Aging *34*
Area Director (AD) 104
Armstrong, C. 94, 176, 201–202, 207, 257, 262

Army Corps of Engineers 78, 140
artificial intelligence (AI) 23, 179, 287–290
Association for Retarded Citizens (ARC) 260
associations 121, 200, 282; business *37*, 79, 174, 268; industry 262; professional 60, 291; state 101, 258, 260; trade **206**, 260, 268
autonomy *13*, 21, 44, 79, 81, 110, 143, 150, 201, 210, 279, 286; bureaucratic 21, 152–153, 212; jurisdictional 175; organizational 241

Bardach, E. 143, 152, 210, 212, 223, 237, 239, 252
bargaining and negotiation 5, 106, 254
Battelle Corporation 89, 250
Benson, G. 168
big data 168, 286, 288
"Big P" politics 5–7, 22, 149–151, 156–158, 197, 200
Black, J. 179
block grants **37**, 74
blueprint strategies 57, 216
Borins, S. 35
bottom-up activity 13, 286
bottom-up processes 41, 181
boundary spanners 19
boundary-spanning: activity **29**, 255; interactions **251**
Bourgon, J. 122
Brodkin, E. 137
Brody, R. 269
brokering 59, 235–237
Brown, T. 36, 108–112, 174, 258
Bureau of Land Management (BLM) 110

296   *Index*

Campbell, E. 224, 228
capacity building 60, 87, 110, 183, 185, 237, 286
Capital Improvement Project (CIP) 5
carbon dioxide (CO_2) 151
Carpenter, D. 21, 152, 212
Castells, M. 18, 79, 286
centralization 58, 114, 209
chartered networks 32, *73*, 74
Chief Information Officers (CIO) 107
citizen involvement 13, 182, 267–269, 272, 286
citizen participation 4, 262
civic engagement 180, 268
coalition building 218
collaborarchy 62, 127–128, 131–132, 146
collaboration: activity 264; cross-sector 28; external 256; fostering 178; interagency 150, 208; interlocal 46–47; interpersonal 115, 117–118; legal 35; negotiations 152; outcomes of 138, 213; power 20; process 59, 133, 163, 178, 240; scientific 236; theory 12; *see also* collaboration knowledge; collaborative process
Collaboration Among State and Federal Agencies to Improve California's Water Supply (CALFED) 10–11, 19, 135, 138, 150, 156, 161, 226, 231–232
Collaboration Assessment Rubric (CoPCAR) 115–116
collaboration knowledge 116
collaborative agenda 215–216
collaborative capacity 156, 235, 237, 252, 255
collaborative GIS programming 228, 288
collaborative governance 16–17, 19, 44–46, 67, 134, 153, 161, **206**, 211, 224, 282–283; challenges of **206**
collaborative governance regime 19
collaborative inertia 214–215
collaborative leadership 128, 282–283, 290
collaborative learning 241
collaborative management 8, 11–12, 15–17, **15**, 20, 22, 39–40, 46, 55, 60–61, 65–66, 67, 98, 110, 115, 121, 126, 131–132, 139–142, 153, 167, 174–175, 179, 181, 194, 200, 202, 207, 212, 217, 224–225, 226, 242, 249, 254, 256, 276; competencies 237;

era of 243; forms 208, 230, 277; players 5; practices of 285; process of 218; rules of 181
collaborative performance management 23, 223–224, 228, 240–241, 288; activities 240; assessing 226; challenge 223; importance of 223; measuring performance 116, 181, 223, 226, 233; outcomes 240; outputs 240; process 255; process analysis 226; research 227; systems 241; value-adding performance management approaches 240; *see also* Interoperability (IOp); Continuous Improvement (CI)
Collaborative Politics (CP) 2, 8–15, 20, 23, 28, 163, 167, 191, 195
collaborative process 3, 28, 55, 111, 133, 150–151, 179, 210–211, 213, 241
collective action 11, 61, 87, 283
communities of practice 57, 99, 115–116, 179, 253, 263, 265–266
Community Economic Development (CED) program 74
complex adaptive systems 56, 284
conductive bureaucracy 57, 93
conductive organization 23, 29, 74, 94, 257
conductive programming 207
consensus: accommodation and 51; brokered 216; building 160, 252; decision-making by 132; forum for 78; goals 46; process 106; reaching 99, 215
Continuous Improvement (CI) 224–228
Continuum of Care (CoC) 2
contracting 16, 18, 37, 70, 109, 111, 121, 123, 195–196, 200, 233–234, 258, 268; complex 108, 111–113; intergovernmental 200; public 108, 111; *see also* relational contracting; stewardship contracting; types of contracting
Contractor, N. 227
contracts 1, 13, 16, 21, 31, 32, 35–36, 39, 69, 72, *73*, 74, 108, 110–112, 122, 170, 173, 206, 229, 234, 257, 262; monitoring 237; simple 111, 240; subcontracts 230
cooperation: interagency 152; intergovernmental 114; interorganizational 35; program 168; regional 52

Index 297

cooperative agreements 19, 187, 210
corporate libraries *71*
Critical Internet Resources (CIR) 104
cross-agency transactions 12, 16–17, 126, 171, 179
cultural change **178**
Cultural Theory (CT) 160–161

Darby Partnership 10, 127–128, 153–154, 160, 183
database **177**, 178, 185, 240, 258, 287; collaborative 240; external 265; local service 288
Davenport, T. 139, 175–176, 179, 217, 263–264
Davenport, Thomas 211
Davis, David 19
decentralization 197, 209
decision-support systems **177**
dedicated task forces 175, 176
dedicated task forces **33**
Deepwater Program 108–109
Deepwater Program (Coast Guard) 153, 154
default position requirements 63
DeHoog, Ruth 130, 154
Democratic-Farmer-Labor (DFL) 156, 199
democratic network governance 190
Denters, B. 243
Denver, Colorado, metropolitan plan- ning organization 217
Department of Health and Human Services (DHHS) 7, 68, 81–82, *83*
Department of Transportation (DOT) 130
Departments of Human Resources (DHR) 82
Developmental Disabilities, Aging and Rehabilitation Services (DDARS) 260
developmental networks 86–87
digital impact 288
digital social networks 286
digital techniques 287
direct loans **37**
discussion groups **177, 178**
Domain Name System (DNS) 103–104

economic development 4, 6, 8, 30, 31, 33, *37*, 39, 70, 74, 76, 79, 115, 132, 193, 202, 237–239, 260; agents 174, **177–178**; local *75*
Economic Development Administration 140

EcoPeace Middle East 52
Edelenbos, J. 133, 151–152, 156, 215, 217–218, 235
Educational Council (EC) 89, 231, 250
Egger, R. 191
Elazar, D.J. 123, 170
electronic archiving **177**
electronic decision-support group work **178**
electronic informational networks 236, 262
emergency management 2, 60, 91, 230–231, 235, 271, 285
Environmental Protection Agency (EPA) 50, 51, 140
exemption 171
expert interviews **178**
externalization 12, 18, 123, 249, 256, 259, 261, 268, 271

face-to-face communication 11
face-to-face skills 249
Family and Social Services Administration (FSSA) 6, 10, 198, 260
Faust, K. 227, 232
Federal Bureau of Investigation, Joint Terrorism Task Force 71
Federal Emergency Management Agency *80*
federalism: collaborative 169; cooperative 169; dual 173; inclusive 167
Federalist Papers 67
federal–state collaboration 169
federal systems 172
fiscal capacity **206**
Fleishman, R. 93
food stamps *37–38*
Forester, J. 267
Frederickson, G. 235, 256
Freeman, J. 111, 186
frontline workers 76, 110–111, 191
functional specialization 2
fusion centers (DHS) 76–79

Gaebler, T. 235
Gash, A. 44–46, 211
Gazley, B. 9, 161
Geographic Information System (GIS) 33, 130, **178**, 287
Girth, A. 36, 108, 234
globalization 41, 238, 256, 285–286
Gofen, A. 137, 174, 201
Goldsmith, S. 111, 235
Goodnow, F. 4, 170

298 *Index*

governance: bottom-up 122; internet 99, 103–105; meta-governance 13, 281–283, 286; modes 175; multiactor 122; network 59, 89, 134, 207; processing 250, 270; shared 122; systems 11–12, 20, 219; theory 228; transferred 252; *see also* collaborative governance; collaborative governance regime; Multi-Level Governance (MLG)

grants 39, 72, 74, 78, 107, 121, 170, 193, 229, 240; acquisition 114; administration/management 84, 114; challenge 236; contracts 173; grants as formal ties 122; implementation of 69; intergovernmental 194; procedure 239; programs 168; rural business enterprise *75*

Grodzins, M. 170

Haas, P. 253, 266
Hage, J. 86, 240
Hanemann, M. 10–11, 138
Health and Human Services (HHS) 7, 50, 81, 82, 85
Health, Education, and Welfare (HEW) 82
highway construction 174
hollowing out 14
Home and Community-Based Services (HCBS) 93, 133–134, 158–159, 208, 211
Home and Community-Based Services (HCBS) Waiver program 86–87, 149, 151, 180–183, *181*, 186
Homeland Security (DHS) Department 168, 169–170, 217
home rule 196–197
Homestead Act (1862) 39
Hood, Christopher 122, 158
Hooghe, Lisbet 243
Hoover, Herbert 76
human capital 35, 94, 176, 210, 236, 238–239, 263–264
Hurricane Katrina 49, 81
Huxham, C. 142, 181

Indiana Association of Rehabilitation Facilities 260
Indiana Economic Development 127
informational networks 86–87
information: bases 290; broker 30; contextual information 138;

creation *34*; definition of 175; exchange 10, 32, *33–34*, 45, 56–57; flow of 1, 58, 175; gathering 39, 168, 231, 270; management 179; portals 177; retrieval 40; seeking 114; services 84, 287; sharing 33; societies 184; transformation to knowledge 176; *see also* Geographic Information System (GIS)

Information Communication Technologies (ICT) – 30, 50, 65, 77, 86, 177, 258, 287

Ingram, H. 3, 135, 267–268
Intellectual and Developmental Disabilities (ID/DD) 259
Intergovernmental Management (IGM) 99, 113, 167, 172, 175, 187, 192, 194, 256
intergovernmental relations 12–13, 123, 167–169, 171, 174, 243, 256; rural 113
interjurisdictional politics 259
interlocal agreements 46–47
Interlocal Cooperation Act 47
interlocutors 269
Internal Revenue Service (IRS) 50
International City Management Association (ICMA) 194, 285
International Convention on the Rights of Persons with Disabilities 285
internet 1, 29, 104–106, 176, 279–280, 284–286, 288; connectivity 184; domain 103, 105–106, 119, 143, 152, 200, 210, 212; *see also* governance, internet
Internet Corporation for Assigned Names and Numbers (ICANN) 105
Internet Engineering Steering Group (INARF) 104
Internet Engineering Task Force (IETF) 104
Interoperability (IOp) 106–107, 224, 230, **251**, 270, 284, 288; components 231–232; definition 254; mapping practices *228*; process 225; requirements 225; research 91; standards 50; steps 106
interorganizational collaborative disincentives 208
Intranet **178**
Iowa Geographic Information Council 87, 183

Jenkins, W. 230, 254
Johnston, Jocelyn 233–234, 258
joint commissions *34*
joint policy-making 183
Joint Terrorism Task Force (FBI) 71

Kapucu, N. 231
Keast, R. L. 213, 226, 240, 290
Kenis, P. 59–50, 79, 175, 237, 290
Kickert, W.J. 240
Kilduff, M. 32
Klijn, E-H. 18, 57–58, 127, 150, 156, 208–210, 215, 216, 218, 224, 228, 235, 240, 242, 284, 290
knowledge: activities 178; architectures 185; bases 232, 282; collective 159; development process 179; exchange of 86; explicit 176, **177**, 180, 185, 265; flow of 217; holders 266; infrastructures 183, 240; institutional 176, 265; interagency 240, 265; maps **177**, 179; shared 163, 179; systems 179; tacit 115, 149, 176–177, 179–180, 187, 237; workers 263; *see also* collaboration knowledge; communities of practice; knowledge-based power; Knowledge Management (KM)
knowledge-based power 22, 55, 138, 140, 162, 200
Knowledge Management (KM) 16, 57, 89, 115, 119, 180, 185, 187, 270; aims 264; tools 177–**178**; vehicles 176; *see also* communities of practice
KnowledgeWorks 89, 250
Koliba, C. 4, 32, 60, 88, 92, 115, 118–119, 175, 179, 215, 224, 226, 228, 284, 288
Konno, N. 176
Kooiman, J. 12, 281
Koontz, T. M. 10, 133, 150, 153, 211, 213
Koppenjan, J. 18, 58, 156, 186, 208, 210, 216, 218, 224, 228, 240, 290

law and politics: as approach to IGR 173
leadership: distributed 57, 269; horizontal 180; mobilization 235; policy 203; skills 101, 268; visionary 209; *see also* collaborative
lead system integrator 108
learning: communities of practice 57, 99, 115–116, 179, 253, 265–266; collective 101, 241; distance

learning cooperatives 66; informal 253; joint 16, 45; mutual 58, 181; network learning 91, 177, 232; opportunities 23; organizational 100–101, 225; process 106, 186; professional communities 115–116; shared 45, 235; structures 241; *see also* collaborative learning; learning organization
learning organization 241, 254
Lejano, R. P. 3, 135
leveraging: collaboration by 29; resources 41, 230
Lichterman, P. 161
listservs **177**, 178
Lower Platte River Corridor Alliance (LPRCA) 78

Mahler, J. 225
management: across boundaries 91, 174–175; relational management 175, 250; *see also* collaborative management; Knowledge Management (KM); New Public Management
mandatory collaboration 48–49
Mandell, M. 34, 58, 70, 98, 207, 210, 214, 226, 290
map libraries 179, 265
mapping: augmentative 288; operational 250, 270
March, J. 4, 94, 172, 281
Margerum, R. 3, 11, 15, 18–19, 35, 156, 213, 230
McGuire, M. 6, 10, 14, 60–61, 66, 79, 89, 91–92, 99, 101, 109, 118–119, 122, 131–133, 138, 153, 174, 194–195, 208–210, 214–218, 224–225, 229–232, 237, 240, 242–243, 250, 252–256, 271, 290
McKinney Act 2
mentoring: formal **178**; informal **178**
metagovernance 13, 281–283, 286
Metropolitan Partnership Group (MPG) 89
Metropolitan Planning Organizations (MPO) 133, 151, 188, 189
Metro School (Columbus, Ohio) 89, *90*, 91, 94, 153–154, 226, 230–232, 250–251, 254–256
Milward, H.B. 18, 59, 88, 131, 153, 252, 290
monitoring 79, 112, 135, 181, **206**; collaborative activity 181; costs

of 11; cross-agency monitoring mechanisms 230; oversight **29**; performance **206**; *see also* contract, monitoring; monitoring networks
monitoring networks 79
Moynihan, D. 177
Multi-Level Governance (MLG) 8
multiparty agreements 253

naarative 58, 62, 191, 280–281
National Aeronautics and Space Administration (NASA) 225
National Incident Fire Command (NIFC) 230
National Oceanic and Atmospheric Administration (NOAA) 50, 65
negotiating *see* bargaining and negotiation
network accountability *see* accountability
network activity 18, 32, 217, 243
network champion 60, 127, 131, 235, 290
network collaboration 60, 120
network governance 59, 89, 134, 207
networking 14, 17, 19–10, *34*, 60, 70, 91, 114, 127, 157, 173–174, 185, 187, 206–208, **206**, 211, 217, 226, 231, 262, 271, 276, 286; behavior 20, 219; interactive 250; peer 265; social 181
network leadership 215
network managing activities: activating 57, 119, 133; facilitating 119; framing 119, 290; mobilizing 119, 290
networks: era of 256; for intellectual and developmental disabilities 259; global 285–286; *see also* action networks; developmental networks; informational networks; monitoring networks; non-chartered networks; outreach networks
network typology *see* action networks; developmental networks; informational networks; outreach networks
New Public Management (NPM) 233
non-bargaining 59
non-chartered networks *73*
non-collaboration 197
Non-Governmental Organizations (NGO) **177**, 259

Obama, B. 69
Occupational Safety and Health Administration (OSHA) 50
Office of Personnel Management (OPM) 49

Ohio State University (OSU) 89, 250
Olsen, Johan 4, 11, 281
operational localism 23, 136–137, 201
O'Toole, L. 19, 32, 60, 88, 135, 171, 216, 219, 238–240, 252
Outcome and Assessment Information Set (OASIS) 260
outreach networks 86–87

parallel action 33, 78
parties: external 100, 174; independent 29; interested 58, 197, 236; political 4, 156; private 16, 58; public 58; *see also* collaboration
partnership fatigue 181
partnerships 1, 12, 16, 18, 32, *34–35*, 36, 69–60, *73–75*, 76, 87, 94, 110, 113, 122, 173, 179, 205, 224, 227, 236, 239, 241, 252, 257, 262, 267, 271, 284, 287
PAST Foundation 89
performance: assessing 240; collaborative 240–241, 255; job performance 263; standards 108, **206**; *see also* collaborative performance management
Peters, G. 286
policy implementation 136–137, 169, 174
policy implementation *see* joint policy-making
Pollitt, C. 277–278
POSDCORB (planning, organizing, staffing, directing, coordinating, reporting, and budgeting) 72, *73*, 290
Posner, B. 270
Potoski, M. 36, 89, 108–111, 174, 258
power: agency 21, 55, 138, 162, 200, 210; bases 62, 127, 131, 146, 159, 162; collaborative 131, 138, 141, 144; deliberative 20, 126, 141, 162, 181; distribution of 12; exercise of 20, 59, 126; exertion of 126, 143; games 138, 158; limited powers *34*, 70; operational 138, 140, 160, 162; power over 20–22, *34*, 59, 139–130; power structures 127, 136, 208, 290; power to 20–22, 58, 132, 139, 140, 145, 162–163, 180, 216; shared 122, 130, 207, 216; *see also* knowledge-based power
president 6, 68–69, 81, 98, 113, 169, 250, 271, 277

process analysis 3, 225–226
process costs 125, 135
procurement 13, 35, 47, 72, *73*, 74, 99, 111, 175, 276; privatization 268
program implementation 93, 114, 136, 167, 176, 201, 207
Provan, K. G. 18, 59–50, 88, 131, 153, 237, 252, 255, 284, 290
Prusak, L. 139, 175–176, 179, 264
public service 13, **15**, 169, 170, 224, 234, 268
public value 14, 16, 23, 67, 103, 223, 238; adding 176, 284; definition of 223; increasing 223

Radin, B. 113–115, 132, 158, 167, 170, 173–174, 207–208, 266
Reed, D. 136, 201
Regional Internet Registration (RIR) 105
Reinventing Government (Osborne and Gaebler) 235
relational contracting 110
Rhodes, R.A.W. 4, 9, 12, 13, 57, 60, 79, 122, 127, 134, 138, 161, 208–209, 224, 242, 281
Romzek, B. 233–234, 258
Rural Development Council (RDC) *75*, 113
Rural Governance Initiative (RGI) 41

SAFECOM Interoperability Continuum 99
Saint-Onge, H. 94, 176, 207, 257, 262
Salamon, L. 19, 36, 39, 173
Saz-Carranza, A. 20, 119, 162, 175, 226, 241
Scharpf, F. 207, 215
Schrage, M. 176, 264
Science, Technology, Engineering, and Mathematics (STEM) 75–76, *75*, 89, 153, 226, 230–231, 250
Scott, A. 286
Scott, T. 19
Senge, P. 60
Senior Executive Service (SES) 50
shared administration **15**, 168, 170, 258
Silvia, C. 3, 101, 290
Skocpol, Theda 142, 170, 271
Slaughter, A. 18, 20, 41, 59, 285
Small Business Development Center (SBDC) *33*, *95*, 130
"small p" politics 9, 22, *33*, 149–140, 157–163, 181–182, 200–201
social networks 56, 79, 176, 264; internet-based 79
social production model 139

soft power 20
sovereignty 126
special districts 172
Spires, R. 107
staff and stakeholders 111
Steelman, T. 210
Steinberg, P. 158, 291
stewardship contracting 99, 110
Stone, C. 20, 65, 99, 138–139, 141–142, 162, 217, 237, 241, 267, 290
storytelling: analysis 202; efficacy of xx; organizational advantages 201–202
Sydow, J. 176, 241

Tapscott, D. 287
task force 1, 6–7, *33*, 49, 68, 71, *75*, 104, 140, **178**, 182, 197, 198, 200, 215
Taylor, M. 18
Temporary Assistance for Needy Families (TANF) **57**, 81
Tennessee Valley Authority (TNA) 169, 212
Thomas, C.W. 19, 143, 152–153, 155, 210, 239, 243, 267
Thompson, F. 208, 230
three-dimensional power 162
top-down processes 181, 281
Torfing, J. 11, 57–58, 132, 163, 179–170, 186, 218
Toyama, R. 218
trade associations **206**, 260, 268
transaction costs 135, 215, 234
transactions: bureaucrat- client 201; collaborative 12, 158–159, 171, 229, 259; formal 22; formal 22, 171; graduated 11; interoperable 107; online 249, 278; routine 126
transfer of functions *34*
trust: as a norm 11, 110; building 112, 214, 242, 262, 270, 283; creating 218; fostering 91, 231; intragroup 55; mutual 44
Tsai, W. 32
types of contracting: fixed price contracts 108; incentive contracts 108; post-reimbursement contracts 108; time and material contracts 108

unemployment insurance **37**
United Nations Convention on the Rights of Persons 8
universities 2, 50, 140, 239, 279
US Coast Guard (USCG) *80*, 99, 111

302 *Index*

US Department of Agriculture/Rural
    Development (USDA/RD) 74
US Department of Agriculture (USDA) 49, *75*
U.S. Forest Service (USFS) *75, 110*

Vandeventer, P. 207
Vangen, S. 181–182, 214–215
Van Slyke 36, 111, 164, 174, 234, 258
vexing policy dilemmas 44
virtual organizations **177**, 178
voluntary associations 185, 234
vouchers 13, **38**, 39, 84, **206**

waivers 20, 114, 140, 192, 200
Waldo, W. 169
Walker, D. 168
Walzer, M. 282
Wasserman, S. 227, 232, 234
Weber, E. 135, 152, 156, 212

Weber, M. 1, 250
Weiss, T. 285
welfare programs: social 234
welfare state 70, 173–174
Wenger, E. 60, 100, 253, 266
White, L. 12
wicked problems 121, 181
Williams, W. 136
Wilson, W. 4, 58
Wise, C. 230
Wondolleck, J. 182, 210
work group 160, 176, **178**
Wright, D. 167–168, 174

Yaffee, S. 182, 210, 261
Yildiz, M. 287, 292

Zia, Asim 4, 32, 60, 88, 175, 224, 228,
    284, 287

Printed in the United States
by Baker & Taylor Publisher Services